Old Abbey Farm, Risley

Building Survey and Excavation at a Medieval Moated Site

Richard Heawood
and
Christine Howard-Davis
Denise Drury
Mick Krupa

with contributions by
Nigel Neil, David Hodgkinson, Harry Kenward, Paul Hughes,
Allan Hall, Charles Lee, David Michelmore, Nigel Nayling,
Alison Plummer, W John Smith, Wendy Carruthers,
Caron Newman, Colin Peacock, Shaun Rainford

2004

Published by
Oxford Archaeology North
Storey Institute
Meeting House Lane
Lancaster
LA1 1TF
(Phone: 01524 541000; *Fax:* 01524 848606)

Distributed by
Oxbow Books
Park End Place
Oxford
OX1 1HN
(Phone: 01865-241249; *Fax:* 01865-794449)

Printed by
The Alden Group, Oxford, UK

ISBN 0 904220 34 6
ISSN 1343-5205

Series editor
Rachel Newman
Indexer
Peter B Gunn
Design, layout and production
Jo Cook and Emma Carter

Front Cover: Reconstruction of the Phase 2 timber hall

LANCASTER IMPRINTS Lancaster Imprints is the publication series of Oxford Archaeology North. The series covers work on major excavations and surveys of all periods undertaken by the organisation and associated bodies.

Contents

List of Tables

Plates

Contributors

Richard Heawood
AOC Archaeology Group, Edgefield Industrial Estate, Edgefield Road, Loanhead, Midlothian, EH20 9SY

Denise Drury
Archaeological Project Services, The Old School, Cameron Street, Heckington, Sleaford, Lincolnshire NG34 9RW

Mick Krupa
85 High Street, Snainton, Scarborough, Yorkshire YO13 9AJ

Nigel Neil
Nigel Neil Archaeological Services, 5 Hillside, Castle Park, Lancaster,   LA1 1YH

Christine Howard-Davis
Oxford Archaeology North, Storey Institute, Meeting House Lane, Lancaster, LA1 1TF

David Hodgkinson
Wardell Armstrong, Lancaster Building, High Street, Newcastle under Lyme, Staffordshire ST5 1PQ

Harry Kenward
Environmental Archaeology Unit, Department of Biology, University of York, PO Box 373, York YO10 5YW

Paul Hughes
School of Geography, University of Southampton, Highfield, Southampton SO17 1BJ

Allan Hall
Department of Archaeology, University of York, The Kings Manor, York YO1 7EP

Charles Lee
Building Conservation Services, Horbury Hall, Church Street, Horbury, Wakefield WF4 6LT

David Michelmore
Building Conservation Services, Horbury Hall, Church Street, Horbury, Wakefield WF4 6LT

Nigel Nayling
Department of Archaeology, University of Wales Lampeter, Ceredigion, SA48 7ED

Alison Plummer
Oxford Archaeology North, Storey Institute, Meeting House Lane, Lancaster, LA1 1TF

W John Smith
30 Penrhyn Avenue, Alkrington, Middleton, Manchester M24 1EQ

Wendy Carruthers
Sawmills House, Castellau, Llantrisant, Mid Glamorgan CF72 8LQ

Caron Newman
Egerton Lea Consultancy, Victoria Hall, Main Street, Grange-over-Sands, Cumbria LA11 6DP

Colin Peacock
Department of Biological Sciences, Faraday Building, Lancaster University, Lancaster LA1 4YQ

Shaun Rainford
Collex Waste Management Pty Ltd, Level 4, Bay Centre, 65 Pirrama Road, Pyrmont, NSW 2009, Australia

Summary

During the 1990s Lancaster University Archaeological Unit (now Oxford Archaeology North) carried out a large-scale programme of archaeological investigation on behalf of UK Waste Management Limited (now Biffa Waste Services Limited and previously Wimpey Waste Management), at Old Abbey Farm, Risley, Warrington Borough (SJ 6624 9356) in the present day county of Cheshire. The farm was the site of a moated platform, thought to be medieval in origin; a Listed seventeenth century brick farmhouse stood on the platform, and a Listed brick barn was sited a short distance to the south-west, beyond the line of the moat. Archaeological investigation of the site began in 1990, following an application to Cheshire County Council to extend the adjacent landfill facility. The fabric of the farmhouse and barn was evaluated, several trial trenches were cut by machine, and the potential of relevant documentary sources was assessed. Subsequently, planning permission for the landfill extension was granted and Listed Building Consent gained for the demolition of the structures, and a programme of archaeological recording was put in place to allow the 'preservation by record' of the site.

The mitigation investigation consisted of two main components, carried out in 1994-5: the controlled demolition and recording of the farmhouse and barn, and the excavation of large open areas both on and off the moated platform. However, multi-disciplinary analysis of the results of the building survey and excavation, and a programme of dendrochronological sampling, has allowed an account of the chronology and development of the site to be constructed. Specialist study of re-used timbers dated by dendrochronology has suggested that a late thirteenth or possibly very early fourteenth century open hall formerly stood on the site of Old Abbey Farm. The hall is thought to have been fully aisled, with a steeply-pitched hipped roof, but all the timbers from this phase were found re-used in secondary positions, so that many aspects of the building's form and appearance remain uncertain. In the late medieval period it is probable that the aisles were removed, with new timber-framing built below the arcade-plates. A clay floor found by excavation either relates to the modified hall, or to an earlier structure. The medieval hall stood on a moated platform; the moat and platform could not be independently dated, but appear to be at least as old as the re-used timbers. It is not clear how the moat was crossed earlier in the medieval period, but waterlogged timbers were recovered demonstrating that a substantial timber bridge was constructed in the mid fifteenth century. Documentary sources indicate that the site lay at the centre of the manorial estate of Pesfurlong, created in the mid thirteenth century.

A crosswing was added to the medieval hall in the mid sixteenth century; elements of the timber frame were found within the farmhouse, and represent the earliest *in situ* remains found within the standing structure. The footings of a sandstone bridge may also date to this period. Subsequently, the house was subject to piecemeal underpinning and rebuilding in brick, beginning in the early to mid seventeenth century, and was extended in the mid eighteenth century. The brick Lancashire-type barn was also built at this time.

The project provided a rare opportunity to excavate below a standing structure that had been archaeologically recorded. In order to examine the effectiveness and validity of the twin techniques of building survey and excavation, and the inter-relationship between standing structure and buried evidence, a unique research experiment was designed, whereby the two elements of the project were carried out by separate teams of archaeologists, who did not communicate until the completion of the fieldwork stages. The results of the experiment formed the basis of a television documentary compiled for the BBC's 'Countryfile' programme.

Acknowledgements

The project as a whole would have been impossible without the generous funding of the client, UK Waste Management Limited (now Biffa Waste Services Limited and formerly Wimpey Waste Management), for whom it was undertaken. Thanks are due to a number of individuals within UK Waste Management Limited, who held different responsibilities at various times during the project, particularly Andrew Carrington, Barbara Herridge, Mark Jones, John Ratcliffe, David Ringwood, Robin Tweedale, and Andy Vosper. Adrian Tindall, Principal Archaeologist for Cheshire County Council, monitored the project throughout its duration, giving it immense support, encouragement, and practical assistance.

Any excavation or building survey report represents a collective effort. However, the present project team is particularly indebted to the individuals who conducted the fieldwork elements of the programme, but who moved to new employment before the completion of the project. Mick Krupa directed the building survey of the Listed farmhouse and barn, whilst Denise Drury was responsible for the excavation. They jointly carried out the archaeological assessment of the archive, beginning the interpretation of the site and formulation of the phasing.

These major phases of fieldwork were the culmination of several years of work carried out on behalf of the client. Initial evaluation of the buildings, the below ground deposits, and the available documentary sources, was conducted for Lancaster University Archaeological Unit (now Oxford Archaeology North) by Nigel Neil in 1990. Subsequently, Rachel Newman assisted Aspinwall and Company with the preparation of the client's Environmental Statement, represented the client at public inquiry, and wrote the project design for mitigation excavation in response to a brief from Adrian Tindall. Jason Wood prepared the brief and specification for building recording and controlled demolition, and the integrated project design. He also acted as the client's managing agent, chairing all site meetings with assistance from Sarah Fitchett. The building survey was managed by Jason Wood, and the excavation by Mark Fletcher. Additionally, Oxford Archaeology North (OA North) would like to thank all the field staff who worked at Old Abbey Farm, particularly David Hodgkinson, Ian Scott, Richard Short, Rebecca Smith, and Chris Wild (building survey), and Richard May, Ian Miller, Karen Miller, Jon Onraet, and Jeff Speakman (excavation).

The report was compiled by Richard Heawood, but contributions by other OA North staff and by several external specialists have been incorporated directly into the text. These include Denise Drury, David Hodgkinson, and Mick Krupa (formerly LUAU); Harry Kenward, Paul Hughes, and Allan Hall (Environmental Archaeology Unit, University of York: plant and invertebrate macrofossils); Charles Lee and David Michelmore (Building Conservation Services: historic carpentry); Nigel Nayling (University of Sheffield: dendrochronology); Nigel Neil (Archaeological Services: documentary study); Alison Plummer (LUAU: vernacular architecture); Christine Howard-Davis (coordination of finds); and W John Smith (brick foundations). Free-standing contributions have also been made by Wendy Carruthers, Nigel Neil, Caron Newman, Colin Peacock, Shaun Rainford, and W John Smith. OA North wishes to thank all the above, and also John Carrott, Environmental Archaeology Unit, University of York, who liaised over the environmental evidence, and the staff of Warrington Museum, who provided archival information regarding unpublished excavations. Other specialists contributed to earlier stages of the project, including Cathy Groves (University of Sheffield: dendrochronology); Phil Howard (University of Durham: geophysics); and C Stephens (Geophysical Surveys of Bradford: geophysics).

The CAD drawings were produced by Mark Tidmarsh. Artist's impressions of the house in Phases 1 and 2 were by Anthony Padgett, and the finds were drawn by Karen Guffogg. The illustrations for the publication were produced by Emma Carter, following conventions from Adkins and Adkins (1994). Project management of the post-excavation analysis was by Richard Newman and Alison Plummer, both of whom gave support and encouragement during the writing of the report, and edited the text. Particular thanks are due to Jennifer Lewis, Nigel Neil, Rachel Newman, Adrian Tindall, Ian Miller, and Jason Wood for their detailed comments on the draft text, but any errors or omissions which remain are the responsibility of the authors. Jennifer Lewis also very kindly provided the draft text of a forthcoming publication (Lewis *et al* forthcoming).

Additionally, Nigel Neil and LUAU wish to the thank the many individuals and organisations who assisted with the documentary research programme. Paul Booth (History Department, University of Liverpool) transcribed and translated original documents, and gave editorial assistance during the preparation of Nigel Neil's report (Neil 1998). Michael Wareing and family generously loaned family deeds, other papers, and photographs, and provided information about the recent history of the farm. Rosemary Keery and John Winterburn gave information from their own researches into the history of Culcheth, and William Walker from his work on the Standishes of Duxbury. Assistance was also provided by the staff of Lancashire Record Office, especially Bruce Jackson (county archivist), Sylvia Birtles (search-room supervisor), and Anna Watson; Cheshire Record Office, Chester; Manchester Central Library (Local Studies - Archives); Chetham's Library, Manchester; Leigh Local History Library; Wigan Archive Service (Nicholas Webb); the British Library (Manuscripts and Reproductions Departments); Warrington Library (Local Studies); the Public Record Office (Reproductions Department); Cheshire Sites and Monuments Record, Chester (Dr Jill Collens); and the National Monuments Record, Swindon (Archaeology, Buildings, and Aerial Photography sections). Thanks are also due to the John Goodchild Collection, Wakefield, Dr Jennifer Lewis (formerly Department of Continuing Education, University of Liverpool), and Dr David Higgins (formerly University of Liverpool Field Archaeology Unit).

The project was afforded a high profile thanks to Jane Fletcher and the BBC *Countryfile* team, which broadcast the results of the experiment. The project was also a runner up in the British Archaeological Awards for 1996.

Figure 1: Location Map

1

INTRODUCTION

Old Abbey Farm and its Location

In 1988, a small farmstead in the Mersey Basin was purchased by a major landfill operator, Wimpey Waste Management Limited (which became UK Waste Management Limited and is now Biffa Waste Services), in order that the adjacent landfill site might be expanded. The farmstead, known as Old Abbey Farm, then consisted of agricultural land, a farmhouse, and a small scatter of agricultural buildings (Pl 1). However, the farmhouse and a brick barn were both Grade II Listed buildings, and as such were recognised in law as historically and architecturally significant. Furthermore, depressions in the ground to the north and south-east of the farmhouse appeared to be the remains of an encircling moat, the earthwork to the north still holding water. The farmhouse was a rendered brick structure, thought to date to the early to mid seventeenth century, with later additions, whilst the barn was considered to be slightly later. The farmhouse was significant in its own right because it appeared to represent a relatively early use of brick in the Mersey Basin (*see Ch 11*), but the presence of the moat enhanced the importance of the site, suggesting the possibility that the farmhouse might contain medieval features, and that buried archaeological remains might exist, within the moated platform, immediately beyond, or in the bottom of the moat itself. This proved to be the case, and the integrated archaeological programme which followed demonstrated that Old Abbey Farm had been more or less continuously occupied for over 700 years.

The Old Abbey Farm site lies at National Grid Reference SJ 6624 9355, at a height of *c* 26 m OD (Fig 1). The site is approximately 5 km north of the River Mersey, with the land dipping down very slightly towards the Glazebrook, a small Mersey tributary *c* 2.5 km to the east. The farm is approximately 1.5 km north-east of the village of Risley, and 6 km north-east of Warrington, the M62 motorway crossing the modern landscape from east to west 0.3 km to the south of the site (Fig 2). The farm buildings were formerly

Plate 1: Aerial view of Old Abbey Farm

surrounded by flat agricultural land, and were underlain by glacial drift deposits of boulder clay, with solid geology of Triassic Keuper Sandstone below (British Geological Survey 1980). Quaternary peat deposits associated with Pesfurlong Moss and Holcroft Moss lie within 0.5 km to the east of the farmstead. Although Moss Side Farm, on the western edge of the mosses, is known to have been established by 1757 (LRO DDRf 11/54(1)), reclamation of the bulk of the mossland seems to have begun in earnest in the nineteenth century (Leah *et al* 1997, 39). The farm was historically the principal residence within the estate of Pesfurlong, created in the thirteenth century when the manorial estate of Culcheth was subdivided into Pesfurlong, Risley, Holcroft, and a reduced Culcheth (*see Ch 2*). All four estates remained within the township of Culcheth, which was a part of the larger ecclesiastical parish of Winwick. The site is now within the modern civil parish of Risley, which was part of Lancashire until 1974, subsequently fell within the county of Cheshire, but is today in the Warrington Borough Unitary Authority.

The archaeology in the vicinity of Old Abbey Farm has been studied recently as part of the North West Wetlands Survey (Leah *et al* 1997, 20-24). During that project, previous research was synthesised, and a large amount of intensive new fieldwork carried out, primarily fieldwalking and augering. Previous finds from the wetlands themselves consisted in the main of pieces of Bronze Age metalwork, though finds of Roman metalwork have also been recorded (*ibid*). The new fieldwalking of the mosses produced a concentrated scatter of Mesolithic or early Neolithic flint, located roughly 3 km south of Old Abbey Farm, on the western fringe of Woolston Moss, but little else.

However, evidence of settlement is known from the mineral soils fringing the peat lands (*ibid*). An enclosure of *c* 1 ha in extent straddles the Glazebrook close to Great Woolden Hall, *c* 3 km east of Old Abbey Farm. Selective excavation of the interior has identified several circular structures within the enclosure, which was probably occupied during the first century BC. An important stratified assemblage of late prehistoric pottery was also recovered (Nevell 1994, 40-51, cited in Leah *et al* 1997, 20). Further afield, two more enclosures are known from the Sink Moss area, and three from Winwick, to the north of Old Abbey Farm, whilst aerial photographs suggest the possibility of two additional enclosures close to the Glazebrook site. It can be suggested that there was an identifiable pattern of dispersed late prehistoric/early Roman settlement in this part of the Mersey Basin (evidence

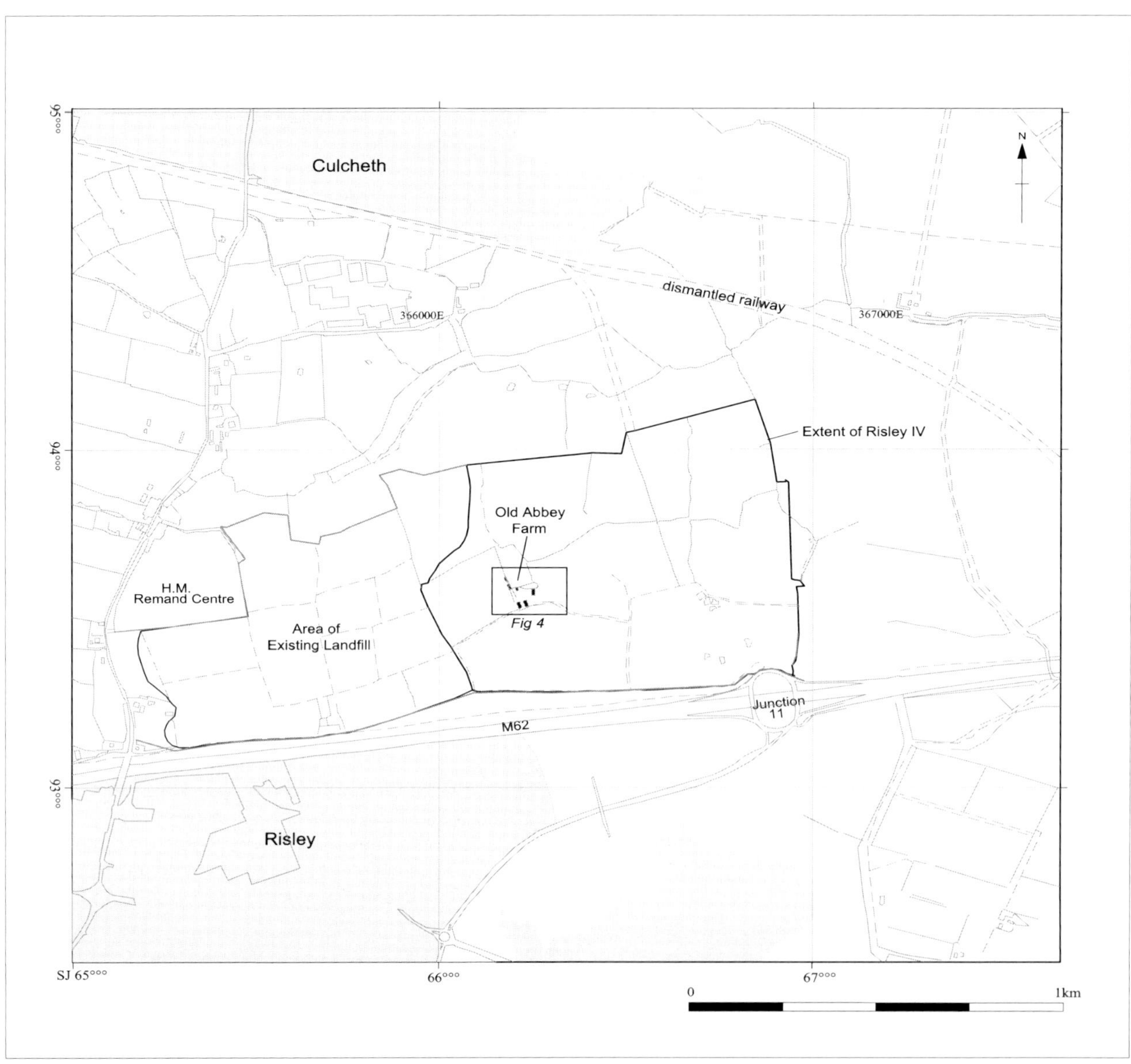

Figure 2: Location of Old Abbey Farm, and area of additional landfill (Risley IV)

summarised by Leah *et al* 1997, 20). For other periods, there is limited evidence of burial, which can be used to suggest occupation: a cemetery site, perhaps of Anglo-Saxon date, and with possible indications of a chapel, was found and excavated in 1980 at Southworth Hall, *c* 3.5 km to the west of Old Abbey Farm (Freke and Thacker 1990). It appeared to overlie a Bronze Age burial mound (Freke and Holgate 1990).

Fieldwalking by the North West Wetlands Survey on the mineral soils fringing the mosslands produced little new evidence, however, and finds were mainly of struck flints of probable late Neolithic and Bronze Age date, mostly occurring singly or in pairs (Leah *et al* 1997, 24). This fieldwork encompassed an extensive area around and immediately to the east of Old Abbey Farm, with only more limited coverage possible to the west, and it seems likely that the heavy clay soils and extensive mosses discouraged intensive settlement before the medieval period. The evidence for the medieval landscape is discussed below (*see Ch 11*), but Old Abbey Farm is one of several moated sites known in Culcheth township (Lewis 2000, 2, 505-16; Freke 1995), and it can be suggested that, in this locality, they may have been associated with assarting and the intensification of agricultural exploitation of the landscape. The moated sites of Cheshire were reviewed by David Wilson in 1987 (Wilson 1987), and he lamented the lack of large-scale excavations on such sites within the county, fearing that limited sample excavation of platforms, and a lack of investigation of areas beyond moats, might be giving misleading results. It appears that, until recently, moated sites such as that at Old Abbey Farm had been disappearing without adequate investigation.

The southern fringe of the historic county of Lancashire seems to have remained economically backward, largely because of the continued inhospitable nature of the landscape. The area was isolated from the south and east of the county by moss and moorland, and suffered poorer soils and wetter climatic conditions than western Lancashire. Consequently, it saw little improvement in its economic status until the rise of the Tudor woollen trade (Tindall 1985a, 16-17). Examples of vernacular architecture dating from the pre-industrial era are scarce, enhancing the local significance of the seventeenth century farmhouse at Old Abbey Farm (Pl 2).

The Re-development of the Site

The original Risley landfill facility lay to the west of Old Abbey Farm, extending to within 0.25 km of the farm buildings (Fig 2). By the late 1980s, the remaining capacity of the existing site was very limited, yet it was clear to the owners that demand was increasing rapidly, particularly from the Greater Manchester

Plate 2: View of the farmhouse in 1991, looking north-east

metropolitan area. As a result, proposals were prepared for the development of the land immediately to the east, with the intention of developing a new landfill facility, Risley IV, which would have a life of approximately 13 years. In pursuit of this objective Old Abbey Farm was purchased from Mr Michael Wareing and family, and in 1990 the then Lancaster University Archaeological Unit (LUAU), now Oxford Archaeology North, was commissioned to conduct an archaeological evaluation of the moated site. The evaluation was carried out in accordance with the terms of a brief produced by Cheshire County Council's Principal Archaeologist, and was designed to provide an assessment of below ground archaeological remains, an appraisal of the historical and architectural value of the two Listed buildings, and consideration of the availability of documentary evidence relating to the site.

The archaeological evaluation suggested that elements of the farmhouse, in particular the stone plinth, a beam in the first floor structure, and a wall-plate, were of medieval origin. This implied that a medieval house might have been encased by later rebuilding in brick. Re-used medieval timbers were also found within the barn. It was further demonstrated that waterlogged primary silting fills were present within the moat which might be of medieval origin, and that cut features survived on the platform that might represent the foundations of early ancillary buildings (trench locations are shown on Figure 3). Documentary research indicated that the farmstead was the likely centre of the manorial estate of Pesfurlong, probably founded in the mid thirteenth century. A small-scale programme of geophysical survey was carried out, the results helping to define the course of the moat (LUAU 1990). However, despite the interest of the site, the application of the English Heritage Monument Protection Programme scoring system suggested that it should not be considered to be of national importance. It was recommended that the site and buildings should not be preserved *in situ*, but that a programme of further excavation and building recording should be implemented.

Subsequently, UK Waste Management Limited received planning permission from Cheshire County Council to proceed with the redevelopment of the site, subject to the implementation of a Section 106 Agreement to fund a comprehensive programme of archaeological fieldwork. However, the granting of Listed Building Consent lay outside the remit of the County Council, and permission to demolish the two Listed buildings had to be sought from Warrington Borough Council. The application was considered by public inquiry, and it was decided that demolition could proceed, provided that it was accompanied by appropriate archaeological recording.

The Fieldwork Programme

The programme of further archaeological fieldwork consisted of two elements, the controlled demolition and archaeological recording of the farmhouse and barn, and the excavation of substantial open areas both on and off the moated platform. The requirements for the former were set out in a *Brief and specification for controlled demolition*, written by Jason Wood of LUAU in 1993, and subsequently adopted by Cheshire County Council. The scope of the excavation was dictated by a *Brief for archaeological recording* written by Adrian Tindall, Principal Archaeologist, Cheshire County Council, in 1992, and a project design was submitted in response to it in the same year by Rachel Newman of LUAU. An integrated project design for the whole programme was later prepared by Jason Wood in 1994, reflecting the terms of both the earlier briefs.

The prime aim of the project design was to examine in detail the construction and earliest uses of the moat and platform, and to chart its changing use and status to the present. Objectives included investigation of the possibility of subsidiary farm buildings existing across the moat; investigation of any evidence for structures pre-dating the standing farmhouse within the platform; investigation of the uses and infilling of the moat; and the detailed investigation of the architectural components of the two Listed buildings, in order to establish and date their construction sequences. It was also expected that the project would contribute to three academic research themes prioritised by English Heritage (English Heritage 1991a).

1)   **The archaeological study of buildings:**
     the importance of excavations on sites of buildings which have been recorded prior to their demolition was stressed, together with the need for examination of the relationship between excavated features and upstanding structures, and exploration of changing plan forms.

2)   **Processes of change:**
     it was noted that the transition from the late medieval to early post-medieval periods is poorly understood.

3)   **Landscapes:**
     it was noted that the factors behind the development of rural settlement are not fully understood, and that a range of settlement types should be investigated, including moated platforms.

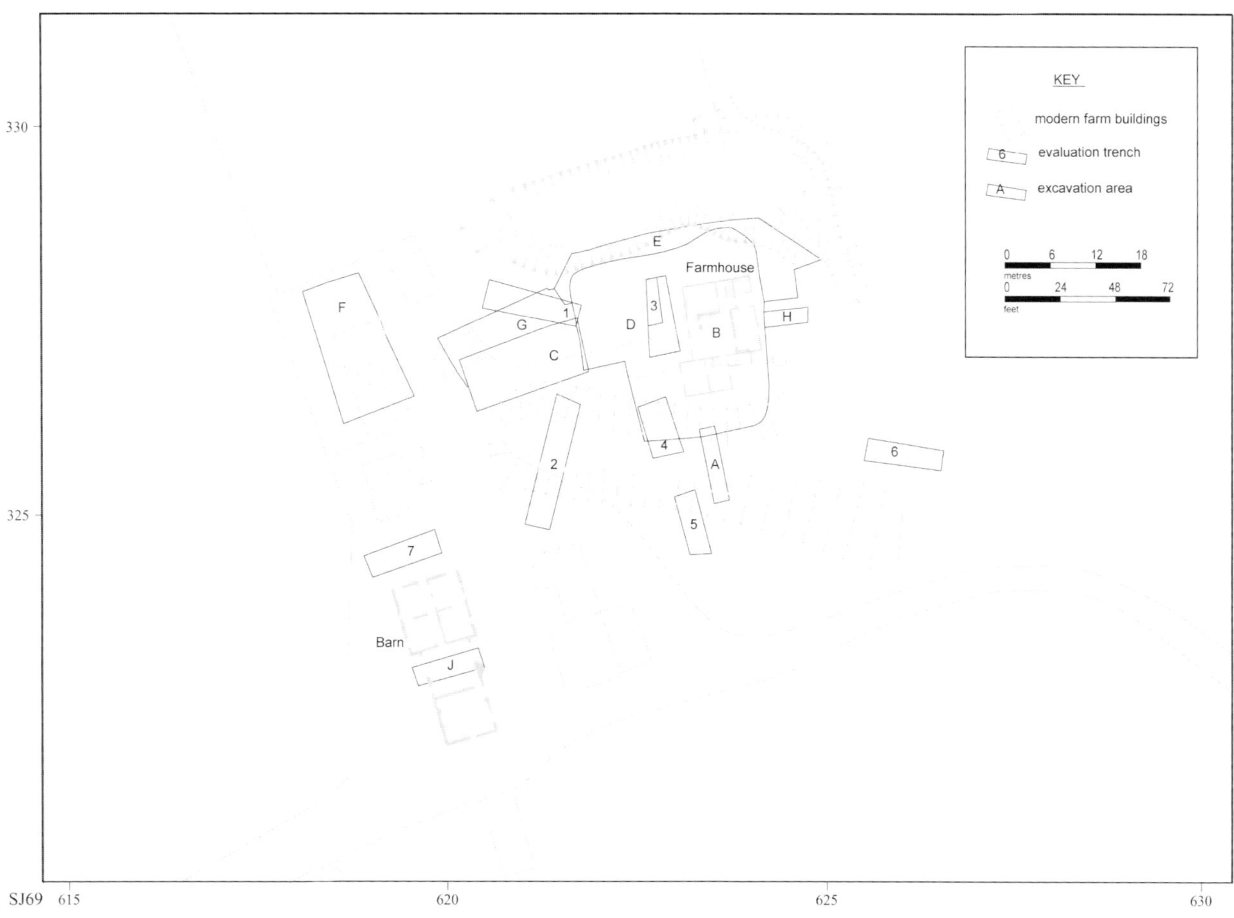

Figure 3: Trench location plan, showing buildings and topography at start of project

In pursuit of these aims, it was intended that the building survey and excavation components be carried out 'blind' by different teams, as a research experiment to assess the validity of the different 'above ground' and 'below ground' methods in use in contemporary archaeological practice. This element of the research, 'The Risley Experiment', as it became known, is described in more detail below (*see Appendix 1*).

When the programme was implemented, LUAU acted as 'managing agent' for the client, co-ordinating the activities of several different contractors and specialists. The first element of the fieldwork involved the recording and controlled demolition of the two Listed buildings. When work began, protective structures had already been erected around the buildings by UK Waste Management Limited, and these served to shelter the farmhouse and barn from the elements as they were dismantled (Pl 3). Demolition was carried out by a specialist contractor under archaeological supervision. Before and during this process, instrument-based survey data were collected in order to allow the production of detailed plan and elevation drawings, and this was enhanced by manual survey and rectified photography as appropriate. Data were downloaded to a CAD system,

on which drawings were produced and manipulated on site. In parallel with this work, a *pro forma*-based context recording system was used to produce a complete stratigraphic record of the development of the buildings, and a photographic record was kept in monochrome, colour transparency, and colour print formats. Samples were taken for materials' analysis, and, as dismantling proceeded, structural timbers were retained in storage for specialist analysis of historic carpentry, including production of detailed timber drawings. This element of the project was conducted over a period of seven months, in 1994 and early 1995.

A two month excavation phase followed in late March 1995. By that time, a further magnetometry survey had been conducted to the south of the farmhouse, covering an area measuring 20 m x 20 m, located in part on the line of the moat, in part beyond it to the south. The results were poor, and demonstrated only the widespread dumping of ferrous material (Geophysical Surveys of Bradford 1994). The farmhouse had by now been completely reduced to the level of its floors and foundations, and its entire footprint formed one excavation area (Fig 3). In addition, a large open area surrounding the farmhouse was stripped of topsoil by machine. This included the interior of the platform, with the exception of its south-west corner (Area D); the southern edge of the moat to the north of the platform (Area E); and the causeway across the moat, together with part of the moat immediately to the north (Areas C/G). Two further trenches were cut across the line of the moat (Areas A and H), a trench was opened across the centre of the Listed barn, now demolished down to floor level (Area J), and a small open area was stripped of topsoil beyond the moat to the west of the causeway (Area F). All further excavation was carried out by hand, with the exception of the use of a machine with toothless ditching bucket to part-excavate sections across the moat, and to excavate two sondages across the eastern fringe of the platform.

Archaeological features and deposits were recorded by means of a standard *pro forma*-based context recording system. Plans were generated by the use of a total station survey instrument, with data being downloaded into an on-site CAD system so that plots could be made at a scale of 1:20 and manually enhanced where necessary. Sections were drawn by hand at a scale of 1:10, and a full photographic record was maintained, in monochrome, colour transparency, and colour print formats. A separate run of object record numbers was used for the identification of finds and environmental soil samples.

Assessment of the Archive and Analysis

When fieldwork had finished and the site archive had been completed, an assessment of the archive was carried out according to English Heritage guidelines (English Heritage 1991b). All categories of data were reviewed, and an updated project design was compiled, which directed the course of a programme of detailed post-excavation analysis conducted during 1998. The aims and objectives of the analysis were as follows:

1) Thematic aims
- to date and characterise the chronological development of the site, particularly the earlier phases of occupation (thirteenth to eighteenth centuries)

- to establish the setting of the site within its broader landscape context, where possible examining patterns of rural settlement, resource territory, and estate/manorial dependency

- to produce an account summarising and synthesising on a chronological basis the results of the building recording and excavation at Old Abbey Farm

2) Specific objectives
- to date accurately the structural and stratigraphic phases by application of dendrochronological analysis to structural and waterlogged timbers

- to appreciate the development of the site in relation to its local environment and within its socio-economic context

- to review the changing status, fortunes, and lifestyles of the site's inhabitants

- to develop a better understanding of excavated features in relation to standing structures

- to set the site within the context of the development of the region's medieval settlement pattern and vernacular architectural tradition

The analysis programme was targeted towards the achievement of these aims and objectives. Separate stratigraphic studies of the excavation and building survey contexts were carried out, together with study of documentary sources, selected categories of finds, structural timbers, dendrochronological samples, and environmental soil samples, specialists being given access to stratigraphic information when available. The stratigraphic and specialist reports were later integrated to produce a single site narrative, the integration process allowing the results of 'The Risley Experiment' to be assessed (*see Appendix 1*).

Further research on other categories of material could not be justified, often because the material was of recent date, and its study would not advance the research aims. Documentary study was targeted towards the elucidation of the fieldwork results, concentrating on the early ownership of the site, and clarification of the origin of the 'Old Abbey Farm' name.

The Excavation and Building Survey Report

The project results have been presented in terms of an integrated, chronological site narrative, divided into chapters by phase. Each phase begins with an identifiable and discrete episode of building construction, and continues until the next such episode, encompassing excavated features which may be less precisely datable. The chapters consist of blocks of more general discussion of a part of the site, each followed immediately by more detailed description. The intention is that the reader should be able to navigate around the text, choosing where to access the more detailed description. Context numbers, allocated during the course of the fieldwork, have been retained: those in the sequences 1-958 (barn) and 2000-3250 (farmhouse) refer to contexts generated by the building survey; those in the sequence 4000-4795 to the excavation. Significant excavation contexts have been shown on the phase plans. Where such contexts have been illustrated, they are cross-referenced in the text to the relevant figure; where not cross-referenced, excavation contexts are not on plan. Dendrochronological dates have been given in accordance with the *Proposed convention for the publication and quoting of tree-ring dates* suggested by English Heritage (English Heritage nd, 27, table 5). Thus, where 'Sheffield, 1998' follows a date, this is a laboratory reference, not a bibliographic reference. The letter 'B' after a date indicates that the bark edge was present on the sample, whilst '?' before a date indicates that the heartwood-sapwood boundary was probably present. All dendrochronological dates have been taken from the relevant specialist report (Nayling 1998).

The site narrative contains information drawn directly from the specialist documentary, structural timber, dendrochronology, and plant and invertebrate macrofossil reports, and the significant contribution of the relevant authors is gratefully acknowledged. Their reports have been referenced within the text, and are available in the project archive; with the exception of a précis of the documentary study (*Ch 2*), and an extract from the plant and invertebrate macrofossil report (*see Ch 10*), they have not been reproduced in their original format. Information has also been drawn from specialist assessment reports, for material categories which did not justify further analysis. These have again been referenced within the text, and the reports on brick, daub, mortar, and building stone samples have additionally been reproduced as part of *Chapter 10*. Finds information has been integrated within the site narrative where relevant to the interpretation of the results; more comprehensive finds reports are again presented in *Chapter 10*. Finds have been referred to by their catalogue numbers where appropriate (*see Ch 10*), but are otherwise identified by context number followed by object record number.

Information from the 1990 evaluation has also been incorporated within this report where not replicated by data from the later investigations.

The Archive

The project archive, incorporating artefacts and paper/digital records, is to be housed at the Warrington Museum (artefacts) and Cheshire Record Office (paper/digital archive). A large proportion of the

Plate 3: The controlled demolition of the barn within a protective cover

finds and samples collected during both the building survey and excavation proved to be of very recent date, with no potential to contribute to the aims of the project. A discard policy was formulated, and these finds and samples were discarded after the completion of the assessment phase of the project, in line with best practice (English Heritage 1991b). The structural timbers were also disposed of, after they had been subject to detailed specialist study; they were shipped to Ireland, where they have been used in the restoration of a standing building. However, the archive includes full finds' catalogues and assessment reports quantifying the discarded material, as well as the unpublished specialist reports on the finds and samples which were subject to further analysis.

The primary record of the building survey is of particular interest. It contains a very large number of detailed plan and elevation drawings of the Listed barn and farmhouse, which exist both on drawing film and in digital format as CAD files. Only a small number could be reproduced within this report, and so, for this project, the archive constitutes a particularly important part of the lasting record of Old Abbey Farm.

2

HISTORICAL BACKGROUND

By Nigel Neil

Introduction

The earliest date at which the 'Old Abbey' element of the Old Abbey Farm place-name can be attested is only 3 June 1803, the burial date of John Warburton, when 'Old Abbey of Culcheth' was recorded in the Newchurch parish registers (Kaye and Kaye 1905, 202). The earliest manuscript reference is *c* 1806-7, in an estate survey (LRO DDRf 11/2), with the first appearance in print being 1818 on Christopher Greenwood's *Map of the County Palatine of Lancaster* (Fig 4). Prior to this, and in some later documents including the 1864 sale particulars (LRO DDRf 11/63; WAS D/DX EL 122/16), the name 'Old Pesfurlong Demesne' is used, the use of which can be traced back to a survey of 1756 (LLHL B/333 PES; Rose 1881, 152-3). This is the form of the name used by the Ordnance Survey (1849) first edition 6″: 1 mile map (Fig 6), and which will be used throughout the report, though the *Victoria history of the county of Lancaster* (Farrer and Brownbill 1911, 159-61) uses 'Peasfurlong'; 'Pestfurlong', and various other spellings, have been used over the centuries.

Pesfurlong was the name given to part of the estate of Culcheth, which itself is first recorded in 1212, by which time it was in the fee or barony of Warrington (Farrer and Brownbill 1911, 156). In 1246, on the unlawful killing of Gilbert de Culcheth, who held it by knight's service from the Lord of Warrington, Culcheth was divided into four smaller estates (*op cit*, 159) - a reduced Culcheth, Risley, Holcroft, and Pesfurlong - to be assigned to Gilbert's four infant daughters (the positions of the estate centres are shown on Figure 5). The daughters automatically became wards of the Lord of Warrington, William le Boteler, who subsequently consented to their marriages to the four sons of Hugh de Hindley. Pesfurlong was assigned to Elizabeth (also known as Isabel), Gilbert's second daughter, who was given in

Figure 4: Extract from Greenwood's Map of the County Palatine of Lancaster, *1818. By kind permission of Lancashire Record Office © Copyright*

marriage to Adam de Hindley, who thereafter took the name of Adam de Peasfurlong. He reverted to the de Hindley name after Elizabeth's death, sometime between 1278 and 1284 (Farrer and Brownbill 1911, 159 n52). Previous writers (*eg* Winterburn 1974; 1977, 30) have thought it likely that Adam was already living in Pesfurlong before the division of the estate, and that the site of his home, therefore, became the homestead of the new estate, but no reliable evidence for this has been found.

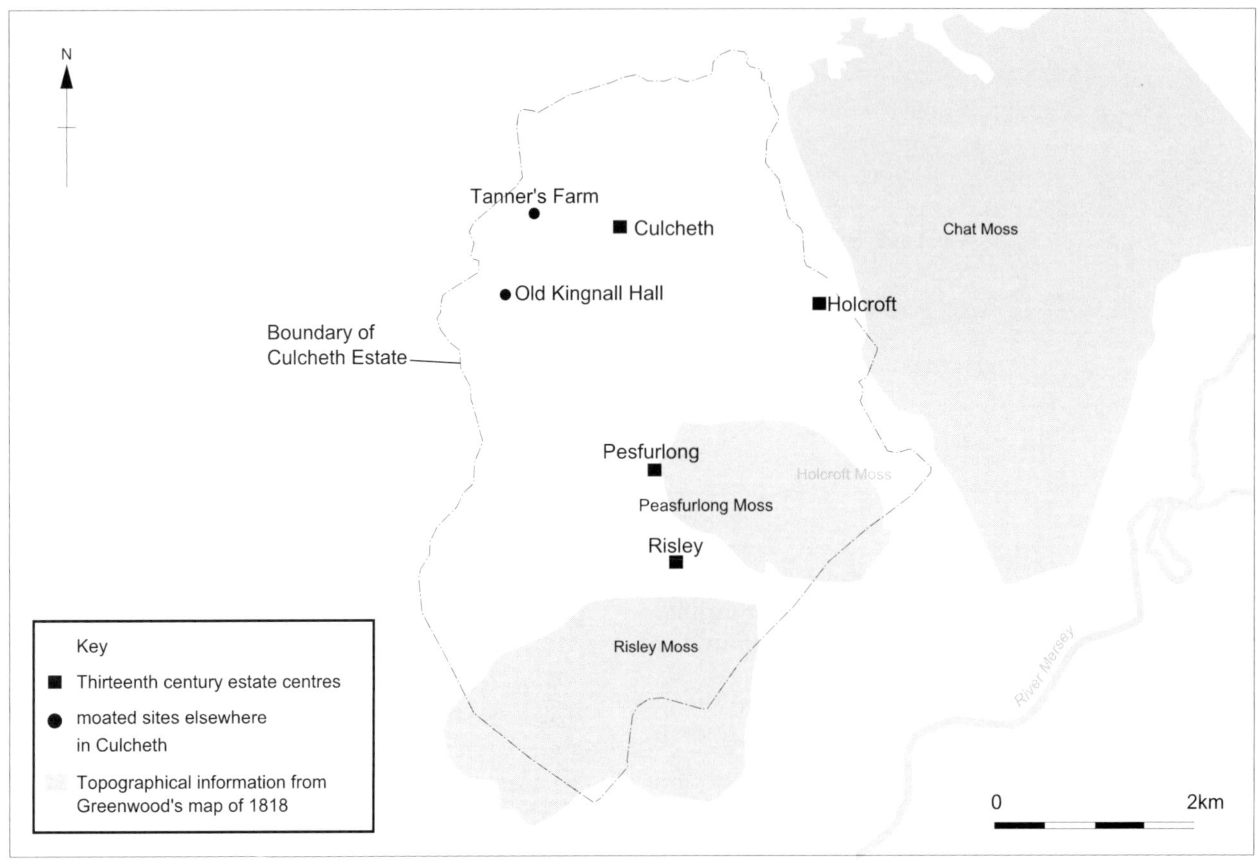

Figure 5: Principal places in the medieval township of Culcheth (after Lewis 1991a, fig 93.12a)

Place-name Evidence

No entirely satisfactory explanation has been found for the 'Abbey' farm name, other than a strong possibility of 'nineteenth-century romanticism'. Keery (1992, 29) notes that 'its last owners and the other long-term residents of the rural community consider that the farm replaced a manor which itself was built on the site of an eleventh-century monastery'. Although the Parish of Winwick, within which Culcheth was situated, undoubtedly has early ecclesiastical importance, St Oswald's church being mentioned in Domesday Book (Beamont 1875, 9-10; Farrer and Brownbill 1911, 125), there is no immediately apparent reason to associate Old Abbey Farm with the church. Furthermore, it is clear from the Public Record Office's (1964) *List and index of the lands of dissolved religious houses* that neither Pesfurlong, nor Culcheth, was a possession mentioned in its own right as a monastic property in the Ministers' Accounts at the time of the Dissolution, indicating no continuity of any monastic connection into the sixteenth century let alone through to the adoption of the Old Abbey Farm name. One possible origin for a mistaken monastic connection lies in the Christine Howard-Davisfield name 'Munk's' or 'Monk's' Wood, which

adjoined Old Pesfurlong Demesne to the south. This field was, in 1757, part of the holding of Thomas Warburton, tenant of what was to become Old Abbey Farm (LRO DDRf 11/1; DDRf 11/54 (1)), and was thus connected with the farm in the later eighteenth century. The field may have taken its name from a 'Monk' or 'Monks' family (the 1588-1812 Newchurch parish registers include many people of the surname 'Monks' (Kaye and Kaye, 1905)); Newchurch in the village of Culcheth was the nearest chapel to Pesfurlong (Fig 5), and became a parish church in 1845 when the parish of Newchurch was split from Winwick (Farrer and Brownbill 1911, 165)), thus providing an opportunity for local people to have incorrectly assumed former monastic ownership. In view of the uncertainty, it has even been suggested that the name might derive from 'abele', meaning 'white poplar', from the medieval Latin *abellus* (J Lewis pers comm). The name was in common usage in the seventeenth century, when the tree, which favours wet ground, was often grown.

The name Pesfurlong perhaps means 'the furlong where peas were grown' (Ekwall 1922, 97). 'Pease' is the common early form of 'peas' (Halliwell 1924, 618), but 'pes' and 'pess' are among the many alternatives listed by the *Oxford English Dictionary* (Murray 1909, 594). 'Furlong' usually means 'a division of an unenclosed field' (Ekwall 1922, 11), perhaps implying that at least part of the new estate had previously been arable land. Winterburn (1974, np) gives a possible alternative derivation from the obsolete word 'pease' meaning 'thing of little worth', or of 'very small value or importance'. *The Oxford English Dictionary* (Murray 1909, 595) dates the use of these to between *c* 1300 and 1598. Another possibility is the meaning of pease found from the mid thirteenth to mid seventeenth centuries of 'to make peace with or reconcile'; pesse and peese are among the forms found (*ibid*). In view of the holding apparently being created during the settlement of Gilbert de Culcheth's estate in *c* 1246, this would be a most interesting, if somewhat unlikely, derivation. Alternative spellings for Pesfurlong include Peysporlange in 1500 (Farrer 1905, 148-149), Pesporlange in 1548 (Farrer 1910, 68), and Peasfurlong in 1910 (*op cit*, 181).

In the description of the agreement setting the limits of the four holdings carved from Gilbert de Culcheth's estate in 1246 (Farrer and Brownbill 1911, 159n52; MCL L1/51/9/12 f107-9, Bod Lib Dodsw v142, f113) 'part of Halghus Carr' is included. According to Winterburn (1974, np), Halghus Carr means 'a field reclaimed from the moss by drainage with holly trees.' However, a more realistic interpretation would be a derivation from the Old English *halh* 'a corner or

nook', often found in the names of Lancashire places 'situated on rivers or streams, or at the edge of mosses' (Ekwall 1922, 11), names similarly derived including Ringstonhalgh, Comberhalgh and others. The 'carr' element is from the Old Norse *kiarr* 'brushwood', or figuratively 'wet ground, especially that where brushwood grows', generally used for 'bog, overgrown with bushes' (Ekwall 1922, 9). The northern and eastern boundary of Culcheth township is formed by the Glazebrook and its tributary the Carr Brook (Farrer and Brownbill 1911, 156). The body of moss at the eastern edge of Pesfurlong, described as wooded on the 1757 plan (LRO DDRf 11/54(1)), is shown on the tithe map of 1838 (LRO DRL 1/21) and the first edition Ordnance Survey map (1849; Fig 6) as being divided into Holcroft, Pesfurlong, and Risley Moss.

Origins of the Pesfurlong Estate

Neither Culcheth nor Pesfurlong are mentioned in Domesday Book in 1086, and the Fee or Barony of Warrington, of which they were to become a part some time before the Great Inquest of 1212 (Farrer 1903, 9), was not created until *c* 1118. The 1212 Inquest allows us to people the early tenure of Culcheth slightly: 'Reginald [or Reynold] held four carucates of

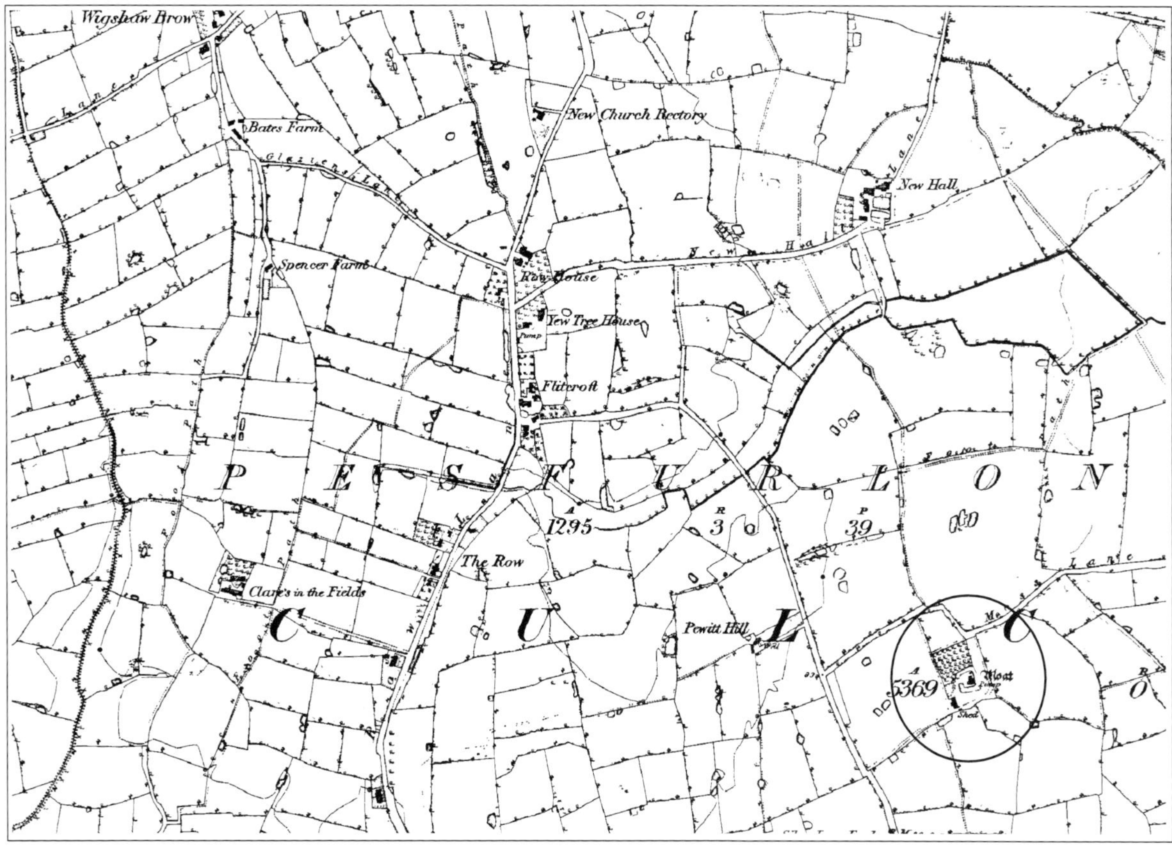

Figure 6: Extract from the OS 6":1 mile First Series map sheet Lancashire 107, 1849. By kind permission of Lancashire Record Office © Copyright

11

land of Pain de Vilers [the first Lord of Warrington] by knight's service. And now Hugh son of Gilbert holds those carucates of William le Boteler for four marks [yearly], and does knight's service where ten carucates make the fee of one knight' (Farrer 1903, 9). Later, it is recorded that, in 1246, one Gilbert de Culcheth was killed by 'unknown malefactors', soon after being recorded as a defendant in the Assize Roll of that year, and the township was fined because it did not pursue the culprits (Farrer and Brownbill 1911, 156). Gilbert seems to have been still a young man, and left a widow, Dame Cecily de Layton (died 1291 or 1292; Farrer and Brownbill 1911, 156n14-15) and four infant daughters, who were thus co-heirs. In due course (the deed is undated) William le Boteler, Lord of Warrington - whose wards they had automatically become by dint of Gilbert's knight's service - granted their marriages to Hugh de Hindley (LRO DP 398 Box 2; Beamont and Rylands 1881, 23, no 20; Warrington Lib MS 74, no 48), who married them to his four sons, each of whom took the name given to the newly created estate. Hindley is in Wigan parish, immediately north of Winwick parish. By a further deed, the sub-division of Gilbert's holding in Culcheth, termed a 'manor', was set out. Culcheth was assigned to Margery wife of Richard, Pesfurlong to Elizabeth and Adam, Holcroft to Joan and Thomas, and Risley to Ellen and Robert. Interestingly, the full text of the deed indicates that only the eldest would have tenure by knight's service from William le Boteler, the others holding their estates of the eldest (LRO DP 398; Beamont and Rylands 1881, 23, no 21; WCL MS 74, no 30).

The area assigned to Adam as the estate of Pesfurlong was: 'all the waste between the Southwood and the Westwood and between Pesfurlong and Croft which could be ploughed and sown [and] all the land and wood which he had inclosed between his house and Southwood, with part of Halghus Carr' (Farrer and Brownbill 1911, 159 n52). The remainder of the 'waste' was to remain in common. Pesfurlong, in this context, may be the name of part of the townfields, or may refer to the house. Winterburn (1977, 30) states that: 'The Westwood was probably the wooded district still remaining in the Broseley district of Culcheth, and the Southwood may have been an area of woodland in the neighbourhood of the present Pesfurlong Moss.'

The boundaries of the four manorial estates were only briefly set out in the first deed of division and, not surprisingly, disputes seem to have arisen. A lost manuscript, then in the hands of Edward Calveley of Great Woolden Hall, transcribed by Roger Dodsworth in 1634 (Bod Lib Dodsw v142, f113-15; MCL L1/51/9/12, f 107-9), defines the boundaries in more detail:

> 'There has been a disagreement between Richard de Hyndelegh and Robert, Adam and Thomas, his brothers over various properties, which has been submitted to the arbitration of Sir Robert de Holand, Robert son of Adam de Holand, Jordan de Gleight and Elias de Leuse. They have awarded as follows: that the whole waste which is capable of being ploughed and sown between Sothewode and le Westwode, and between Pesturlonge and Croftes, shall remain to Adam and his heirs. However, the land within the aforesaid bounds which cannot be ploughed to bear corn, shall lie in common to himself [ie Richard] and his brothers and their heirs and free tenants. Adam is to provide a sufficient right of way between Sothewode and le Westwode to the common for Robert and his co-parceners and their men and free tenants, namely three perches wide in the place set by the arbitrators. Adam is to keep all his land and woodland which he has enclosed at the time of this award between his house and Sothewode, together with part of Halghuscar, beginning at the angle of the hedge which separates the bound of Adam and his brother Thomas [lord of Holcroft], and then straight across le kar up to the moss, and following the moss as far as the hedge which encloses the encroachment of Adam at his house, and [as far as] the house of his brother Robert [lord of Risley]. It is ordered that the land which Adam has let to Robert son of William de Sonky shall not be challenged by the co-parceners. His brother Robert shall have all his encroachments which had been enclosed by this time, except for twelve acres in Rossale. Robert is to have the pasture of the moss between Riselegh and the boundary of Crofte without opposition from Adam. Richard [lord of Culcheth] five encroachments in le Lytultwysse and le Blindehurst, Kinkenhale and le Milnehouses shall remain as they are, and he shall let the twelve acres which he had enclosed next to Kynebroke without challenge. Richard shall also have the course of the brook and the fledegates [floodgates] which he once had on his brother Thomas's land, and he will excuse his brother Thomas from his claim on a site for a mill as long as Thomas does not build a mill there himself. It is also ordered that Richard shall have his mills in Cuichit [sic], built and to be built, and his house, without challenge. It is established that Robert de Ryselegh [Risley] shall have twenty acres in Roghhurst next to Croftewede, allowing his brothers' right to take their beasts to water. The twelve acres that Robert has enclosed in Rossale shall lie in common. Robert's horse-mill is to be demolished. Thomas shall have

30 acres beginning at the head of the twelve acres formerly granted, as far as the mill, and then ascending between Lynebroke and le Hursteshorde until 30 acres is reached. None of the brothers shall enclose land to prevent the others and their tenants from having access to pasture or woodland'.

The de Radclyffe Family

Adam de Peasfurlong reverted to the de Hindley name after Elizabeth's death, sometime between 1278 and 1284. He was still living in 1292. Adam and Elizabeth de Peasfurlong had two daughters, Margery and Beatrice, and, in or before 1303, Margery married William de Radclyffe (1280-1333). In 1309, William's father settled upon him and his heirs the manors of Radclyffe, Oswaldtwistle, and Quarlton. The Pesfurlong estate then remained with the Radclyffe family up to the early sixteenth century, presumably descending with the estates inherited by William from his father (Farrer and Brownbill 1911, 159).

Few records have been located relating to Pesfurlong during the Radclyffes' 210 year tenure. In 1349, Margaria - possibly daughter of a Gilbert de Culcheth who died in *c* 1342 - a widow, released to Richard Radclyffe (the eldest of William de Radclyffes's and Margery de Peasfurlong's three sons and six daughters) all claim to the lands which he had by gift of her father (Farrer and Brownbill 1911, 159n55; Bod Lib Dodsw v39, f123b; MCL L1/51/9/12, L743). Pesfurlong is not specified as being amongst these lands, however.

Richard Radclyffe, third son of James Radclyffe, inherited the Pesfurlong moiety of Culcheth but, dying *c* 1441 before his father (d 1446), the lands reverted to his eldest brother John (Hampson 1940, 29-30). John was involved in 1483 in a dispute with Sir Christopher Southworth about lands in Culcheth, which was decided in Radclyffe's favour (Farrer and Brownbill 1911, 160n56). He was killed at Bosworth Field in 1485, fighting on the Lancastrian side. His *Inquisition Post Mortem* (Langton 1876b, 120-2) showed that he held the manor of Radclyffe of the King as Duke of Lancaster, in addition to Oswaldtwistle and part of Culcheth (*ie* Pesfurlong). His eldest son, Richard (d 1502), succeeded to the Pesfurlong lands, his (second) wife Alice (d 1531) having lands in Pesfurlong, Crumpsall, Moston, and Lowton, worth £40 3s yearly, as dower (Langton 1876b, 147-8; Hampson 1940, 31). Richard had no surviving issue and his brother John succeeded to the title at the age of 42 years. He seems to have been in possession of Pesfurlong before his brother's death, since, in March 1500/01, he is described as John Radclyffe of Peysporlonge, senior,

in a case heard at Lancaster between him, Roger Longworth, clerk, Richard Barker, chaplain, and Nicholas Jackson, against Richard Radclyffe of Radclyffe (Farrer 1905, 148-9). This John died in 1512 or 1513, leaving two daughters (Farrer and Brownbill 1911, 59) and his lands passed to his nephew, also John, son of Roger Radclyffe, then aged 14 years. Wardship of the boy was given in February 1513/14 to Queen Katherine, but he died in 1517 before attaining his majority. With the death of John Radclyffe in 1517, the estate passed to a younger branch of the family, represented by Robert Radclyffe, Lord Fitzwalter, created Earl of Sussex in 1529 (Farrer and Brownbill 1911, 59-60; Hampson 1940, opp 17). The estate and others in Lancashire were sold to provide the dowries for his daughters.

Holcroft and Calveley Families

Pesfurlong was bought from Robert Radclyffe in 1549 by Sir John Holcroft of Holcroft Hall (d 1559 or 1560), when the rent payable to the Lord of Warrington was 3s 6d. The *Foot of Fine* of the conveyance to Sir John Holcroft in 1549 states that 'Pessuerlonge' comprised: '16 messuages, three cottages, 400 acres of land, 40 acres of meadow, 100 acres of pasture, six acres of wood, 300 acres of moss, 40 acres of heath and moor and two water mills' (Farrer 1910, 73-4, MCL L1/50/35/7 bdl 13, m77). Since Sir John's estate centre was elsewhere, it is likely that the Pesforlong manor was tenanted. The estate was settled in 1574 on Hamlet Holcroft, third son of Sir John Holcroft, his younger brother Alexander having died without issue and his eldest brother (another Sir John, b *c* 1520) having only one child, Alice, later wife of Sir Edward Fitton (Rylands 1887, 13-15). The 1574 *Foot of Fine* conveys:

> 'between Francis Holte, esq, and William Hilton, plaintiffs (*ie* purchasers) and John Holcrofte, knight, and Hamlet Holcrofte, esq, deforciants (*ie* present owners) the manor of Pesforlonge, with the appurtenances, and of 100 messuages, 20 cottages, 60 tofts, two water-mills, two dovecotes, 100 gardens, 100 orchards, 1000 acres of land, 300 acres of meadow, 600 acres of pasture, 100 acres of wood, 600 acres of furze and heath, 500 acres of moor, 400 acres of turbary, 100 acres of moss, and 20s of rent in Culcheth, Pennyngton, and Lawton, and free fishery in the water of Glazebrake.'

In 1575, Hamlet Holcroft and his wife Isabel, daughter of Thomas Clifton of Westby, were returned as Recusants in the Deanery of Warrington (Farrer and Brownbill 1911, 160 n59; Rylands 1887, 15). Whether Hamlet ever lived at Old Abbey Farm is unclear, as is the duration of his possession of the manor, as the legal wranglings and re-mortgagings concerning the Pesfurlong manor and other Holcroft estates are convoluted and opaque. Even so, what is clear is that, despite problems with debt, the Holcrofts had by 1590 caused to have built a new capital messuage for Pesfurlong, New Hall, *c* 1 km to the north (Fig 5; LRO DP 398, Box 1). From that date the farm later called Old Abbey Farm was known as Old Hall or Old Pesfurlong Demesne. Clearly by the later sixteenth century it must have been tenanted and no longer the principal residence on the estate.

In 1605, Hamlet's son, John Holcroft, sold the manor to Ralph Calveley (d 1619) of Saighton, near Chester (Farrer and Brownbill 1911, 160 n60) when it was said to comprise:

> '30 messuages, 20 tofts, 10 cottages, 30 barns, two dovecotes, 40 gardens, 1000 acres of land, 200 acres of meadow, 1000 acres of pasture, 100 acres of wood, 1000 acres of furze and heath, 1000 acres of moor, 1000 acres of turbary, 1000 acres of moss, 100 acres of land covered with water, 14d rent in Pesfurlong, Holcroft, Risley, and Culcheth, and common of pasture for all cattle in Holcroft, Risley, and Culcheth' (MCL L1/50/28/3/6, f232, bdl 68, m6).

The following 50 years are a very complex period in the history of Pesfurlong. By his death in 1619, Calveley had also bought the manor of Holcroft. In addition, as a trustee or tenant under Dame Alice Fitton, he was in possession of the adjacent former Stanlaw/Whalley Abbey property of Cadishead, including Great and Little Woolden, which had been granted to Sir Thomas Holcroft at the Dissolution. The title to the de Culcheth deeds transcribed by Roger Dodsworth (Bod Lib Dodsw v142, f113; MCL L1/51/9/12, f107) states that one Edward Calveley was Lord of Pesfurlong, Holcroft, Barton, and Wigshaw in Culcheth in September 1634, and he died in 1636. The Holcrofts regained possession of Pesfurlong along with Cadishead and Holcroft in or before 1652 (Farrer and Brownbill 1911, 372n98) but, from 1634 to 1661, the Calveleys laid claim to the estate, citing a fraudulent sale. Nevertheless, until *c* 1686, Pesfurlong descended with the principal manor of Holcroft.

Lt Col John Holcroft and his wife, Margaret Hunt, held Pesfurlong and Holcroft in 1652. Their eldest son Thomas became heir on Lt Col Holcroft's death in 1656, but seems to have sold the Pesfurlong and Holcroft manors to John Holcroft, as described in statements of 'defendant's title' in *c* 1657 (LRO DP 397/25/4). There were further equity proceedings in the Chancery Court of the Palatinate of Lancaster in

March 1665 (Barlow 1989; PRO PL 6/v24, no 86; PRO PL 7/v42, no 59), and as late as December 1690 (PRO PL 6/v41, no 77). Depositions dated 3 November 1666 by Leonard Egerton of Shawe, esq, Holcrofte Linford of Little Walden [Woolden], gentleman, and John Peers of Glasbrooke [Glazebrook], yeoman, in the case of Leonard Egerton v John Holcroft of Holcroft, esq, concern money borrowed for the purchase of the manors of Holcroft and Pesfurlong from the Calveleys (LRO DP 23). Thomas Holcroft died in August 1667, and his younger brother Charles succeeded, but he died without issue in 1672.

John Holcroft was named as having three hearths in the Hearth Tax returns for 1663, which combined Pesfurlong with Risley. It is unclear where his property was but it is perhaps most likely that it was New Hall (LRO MF 1/27, from PRO E 179/250/8/pt 5, f4-5). In 1666 Thomas Holcroft, with four hearths, is at the head of the Lordship of Pesfurlong list (LRO MF 1/27, from PRO E 179/250/9/f194), this time subdivided from Risley. Second in the Pesfurlong list – occupiers were generally listed by status – was Francis Jackson, also with four hearths, amended from two (P Booth pers comm). It is unclear where he resided, and the archaeological investigations produced no evidence for more than a single hearth in the seventeenth century buildings at Old Abbey Farm.

Following the death of the last male heir, Charles, the estate was divided between Thomas Holcroft's two daughters. The elder, Eleanor, had married Thomas Tyldesley of Myerscough and Morleys, while the younger, Margaret (1656-1735), married Sir Richard Standish of Duxbury. In 1680, two moieties of the manors of Holcroft and Pesfurlong were settled, one on the Tyldesley couple and one on the Standishes (MCL L1/50/28/7, f496), and it is the latter which included the manorial demesne of Pesfurlong.

The Standish Family

The Standish tenure is punctuated by several quite complex legal cases, and a large quantity of documentation survives for their ownership, including surveys, rentals, correspondence, and latterly some notes on repairs and improvements. Despite an attempted sale of the estate in parcels in 1864, Old Abbey Farm remained in Standish possession until 1950, one of the last of their tenanted properties in Lancashire to be sold off. A schedule of Standish deeds compiled in December 1845 by Wigglesworth & Co of Grays Inn (MCL L1/27/8) mentions several papers no longer in existence, or perhaps still in private hands. The earliest listed for 'Pestforlong' is a partition deed of 13 August 1686,

between Tyldesley Standish, Sir Richard Standish -
latterly mayor and Whig Member of Parliament for
Wigan (Farrer and Brownbill 1911, 210n10) - died in
1693 (Walker 1995, 15), and Lady Margaret, re-married
to Sir Thomas Stanley, a further conveyance being
settled in August 1700. In July 1737, Counsel's opinion
was sought, thought to be from Richard Standish of
Barnard's Inn, regarding 'Sir Thomas Standish's case
touching his mother's [Dame Margaret's] power of
leasing'. The document is damaged, but it appears
that to raise funds ('portions') for the upbringing of
her younger children, Dame Margaret:

> ' ... did grant and convey the said Mannor of
> Pestforlong and all her lands in Pestforlong
> [sic] and Holcroft aforesaid unto Thos Worsley
> and other Trustees and their heirs, To the use
> of the said Trustees for 50 years if the said
> Dame Margaret should so long live. In Trust
> to permit her to receive the rents for the
> maintenance of her younger children and the
> surplus for her own use….And ... raising
> certain portions and maintenances [for the]
> daughters and younger sons of the said Dame
> Margaret Standish…With a remainder to Sir
> Thomas Standish her oldest son in fee…And
> in the [June 1696 settlement] of release there
> is a provision or power for the said Dame
> Margaret to make leases of lands usually
> leased for three lives or twenty one years
> reserving the ancient rents boons and services
> ...' (LRO DP 397/13/27).

In August 1702, a settlement between the Stanleys
and Lady Margaret's eldest son, Sir Thomas Standish,
gave the extent of a moiety of the manors of Holcroft
and Pesfurlong as:

> '30 messuages, 20 cottages, 300 acres of land,
> 100 of meadow, 500 of pasture, 1000 of moor,
> 1000 of moss, 1000 of furze and heath, 20s rent
> in Pesfurlong. [Also] one water grain mill,
> one melting house [malt kiln], and 300 acres
> of moor, 300 of moss, 300 of furze and heath
> in Holcroft and Pesfurlong' (MCL L1/50/
> 28/7, f553).

Sir Thomas Standish, who was High Sheriff of
Lancashire in 1711, died in 1746. His son, also Thomas,
married Katherine Smith or Frank, a widow, in 1739.
It was during this Thomas' life that part of the manors
of Culcheth, Holcroft, Risley and Pesfurlong - the area
north of Old Abbey Farm known as Twiss Green - was
enclosed in 1749-51 (transcript of 1910, WAS RD Lei/
E1/1). Thomas died in 1756 and was succeeded by
Frank (b 1745; Farrer and Brownbill 1911, 210, n12;
Walker 1995, 18), who, it has been suggested, was
more interested in horse racing than in managing his

inheritance (Walker 1990, 35, 1995, 19-23). In
September 1768 he redeemed a £2000 mortgage on
Pesfurlong (LRO DX 1030), it having perhaps the best
farmland on the estate. This mortgage had been raised
originally by his father in April 1740 through Messrs
Worsley and Wentworth. However, he immediately
re-mortgaged it for £5000, increased to £7500 in 1770,
and to £10,000 in 1790. He finally held Pesfurlong in
fee again by 1806 (MCL L1/27/8; Walker 1995, 25).

Sir Frank died unmarried in 1812, his nominated heir
being Frank Hall (b 1799) of Egglescliffe, County
Durham, the grandson of Sir Frank's aunt, whose
guardian Sir Frank had become in 1807. Taking the
name Frank Hall Standish, this young man is dubbed
'the dilettante debtor' by Walker (1995, 27-41), and was
described by Disraeli as 'exceedingly affected' (Robinson
1991, 180). He spent much of his time abroad.

There was lengthy correspondence concerning a
partition dispute on Pesfurlong Moss in 1837-38, with
Frank Hall Standish as one of the protagonists, which
was only barely settled prior to the mapping of the
township by the tithe commissioners (LRO DX 999-
1022). Following the death of Frank Hall Standish in
1841, the estate passed to William Carr of Cocken Hill,
County Durham, who had changed his name to
William Standish Standish in May 1840. This heir
again increased the debts of his inheritance, by taking
out a massive mortgage for £130,000 in 1853 with Law
Life Assurance of Fleet Street; this cost £4500 *per
annum*. Unlike the Clifton and other Lancashire estate
owners who at this time were taking up grants from
the government and raising loans to provide land
improvements such as tile drains, William Standish
Standish used the mortgage to fund the ultimately
unsuccessful career in the 8th Hussars of his son,
William Standish Carr Standish (1835-78).

Amid all this, Pesfurlong appears to have been
amongst the Standish's best inheritances. A report on
the estates in 1844 says:

> 'The detached estate at Pestfurlong is a very
> desirable one and on the whole much better
> farmed than any other part of the property
> and is within about five miles of the town of
> Warrington and very near to the Kenyon
> Station on the Manchester and Liverpool R'y.
> The payments of tithes and poor rates I think
> are moderate' (MCL L1/27/2/11, f5).

William Standish Standish died in 1856. A few years
afterwards, on 6 October 1864 (LRO DDRf 11/63; WAS D/
DX EL 122/16), the Pesfurlong estate was put up for sale by
Claytons, solicitors, of Newcastle upon Tyne, but only
parts of Bates' and Flitcrofts' Tenements on the west side of
the holding were sold (map DDRf 11/54 (2)). The

valuation, done by Mr Taylor Wainwright of Castle Street, Liverpool on 4 November 1909, gave the whole of the Pesfurlong estate as totalling 830a 3r 36p (acres, roods, perches), with one year's rent and tithe being £1404 5s 0d. George Green was the occupier of Abbey Farm, Gleaves Farm, and part of Pestfurlong Moss, an area of 126a 3r 27p. Elsewhere in the valuation, Hugh and Peter Wareing are shown to have occupied 'part of Pestfurlong Moss', 28a 1r 39p, for £25 rent per year, with no tithe to pay.

The Wareing Family

On the deaths of William and Ann Green in 1900 and 1903 respectively, Hugh Wareing (1880-1959) [an elder brother of the same name, 1874-6, had died in infancy] and his family became guardians of the Greens' children. The Wareings became tenants of the Standish Trustees at Old Abbey Farm in *c* 1911, and also of Unsworths and Pestfurlong Moss Farm by 1920 (sales particulars LRO DDRf 11/75).

In October 1939, a large part of Old Abbey and Moss Side Farms, south of the Occupation Road (parallel with the M62), which continued the line of Silver Lane, was claimed by the Ministry of Supply, for construction of the Royal Ordnance Factory Lane (annotation on Wareing copy of 1920 sale particulars). In April 1950, Fair & Rea wrote to Hugh Wareing at Abbey Farm stating that:

> 'The Trustees of the ... Estate have decided to sell their Properties. They have expressed a wish that they would like the Sitting Tenants to have the chance of purchasing their respective Holdings. If you are interested in purchasing the Property you tenant belonging to them, kindly let us know within ten days ...'.

A schedule of assets taken over at 2 August 1950 indicates that New Hall Farm was to be sold to Hugh Wareing, and Old Abbey Farm to Peter Wareing. One or both of these men appears to have been the next generation - that is Hugh (b 1923, living 1998 at New Hall Farm) and Peter (1921-89), the sons of Peter Wareing (1882-1929), younger brother of Hugh (1880-1959). The schedule specifies £190 for sheds, and £1697 10s of growing crops at Old Abbey Farm, from a total valuation of £2509 10s, though pen amendments indicate that this was later reduced slightly, the purchase price including the house being £3150. The house was in effect divided in *c* 1972-3 to provide more private accommodation for Peter and Winifred Wareing's son Michael (b 1954) when he married the following year. In November 1988, just before the

Figure 7: 1757 Estate map showing Old Abbey Farm in mock-perspective and a causeway across the moat. By kind permission of Lancashire Record Office © Copyright

death of Peter Wareing, sale of the property to UK Waste Management Limited was concluded, correspondence being addressed to Mrs Winifred Wareing. Michael Wareing and his family were the last residents of the house. After their departure the house fell into disuse.

Old Abbey Farm between the Eighteenth and Twentieth Centuries

T he earliest estate map of Pesfurlong was produced by the well-known Lancashire surveyor R Lang for Sir Frank Standish in 1757 (Fig 7; LRO DDRf 11/54(1)). Other individuals who owned land in Pesfurlong alongside the Standishes at this time were Ellen Clare, James Thompson, Thomas Blackburn, James Tyldesley, a Mr Merrick, William Clough, Thomas Bait, Thomas Guest, and Thomas Risley. Some of the pattern of landholding can be projected back to 1736 by comparing the names of tenants and acreages with those given in a rental of that year (MCL L1/27/2/1). A simplified valuation of all the Standish lands in Culcheth (MCL L1/27/2/2) was also made in 1750, under the terms of the Twiss Green Enclosure Act, which - in addition to the Common to be enclosed - included 'Pesfurlong Hall' (formerly New Hall) with 94 acres, which was tenanted by Edward Unsworth in 1736 and 1757, and is the first-named on each list. It had a yearly valuation of £100 in 1736, £99 16s 3d in 1750, and £114 10s 9d in 1757, though the last figure is for a little over 102 acres, compared with the 94 acres in 1750 (acreages are not given in the 1736 survey).

Second in the order of precedence is clearly Old Pesfurlong Demesne. In 1736 it was leased to Thomas Richardson, with a valuation of £21 yearly, this being the only mention we have of this tenant. In 1750 John Warburton had $33^1/_2$ acres, with a valuation of £39 11s $10^1/_2$d. In 1757 'Thomas Warburton for Old Pestforlong Demesne' had 32a 2r 18p, of which 29a 3r 12p were pasture. The total yearly value was £40 2s 0d, of which £2 0s 0d was for the 'house, garden, mote, fold, & lane', and the fields were valued at between £24 and £30 per acre. Clearly by the early eighteenth century Old Abbey Farm was no more than the farmstead of a small tenanted farm, even if it was still considered the second most important property within Pesfurlong. This may be a reflection of its past importance rather than a real reflection of its contemporary standing.

In the Culcheth township books, the Henry Warburton named as a constable in 1733 may have been a relation of Thomas Warburton of Old Pesfurlong Demesne (LLHL B Cul 352 Nor, f8). A James Richardson is named as a Surveyor of the Highways in 1771 (*op cit*, f33), and Roger Richardson of Culcheth, husbandman, holder of one cottage in Culcheth, leased from Thomas Culcheth, registered a Papist estate in 1717.

The estate map of 1757 (Fig 7) shows Old Abbey Farm in mock-perspective, looking broadly similar to its 1990 appearance, though with the projecting wing at the south appearing as large as the rest of the house. Three chimney stacks are shown. The 1757 map also shows two other (smaller) buildings, south of the moat and east of the barn. Gates and tracks are also shown. Access across the moat is clearly by the causeway rather than a bridge, refuting popular belief (Newchurch Girl Guides 1953, 59) that a bridge had been used within living memory.

Old Pesfurlong Demesne comprised the same fields from this date until *c* 1864. They were the Stack Yard (north of the moat; tithe 757), Hemp Croft (759), Great Back House Field (756), Less Back House Field (part of 756 by 1834), Further Four Acre (755), Nearer Four Acre (754), Long Meadow (not part of Demesne by the tithe), Barley Croft (753, called Bailey's Croft on the tithe), Shippon Field (760), Little Ox Hey Meadow (761, 763), Great Ox Hey Meadow (762), Berchell Meadow (Birchall's Meadow on the tithe, 752), Five

Rood Land and 20 Acre (767, part of Moss Side Farm by the tithe), Intack (774, part of Moss Side Farm by the tithe), and Rough (not identified).

A later map 'reduced and copied by James Derham, Chorley' (LRO DDRf 11/54(2)), apparently from the tithe map of 1838, since it shows the tithe field numbers, shows a small projection to the north of the house, and an extension along half of the east side. The two small sheds, lying to the south in 1757, are not shown. 'Pestforlong Moss' is shown, and annotated 'woods'.

James Green was the tenant at the time of the tithe apportionment of 1838 (LRO DRL 1/21; WCL MS 2549a), in rentals of 1841-2 (MCL L1/27/2/5), in 1843 (LRO DX 1200), when he had arrears of £2 2s, and in 1845 (MCL L1/27/2/8). In the first of the 10-yearly censuses, in 1841 (LRO MF 24/24 from PRO HO 107/524/6), he was aged 40 years, and shared the house with his wife Ann (aged 35), and Sarah Banks (five), Sarah Wilkie (13), two man servants, Joseph Milburn (20) and Thomas Guest (18), a 'man of independent means' John Banks (68), and George Whittle (40), a 'wolin weaver' [*sic*]. The next entry is for Moss Side Farm, which was a century later to become part of the Old Abbey holding, which was occupied in 1841 by Ephraim Stringer (60), and his wife and five children.

By the end of the 1840s the tenancy had changed to Joseph Green, whose relationship to James Green is not known. He is named in the survey report of 1848/53 (DDRf 11/77, f62-3 and 71), and in the census of 1851 (LRO MF 25/66 from PRO HO 107/2204, f194-5) Joseph (aged 53) shared the house with his wife Mary (44), and nine children, namely James (24), Phobe [*sic*] (21), Richard (19), Thomas (16), John (13), Joseph (nine), George (six), William (four), and Margaret (two).

The children gradually moved away - James, Phobe [*sic*], Richard and Thomas by 1861, by which time they had another child Peter (aged eight), and a grandson Samuel (aged seven) also living with them (WCL MF 22, reel 4, from PRO RG 9/2801, dist 14C, f19). Joseph farmed 74 acres in 1861, his widow Mary 104 acres in 1881, but they do not seem to have employed anybody outside the family (this would have been shown in the census).

Joseph died sometime between 1871 and 1878 since, in the valuation of 1878, Mary alone is named as the tenant of Old Pesforlong Demesne and Gleaves Tenement (the latter being in two parts, in the tenancy of Peter Meredith and William Westwell, in the 1864 sale particulars, LRO DDRf 11/63). Mary was still head of the family in 1881 (WCL MF 28, reel 6, from PRO RG 11/3804, dist 14, f62), but her son William, then single, is recorded as the tenant in the 1891 census (WCL M/Fiche ED 15, fiche 4, from PRO RG 12/3085, f154). He still shared the house with his brothers and sisters, George, Margaret, and Peter, a niece Mary (aged 28), and a farm labourer, Thomas Croston (aged 21).

In a list of tenants and record of repairs and improvement done and needed 1894-9 (LRO DDRf 11/16, f5) Old Pestfurlong Demesne and Gleaves Tenement are recorded as being let to the 'Representatives of Mary Green', with an acreage of 106a 2r 25p. The year's rent was by then £145. Work done is noted as 'Repairing & cementing walls of farm house. Repairing roofs, building harvest mens house, piggeries, etc', and the estimated cost of work in 1899 was £235 17s 4d.

The Census of 1901 was not available for public consultation during the documentary research, but the Wareing family documents indicate that William Green died in July 1900, leaving a widow Ann, who died in November 1903, leaving Annie, a minor, and Mary and Elsie, infants, as her only next of kin. Hugh Wareing, uncle of the children, became their guardian, and formally became tenant in May 1911, unless this replaces an earlier agreement (letter found in house 1990).

A notebook containing a rent audit for Pesfurlong in December 1903 has nothing to say about Old Abbey Farm, but notes that *John* Green was 'much in arrears and should be sent off the estate'. He was £232 1s in arrears and signed a pencilled request to be relieved of the tenancy, authorising the estate to sell produce and implements as part payment. From the 1894-9 list of tenants, he occupied Shaws Tenement. This may be William Green's brother, who would have been aged about 65 by this time (LRO DDRf 11/83).

In the abortive sale of 1920, the particulars state that 'The Dutch barn at Old Abbey farm belongs to the tenants and is not included in the sale' (LRO DDRf 11/75). This seems to have been replaced in 1937/8 by the six-bay structure still standing in 1990, for which an estimate was to be sought in November 1937, after the resolution of the following disagreement.

Correspondence in the Wareing family collection indicates that Hugh Wareing served Fair & Rea with Notice to Quit Abbey and Pesfurlong Moss Farms in November 1932, but after interviews withdrew it in September 1933, and signed a fresh form of agreement with the Standish Estates in March 1934, with a rent of £200, instead of £300 'for the first two years of the tenancy, commencing February 1934 and for it to be reconsidered at the end of the second year ...' (from correspondence in the hands of the Wareing family). At the same time, Hugh Wareing agreed to take over the tenancy of Moss Side Farm from G Nicholson, for £75 *per annum*, the low rent being 'in consideration of the farm being in such poor and dirty condition and of the cost of cleaning and getting it back into tenantable order and to do all repairs and painting' (*ibid*).

3

PHASE 1 - THE MEDIEVAL MOATED PLATFORM, TIMBER-FRAMED HALL, AND BRIDGE

MID THIRTEENTH TO MID SIXTEENTH CENTURY

Specialist study of re-used timbers dated by dendrochronology has suggested that a late thirteenth or possibly very early fourteenth century open hall formerly stood on the site of Old Abbey Farm (Fig 8). The hall is thought to have been fully aisled, with a steeply-pitched hipped roof, but all the timbers from this phase were found re-used in secondary positions, so that many aspects of the building's form and appearance remain uncertain. In the late medieval period it is probable that the aisles were removed, with new timber-framing built below the arcade-plates. A clay floor found by excavation relates to this building or to a slightly earlier structure (Fig 9). The medieval hall stood on a moated platform; the moat and platform could not be independently dated, but appear to be at least as old as the clay floor and re-used timbers. It is not clear how the moat was crossed earlier in the medieval period, but waterlogged timbers were recovered demonstrating that a substantial timber bridge was constructed in the mid fifteenth century.

The Timber-Framed Hall

The building survey demonstrated that some timbers re-used in the farmhouse and barn in Phases 2 - 6 had been drawn from one or more medieval timber-framed structures. Specialist analysis of this limited body of timbers suggests that many were re-used from a medieval hall (Lee and Michelmore 1998). Although its exact position has proved difficult to establish, it has been possible to gain a relatively good understanding of the construction and appearance of this early hall (Figs 8, 12; Pl 4). Some of the medieval timbers appear to have been derived from another similar building, perhaps a barn.

Two small groups of timbers employed within the Phase 5 central hall of the farmhouse (Room G1, *Ch 11* Fig 69) were identified as particularly likely to be derived from the Phase 1 build of the same structure (Lee and Michelmore 1998). One group (Figs 10, 12) was found within the frame of the first floor of the hall. Six flooring joists were recognised as being cut

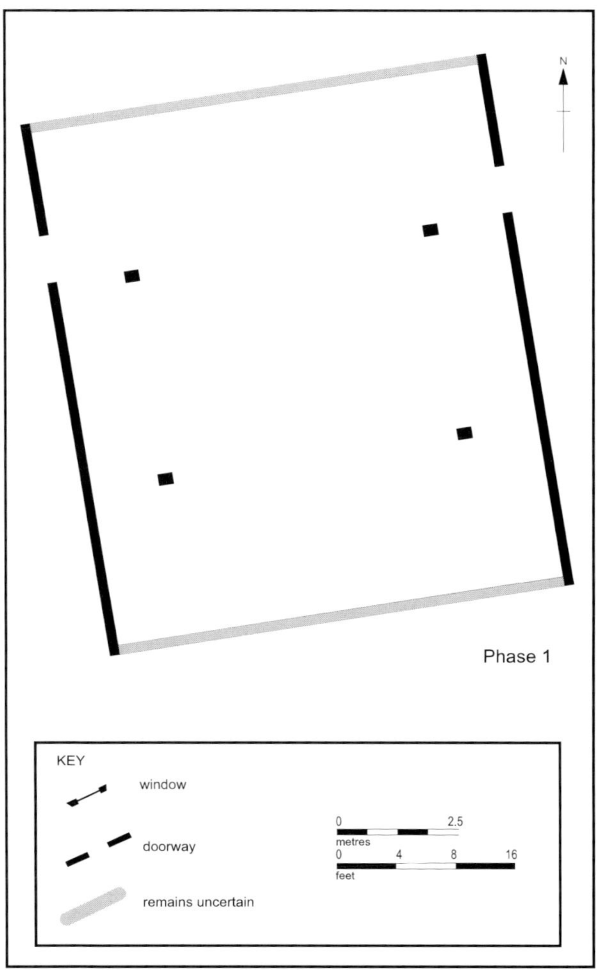

Figure 8: Suggested plan of the timber-framed hall, Phase 1

down sections of former A-frame rafters (Fig 13); disused joints present on the timbers allowed the angle of the former rafters to be reconstructed. The joists were jointed to a bridging joist, which may have been cut down from the tie-beam of an open truss belonging to the same roof; the fact that the central hall roof is known to have been replaced in Phase 5 strongly suggests that these former roof timbers had been liberated from within this structure. Dendrochronological analysis demonstrated that two of the rafters were from trees felled after AD 1249 and AD 1261, and that the tie-beam was from a tree felled after AD 1268 (Hillam *et al* 1987 for 10-55 sapwood estimate). As there was no sapwood on any of the samples from these timbers, ten years has been added to the date of the last tree ring in order to arrive at the earliest possible calendar date for the sample, because ten is the minimum number of sapwood rings usually present on British oak between the heartwood and the bark (*ibid*). It is impossible to estimate how many heartwood rings may have been lost, though it might be argued that the figure is likely to have been low, unless the timber conversion had been wasteful.

A second group of two timbers was found lying horizontally between the top of the Phase 3 brick east wall of the central hall (Room G1, Fig 69), and the probable Phase 5 wall-plates above. The timbers had formerly been the top part of an arcade wall-post (Fig 10), and an arcade wall-plate (Fig 12). The lack of side mortises for girding mid-rails on the post indicated that this was a free-standing aisle post, rather than part of a wall-frame. The clean face of the post, without stave holes or infill grooves, demonstrated that, as with the former tie-beam, it was from an open truss. Dendrochronological analysis showed that it was derived from a tree felled after AD 1240 (*op cit*; the considerations outlined above also apply to the true felling date of this timber). The good condition of the plate, as well as its carpentry features and the presence of the aisle post, suggested its origin as an arcade-plate. In aisled structures, the arcade wall-plate and posts, being internal, are normally well protected from the agents of decay, and usually survive longer than external posts and plates. It is notable that these two timbers survived together, and were available for mutual exploitation later. A further isolated re-used timber deriving from Phase 1 was found within the structure of the Phase 2 crosswing. It appears to be a truss collar (Fig 10).

The evidence of these timbers, and of the carpentry joints preserved on them, was used to create a span matrix. Timbers re-used as wall-plates in the Phase 6 barn were added to the matrix; they included one near complete former tie-beam (Fig 12), and two or possibly three short sections of tie-beams (*see Ch 3 p25*). The basic geometry and angles of the mortises were found to correspond to the matrix, and these timbers may also have originated in the farmhouse. However, it must be stressed that they may come from a comparable structure, such as an aisled barn, of roughly the same date and size as the house. Furthermore, the pattern and nature of the joints on these timbers was not compatible with those on the possible tie-beam re-used as a bridging joist referred to above, so the barn timbers or the bridging joist must have originated in another building. Two re-used tie-beams from the barn have angled mortises in

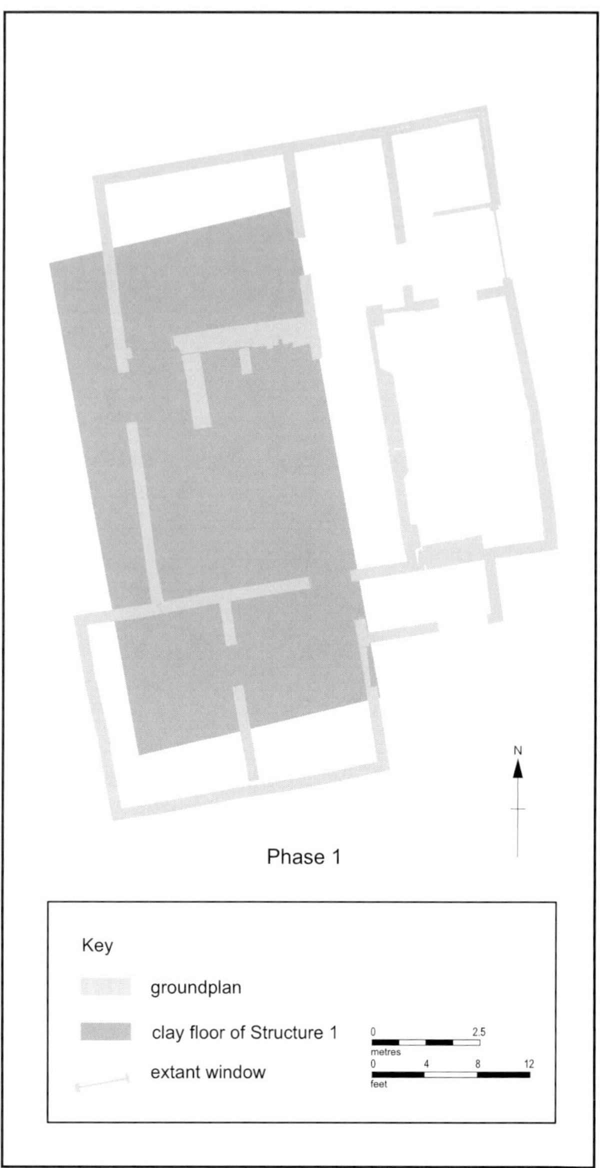

Figure 9: Plan of timber-framed hall showing physical evidence, Phase 1

their upper faces, suggesting that the building from which they came had a double-raftered roof (Fig 12).

Study of this evidence has allowed some of the key dimensions and angles of the Phase 1 hall to be reconstructed (Lee and Michelmore 1998). The span of the nave was derived from the length of the possible tie-beam re-used in the Phase 5 floor (not illustrated); on this basis the nave may have measured 5.8 m in width. This corresponds to the width of the clay floor recorded during excavation (Fig 9), and to the width of the central room of the later farmhouse. The length of the arcade from the upper face of one post to the lower face of the next post could be derived from carpentry features within the arcade-plate (Fig 12). This gives a bay length of *c* 4 m, a figure which matches the distance from the north side of the Phase

Plate 4: Reconstruction of the timber-framed hall

2 crosswing to the likely southern side of a putative Phase 1 cross-passage. The correspondence in figures suggests that the re-used arcade-plate had originally been positioned above the central bay of the timber hall. It was also possible to calculate the pitch of the roof, the angle of a collar mortise surviving on one of the former rafters demonstrating that the pitch was 58-60° (Fig 10).

Further inferences can be drawn about the likely overall layout and appearance of the hall (Lee and Michelmore 1998). The evidence of the arcade-post and plate indicates that the hall had an aisle to the rear, and it seems probable that it would have been a fully aisled building, with further aisles along the front and at either end (Fig 8). The external aisle walls probably had large wattle and daubed panels, with arch-braces only being used in the arcade of the main structure. There was no direct evidence from the re-used timbers for the length of the building, or the number of bays. However, if the clay floor (*see below, Structure 1, p 24*) relates to this build of the hall, it may have been relatively short. To reflect this possibility, reconstructions (Fig 12, Pl 4) have been prepared which depict a hall of a single bay, defined by two pairs of nave arcade-posts. Additional space was provided at either end by cantilevered arcade-plates extending beyond the aisle posts, and end aisles (Fig 12). Fully aisled structures with cantilevered arcades

have been recorded elsewhere, at Sandal Castle in West Yorkshire (dating from the twelfth century; Michelmore 1983), and at Lime Tree House, Berkshire (built in two Phases in the mid and late thirteenth century; Fletcher and Currie 1980; Fletcher and Tapper 1984).

The building would have had an open hall, probably with an inner solar room at one end, and a cross-passage and service at the other. Parlour and service may have had upper rooms, and may have been partitioned off from the main hall on the ground floor (though the inner face of the surviving aisle post contained no carpentry features). In the hall, it is likely that there would have been a central open hearth, and some evidence of this was gained by excavation (*see below, Structure 1, p 24*). The hearth would have been ventilated by gablets at either end of the roof, which was probably hipped. The gablets would also have served as small windows. Additional light probably came from windows placed in the aisles. The early roof had A-frame rafters, and may have been of crown post construction, though there is no obvious evidence for crown post trusses. The size and quality of the early timbers are indicative of a relatively high status building.

The later layout of the farmhouse can also be used to add to knowledge of its likely Phase 1 groundplan. Evidence that the early structure took the form of a

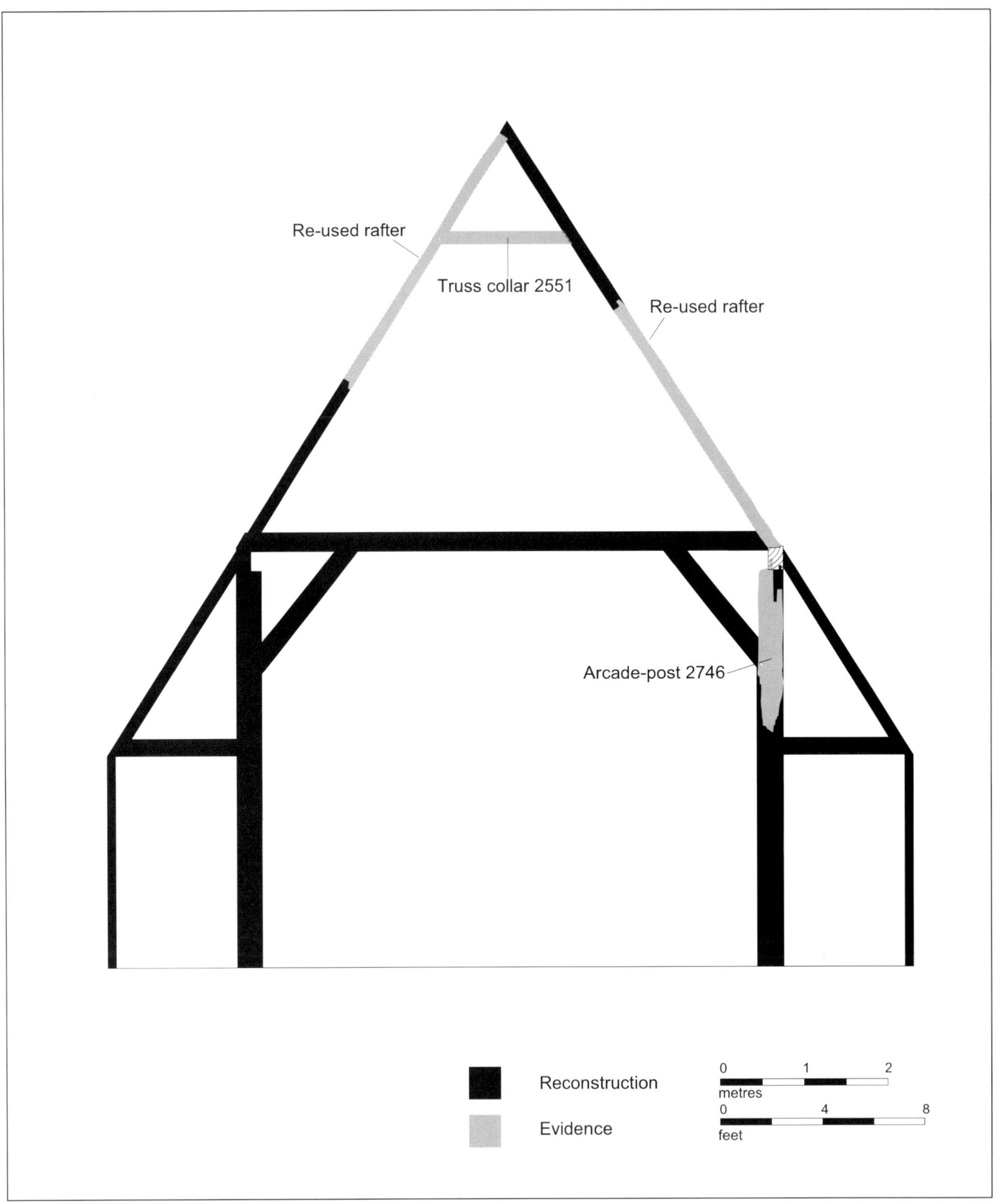

Figure 10: Reconstruction of the roof pitch of the Phase 1 timber-framed hall, based on evidence of rafters and collar

hall with a cross-passage to the north derives from the position of the main west door and fireplace in the later Phase 3 brick build of the central room. Their location suggests that a baffle entrance and inglenook had been inserted into a previous cross-passage. This is reinforced by a blocked doorway in the east wall, opposed to the western entrance. If the typical plan of a medieval open hall had been followed, it is to be expected that the service bay would have been located immediately beyond the cross-passage, in this case to the north, in the area subsequently occupied by rooms G2 and G2A (Fig 69). The solar would have extended beyond the later south wall of the central hall, into the area occupied in Phase 2 by a southern crosswing.

These conjectures about the form of the Phase 1 hall are drawn from limited direct evidence, and it cannot be proved that the dated timbers did in fact come from this building. However, the match of postulated nave width and bay length with the dimensions of the later central hall further suggest that this may be the case.

The subsequent excavation provided support for the general premise that a medieval open hall pre-dated the later brick farmhouse (Fig 11), but the exact relationship between the early hall indicated by excavation evidence, and the later structure, remains problematic. A probable beaten clay floor bounded by padstones to the east lay beneath the central room of the farmhouse, and extended beyond it to the north and south; this is considered to be the footprint of a medieval building, Structure 1. It measured *c* 10.7 m x 5.8 m, and was surrounded by a deposit of redeposited clay, probably a rough surface into which it appeared to have been set. If the floor related to the notional building which can be reconstructed from re-used timbers and the later farmhouse, then the dimensions suggest that the floor was confined to the nave and end aisles, or dates to a period after the side aisles had been removed to give greater light (*Phase 1b, p 34*). A shallow cut feature, which truncated the clay floor, may represent the remains of a subrectangular hearth (4582, Fig 11); it was bounded to east and west by patches of burnt clay. The cut was stratified directly above the floor, but its fill contained a sherd of late seventeenth century pottery, as well as fragments of ceramic building material. Although these finds might derive from later consolidation of a feature backfilled earlier, their presence casts doubt as to whether this shallow cut could be a hearth pre-dating the Phase 3 inglenook fireplace.

Further difficulties remain in demonstrating that this early floor surface relates to the hall inferred from re-used timbers. This is because, whilst the floor surface matched the width of both the nave of the hall suggested by the re-used timbers, and the central hall of the later Phase 3 house (Room G1, Fig 69), the floor was displaced *c* 1 m to the west of the later central hall. This implies that the floor belonged to a different structure which was demolished at an early date, or that the whole Phase 1 timber-framed building was subsequently moved. Both possibilities need to be considered (*see Ch 11*). On the one hand, documentary sources and dendrochronology indicate that a period of at least 22 years elapsed between the death of Gilbert de Culcheth and the earliest date for the construction of the hall indicated by re-used timbers, and it might be thought that an earlier building, perhaps represented by the clay pad, existed on the site during the interval. However, it remains possible that considerable alterations were made to the central hall in Phase 2, when the southern crosswing was erected. The central hall may have been partially rebuilt and shifted east towards the moat at this time.

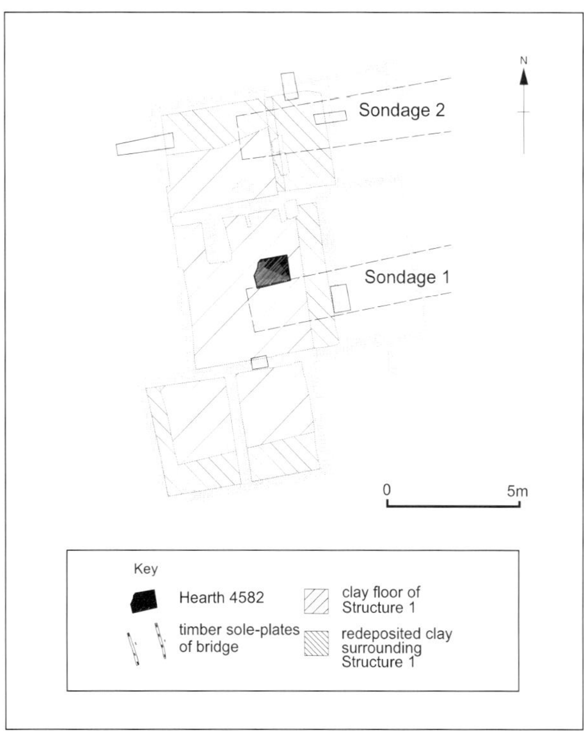

Figure 11: Excavation evidence for the Phase 1 timber-framed hall

Hard standing around Structure 1

Four similar clay deposits, divided by later foundation trenches, together represented a final episode of ground levelling prior to the laying of the clay floor for a probable timber building (Structure 1). In contrast to the underlying consolidation deposits, it was possible to record these layers in plan (Fig 11). They appeared to flank the probable floor surface (*described below, p 24*) to the north, east, south, and south-west, rather than underlying it, thus creating areas of hard standing around the probable building footprint. The hard standing had total dimensions of at least 13.5 m (north / south) by 10.5 m (east / west), leaving an area of *c* 11 m x 6 m clear in the centre where the clay floor appears subsequently to have been laid. The deposits were investigated by means of two machine-dug sondages aligned east / west. They were also partially excavated when small hand-dug sondages were dug across the foundation trenches of the later farmhouse.

Layer 4759 represented the northern end of this area of clay. It lay within the area of room G2 (Fig 69) of the later farmhouse, and was truncated by that room's foundation trenches (Phase 6) to the north and west. It was observed that 4759 was also present beyond the foundation trench to the north, but it was not possible to record its full extent. One rim sherd of pottery (Fig 53.2), of probable mid twelfth to mid fourteenth century date, was found within the deposit. It was one of only seven sherds of medieval pottery recovered during the excavation, and was the only such sherd

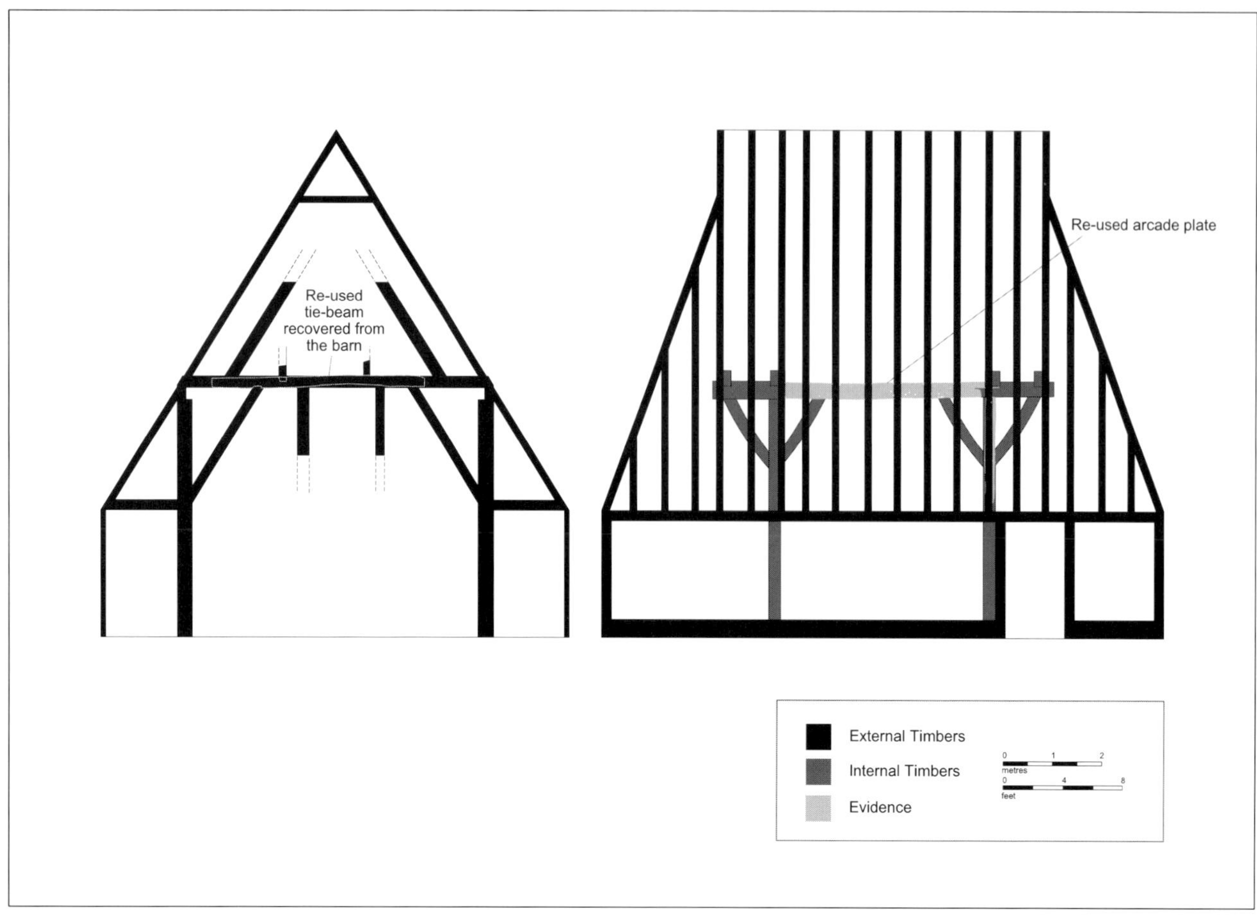

Figure 12: Phase 1: Reconstruction of the Phase 1 timber-framed hall, based on evidence of re-used timbers

not from a very mixed context. In common with the other medieval sherds, it was in an oxidised, gritty fabric, with a splash of green glaze, and was abraded, suggesting that it may have been moved around before coming to reside in this layer.

Layer 4287 lay immediately to the east, within the footprint of later farmhouse room G2A. Three sherds of eighteenth to nineteenth century pottery (Fabric 3) were recovered from the layer, but were thought to be intrusive; modern deposits were stratified directly above the layer, and it was truncated to north and east by that room's foundation trenches (Phase 6). Layer 4287 was composed of redeposited clay.

Layer 4772 flanked the floor surface to the east. This clay layer was subsequently truncated to the east by the Phase 3 wall trench of room G1 of the later farmhouse (*see Ch 5*). Clay floor layer 4265 was thought to have been laid over the western edge of 4772.

Layer 4766 lay to the south and south-west of the central floor surface, and was itself truncated to the south and south-west by the foundations of later farmhouse room G4/G5/6. As with the related layers, it is thought that the clay floor to the north was stratified above 4766.

Structure 1

This was represented by a probable rectangular clay floor surface 0.07-0.08 m thick, with dimensions of *c* 10.7 m north / south by 5.8 m east / west (Fig 9). The floor surface appears to have been set into the final layer of clay make-up which surrounded it to the north, east, south, and south-west, and was composed of greyish yellow silty clay with no coarse component, more compact and smooth than the surrounding make-up, perhaps suggesting that it had been beaten when deposited. The floor surface was truncated into separate areas by the foundation trenches of the later farmhouse, 4265/4767 and 4390 referring to the portion surviving within the central room G1 of the later building, whilst 4390 again and 4531 were used for the portion to the south within later rooms G5/6 and G4. Context 4760 refers to the northern part of the floor located within later room G2. The floor was recorded in plan, but it was also seen in section where two machine-dug sondages were excavated, and when sondages were hand-dug across the foundations of the later farmhouse. Two sherds of pottery (Fabric 4), possibly dating to the late seventeenth century, were recovered from 4531. It is thought that these sherds were introduced into the floor from above; the overlying deposits were post-medieval in date. The building survey demonstrated that the crosswing,

24

comprising rooms G4 and G5/6, contained *in situ* remains dating to the sixteenth century. The clay floor surface, which does not correspond in plan to the surviving building footprint, must have been earlier.

A possible hearth (4582) lay roughly halfway along the length of the floor, but close to its eastern edge (Fig 11). It measured 1.20 m x 0.95 m by 0.18 m deep, with relatively steep sides and an uneven base. Irregular patches of burnt clay lay immediately to the east and west, and may have been burnt *in situ*.

Three possible padstones were recorded which may have supported vertical timber posts, one of which (4673) was set within a shallow foundation cut. The three stones were oriented north / south, and were aligned along the edge between the exterior make-up and probable internal floor surface. It is suggested that they were the surviving remnant of foundations for the east wall of Structure 1. Stones 4671 and 4672 were thought to be laid over the edge of the clay floor surface; cut 4791 for stone 4673 was recorded truncating the edge of the surface.

Stone 4671 was sub-rectangular in plan, with dimensions of 0.65 m x 0.50 m. It lay 1.0 m to the south of 4673. Stone 4763 was 0.80 m long, but varied in width between 0.50 m and 0.30 m, whilst foundation cut 4791 for stone 4673 was 0.58 m wide by 0.26 m deep. Stone 4672 was a similar shape, and measured 0.60 m x 0.40 m. It lay almost immediately adjacent to 4673, again to the north.

Re-used timbers from the Phase 1 hall

The re-used timbers were studied by Building Conservation Services (Lee and Michelmore 1998). Two such timbers (2745 and 2746), jointed together using a relatively unsophisticated scarf joint, were being re-used below the Phase 5 wall-plate at the top of the east wall of the central hall of the farmhouse. They lay resting on top of the Phase 3 brick rebuild of that wall.

One, a short extension piece, was the top part of an arcade wall-post (2746) and the other a re-used wall-plate (2745). The wall-plate was 4.20 m (13'9") long and had seatings for eight rafters on the original top. It had two pegged arch-brace mortises in its soffit, angled towards each end. At one straight cut end, there was visible evidence of a post mortise but at the other end the creation of the scarf joint had cut away any evidence for the other post. Running on the outer edge of the soffit and across the front of the arch-brace mortises was a 35 mm wide by 50 mm deep square-cut slot. This ran from the square-cut end up to a point just beyond the second windbrace, stopping 350 mm (14") short of the assumed wall-post position. The inside soffit had been reduced by 12-25 mm ($^1/_2$-1").

On the outer face, were two 35 mm ($1^1/_2$") face pegs, 150 mm (6") above the soffit, 1.05 m ($3'5^3/_4$") and 220 mm (9") from the back of the first arch-brace mortise. On the outer face was a series of small mortises and drilled holes which were for window 2767 from Phase 3 (*see Ch 5*).

The wall-post produced a dendrochronological felling date of AD 1240+ (Sheffield, 1998; Hillam *et al* 1987 for 10-55 sapwood estimate). It was scarfed to the wall-plate and was 2.00 m (6'6") long. There were three arch-brace mortises on the post, two for lateral braces and another for an arch-brace to a tie-beam. The two side mortises were 250 mm (9-10") long, set slightly lower than the front brace. The existence of these mortises shows that this was not a corner post. The front brace mortise was 340 mm (13-13$^1/_2$") long. The face was clean, without stave holes or infill grooves, and indicates that this was from an open truss. During the thirteenth century, construction methods changed and posts with jowls were used; the tree was cut down and turned upside-down in use, with the thickening of the bole being cut to provide the jowl. Prior to this, the posts were cut from timbers which were used the natural way up, with the bole at the bottom. As it is suggested that the building as a whole was constructed after AD 1268, it is possible that the posts had jowls; unfortunately, due to surface decay on the face, it was not obvious whether this example had been cut back or not. The post had no side mortises for girding mid-rails which would normally appear as extensions to the brace mortises, or separately, just below them. In this case, there was nearly 400 mm (15") below them clear before the decayed post's lower end. Their absence indicates that the post was a free-standing aisle post, but there is no evidence of a mortise for an aisle-tie to the rear of the post. In its use as part of a Phase 3-4 wall-plate, a deep tapered groove was noted across the post, tapering from 180 mm down to 100 mm (7- 4"), which lines up where a Phase 3-4 tie-beam was probably housed. A tie-beam was still located above this in the secondary wall-plate on top of the early timber.

Bridging joist 3169 appears to have been cut down from a tie-beam in an open truss, possibly supported by the postulated arcade-plates above one of two pairs of aisle posts. It produced a dendrochronological felling date of AD 1268+ (Sheffield, 1998; Hillam *et al* 1987 for 10-55 sapwood estimate). The dimensions of the timber were 300 mm x 320 mm x 5.80 m (12"x 13" x 19'0"). It had been ripped down its face length, had one end cut with a seating for installation into the west wall, and the other chopped rough to be built into the Phase 3 wall on the east. On the face of the timber were five large pegholes of 35 mm diameter ($1^1/_2$"), three to the centre of *c* 300 mm diameter (1'0"), and others of *c* 1.60 m (5' 3"). As they have nothing to

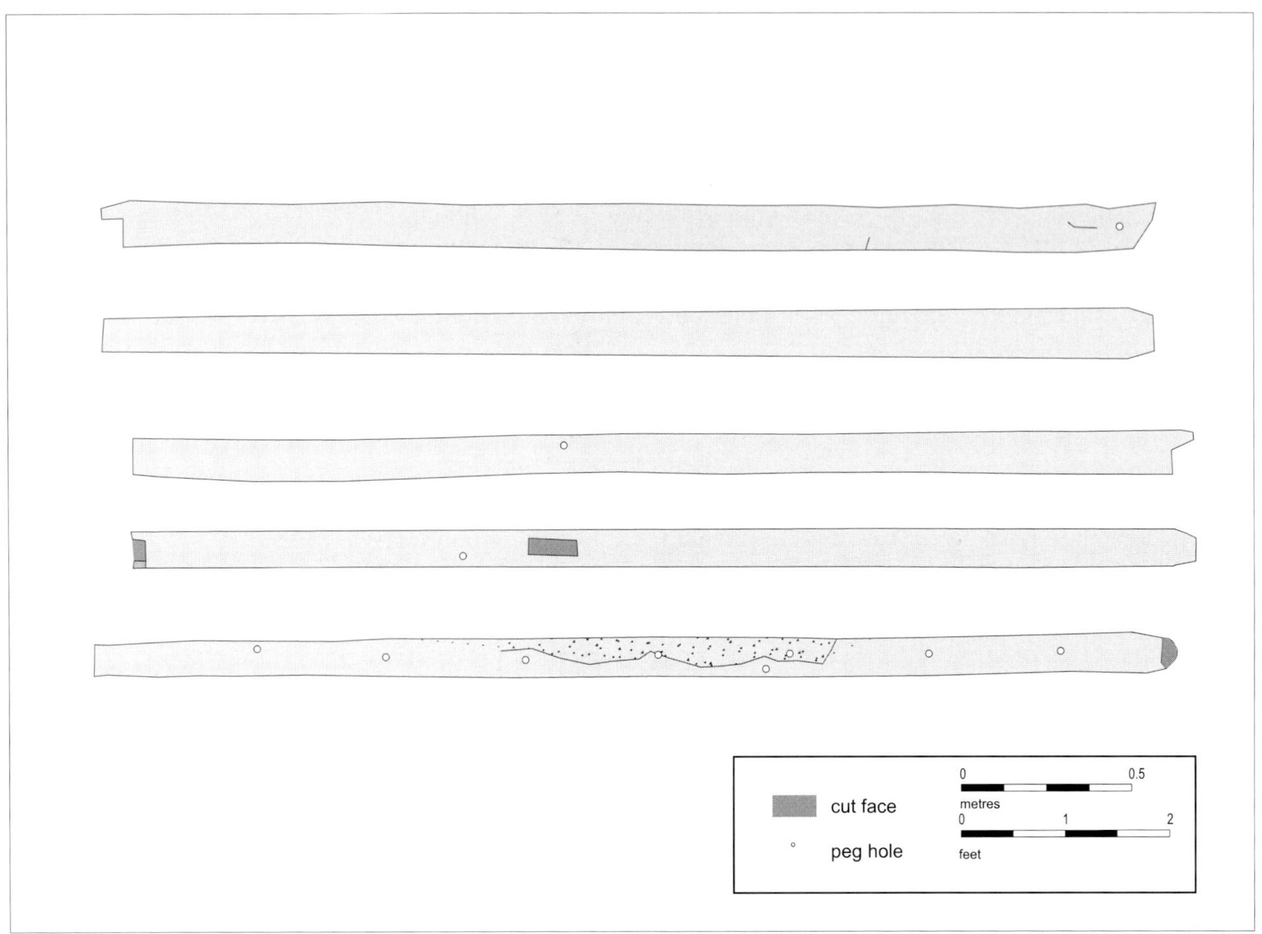

Figure 13: Re-used rafters 3167 from the Phase 1 timber-framed hall

do with its later use as a floor beam, they must be from its previous use. The outer two appear to be left from long passing braces after the face was sawn off.

Six flooring joists from the central hall of the Phase 5 farmhouse were identified as cut down sections of former A-frame rafters (Figs 12, 13). Joist 3167C produced a dendrochronological felling date of AD 1249+ (Sheffield, 1998; Hillam *et al* 1987 for 10-55 sapwood estimate), and 3167L a date of AD 1261+ (Sheffield, 1998; Hillam *et al* 1987 for 10-55 sapwood estimate). Tapering from 150 mm x 125 mm to 100 mm x 87-100 mm (6" x 5" to 4" x 3^1/$_2$"), the joists have pegged mortises for collars and may have been close spaced. One joist gave the rafter length from the upper coupling tenon to below the collar mortise, whilst another ran from the rafter foot and had been cut off below the collar mortise. The angle of the collar is drawn from the angle of the mortise which is taken as horizontal. This gives a pitch of 58-60°.

That this is correct is further supported by what appears to be a truss collar (2551, Fig 10). This timber measured 127 mm wide by 127 mm deep (5"x 5"), with a clear span of 1.40 m (55"), and had been re-used in the Phase 2 crosswing. It had a pegged, square-cut, bare-faced tenon, with a sloping shoulder. The opposite end was slightly decayed without a tenon, although it was the full length. The length and angle of this corresponds closely to the evidence of the former rafter described above. On the top of this collar there was a series of shallow drill holes, two of them extending through to the soffit, with ratios of 0.25, 0.5, 0.25 (^{1}/$_4$, ^{1}/$_2$, ^{1}/$_4$). There were two pegholes on the lower face, one central, and the other 300 mm (12") to the side of it. Several timbers from the site exhibit this type of flush-cut end to a tenon (for example, 3168).

Evidence for Other Timber-Framed Structures

Several re-used timbers of possible medieval date were identified among the wall-plates of the mid eighteenth century barn (*see Ch 8*). The basic geometry of three of these timbers, and the angles of their mortises, correspond to the matrix constructed from the re-used farmhouse timbers, implying that some of these timbers could have originated within the medieval hall (*see above, p 19*). However, the positions of the former joints showed that they could only be derived from the Phase 1 hall if bridging joist 3169 had originated elsewhere. A fourth timber was of different character, and appeared to be a medieval mid-rail. On the basis of this evidence, it is suggested that some of the re-used timbers found in the barn may have come from a structure comparable to the aisled hall, perhaps an aisled barn of roughly the same date and size as the hall, but constructed using timbers of lesser dimensions (Lee and Michelmore 1998, 11). It cannot be proved that this structure stood on the Old Abbey Farm site, rather than elsewhere in the vicinity, but the possibility can at least be suggested.

Several re-used timbers were also found among the barn purlins. These were more difficult to date on stylistic grounds than the wall-plates, but have been attributed to the sixteenth century or earlier (Lee and Michelmore 1998, 11). They are discussed in *Chapter 4.*

Re-used timbers employed as wall-plates in the Phase 6 barn

Among the re-used wall-plates of the mid eighteenth century barn, one near complete tie-beam, and two, or possibly three, short sections of tie-beams were found (141, 127 and 492). The geometry and mortise angles of these timbers were comparable with those of re-used timbers found in the farmhouse, thought to suggest the former existence of an aisled hall.

A fourth wall-plate (410) showed clear evidence of re-use, and was also of medieval appearance. It was 3.40 m long, 150 mm square and had three full mortises and one quarter mortise unevenly spaced along the bottom. Wattle infill stave holes were placed between the second and third mortises, but not up to the first, or up to the second. A chamfer on the outside edge, running between the first and second studs, indicated an opening. The chamfer was extended and the second stud had been moved to the side to widen the opening. On the top of the timber, there were no mortises and only one peg hole straight down between the second and third mortise. Seatings 180 mm wide were cut 30 mm deep on either side of the first stud mortise, indicating that this may have been some kind of internal partition. This timber could have been a cut-down section of re-used mid-rail (Lee and Michelmore 1998, 11).

The Moat and Moated Platform

The excavation, and the earlier evaluation trenching conducted in 1990, demonstrated that Old Abbey Farm had formerly been surrounded by a substantial subrectangular moat. The moat was most thoroughly investigated to the west of the farmhouse in Area C (Fig 3), where the impact of recent disturbance appeared to be limited. Here, sections were excavated across the feature (Pl 5), and it was found to measure 14-15 m in width at the top, and *c* 3.2 m in depth (Fig 14). It enclosed a platform measuring *c* 25 m east / west by 22 m north / south. Comparison with other moated sites in north-west England suggests that this should be regarded as a relatively substantial moat enclosing a small platform (*see Ch 11*).

Clay from the excavation of the moat appears to have been dumped to build up the platform at its eastern edge, but was not used to increase the height of the platform surface significantly above the level of the surrounding landscape. Several dumped consolidation layers were identified close to the platform's eastern margin, within two machine-excavated sondages (sondages 1 and 2, Fig 14). Together these layers extended for *c* 7 m, from within the probable footprint of the medieval timber hall, to the eastern arm of the moat, appearing to fill a shallow hollow in the underlying boulder clay. The layers built up the ground surface here by a maximum of 0.9 m, so that it corresponded to the height of the platform further west, allowing building on this part of the platform. A 'V'-shaped cut, seen only in section within the deposit sequence, remains an uncertain feature.

No direct artefactual dating evidence was recovered to indicate when the moat was dug and the platform constructed, but an origin for both features in the later thirteenth century can be suggested on the basis of stratigraphic relationships. The consolidation layers at the east of the platform underlaid a further area of clay make-up, and an associated rectangular clay floor which may have related to the Phase 1 timber hall. The dating of this hall is discussed above (*see p 19*), but dendrochronological analysis of re-used timbers found within the later fabric of the farmhouse suggested construction of an open hall in the late thirteenth century. If such a building stood largely within the footprint of the later farmhouse, as is suggested, the consolidation layers must also date to the late thirteenth century, or earlier. Seventeenth century pottery was recorded as deriving from the lowest of these deposits, but this was almost certainly intrusive material introduced when the foundation trench for the Phase 3 east wall of the farmhouse was dug; the consolidation layers must have been laid down before the mid sixteenth century at the very latest as they were stratified below *in situ* elements of the Phase 2 timber-framed crosswing also revealed during building recording (*see Ch 4*).

If the construction of the platform occurred in the later thirteenth century, the digging of the moat can probably be attributed to the same episode of activity, and is likely to have provided a source of clay for the levelling of the platform. It is perhaps to be expected that the earlier fills within the moat might have been lost in antiquity through regular cleaning, so the absence of basal fills containing thirteenth century artefacts is not surprising. A later thirteenth century date for the construction of platform and moat, indicative of occupation of the site by people with some degree of local status, corresponds to the dating suggested by the available documentary evidence. The creation of the satellite sub-manor of Pesfurlong occurred on the division of the Culcheth estate, following the murder of Gilbert de Culcheth in 1246 (*see Ch 2*).

The moat was certainly in existence by the mid fifteenth century. Waterlogged timbers recovered from the base of the moat in Area C to the west of the farmhouse had formed part of a wooden bridge giving access to the platform from the west. Several of these timbers were subject to dendrochronological analysis, and all that were successfully dated had been felled in the mid or late fifteenh century. The earliest fills recorded within the moat appeared to post-date the erection of this bridge, and one contained artefactual evidence from a similar period (*see below, p 32*).

It seems likely that the late medieval timber bridge replaced an earlier structure in a similar location, but this cannot be demonstrated. If the moat was of thirteenth century date, the original means of access to the platform is unknown.

The moat

Several trenches were excavated across the moat, allowing its extent and shape to be demonstrated (Figs 14, 15).

Area A

A sondage was excavated across the moat by machine directly south of the farmhouse (Area A). The trench was too deep and unstable for detailed recording, but measurements were taken from the surface. The moat, here numbered 4035, was found to be c 2.9 m deep, and had a rounded base, perhaps the product of repeated cleaning out. The profile was asymmetrical; to the north, the 'inner' edge was relatively steep and convex, with an overall gradient of c 1:1. The southern edge was straight sided, and cut at a slightly more gentle gradient. It is possible that the final profile was a product of repeated cleaning out, during which it seems probable that detritus would be removed up the outer side of the moat, away from the habitation area.

Areas C and G

The cut of the moat was most completely revealed by sondages excavated across the feature by machine in Area C. The moat was found to be c 14-15 m wide and c 3.2 m deep, the cut being traced from a height of

Plate 5: Composite section across the moat, during excavation as part of the archaeological evaluation in 1990

26.32 m OD down to 23.08 m OD at the base (Fig 15). However, there is no doubt that the original profile had been disturbed here by the excavation of steps to allow the construction of later timber and stone bridges, so that the profile recorded cannot be regarded as representative of the original moat cut. In addition, later disturbance had clearly exaggerated the convex profile of the moat. The cut had an overall gradient of 3:2 (x:y), with the base gently rounded. The top of the inner, eastern side of the moat cut was not completely exposed in the sondage, but it must have fallen gently away from a gradual upper break of slope. There was then a second break of slope at c 24.6 m OD, below which the cut (4577) was inclined more steeply. It was here slightly concave, so that there was no discernible break of slope to the rounded base. The outer, western, side of the moat was of similar profile, but the middle break of slope was situated lower down the moat edge at c 24 m OD. The cut then fell away near vertically to a relatively sharp break of slope with the base. The breaks of slope part way down each side reflected the alteration of the moat profile to allow two substantial stone piers to be built to support a later bridge (*see Ch 4*).

Area G provided a sondage across the upper part of the moat immediately to the north of the later bridges

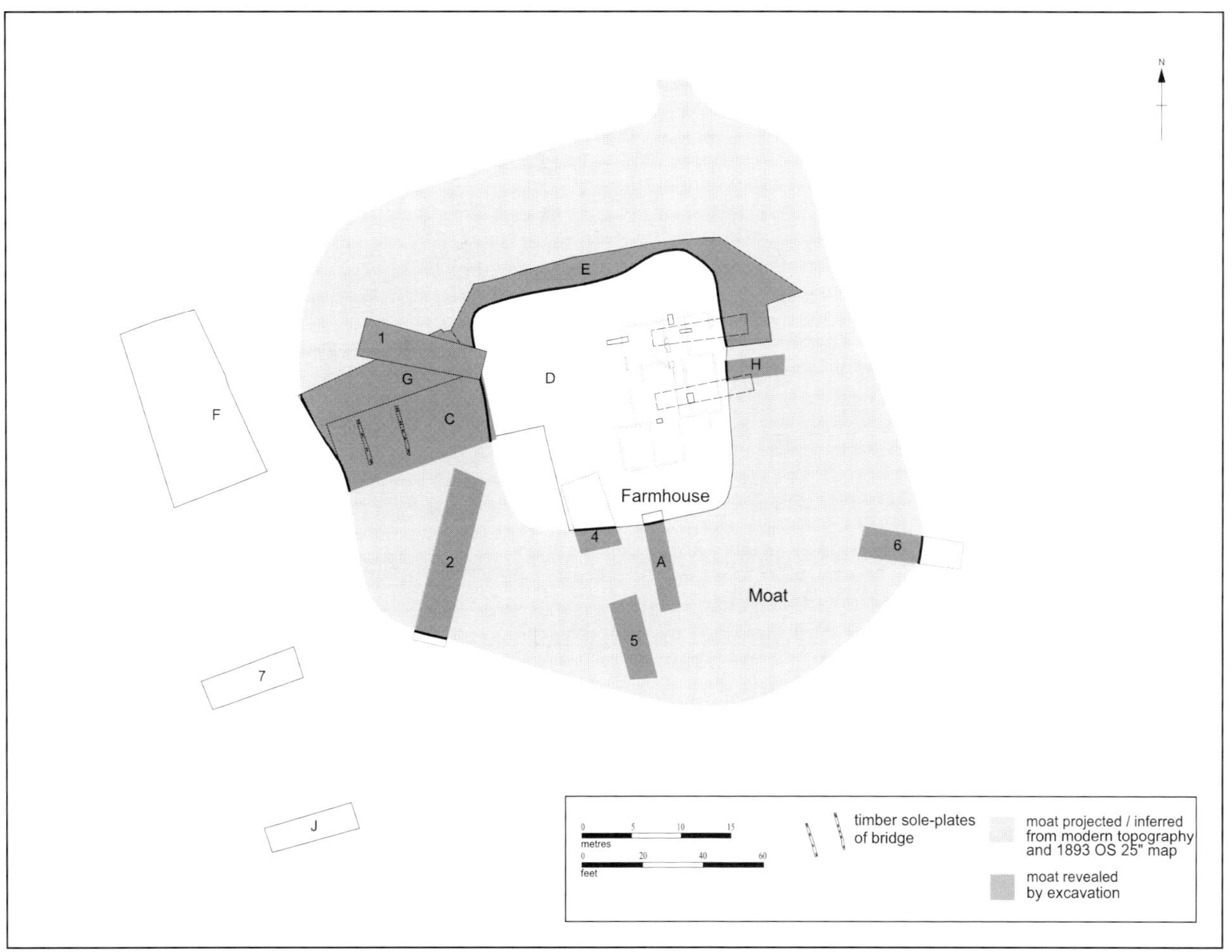

Figure 14: Excavation evidence for the Phase 1 moat

and causeway. The cut was not revealed to the east, but the western side of the moat was again clearly convex in shape, with an overall gradient of *c* 3:2 (x:y). Here, the gradient of the steepest part of the cut was at most *c* 1:1. This may be regarded as a truer approximation to the original shape of the moat profile, although the sides may still have been affected by centuries of cleaning out.

Areas E and H

The upper portion of the inner edge of the moat cut was also revealed by machine clearance within Areas E (north of the platform) and H (east of the platform). In neither area did excavation continue to the bottom of the moat. The deposits removed appeared to consist of relatively recent twentieth century infill, and are discussed in *Chapter 9*.

Evaluation Trench 1

Five evaluation trenches excavated in 1990 contributed further information on the position and shape of the moat (Fig 12). Trench 1 was excavated west of the platform and north of the causeway. In the 1995 excavation, Area G was opened obliquely across the backfilled assessment trench, with Area C immediately to the south. The moat profile revealed in section in Trench 1 was very similar to that recorded in the north-facing section of Area C, *c* 8 m to the south. The moat had a relatively steep eastern, inner, side (gradient *c* 3:2, x:y) and a rounded base. The western side of the moat was not revealed within the trench.

Evaluation Trenches 2, 4, and 5

Trench 2 was placed at the south-west corner of the moat, and demonstrated that the western arm turned east along the southern side of the platform. Only brief recording of the trench was possible because of the wetness and instability of deposits here. The moat was found to be at least 10 m wide, but its base was not reached. To the east, Trenches 4 and 5 aimed to investigate the northern and southern edges of the southern moat arm. Trench 4 defined the inner margin of the moat, but a raft of concrete in Trench 5 prevented definition of the southern edge. Excavation was confined to the removal of modern infill.

Evaluation Trench 6

Trench 6 was positioned to allow the putative south-eastern corner of the moat to be located. The moat was found to be present within the trench, but a high water table limited both the extent of excavation and the degree of recording that was possible. As a result,

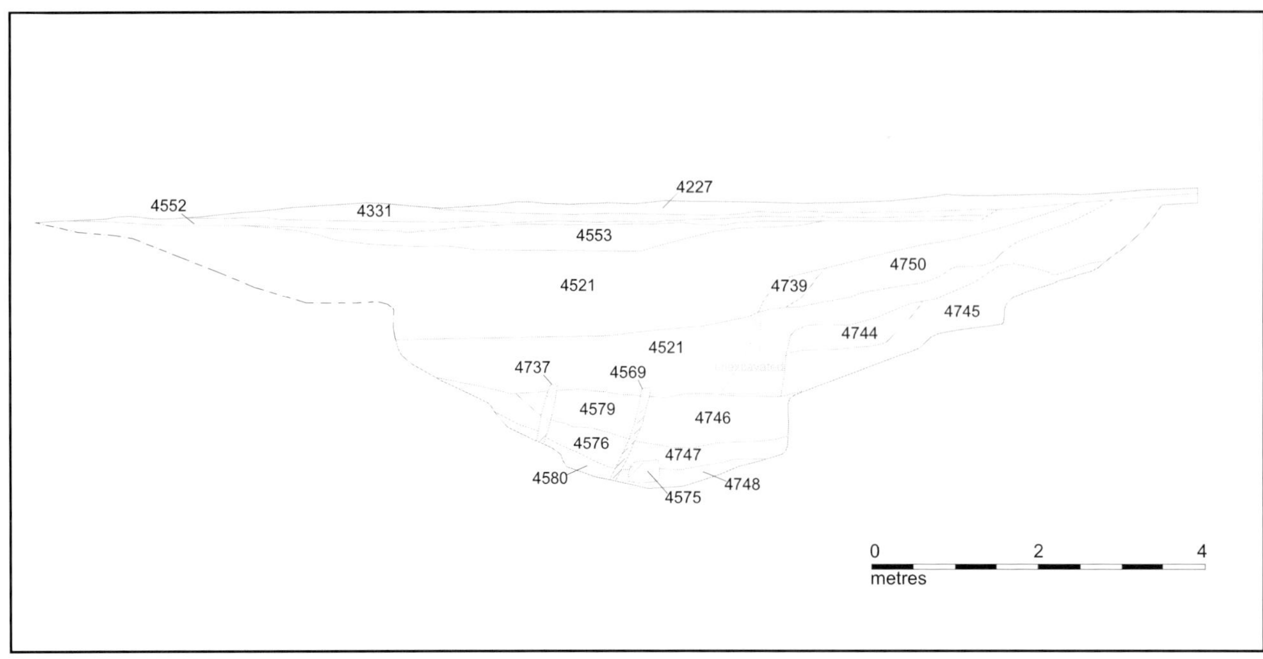

Figure 15: South-facing composite section across the moat

the exact position of the outer edge of the moat cut could not be established. All the layers removed were found to be modern, suggesting that here the final filling of the feature to present ground level had again occurred recently.

Dumped deposits at the east of the platform

Two differing deposit sequences were recorded in section following the excavation by machine of parallel sondages aligned roughly east / west (Sondages 1 and 2, Fig 14).

Sondage 1 was excavated at right angles to the moat, roughly midway along the eastern edge of the platform. The lowest layer recorded here (4778) was composed of dark brown clay. It was of firm consistency and similar to the natural boulder clay, so that it was uncertain whether this was a dumped deposit or natural horizon. It may in fact represent the interface between natural clay and the beginning of the dumping sequence. Above, layer 4710, 0.05-0.10 m thick and extending for at least 5 m, consisted of dark greyish brown silt. Frequent charcoal fragments, occasional fragments of burnt bone and brick, and three sherds of seventeenth century pottery (Fabrics 4 and 12; including Fig 53.3, 46) were recorded as being recovered from the deposit, but it is thought most probable that these derive from trample introduced from the overlying foundation trench (4668) during Phase 3. Although Section 135 (held in the project archive) does not show 4668 extending down as far as 4710 within Sondage 1, Section 124, a section across a hand-excavated portion of foundation trench (4668) (again held in the archive), shows that,

to the south, 4710 was the layer exposed in the base of the foundation trench). Successive layers (4777, 4709, and 4708) were then deposited, respectively greyish brown silty clay, orange to yellow clean clay (redeposited natural material), and mottled grey and yellow clay. To the west, dark brown silty clay with charcoal flecks (4773) overlaid natural clay but was stratified below 4709. Finally, mixed brown clay and silty clay (4774) overlaid 4773 and probably 4708, to which it was very similar. The deposits together had a maximum depth of *c* 0.9 m, producing a level surface above the underlying clay, which dipped down to the east.

The deposits described here were certainly stratified below the first brick foundations for Room G1 (Fig 69) of the Phase 3 farmhouse (*see Ch 5*). They were also clearly sealed by layer 4772, above which Phase 1 floor layer (4265, Structure 1) is thought to have been deposited. Floor 4265 may relate to the open hall erected on the platform during Phase 1.

Sondage 2, *c* 4 m to the north, revealed a similar pattern of deposition, although individual layers could not be correlated. The bottom deposit (4793) was composed of blue grey silty clay, a maximum of 0.25 m thick, with moderate medium and large pebbles and occasional charcoal flecks. Deposits 4792, 4785, and 4784 were successive layers of similar brown silty clay, whilst 4783 at the top of the sequence was formed of redeposited boulder clay. Layer 4786 was deposited on the same level as 4784, the two deposits being separated by later truncation when the foundation trench for the east wall of room G2A was dug (4281 / 4283). The layers extended for a maximum

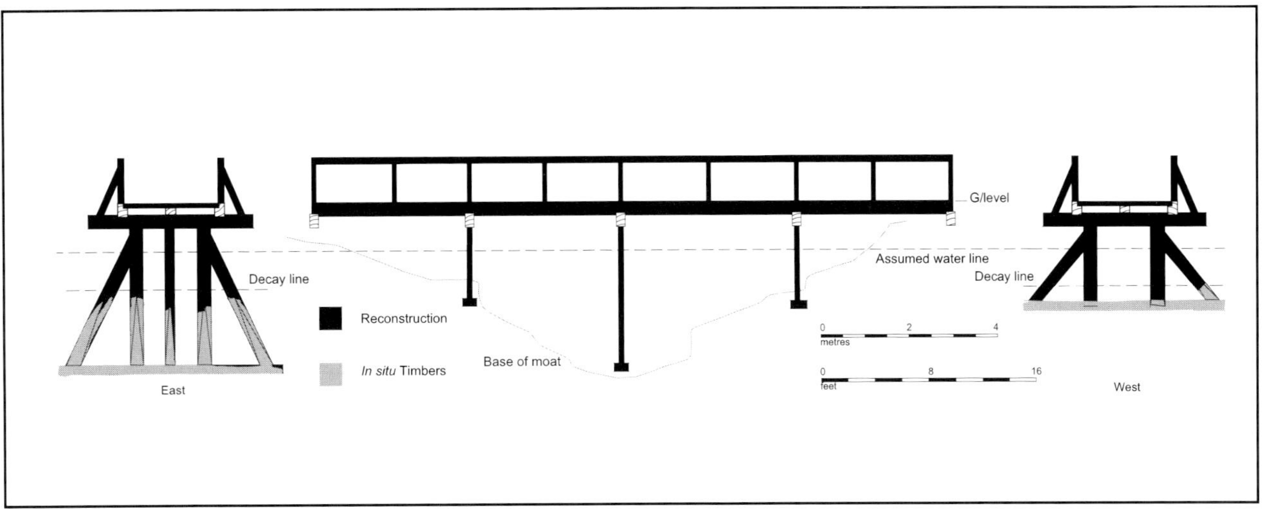

Figure 16: Reconstruction of the timber bridge across the moat

of *c* 7 m from west to east, and had a combined depth of *c* 0.9 m.

A possible 'V'-shaped cut at least 0.3 m deep (4790) may have been dug during this sequence of deposition. It cut through layer 4785 but was completely sealed by layer 4786. It was only revealed in section and its function remains unclear. It was filled by 4787, and probably also by 4788. Both were deposits of dark grey silty clay.

Phase 1b: The Late Medieval Timber Bridge and Early Moat Fills

Parts of a timber bridge were found when a sondage was excavated beneath the modern causeway across the moat. The timbers were waterlogged, and had been preserved by the wet, anaerobic conditions which existed at the bottom of the moat cut. The most substantial timbers were two sole-plates which had survived in their original positions (Pl 6), lying parallel with the alignment of the moat, stratified directly above the cut. Of these, one was centrally located in the moat at its lowest point, the other part way up the western edge (Fig 16), and it is probable that a third sole-plate on the eastern side of the moat had been removed when a later stone bridge was constructed, probably in the sixteenth century (*see Ch 4*). The western sole-plate had supported two central vertical posts, and two shallow angled braces for the posts, one at each end of the plate. The sole-plate at the moat base had held three vertical posts, again with a brace at each end of the horizontal timber. The braces were steeply pitched and would probably have risen to a point just above the water line, and, with the exception of one post, parts of all the posts and braces had survived *in situ*, jointed into mortises in the sole-plates. However, no remains of the deck of the bridge survived. All the surviving timbers were of oak,

and four were successfully dated by dendrochronology: three were found to have been from trees felled in AD 1455, the fourth from a tree felled in the period AD 1448-93. Thus, it is possible that all the timbers for the bridge were from trees felled in 1455, and that the bridge was built shortly afterwards. This seems likely, given that it is believed that the seasoning of wood is a relatively recent phenomenon for all but the highest status structures (English Heritage nd).

The surviving timbers suggest that the bridge derived from a single episode of construction, although it is not clear whether it replaced an earlier structure. The form of the bridge, with sole-plates carrying laterally braced trestles, was typical of timber bridges from the thirteenth to sixteenth centuries (Rigold 1975). The posts of each trestle would have been tenoned into a head-beam, lintel, or tie, of almost the same length as the sole-plate. There would have been three bearers for decking laid above the head-beams: large side beams would have been jointed or lapped onto the trestles at either end of the bridge, with a slighter side-lain central bearer lapped on the central trestle. This would explain the third stud of the central trestle. One would expect the bearers at either side to rest on stone bases to prevent damaging contact with the ground. The outer bearers would have been timbers of about 300 mm square (12"), rebated on the inside and with handrails set along them mortised onto the top of widely spaced posts. The central bearer would have been set lower, and probably trenched into the head-beam to allow for the thickness of the decking. The decking cross-planks would have been oak slabs of no less than 100 mm (4") thick, set into the rebates either side and sparsely secured with expensive iron nails, and the handrail would probably have been braced at the sides by lateral braces from the cantilevers of the head-beams. It was noted by Rigold (*op cit*, 56) that the decking bearers provided the only longitudinal support and that, without this,

Plate 6: Excavated section across the moat showing timber sole-plates on steps to left and right

and until they were in place, the trestles were unstable. He noted that any bracing in this line must have been upwards to the walkway, but that a little stability might be given by laying the plates (decking bearers) in prepared trenches.

The reconstruction presented here (Fig 16) is derived largely from contemporary structures. For the bridge at Old Abbey Farm, there was no evidence for the superstructure above the trestles, as the surviving timbers were cut off or decayed to a point below the water level of the moat, and mortises for any longitudinal support braces are missing. Excavation in Areas C, D, and G found no evidence of stone landing platforms at either side of the moat.

The central sole-plate was sealed by the earliest remaining fills of the moat, consisting of silty clay at the base, with sands and silts above. These deposits survived to a depth of *c* 0.5 m. One of these fills contained the relatively complete sole of a shoe, of a style fashionable in the later fourteenth and earlier fifteenth centuries. This suggests that the fills may have accumulated soon after the construction of the bridge, and that the base of the moat around the bridge was not subsequently thoroughly cleaned out, presumably because to do so was rendered more difficult by the presence of the bridge. The western sole-plate was sealed by patches of firm redeposited clay and silty clay which may be of a similar date to the deposits overlying the central sole-plate.

Two general biological samples from these basal moat fills were selected for detailed investigation of plant and invertebrate (principally insect) macrofossils (Kenward *et al* 1998; *see Ch 10*). One was from the context from which the shoe was recovered. Both samples produced very closely comparable results, with evidence for aquatic vegetation indicating that the moat had held shallow water all year round. The rarity of evidence for marginal plants at the water's edge suggested deep shading by overhanging vegetation. The moat was probably surrounded by a loose hedge-like tangle of shrub, perhaps with a few taller trees. Thorns of sloe or hawthorn and prickles of rose or blackberry were recovered, and are likely to have originated very close by. Further choking of the aquatics may have been caused by dense stands of tall herbs on the banks. The plant remains indicated that water within the moat was relatively unpolluted, and the small number of insects from synanthropic species provided no clear evidence for deliberate dumping of occupation waste into the moat; these individuals may represent a 'background fauna' derived from nearby buildings. The strong representation of disturbed ground plant species may represent proximity to a farmyard, and some pasture or meadow species were also present. However, in general, the significant plant and insect species present seem to derive from the immediate environs of the moat, with the rate of transfer of debris from nearby occupation being low. The botanical and insect evidence from the moat fills was of little value in reconstructing the

Plate 7: Sole-plate 4575 in situ

wider environment of the surrounding fields, or the domestic economy of the inhabitants of the platform.

The bridge timbers

Sole-plate 4765 was located on a step part way up the western side of the moat, at a depth of *c* 24.65 m OD (Pl 6). It was aligned north / south along the moat edge and had been laid within a tightly fitting shallow rectangular cut 0.55 m wide. It measured *c* 4.56 m x 0.39 m. The plate had four mortises in its upper face: one at either end for angled braces, and two *c* 1.2 m apart, towards the centre, for vertical posts. Parts of both braces and one of the vertical posts remained *in situ*. Vertical post 4755 was very badly decayed and was not retrieved; the northern and southern braces (4519 and 4756) survived in better condition and were recovered.

Sole-plate 4575 was located in the base of the moat (Pl 7), the upper surface at a depth of *c* 23.30 m OD. It was parallel with 4765, and had been laid *c* 3.7 m to the east. Five mortises were present in the upper face, with surviving timbers jointed into all of them. Again, there were angled braces to north and south (4571 and 4757). In between were three vertical posts (4572, 4573, and 4574), placed *c* 0.5 m apart.

Dendrochronological analysis of sole-plate 4575 gave a felling date of AD 1448-93 (Sheffield, 1998; Hillam *et al* 1987 for 10-55 sapwood estimate), whilst that of posts 4572, 4573, and 4574 gave a felling date of AD 1455B? (Sheffield, 1998).

The earliest moat fills

Sole-plate 4765 was covered by patches of firm redeposited clay (4763) and dark grey silty clay (4754), through which the vertical post and braces were protruding. No dating evidence was recovered from these fills, though they may have accumulated soon after the construction of the bridge.

Sole-plate 4575 was covered by a deposit of dark grey slightly silty clay 0.20 m thick (4748). This was the same as or very similar to the basal fill of the moat (4580), recorded in section at the bottom of the eastern edge. Immediately above, two pale brown fills were recorded. Fill 4576 (Fig 15) consisted of silt with sandy lenses and a visible organic component, while fill 4747 (Fig 15) was a mix of fine lenses of sandy silt and silty clay. These fills were a maximum of *c* 0.30 m thick, and probably accumulated soon after the construction of the bridge. Their survival seems to suggest that the part of the moat at the base of the timber bridge was not subsequently cleaned out, perhaps because the presence of the bridge made this difficult to accomplish. The broken tips of two wooden pegs (*Catalogues 3 and 4*) were recovered from 4747 and 4748 (*see Ch10*).

The leather sole of a left shoe, with a small fragment of the upper attached, was recovered from 4576 (*Catalogue 1;* Fig 64.1). The sole was from a well-made poulaine-type shoe of turnsole construction (*see Ch 10*), with an exaggerated pointed toe that had been stuffed with moss. This form of shoe was in fashion in the later fourteenth and earlier fifteenth centuries. A row of widely spaced tunnel stitching appears to indicate the position of a repair. Part of a worn sole repair was also recovered during excavation of the sondage across this part of the moat (*Catalogue 2;* Fig 64.2). It did not derive from a stratified context, but stitching on the patch was similar, but not identical, to that on the shoe (*see Ch 10*). This suggests that the patch may have been used to repair a broadly contemporary shoe.

Phase 1b: Late Medieval Alterations to the Timber-Framed Hall

---

Little or no extant evidence was found for works undertaken to the central hall between its initial construction in the late thirteenth century, and the beginning of rebuilding in brick in the seventeenth century. However, the erection of a well-constructed bridge in *c* 1455 suggests that the house itself was being well maintained and regularly repaired. It seems unlikely that no major alterations to the building were made in the two centuries that elapsed between its initial construction and the late fifteenth century. It is thus suggested that the fragments from Phase 1 which do survive must have been from a section of the building around which other alterations occurred.

It is likely that, during the late medieval period, one if not both of the side aisles was removed, to allow more light into a narrowed open hall through higher windows located under the original arcade-plates. The groove on the soffit of wall-plate 2745 probably dates from this time, being cut to allow the insertion of wall-frame studs in the previously open east arcade. The arcade wall-plates at the front of the hall may have been adapted in a similar manner. The two peg-holes noted on the face of the rear arcade wall-plate may be for a pegged-on window to light the back of the hall at the upper end, whilst a timber found re-used in the barn, lintel 867, a re-used seven-light mullioned window head or sill, may derive from a possible front hall window. The roof may have been altered, with the hip removed from the parlour, and the roof run through to a gable end. However, alteration of the roof may not have occurred until Phase 2.

The beaten clay floor, Structure 1, was only as wide as the nave of the original aisled hall. If it was associated with this aisled hall at all, this may imply that only the central nave area was floored in this way, or that floor and padstones were not inserted until after the removal of the aisles.

4

PHASE 2 - CONSTRUCTION OF THE SOUTHERN CROSSWING, AND A POSSIBLE NORTHERN WING
MID SIXTEENTH CENTURY TO EARLY SEVENTEENTH CENTURY

The southern end of the open hall appears to have been cut down and replaced with a forward breaking crosswing (Fig17). The new wing was constructed as a separate timber-framed structure, with close studding to the gables; it had two storeys (Fig 18), and would have provided improved accommodation for the parlour. Part of the framing survived *in situ*, and dendrochronological analysis of three timbers gave felling dates in the mid sixteenth century. It is possible that a second crosswing was also built to house the service area to the north of the house, but surviving evidence for this was minimal. It seems clear that the roof of the central open hall would have been reduced to a lower pitch by this time; direct evidence was lacking, but the original high roofline appears incompatible with the much lower crosswing roof. The late medieval timber bridge may have been replaced with a stone bridge at this time.

The Southern Crosswing

Much better evidence for the second phase of development survived within the farmhouse structure. This comprised the *in situ* remains of a two-storey crosswing constructed on the site of the former southern upper end of the postulated Phase 1 hall (Figs 19, 20). The surviving timbers were studied by Building Conservation Services (Lee and Michelmore 1998); they included a bridging joist, with several attached chamfered floor joists, which was tenoned to the upper section of a post (Figs 17, 18) which was itself tenoned to a section of the north wall-plate. Opposite, a section of the south wall-plate (Fig 17), with mortise holes on the underside, indicated the position of two other posts, with a window position being indicated by empty peg holes. Two further large timbers had been re-positioned, but were thought to have been first used during this phase. Firstly, a valley rafter was found originally to have functioned as a gable end tie-beam, with carpentry features demonstrating the former presence of a first floor gable window immediately below the beam (Fig 17). The lack of pegholes or mortises on the upper face indicated that the gable ends of the roof must have

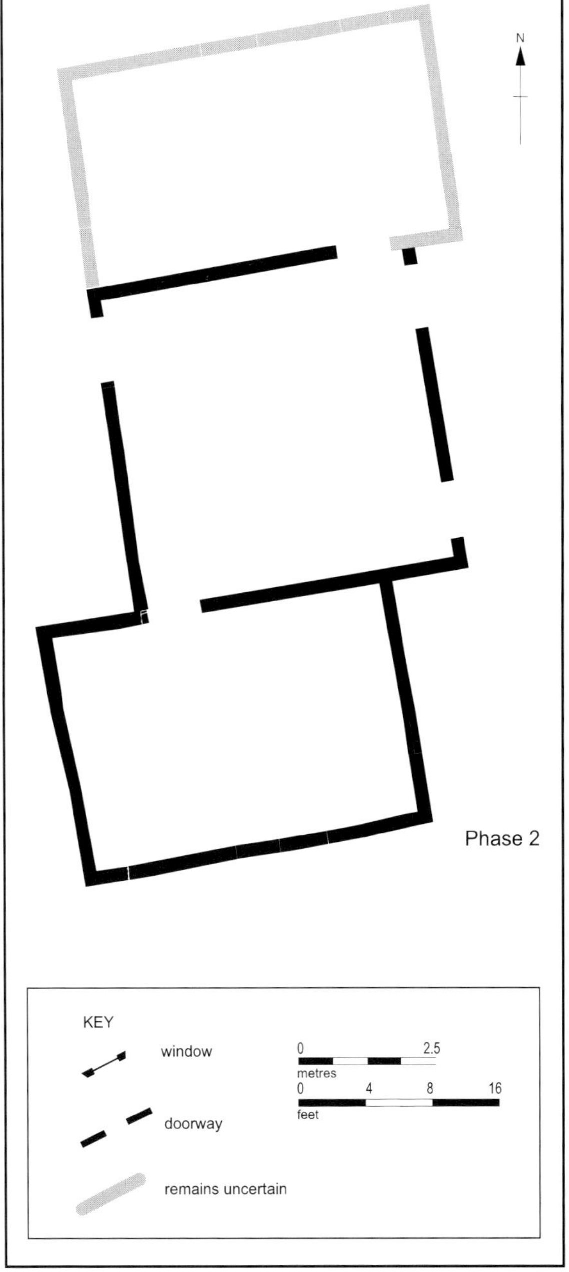

Figure 17: Suggested plan of the timber hall ground floor, Phase 2

been jettied out slightly above the first floor chambers, with knee braces supporting wall-plate projections.

Secondly, a re-used bridging joist found lying east / west appeared to have been re-oriented from its original north / south alignment.

With the exception of a thin strip of brick blocking towards the east of the south wall, where variation in the later brickwork suggested the former presence of a post, no trace of the timber frame of the crosswing was found at ground floor level. However, parts of a stone plinth remained at the base of the later brick walls of the wing (Fig 17), directly below the surviving wall-plates and posts. This appears to demonstrate that the elements of the frame of the crosswing noted at first floor level are in their original position. The plinth was substantially complete to the south and west, though of very irregular construction; single stone blocks survived below the north and east walls. Specialist analysis of the stone showed it to be Triassic sandstone. This rock outcrops in a variety of locations in the immediate area surrounding Old Abbey Farm: the stone is thus likely to be local, but cannot be sourced (Rust Environmental 1995).

Dendrochronological analysis of three of the timbers attributed to this phase indicates that the crosswing was probably built in the mid sixteenth century. It appears to have been constructed from new timbers of smaller dimensions and inferior quality to those attributed to the first phase. This difference in quality has allowed the differentiation of timbers from the episodes of construction, and it has been possible to gain a relatively complete impression of the original appearance of the crosswing. The configuration of mortises within the wall-plates and re-used tie-beam suggests that the wing was a box-framed structure, with large daub panels to the side and close studding to the end gables, which were jettied outwards at the level of the wall-plates (Fig 17). The southern wall-plate showed that a small window was positioned in the upper south elevation, and a six-light mullioned window was centrally placed at first floor level in at least one of the gables. Presumably similar windows existed in the other gable at first floor level, and in both gables on the ground floor. This appears to have been a structure with three bays of wall framing, but with only two bays in the roof, an unusual feature in English timber-framed buildings. The upper storey was divided into two rooms by a central partition, whilst the ground floor may have been divided between the central and eastern bays. The surviving central roof truss was thought to derive from the original roof of the crosswing, as were the purlins and windbraces.

It seems probable that this sixteenth century roof may have had a stone covering, given the relatively shallow pitch of the roof, its solid construction, and the fact that the farmhouse roofs retained a covering of

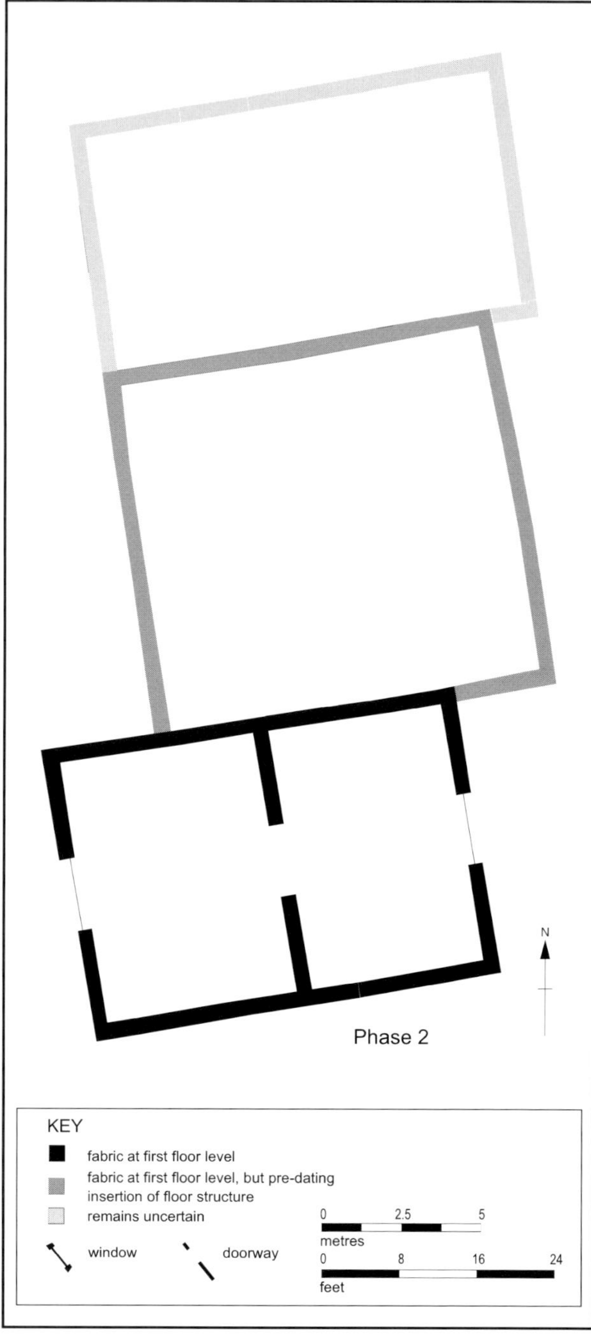

Figure 18 : Suggested plan of the timber hall first floor, Phase 2

sandstone slabs in 1990 (LUAU 1990). The stone slabs noted during the 1990 evaluation appeared to be of fine-grained Triassic sandstone; the site lies in an area of frequent Triassic sandstone outcrops (Rust Environmental 1995, 7), and it must be presumed that this material would have been freely available in the medieval and post-medieval periods. At least three thin slabs of this material were identified within the later fabric of the farmhouse (Phases 3 and 5, *op cit*, table 1), although it is unclear whether they were re-used roof slabs, or slabs which had been cut thinly for another purpose. Ceramic roof tiles were not found on the site, and although some fragments of slate were present in the upper fills of the moat, this seems most likely to have been introduced to the site during the nineteenth or twentieth centuries (Brunskill 1981, 98).

The timber frames of the new wing and central hall to the north appear to have been partially interlinked. A pegged seating was recorded on the outer, northern, face of the *in situ* post which remained within the north wall of the crosswing. The only explanation for this seems to be that it held a relocated brace supporting the front arcade-plate of the old hall. Comparison of the height of the feature with the span matrix constructed for the earlier hall indicates that the bottom of the seating lines up relatively well with the height expected for the bottom of a brace in this position. This suggests that the hall's west wall-plate was no longer supported by its own post, which may have decayed. Comparison of heights suggests that the hall wall-plate lay just above the position of the new crosswing wall-plate. It may have rested on top of the new crosswing wall-plate, directly, or supported by packing.

The new wing presumably offered better and more extensive private accommodation than had been provided by the medieval building. The appearance of the crosswing also shows signs of social aspiration. Features such as the close studding, a six-light gable window, and the roof at right angles to that of the hall would have been visible to onlookers approaching the front of the house (Pl 8). In fact, the effect was achieved 'on the cheap', with timbers of poor quality and a structurally sub-standard timber frame.

The wall-posts, wall-plates, and structural bays

Wall-post 2791 was recorded in the interior elevation of the north wall of the crosswing, at first floor level (Fig 20). The top of the post was still tenoned into a length of wall-plate above, and it extended down to slightly below the first floor, where it appeared to have been cut off. Towards its base, Phase 5 brick wall 2859 had been built up around the post. It measured 190 mm x 130 mm in section, and stood *c* 2.02 m from the contemporary west wall of the crosswing, as inferred from the stone plinth recorded at the base of that wall. Its position suggests that this post marks the east end of the western bay of the wing. Evidence of further posts was derived from a length of wall-plate (2750, Fig 17), also found *in situ* along the top of the crosswing's south wall. An empty mortise demonstrated the former presence of a post opposite 2791, whilst a further empty mortise *c* 2 m to the east indicates the position of the next post, at the division between the central and eastern bays of the structure.

Confirmation of the position of the latter post can be derived from the join between two later areas of

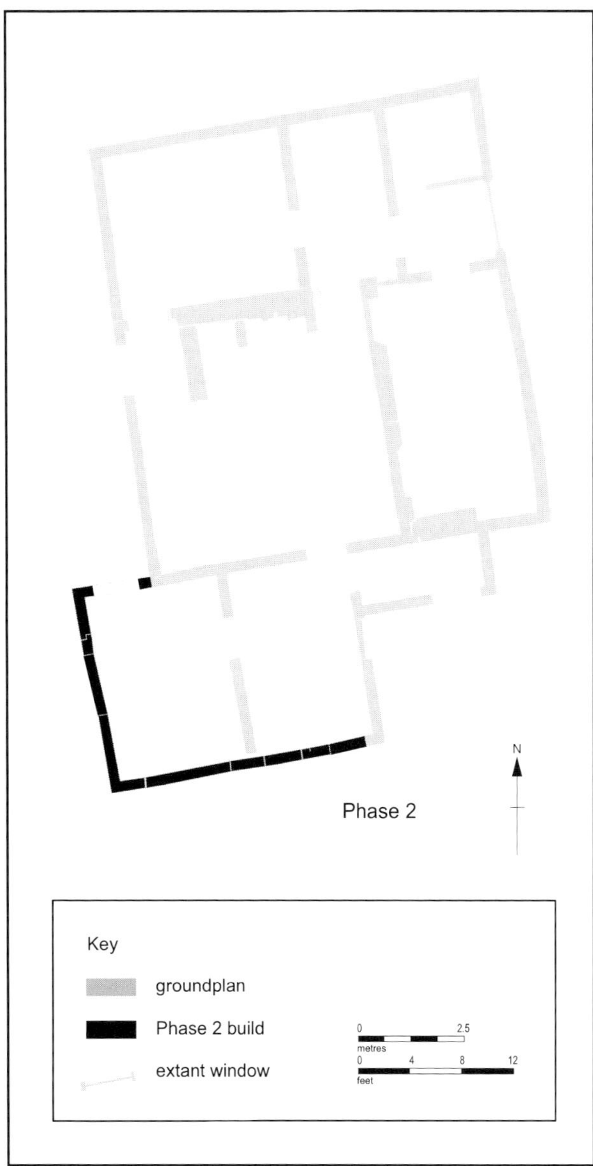

Figure 19 : Plan of the timber hall ground floor showing physical evidence, Phase 2

brickwork in the south wall. At ground floor level, it appeared that 2023 and then 2252 had been built up to a post internally. The post had then been removed and replaced with brick blocking 3078, 0.20-0.58 m wide and a single skin thick, present only on the interior of the wall. The blocking was located immediately below the position of the empty mortise in the overlying wall-plate.

These post positions show that the crosswing was built of three bays, the western two each of *c* 2 m in width. The eastern bay appeared to be *c* 0.4 m shorter. It might be thought that the building had been shortened since the original timber-framed structure was built, but the single stone block remaining at the base of the east wall, and the largely original roof structure, suggest that this was not the case.

The extant post was tenoned to northern wall-plate
2790. Dendrochronological analysis of 2790 gave a
felling date of AD 1534-?1579 (Sheffield, 1998; Hillam
et al 1987 for 10-55 sapwood estimate). It measured
175 mm x 140 mm, and its soffit contained a continuous
line of staveholes for timbers supporting wattle and
daub panels below (Fig 18), completely separating
the crosswing from the open hall to the north at first
floor level. The timber appeared to have been cut off
at the western end. At the top of the south wall,
opposing wall-plate 2750 contained evidence for the
position of a small window as well as for the posts
referred to above. The wall-plate measured 150 mm x
150 mm.

The central roof truss, purlins, and windbraces

A single roof truss survived *in situ*, spanning the
middle bay of the crosswing rather than set directly
above a set of wall-posts. In addition, a tie-beam was
identified as deriving from the eastern or western
truss. It had been re-used as valley rafter 2075 (Fig 22).

The surviving truss was centrally placed relative to
the middle bay, but *c* 0.25 m nearer the west than the
east end of the extant structure of the wing. Tie-beam
2517 (Fig 22) appeared to be attached by dovetail
joints into the upper surfaces of the north and south
wall-plates; its lower face was chamfered. Principal
rafters 2552 and 2553 were jointed to the northern and
southern ends of the tie-beam respectively, with 2552
tenoned into 2553 at the top of the truss. An horizontal
collar provided additional support. The principal
rafters were set on their narrow faces at an angle of *c* 45°.
The western face of the truss had been the upper face
during construction, as evidenced by carpenters'
marks visible on this side of the principal rafters.

A side purlin was present on either side of the roof,
trenched into the central principal rafter. On the north
pitch, 2739 was contained within a halving joint on
2552, whilst on the south pitch, purlin 2741 was
likewise jointed into 2553, both having been pegged
through. The side purlins were roughly square in
section, 2741 having a chamfered bottom edge. A
ridge purlin, 2740, set along the top of the roof, was
square in section, and was attached to southern
principal rafter 2553 with a birds' mouth joint. All but
one of the original windbraces survived, ranging in
length from 0.72 m to 1.10 m, and providing additional
stiffening to the roof structure. On either pitch, they
extended diagonally outwards from both sides of the
central principal rafter to the undersides of the side
purlin above. Four additional braces would have
extended between the principal rafters of the two
outer roof trusses and the side purlins. Three of these
timbers survived *in situ*, still tenoned to the underside
of the purlins, but with their lower ends having been
built into the later brick gable walls after the

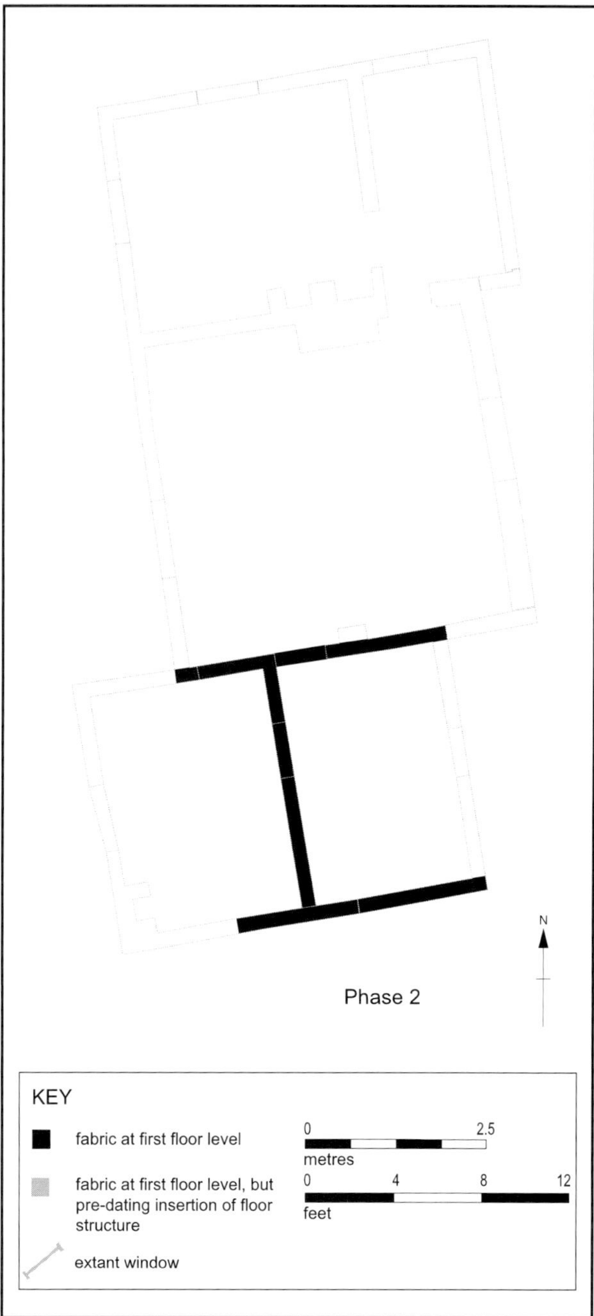

*Figure 20: Plan of the timber hall first floor showing
physical evidence, Phase 2*

replacement of the two outer trusses. The fourth
brace, in the south-west corner of the roof, appeared
to have been removed when the fireplace and chimney
were constructed in the upper west room of the
crosswing, probably during Phase 6. A surviving
mortise in the underside of the purlin confirmed the
former presence of this brace. The braces still attached
to principal rafters were joined to the rafters with
halving joints; they were attached to the side purlins
with pegged tenons. Carpenters' marks on the purlins
and windbraces matched those of the wall-plates,
demonstrating that the main elements of the roof
structure were original features contemporary with
the timber-framing of the wing.

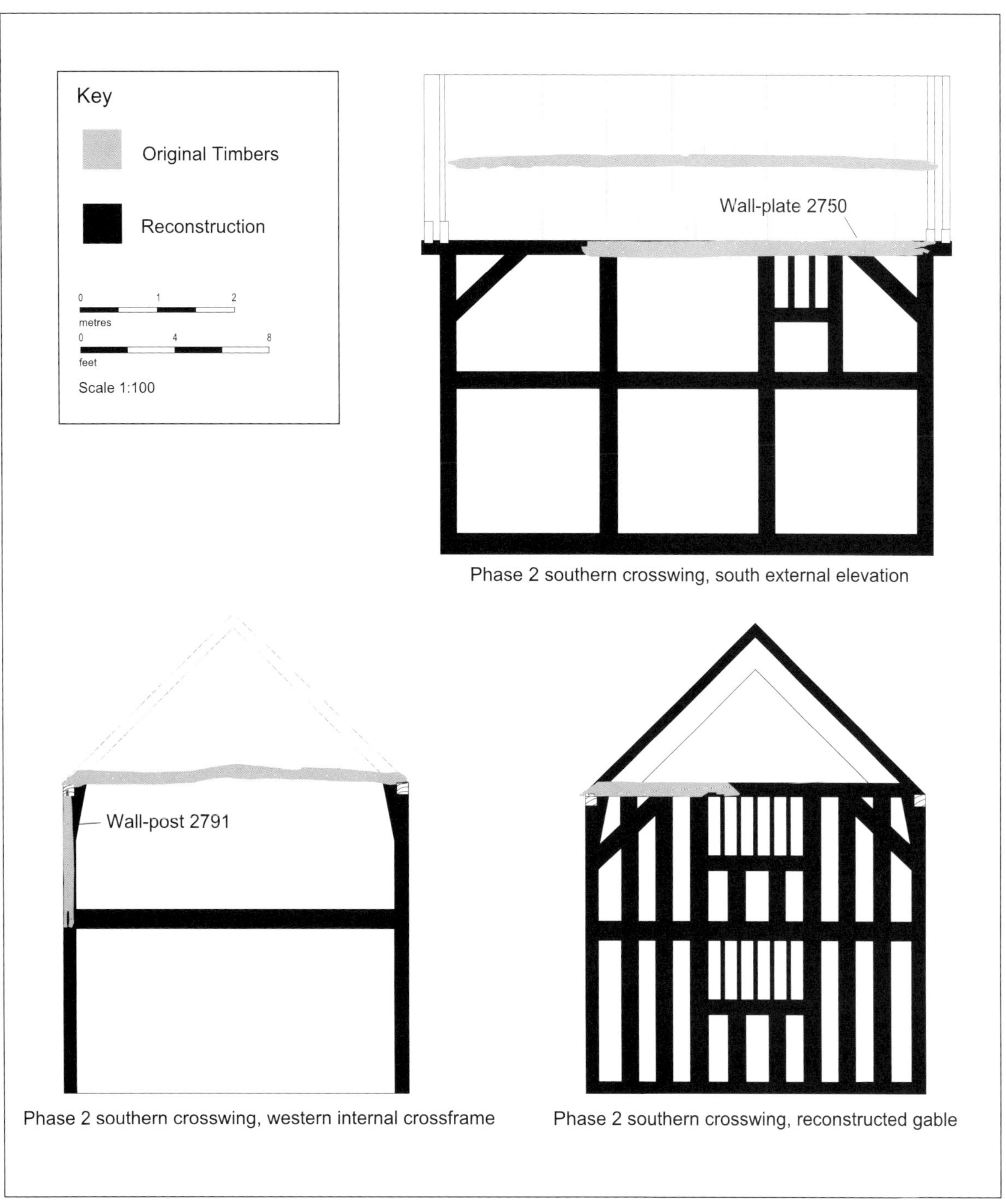

Figure 21: Phase 2, reconstruction of southern crosswing

It is possible that all but three of the rafters on the south pitch of the roof were contemporary with the main elements of the roof structure. This is suggested because these rafters appeared to be pegged to the purlins within the original peg holes. Separate sets of rafters joined the wall-plate and side purlin, and side purlin and ridge purlin, with no attempt made to join the two. The lower rafters had an average length of *c* 1.75 m, and were of rectangular section with dimensions typically *c* 60 mm x 70 mm. The upper rafters were slightly shorter, but of similar shape and dimensions in section. The lower set of rafters were seated in grooves in the wall-plates; the upper set lay in a slight groove in the side purlin. Valley rafters at either side of the roof, and a rafter adjacent to the Phase 6 chimney, were later insertions. On the south pitch of the roof, a single rafter may have been in its original position. Additionally, eleven rafters may have been re-used from the original roof. They spanned the whole distance from the ridge purlin to wall-plate, nailed in position, but peg holes in the vertical sides showed that several had been turned through 90°.

The upper floor structure

The first floor of the crosswing was carried by beams extending across the width of the structure between

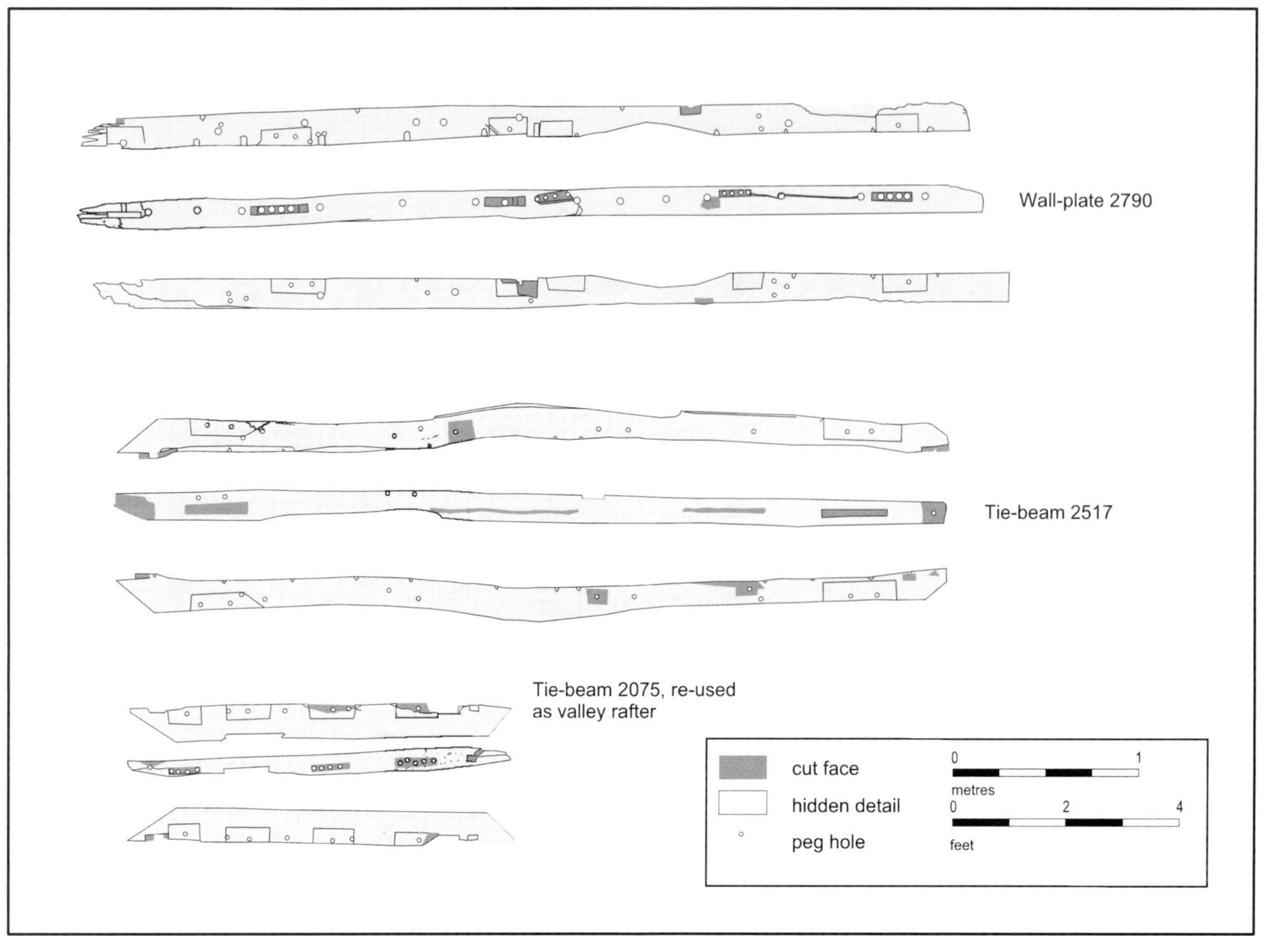

Figure 22: Phase 2, individual timbers

pairs of opposed bay posts. One of these bridging joists (3008) survived, tenoned into northern post 2791 and spanning the wing between the western and central bays. It was a substantial timber of near square section, measuring 250 mm x 220 mm by 4.23 m long, and was chamfered on both east and west sides. Six floor joists (3025 A-F) were attached to its east side, by barefaced tenons with a housed or spurred shoulder. One of these joists produced a dendrochronological felling date of AD 1526+ (Sheffield, 1998; Hillam *et al* 1987 for 10-55 sapwood estimate). The joists are thought to be contemporary with the bridging joist, and had chamfered sides and stop chamfers. They had been sawn off at their eastern ends, leaving them *c* 1.02 m long. Three further joists (3026 A-C), probably also contemporary, were attached to the west side of 3008. The same form of joint was used, here with a housed shoulder in each case, and the joists again had chamfered sides and stop chamfers. They extended for *c* 1.90 m to the west wall, crossing the length of the bay.

The eastern end of the floor structure was remodelled during Phase 5 to allow for the insertion of a staircase, but a bridging joist found aligned east / west was thought to have been re-used from the original floor. It seems probable that, in its primary use, it spanned

the wing from north to south, and lay parallel with 3008. Like 3008, it is likely to have been aligned across a bay division, and was probably jointed to a post in the south wall-frame, the position of which was demonstrated by a thin column of brick blocking, 3078 (*see p 37*). Dendrochronological analysis indicated that the timber was derived from a tree felled in the period AD 1534-72 (Sheffield, 1998; Hillam *et al* 1987 for 10-55 sapwood estimate).

The first floor partition wall

The upper storey was divided into two equal one-and-a-half bay rooms by a wattle-and-daub partition wall (2105), constructed on the line of the central roof truss (Pl 9). Along part of the base of the wall, timber 2825 may represent part of an original mid-rail, cut off to the south. Vertical studs 2551 and 2816 stood on the possible mid-rail, but may be later inserts. The daub was cut through on both sides of 2551, and the face-halved joint at the top of the stud attaching it to the tie-beam was located on the east-facing side of the beam; all other such joints apparent on the base of the tie-beam faced west. Likewise, stud 2816 was only 'notched' into 3178, and encroached upon an earlier mortise. A doorway between the two upper rooms was present at the north end of the partition wall, but

Plate 8: Reconstruction of Phase 2 timber hall

it was uncertain whether this was its original position. Peg holes on the tie-beam suggest that the first doorway may have been centrally placed within the wall. This suggests that the wattle and daub itself, as well as elements of the framing, may have been replaced after the construction of the wing.

The ground floor

The ground floor may have been divided in line with the eastern post. Access to the ground floor of the parlour from the 'Open Hall' would have been via a door to each room. The smaller of the two rooms may have had a ladder access to the first floor.

The foundations of the crosswing

The western and southern brick walls of the crosswing (Phases 4 and 5) rested on one to two courses of large stone blocks (4063), mostly of sandstone (Pl 10). Single blocks were also present below the southern end of the east wall, and the north wall. The dimensions of the individual stones showed considerable variation; the largest, located in the southern wall, measured 1000 mm x 360 mm x 350 mm and the base of the western and eastern walls was up to 0.5 m lower than the base of the southern wall, suggesting that the gable ends of the crosswing required greater strength than the south wall. The height of surviving stonework varied, but did not exceed two courses or *c* 0.5 m. Three stones were allocated individual context numbers. Stone 4049 formed the north-west corner of the crosswing, aligned east / west, and appeared integral to both the west wall and the western portion

of the north wall. Stone 4048 butted this corner immediately to the south, and 4696 was a rectangular block at the south-western corner of Room G5/6.

Corner stone 4049 had maximum dimensions of 860 mm along the east / west axis, and 390 mm along the north / south axis. Its presence appears to suggest that the stone element of the west wall of Room F4 and the western end of the north wall were built at the same time. It may subsequently have functioned as the western jamb for an external doorway leading out of the crosswing to the north, but there is no evidence for the presence of any such feature in Phase 2.

A large rectangular stone block (4044) was located below the later north wall of the crosswing. It was stratigraphically isolated from cornerstone 4049 to the west by later threshold bricks (4689), but may also originally have been part of the plinth. It appeared to have been laid directly onto redeposited clay, and to be earlier than, and butted by, foundations (4389) to the east (Phase 5). Stone 4044 may have been retained in later phases because it served as the east jamb for a doorway to its west, as well as the jamb for an internal door to the central hall positioned to its east. No evidence for the structure of these doorways survived from Phase 2; brick thresholds for the doorways to the west and east probably dated to Phases 3 and 5 respectively.

The western wall of the stone plinth appeared to have been built within a shallow foundation trench (4551). No evidence of a cut was found below the other parts of the plinth, although a modern flowerbed had caused extensive truncation externally at the base of the southern wall of the wing.

Alteration of the Phase 1 Hall

Clear evidence for the improvement of the central hall and northern service bay at this time seems to have been removed by the later rebuilding and re-roofing of these parts of the house. It is thus uncertain how the existing structure was modified, the possibilities ranging from minor alteration to comprehensive renewal of the frame. In part interpretations depend on inferences drawn from the likely state of the property in the mid sixteenth century. It had been standing for nearly 300 years, and was an old building which was likely to have presented maintenance problems. In particular, the sill beams and lower timbers may have been decayed, and the roof may have been re-assembled at a shallower pitch with a stone covering. It also seems likely that changes would have reflected the taste and resources of a new owner. The mid sixteenth century date for the works, suggested by dendrochronology, probably correlates with the purchase of the property in 1549 by Sir John Holcroft. However, despite these more general factors, there are four pieces of evidence, sometimes apparently contradictory, which any interpretation must consider.

1)   The wall-post surviving within the north wall of the southern crosswing contained a seating, thought to have been for a brace attached to the underside of the proposed central hall west arcade-plate (*see above p 35*). This appears to demonstrate that the south-western arcade-post within the hall had been removed, and that the western arcade-plate was thereafter carried on the wall-frame of the crosswing. The seating has further significance: the position of the footprint of the Phase 1 hall could not be established on the basis of the surviving re-used timbers, but, from Phase 2, the seating allows the central hall to be fixed in space.

The use of the new crosswing to support the arcade-plate of the Phase 1 hall suggests that major structural timbers had decayed in places, necessitating at least selective removal. However, it also suggests that the response was pragmatic, utilising whatever support was available, rather than completely renewing the frame. If the west aisle had not already been removed in Phase 1b, it was probably dismantled at this time, with a new west wall of studs and wattle and daub panels installed beneath the existing arcade-plate.

2)   The surviving wall-plate in the north wall of the crosswing had on its soffit a continuous line of staveholes. This demonstrates that there was no access to the central hall from the crosswing at first floor level, and strongly suggests that the central hall was still open to the roof at this time, and not floored over at first floor level. This would have been archaic in the mid sixteenth century in the North West, for a house of relatively high status, and is perhaps an indication that an old hall had been repaired rather than a new structure erected.

3)   Although the earliest brickwork in the northern rooms of the farmhouse is dated to Phase 4, the Phase 5 brick footings at the south-east corner

Plate 9: Phase 2 first floor partition wall with plaster stripped to reveal anatomy

of G2A (*Ch 11*, Fig 69) butt against a substantial stone block. This stone may have survived from a former plinth. Furthermore, the layout of the northern rooms at this point, breaking to the rear of the central hall, mirrors that of the southern crosswing, which broke forward of the hall. It is impossible to be definite about the form of the service structure, but such a structure would almost certainly have existed to the north of the central hall in Phase 2. It is quite possible that this part of the house was rebuilt at this time, and that it took the form of a northern crosswing breaking to the rear of the hall.

4)   As discussed above (*see Ch 3*), a clay floor (Structure 1) revealed by excavation lay displaced slightly to the west of the later central hall, as defined by the brick walls of Phases 3 and 4. The floor relates to a building preceding

the Phase 1 structure, or it indicates that the Phase 1 building originally lay *c* 1 m further west. The fixing of the position of the west front of the house by reference to the seating on a southern crosswing wall-post (*see 1) above*) means that the Phase 2 building work is the latest time at which the old hall could have been repositioned. If the central hall was moved slightly, which remains uncertain, this might have involved partial dismantling, renovation, and re-erection of the existing frame. The question of a possible shift in the building footprint is explored further below (*see Ch 11*).

Features Immediately Pre-dating the Rebuilding in Brick

A small area of cobbling revealed by excavation lay on either side of the east wall of the central hall (Fig 23). This cobbling was truncated by the wall's brick footings, thought to have been constructed in Phase 3, and thus it clearly pre-dated the brick rebuilding. However, the position of the cobbled surface corresponded to that of a doorway through the brick wall, suggesting that there may have been an earlier doorway through the timber-framing in the same location, with the cobbles laid to reinforce an area of heavy wear. A small assemblage of pottery was recovered from the surface, and was dated probably to the mid to late seventeenth century, showing that the cobbles must have been laid by this date at the latest. Although the pottery may have been deposited after the laying of the cobbles and trodden into the deposit, it is possible that the cobbling may have been relatively recent when the east wall was rebuilt.

A single posthole was recorded in section immediately below the cobbling when a sondage was cut by machine through the dumped deposits forming the east of the platform (Sondage 1, Fig 14). It lay within the footprint of the eastern outshut of the farmhouse, but pre-dated that room's construction, and its associations are uncertain. It may derive from Phase 3, or from earlier activity, and was plausibly part of a small ancillary structure located immediately to the east of the hall.

Posthole 4776
The posthole was cut through layer 4708, and was sealed by cobbling (4676), part of a layer which contained mid to late seventeenth century pottery. Posthole 4776 was 0.55 m wide and 0.58 m deep, the sides tapering to a point off centre to the east. The loose dark grey silty clay fill contained at least three large rounded stones which may have been displaced packing stones.

Cobbled surface 4616/4676
The remains of a cobbled surface were recorded, within the footprints of Rooms G1 and G3 but pre-dating the brick build of both rooms. Surface 4616 (Fig 23) within G1 measured *c* 1.25 m x 0.50 m, and was truncated to the east by foundation cut 4668. It contained eight sherds of pottery (Fabrics 4 and 5; including Fig 53.9), the assemblage as a whole being assigned a date in the mid to late seventeenth century,

Plate 10: The stone foundations of the south wall of the crosswing

or slightly earlier. It is clearly possible that the pottery was deposited some time after the cobbles were laid, especially as some of the sherds showed joins with fragments from the overlying layer (4615), assigned to Phase 4. This may suggest that fragments of pottery were lying on the top of an old cobbled surface when the later levelling layer was deposited. The cobbling continued a short distance to the east beyond cut 4668, and was here numbered 4676.

Evidence for Additional Timber-Framed Structures

Many of the re-used timbers recorded within the Phase 6 barn may originally have been used in Phase 2 (Lee and Michelmore 1998). Although several were sampled for dendrochronological analysis, none could be successfully dated, and so they have been attributed to this phase on stylistic grounds. As a consequence, the dating is imprecise, and it must be accepted that many of the individual timbers may be rather earlier or later. Nevertheless, a body of evidence exists to suggest that a cruck-built barn may have stood on the site in the sixteenth or seventeenth centuries, perhaps replacing an earlier aisled barn (*see Ch 2*). The presence of such a building cannot be established beyond doubt, however, because it cannot be demonstrated that the timbers were not brought to the site from a structure elsewhere in the neighbourhood.

Re-used timbers thought to be derived from a cruck-built structure

Purlins 76, 77, 78, and 98 had seatings cut into them which show they were originally used in a structure which had large windbraces, between 1.30 m and 1.80 m (4'6"- 5'10") long. The brace seatings on the purlins show that they were let into the surface rather than lapped-in. Though it is possible that some or all of these purlins were re-used from a large barn, possibly cruck-framed, there is no evidence for cruck principal rafters, cut-down or re-used as tie-beams. It is difficult to date the re-used purlins, and no dendrochronological information was obtained from any of them because a sample from 98 failed to produce a date. As the quality of the conversion was quite good, they may date from before 1600, although such a date is a conservative estimate.

Two further timbers may also derive from a cruck-framed structure. One, wall-plate 140, measuring 2.80 m long x 200 mm x 100 mm, was definitely a re-used wall-frame stud. The stud had two double-pegged mortises on each side, a large double-pegged central mortise in the face below the second rail, and a small single-pegged mortise 300 mm (12") below this. It had been cut top and bottom, but the length of the timber and the configuration of the mortises allowed the height to the eaves of the structure from which it was derived to be estimated at 3.80 m (12' 6"). The spacing of the mortises for rails indicates that this former stud could have been from the wall around a cruck-framed building. The timber is weathered and burnt inside and around a lower mortise.

Timber 744 was 3.30 m (10' 9") long, with a series of mortises on its soffit. These have infill staveholes drilled between them. The distance between the mortises was 0.86 m and 1.24 m, and the timber was cut 30 mm from the end of the first mortise. The timber is clean on the top but has charring from the side inwards, including the second mortise, for a distance of 800 mm. Given that 744 is the inner lintel over the barn door, and 140 was diagonally across near the corner, they must have come from the same building.

Other re-used timbers

There were several re-used timbers for which it is difficult to specify a precise original use, but which must derive from wall-frames and partitions. These may have been obtained from areas in the house such as the service and ground floor of the Phase 2 southern crosswing, or from buildings no longer represented on site. Of these, three timbers had mortises on adjacent faces, indicating an original use in partitions or screens. Even allowing for cutting down, it is felt that their section is too small for them to have been structural corner-posts (132, 137, 2816).

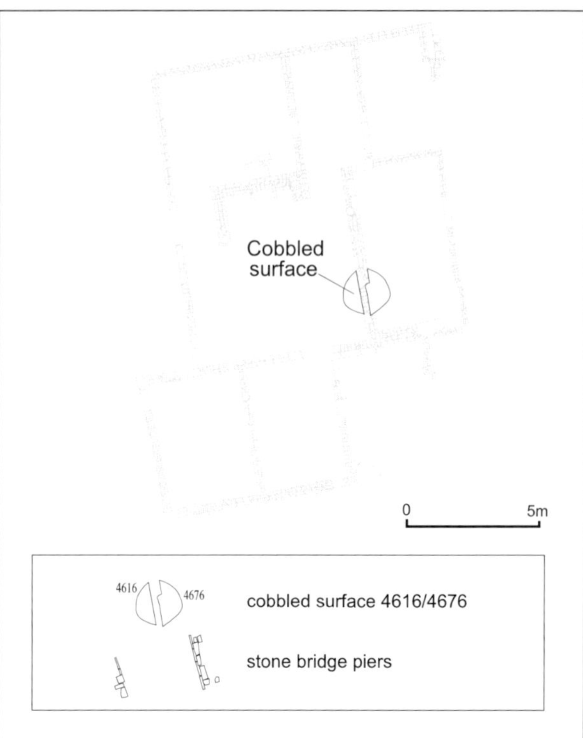

Figure 23: Excavation evidence, Phase 2

The Stone Bridge

The bases of two substantial sandstone piers revealed at the moat bridging point indicated that the Phase 1 timber bridge was eventually replaced by a stone structure. The piers were *c* 4.85 m apart, constructed towards the bottom of each side of the moat. They lay parallel with the timber base-plates described above (*see Ch 3*), but were not symmetrically placed relative to the profile of the cut.

It seems that, in north-west England, stone bridges were erected to give access to moated sites over a considerable period of time. Several sandstone bridges in the region appear to have been late medieval in date, including examples north of the Mersey (within the south of the historic county of Lancashire), at Bryn Hall, Ordsall, and Clayton (Tindall 1985a). However, elsewhere, stone bridges are known to have been built in some numbers in the late sixteenth century (R Newman pers comm), and north of the Mersey, the sandstone bridge foundations at Bewsey are thought to be of sixteenth century date (J Lewis pers comm). However, with only the bases of two piers surviving at Old Abbey Farm, comparative structures can provide no firm indication of date.

The stone bridge at Old Abbey Farm clearly post-dated the late medieval timber bridge of *c* 1455, with construction of the eastern pier probably having removed the eastern sole-plate. The piers had no

Plate 11: Stone pier 4568, stepped into the east side of the moat

direct stratigraphic relationships with the primary moat fills, but a deep fill containing a sherd of late seventeenth century pottery had built up against the western pier, providing a tentative *terminus ante quem* for construction of the bridge. The stone bridge would thus seem to date from the broad period 1455–1700. Within this period, an origin during the Phase 2 rebuilding can be tentatively suggested. The masonry piers of carefully cut ashlar blocks were meant to be seen, and display was certainly a consideration when close studding was chosen for the gable walls of the southern crosswing. This was a time at which the owner may have had both the inclination and the resources to replace the existing structure, although the possibility remains that the bridge was constructed later, and not necessarily at the same time as works were being carried out to the fabric of the house. However, an origin in the seventeenth century seems unlikely. By 1590, Old Abbey Farm was no longer the manorial seat of the Pesfurlong estate, and for much of the seventeenth century, the ownership of the estate seems to have been disputed (*see Ch* 2). Such conditions would not appear conducive to the construction of a new bridge of well-dressed stone.

Pier 4568

To the east, pier 4568 (Pl 11)was also stepped into the side of the moat, but it was laid higher up the moat edge. Below the pier, the side of the moat continued falling away towards the base at an angle of *c* 2:1 (x:y). The pier survived to a height of two courses for most of its length, but there were traces of a third, disturbed course. It was again built of closely fitted, unmortared sandstone blocks, and had overall dimensions of 3.60 m x 0.80 m by 0.62 m high. The lower course consisted of blocks 0.23 m high and up to 0.87 m long; the upper course was of larger blocks, measuring up to 0.90 m x 0.56 m by 0.39 m high. The stones were laid tightly against the step to the rear with no intervening fill identified.

Pier 4752

To the west, pier 4752 was constructed just above the base of the moat, on a step which had been cut into the existing moat edge. It was built of rectangular dressed sandstone blocks, closely fitted and unmortared, one course wide and surviving to a height of two courses. The overall dimensions of the pier were 3.05 m x 0.75 m by 0.60 m high, with individual blocks having dimensions of up to 0.9 m x 0.7 m by 0.3 m high. The stones had been laid tightly against the step. Dark grey silty clay (4753) was recorded to the rear of the footings, but may have been deposited when some of the stones slumped forward. The north end of the pier in particular appeared to have slumped in this way; the large numbers of stones excavated from the moat fill immediately east of this pier were judged sufficient for the original height of the structure to have equalled that of eastern pier 4568.

5

PHASE 3 - COMMENCEMENT OF REBUILDING OF THE TIMBER HALL IN BRICK

EARLY TO MID SEVENTEENTH CENTURY

The timber-framing of the east wall of the open hall was replaced in brick bonded with clay. A brick wall was also built at the north end of the hall, creating an inglenook fireplace and baffle entry in what is thought formerly to have been a cross-passage (Fig 24). The hall was still open to the roof, but a smokehood was erected above the new fireplace. It was supported to the south by a bressumer beam, fashioned from a tree thought to have been felled in the period AD 1615-35.

The Central Hall

In the seventeenth and early eighteenth centuries, the timber hall and crosswing underwent piecemeal renovation, with elements of the timber structure replaced with new walls built from hand-made brick. The bricks were of very varied quality and dimensions, probably because of the employment of unskilled labour for brick production (Smith 1996), and brick dimensions alone gave little indication of the sequence of building. However, analysis of the bonding materials, and of the stratigraphy of the brickwork, has allowed different phases of construction to be discerned.

Phase 3 marked the beginning of this process of rebuilding in brick. A remodelled central hall was defined by new brick east and north walls, predominantly the width of three bricks thick, and built using clay as the bonding material (Fig 25 ; Pl 12). The probable central open fire of the Phase 1 hall was replaced by an inglenook fireplace inserted into the inferred position of the former cross-passage. This in effect converted the building into a *'baffle entry'* house, though it is thought that it still remained open to the roof at this period. The plan is not dissimilar to the baffle arrangement at Barley Castle Farm, near Appleton, Cheshire, where a massive sandstone inglenook has been inserted into an earlier timber frame, probably into the cross-passage (J Lewis pers comm). The short wall protecting the inglenook from the main farmhouse entrance contained a small fire window; this would normally be placed in the opposite wall to light the inglenook (Brunskill 1981, 112), so its

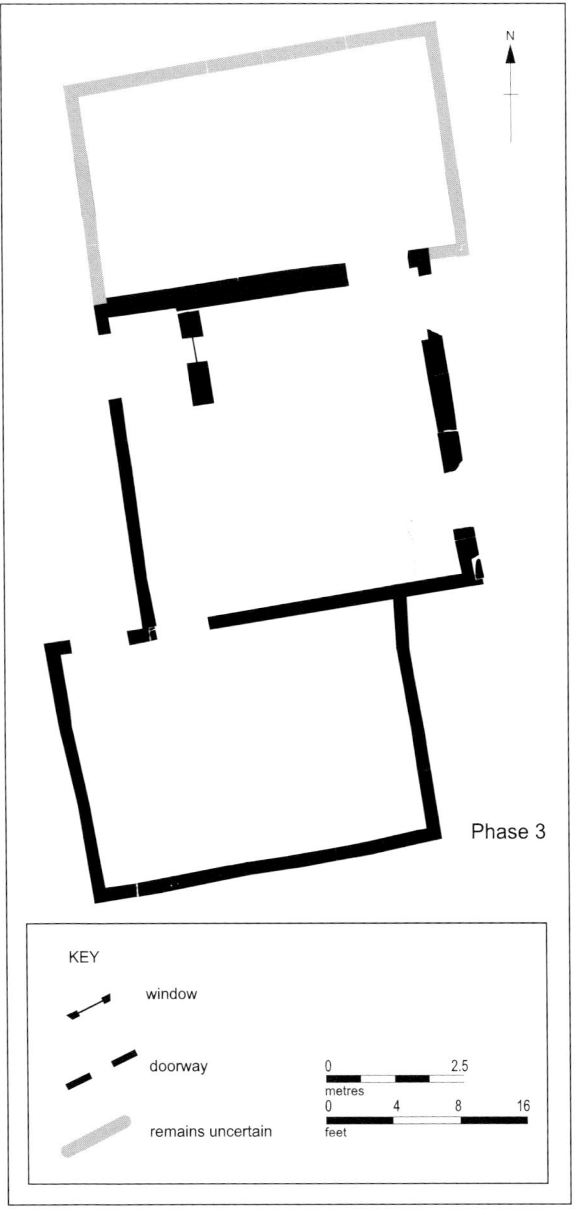

Figure 24: Suggested plan of the timber hall ground floor, Phase 3

position here is unusual, with the window lacking an obvious function. No evidence for the Phase 3 hearth has survived later remodelling, but the surrounding

"

walls of the inglenook and a bressumer beam which probably supported a smokehood were recorded. Blocked holes in the east wall and (later) west wall of the hall demonstrated the position of the bressumer beam, subsequently raised when the hall was floored over in Phase 5. Dendrochronological analysis of two samples from the bressumer beam suggested that it was derived from a tree felled in the period AD 1615-35.

Recording during excavation independently confirmed that the north and east walls of the newly defined central hall were contemporary, and of a single build. The foundations of the two walls shared common constructional characteristics, in particular the presence of layers of red sand between uncoursed brick or stone rubble, and the lowest regular courses of brick. Although the north-west 'heck' wall foundations were slightly different in dimensions and form, the wall above appeared continuous with the north and east walls. Three rectangular voids found within the east wall suggested the possible cladding in brick of studs remaining from the earlier timber frame, probably erected in Phase 1b or 2. Three sherds of pottery (Fabric 4, *see Ch 10*), found sealed within the foundations of the east wall, provided further dating evidence for this phase, to complement that of the dendrochronological date cited above. The sherds were initially dated tentatively to the late seventeenth century, but the black-glazed redware fabric was derived from earlier Cistercian-type wares, and a mid seventeenth century date cannot be discounted; in view of the felling date of 1615-35 obtained for the bressumer beam, the earlier dating of the pottery is preferred. Thus, considering that oak might remain green and workable for up to ten years after felling, it is suggested that the beginning of the rebuilding in brick be placed towards the end of the first half of the seventeenth century.

Some of the door-jambs, thresholds, and areas of brick blocking evident in the east wall were clearly added subsequently, for example the jambs for the southern doorway, which overlaid a concrete floor repair. There is some evidence that these jambs were re-used from an earlier doorway in the same position. The presence of cobbling in this area (*see Ch 4*) suggests that this may have been an accessway into an earlier timber hall before the eastern wall of the central hall was built in brick, and the Phase 3 hall may have retained a doorway in this position. The doorway at the north end of the wall, however, may also have been present in Phase 3, and its location mirrors that of the opposing main baffle entrance to the hall at the north end of the west wall, suggesting that it likewise may have been retained from the earlier building.

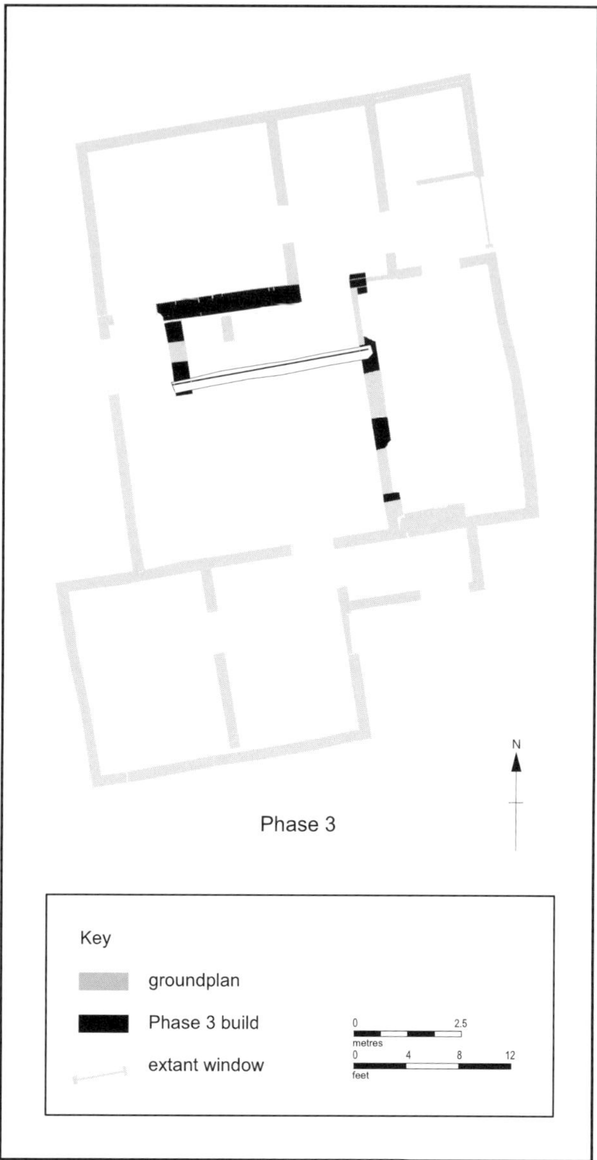

Figure 25: Plan of the timber hall ground floor showing physical evidence, Phase 3

The building survey corroborated the suggestion that the northern and southern doors in the east wall were largely contemporary with the first brick build of the wall, and might have been in the positions of earlier entrances. These doorways pre-dated the Phase 6 outshut to the east (G3, *see Ch 11*, Fig 69), but may have led to two independent storage facilities present before the outshut was built. No evidence of these was found, and they may have been constructed as ephemeral lean-to wooden structures. The northernmost of the doors led directly out of the inglenook. This is relatively unusual, and it is possible that this doorway may have led to a fuel store, which would account for the insubstantial nature of any structure. At Barley Castle Farm, a ladder giving access to the first floor is thought to have been sited at the opposite side of the inglenook to the baffle entrance (J Lewis pers comm). It is possible that a ladder in a similar position at Old Abbey Farm gave access to an upper storey in the putative northern service wing, but this seems unlikely given the inconvenience of also having two doors leading into this confined area.

Plate 12: External elevation of Phase 3 east wall of the central hall, showing original window high up, and late blocking of doors

Blocked holes, probably former purlin holes, high in the north wall of the central hall, appear to demonstrate that, in Phase 3, the roof was carried at a lower height than in the extant structure of the farmhouse (Fig 27, top; only the bottom, western hole shows clearly). If there is evidence for the support of a lower roof in the north wall of the central hall, this ought to be reproduced elsewhere. The clearest such indication of a possible lower roof in Phase 3 is the discrepancy in height of *c* 0.13-0.20 m between the Phase 3 east wall of the hall, and areas of walling built subsequently. Probably as a result of the low height of the east wall, two sets of wall-plates were recorded here supporting the later roof, one laid on top of the other. The lower set is thought to have been retained from Phase 3, and in the case of 2745, from Phase 1, and must have been needed as blocking once the roof had been raised.

It is thought unlikely that the Phase 3 roof retained its original form from Phase 1 (Lee and Michelmore 1998). Purlins were probably now inserted for the first time, not having been used in the original thirteenth century roof, and their introduction suggests considerable remodelling of the roof frame. The purlin holes show a pitch of *c* 45°, certainly much more shallow than was indicated by the Phase 1 re-used timbers, though changes to the pitch of the roof may already have been made in Phase 2, as suggested by the re-use of a rafter collar in the crosswing. This much lower pitch confirms a change in roofing material, already speculated upon for Phase 2, from thatch to a more impervious material, probably stone slabs.

The incorporation of an original Phase 1 tie-beam and of cut down sections of A-frame rafters within the Phase 5 floor may indicate the survival of individual roof timbers to the early eighteenth century rather than wholesale replacement in Phase 2. For Phase 3, it can be demonstrated that a Phase 1 arcade-plate was re-used, probably *in situ* above the newly-built brick east wall, simply being rotated through 90° (Lee and Michelmore 1998). It was extended by the scarfing of a re-used post to the southern end, the post probably liberated by the replacement of the wall-frame with brick. Thus, although the pitch of the roof had certainly been reduced by Phase 3, many of the original timbers may have been retained.

The east wall of the central hall

The timber-framing to the rear, or east, of the hall was replaced by a substantial brick wall (Pl 12), the width of three stretchers thick (*c* 0.38 m), and bonded with clay. In places the bond was irregular, but there were also areas of brickwork laid in English Garden Wall, with four courses of stretchers between each course of headers.

The wall was built on a brick foundation set within cut 4668, a near vertical-sided trench 0.52 m wide. This cut was sample-excavated in two sondages; the base sloped down from west to east in the southern sondage, but where recorded further north the feature was flat-bottomed. The depth ranged from *c* 0.2 m to 0.32 m. Where the base was inclined, it was levelled up with a layer of broken and whole bricks (4662). A single sherd of pottery (Fabric 4) was recovered from this deposit. Foundations (4669) were then laid on a thin layer of reddish sand (4637), which contained two further sherds of pottery (Fabric 4). It has been suggested the three sherds are most likely to derive from the late seventeenth century, but that a mid seventeenth century date is a possibility (*Ch 10;* C Howard-Davis). The foundations consisted of a bed of random brick bats 0.26 m deep, covered by a layer of red sand 0.07 m deep. Above, the lowest course of brick was laid in a double header bond, giving a wall thickness here of 0.48 m.

Three sockets, perhaps representing the positions of vertical timber posts, were recorded in the base of the east wall. Socket 4421 was located at the northern end, and was not enclosed to the north. It had vertical sides and a flat base, measured 0.20 m x 0.14 m, and survived to a height of 0.07 m. Socket 4419 was located *c* 1.7 m to the south of 4421 and 0.45 m south of door-jamb 4075. It measured 0.16 m x 0.14 m, and again had vertical sides and a flat base and survived to a height of 0.07 m. Socket 4417 lay *c* 0.9 m south of 4419 and 0.32 m north of door-jamb 4074. It measured 0.16 m x 0.13 m, survived to a height of 0.36 m, and had the same profile as the other sockets. No further sockets were identified to the south, but if the doorway between jambs 4074 and 4072 was secondary to the original wall-frame, it is possible that it removed evidence for an additional socket. These sockets were all filled with light brown clay silt.

The Phase 3 east wall appears originally to have been constructed with a doorway situated towards each end of its length. Doorway 2302, towards the north, was probably in the position of an earlier doorway at the east end of the proposed cross-passage of the Phase 1 hall. Its south edge was built on a sandstone pad, and was made of chamfered bricks which appeared to have been cut *in situ* rather than moulded. The north edge was straight, built of some cut and some uncut bricks, the presence of the uncut bricks indicating probable contemporaneity with wall 2103. To the south, doorway 2306 was of a similar width. Here the northern edge was built of chamfered bricks probably cut *in situ*, whilst the southern edge was clearly not cut through wall 2103. Stone blocks underlaid the two sides of the doorway, below the brickwork. The lintel was a poor fit, and appeared to be a later insert.

The east wall also had a wooden mullioned window (2546), built in at eaves level (Pl 12). The window contained three mullions, tenoned into the re-used wall-plate above (2745); though common, this type of window can be dated to the sixteenth or seventeenth century. There was no evidence for re-use of the window frame, yet the window appears initially to have been unglazed, being subsequently grooved and fitted with glass held in by nails. It is surprising that an unglazed window should be fitted to a house of even moderate status in the mid seventeenth century, yet this serves as a reminder that, in some respects, the open central hall had changed little since the thirteenth century.

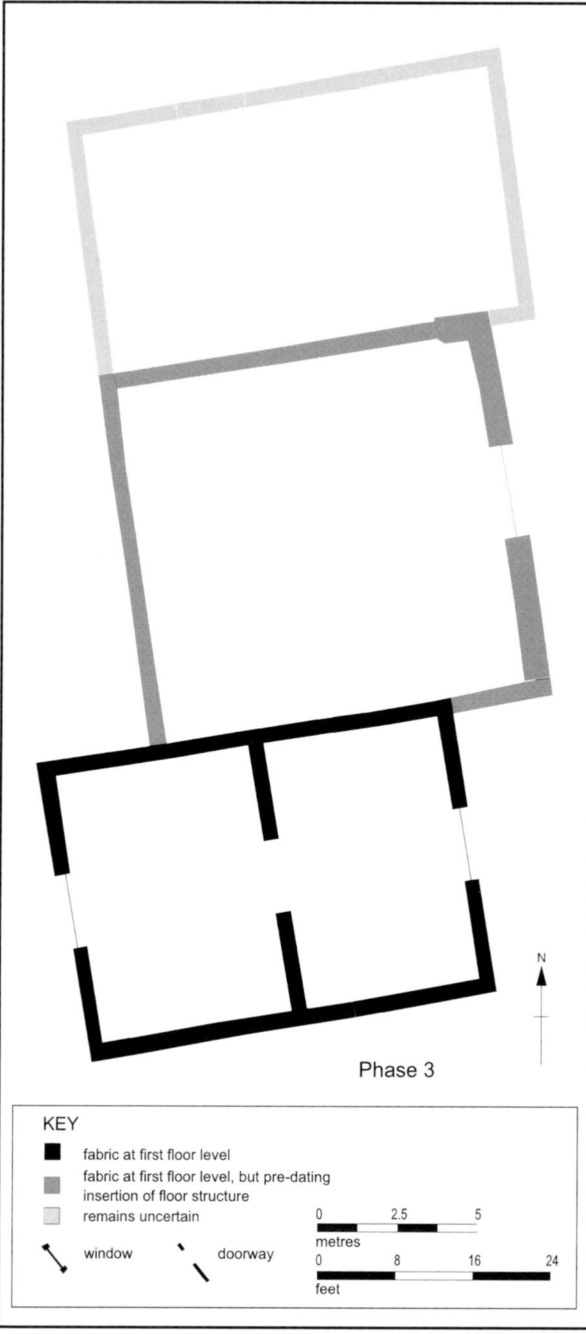

Figure 26: Suggested plan of the timber hall first floor, Phase 3

The north wall of the central hall and the inglenook fireplace

A clay-bonded brick fire-wall was built at the north end of the central hall, up to the apex of the roof, and must have replaced a former roof truss. It was mostly constructed to the width of three stretchers, but towards the east of the upper part of the elevation, wall 2101 was only two bricks thick. It is uncertain if this reflects the original construction of the wall, or if a skin was removed at the time of the construction of

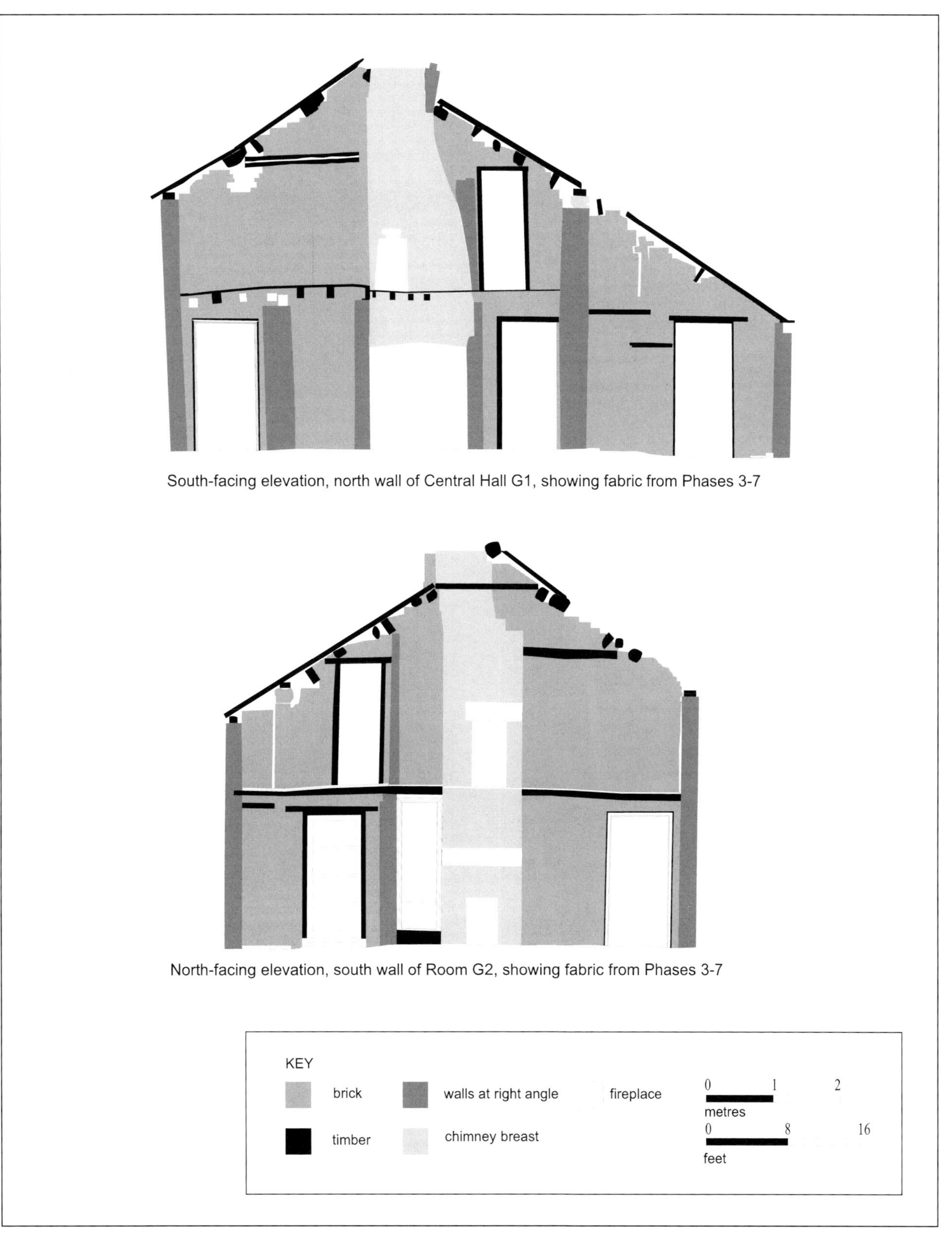

Figure 27: The timber hall of the farmhouse, internal elevations

later first floor fireplace 2766. At ground level the bond of the brickwork was very irregular, and there were many brick bats; at first floor level, the bond was predominantly English Garden Wall, with three courses of stretchers between each one of headers. Despite these differences between the top and bottom of the wall, the upper courses are not thought to derive from a later phase of building. This is partly because of the lack of change in the mortar, and partly because of the presence of former purlin holes in the upper part of the wall, which appear consistent with the height of the Phase 3 east wall, but not with that of later walls (*see p53*).

The wall is thought to have replaced a timber-framed partition, dividing the rear of the putative former cross-passage from the service to the north. At ground level, the wall branched to the south to form a short 'heck' wall, opposed to the main front entrance, and enclosing the fireplace. The bricks here had been laid with greater care than in the fire-wall. The heck wall contained a small fire window. Beyond, the north wall continued to the line of the west wall of the hall at foundation level, and high up in the elevation, where it was numbered 2101. A gap in the wall at ground level for a doorway appeared to be a Phase 6 insertion. Doorway 2169, at the eastern end of brick wall 2101, was a later insert, but there may have been an earlier door aperture in the same position giving access to the probable northern service range.

The foundation cut for the north wall had steep but slightly concave sides and a rather uneven base, and was *c* 0.55 m wide and 0.25 m deep. Where excavated, randomly laid stones covered the base of the trench, supporting a bed of red sandstone, the largest stone measuring 400 mm x 180 mm x 130 mm. Reddish sand (4692) had been deposited above; this seems to have been the same as 4637 underlying the foundations for the east wall. The brick foundations (4092) were again three courses high, and where excavated were two headers and one quarter brick wide (0.56 m).

The foundation cut (4706) for the north-western wall, which formed the rear of the baffle entrance, appeared to be rather wider. It had near vertical sides and a flat base, and measured 0.94 m wide by 0.15 m deep. A brownish grey sandy silt (4646) had been used to backfill the trench, and surrounded the bottom two courses of brick foundations (4080). The foundation was a total of three courses high, and was wider than the upper brickwork, being two headers wide (*c* 0.48 m).

Within the north wall, five voussoirs of a blocked brick arch survived, bonded with clay. They are thought to be part of a brick-built bread oven, contemporary with the wall, the eastern portion of

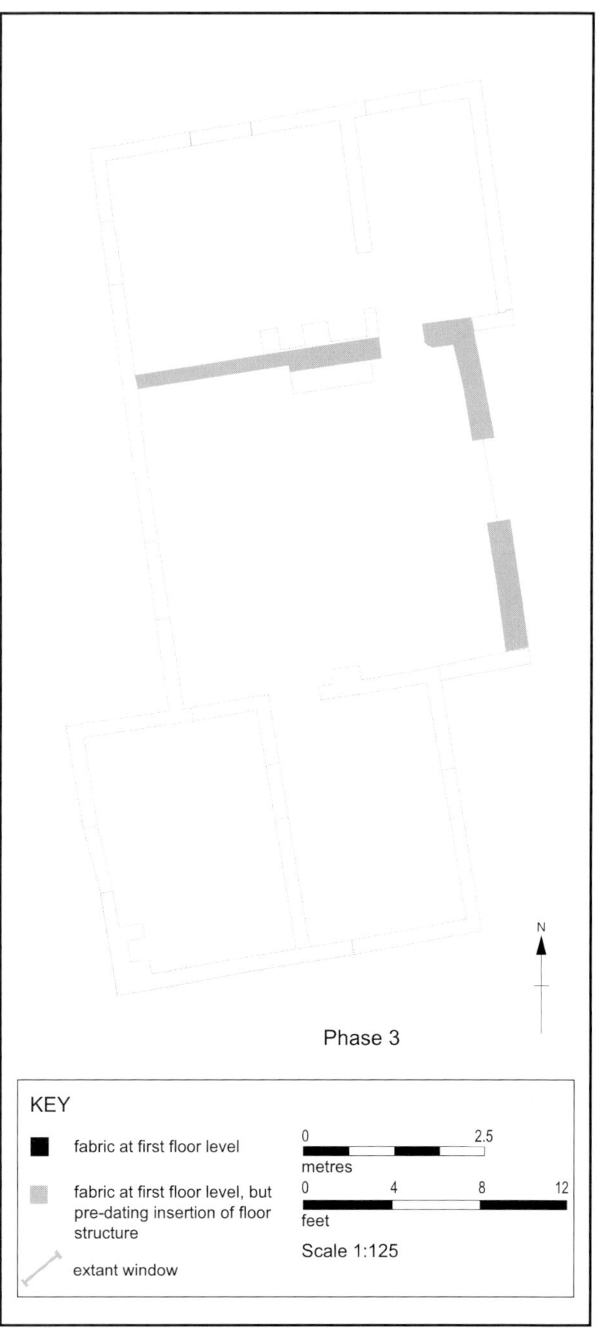

Figure 28: Plan of the timber hall first floor showing physical evidence, Phase 3

which had been destroyed by later fireplaces. This oven was situated to the west of all later fireplace structures, and was probably also on the western side of the original Phase 3 hearth. Below, two sandstone blocks, 3203 A and B, had been shaped and then placed so as to create an aperture measuring a maximum of *c* 0.17 m high by 0.21 m wide passing right through the wall from south to north. Its function is not fully understood, though it might have connected the hearth to a possible water boiler on the north side of the wall.

The smokehood

A bressumer beam (3108) was inserted at this time, extending from the heck wall to the rear, eastern wall of the hall, built into the front of the hearth; it had a groove cut in its upper face into which the spars for a timber-panelled smokehood would have been inserted. Additional evidence for a smokehood lay high up in wall 2101. A beam (2726) had been built into the wall at a height of *c* 5 m and appeared contemporary with it. Its underside contained mortises at either end, *c* 0.84 m apart, which may have been for the studs of a smokehood. Two samples from bressumer beam 3108 underwent dendrochronological analysis, generating felling dates of AD 1550+ (Sheffield, 1998; Hillam *et al* 1987 for 10-55 sapwood estimate) and AD 1615-1635 (*op cit*).

The roof of the central hall

At the time the fabric of the farmhouse was recorded, the roof purlins above the central hall were supported at their northern ends on top of the hall's Phase 3 north wall (2101). However, this seems unlikely to have been the position of the roof in Phase 3, because the north wall was scarred by a series of blocked holes, present on both faces, located directly below each purlin (Fig 27, top; only one hole is clearly visible). The size and position of the blocked holes, coupled with their apparent contemporaneity with the wall, suggest that their purpose was to support a roof which was earlier, lower, and marginally more steeply pitched than the structure extant at the time of recording. This Phase 3 roof was probably retained from Phase 2 or earlier, it being argued that the original medieval pitch must have been reduced before construction of the much lower southern crosswing roof.

The lower area of blocking below the western roof pitch (2727) measured 0.30 m x 0.25 m, the brickwork bonded with cream mortar with frequent small fragments of lime. The blocking higher on the wall (2768) measured 0.38 m x 0.22 m. The brickwork was neat on the northern face of the wall, bonded with hard white mortar with frequent lime inclusions, but on the southern face broken bricks had been roughly packed with mortar and straw. The holes appeared wide enough for only a single purlin, suggesting that the roof of the putative northern bay was supported elsewhere, or, perhaps more probably, given that the holes penetrated the full thickness of the wall, that a single purlin extended through the hole, supporting the roof both of the central bay and of that to the north. Whether or not this was so, there seems to be little doubt that the holes carried the purlins of the Phase 3 central hall roof, whether it was newly built or survived from an earlier phase. This is because the Phase 3 east wall, rebuilt in brick, was lower than the other brick walls of the central hall, built subsequently. There is no evidence for how the Phase 3 hall roof was supported, if not by the blocked purlin holes.

Other Parts of the House

The south and west walls of the central hall contained no fabric attributable to this period. It seems that here the existing timber-framed walls deriving from Phase 1b, and perhaps repaired or re-erected in Phase 2, were again retained (Fig 26). Evidence for alteration to the crosswing was confined to a possible brick threshold, sealed beneath the Phase 4 brickwork of the north-west return wall of the wing (Fig 28). The use of brick for the threshold, and its stratification below a Phase 4 wall, suggests the presence of a Phase 3 external doorway here. Although excavation evidence and the probable 'cross-passage' layout of the Phase 1 house suggest that a further bay existed to the north of the central hall and its newly built brick north wall, no evidence for its alteration during Phase 3 survived.

Threshold 4689

This consisted of half and third bricks laid between stone blocks 4044 and 4049, which are thought to have served as door-jambs. It measured 0.84 m long by 0.35 m wide.

6

PHASE 4 - REBUILDING IN BRICK, AND EVIDENCE OF EXTERNAL COBBLING

LATE SEVENTEENTH CENTURY TO EARLY EIGHTEENTH CENTURY

The north (external) and southern walls of the southern crosswing were replaced, and, whilst no evidence remained, it seems likely that the latter's gable walls were also rebuilt (Figs 29, 30). The timber-framing of the west wall of the central hall was also replaced in brick. Clay was still used to bond the bricks, and the quality of both the bricks and the brick laying appeared to have declined since Phase 3. Evidence was also recovered for a Phase 4 brick build of the northern wing, and for cobbling in front of the farmhouse. It seems that, during this phase, cleaning-out of the moat was discontinued, allowing deep silting fills to form.

The Central Hall

Within the main hall, much of the extant west wall up to eaves level was constructed during Phase 4 (Figs 31, 32). The brickwork was bonded with clay, as the Phase 3 brickwork had been, but several differences between the west wall of the hall, and the north and east walls, demonstrated that the west wall was the product of a distinct, later, phase of construction. The west wall was found to be *c* 0.13-0.20 m higher than the east wall, indicating that it must have been built after the purlin holes in the Phase 3 north wall had been made redundant by a slight raising of the existing roof structure (*see below p 60*). The brickwork itself was the width of two stretchers thick, whereas that in the north and east walls was predominantly built to the width of three stretchers, and it was also observed that the standard of the workmanship and quality of the hand-made bricks had declined. The foundations also differed. The west wall was built in a much shallower foundation trench than the north and east walls, and the foundation of bricks laid in mortared courses rested directly on the base of the trench, without the use of beds of randomly laid stones, or brick bats, as had been employed in the north and east wall foundations respectively. The layer of red sand, common to both the north and east wall foundations, was also absent.

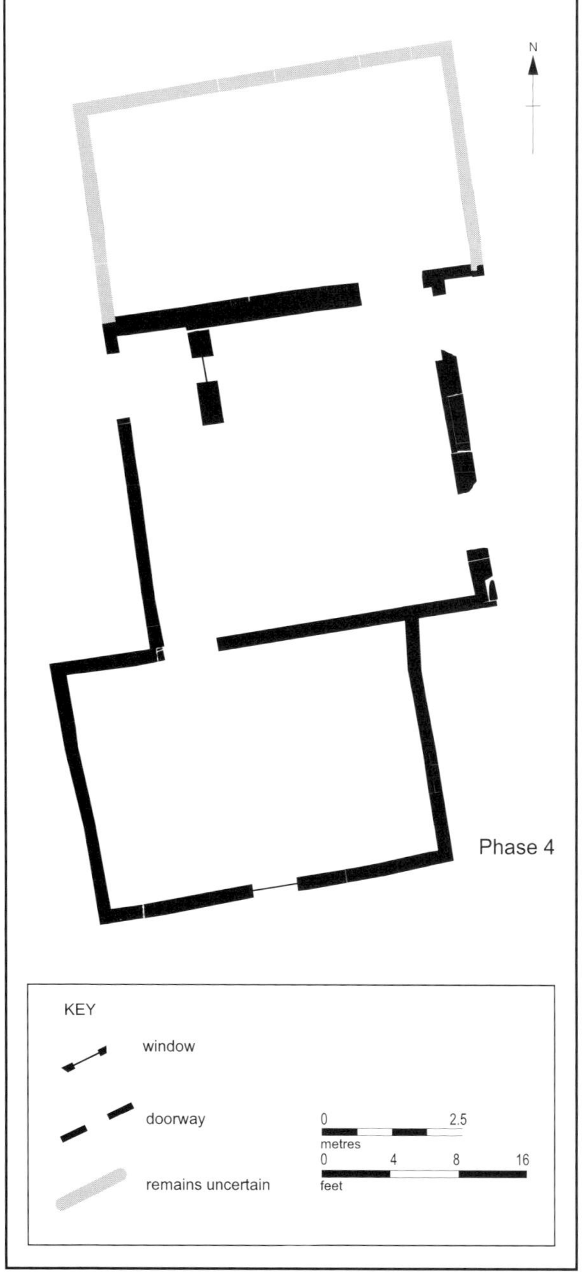

Figure 29 : Suggested plan of the farmhouse ground floor, Phase 4

These differences provide good evidence that the Phase 4 improvements represented a distinct phase of building activity, post-dating Phase 3, but do not allow Phase 4 to be dated with accuracy. No datable timbers were identified, and there is nothing to link external cobbling containing mid to late seventeenth century pottery with any of the Phase 4 walling. A fragment of late seventeenth or early eighteenth century glass was found within brickwork at the base of the west wall of the southern crosswing, but the attribution of the bottom courses of this wall to Phase 4 is not beyond doubt. Thus, the Phase 4 improvements can only be said to lie between Phases 3 and 5, in the period *c* 1635 - *c* 1724.

At the base of the west wall, a course of substantial stones was recorded. It became clear during excavation, however, that this stonework did not represent the *in situ* remains of an original plinth for the Phase 1 hall. Excavation of the wall foundations demonstrated that the course of stones was resting on a broad brick foundation, contrasting with the plinth beneath parts of the crosswing, where the stone blocks had lain directly on the underlying clay. The use of stone below the west wall was probably contemporary with the construction of the brickwork above, though it does seems likely that the stones had been obtained from a dismantled plinth, the original location of which remains unknown. The insertion in the west wall of a course of stones above the brick foundation means that all the Phase 4 brickwork identified within the farmhouse rested on a stone plinth, whether retained *in situ*, or re-used above a new foundation.

No evidence for Phase 4 windows within the wall survived, but fenestration probably existed in the position occupied by a later Yorkshire sash window, inserted at first floor level during Phase 5. Evidence for this is provided by an area of blocking which surrounded the Yorkshire sash window, and was clearly secondary to the original Phase 4 wall. Later brickwork was also recorded towards the north of the wall at first floor level.

Several fragmentary make-up layers and early floor surfaces recorded within the central hall may derive from Phase 4. A single sherd of pottery from an underlying fill appeared to demonstrate that one of these layers post-dated the late seventeenth century, but the absence of a stratigraphic relationship with the Phase 4 west wall means that the deposit cannot be related with certainty to the Phase 4 improvements. The make-up layers and floor surfaces were not all contemporary, but appear to represent successive episodes of repair and reinforcement of the floor area of the hall. Two sandy clay layers were found towards the south-east and north of the hall, and perhaps represent levelling layers dumped to make up the

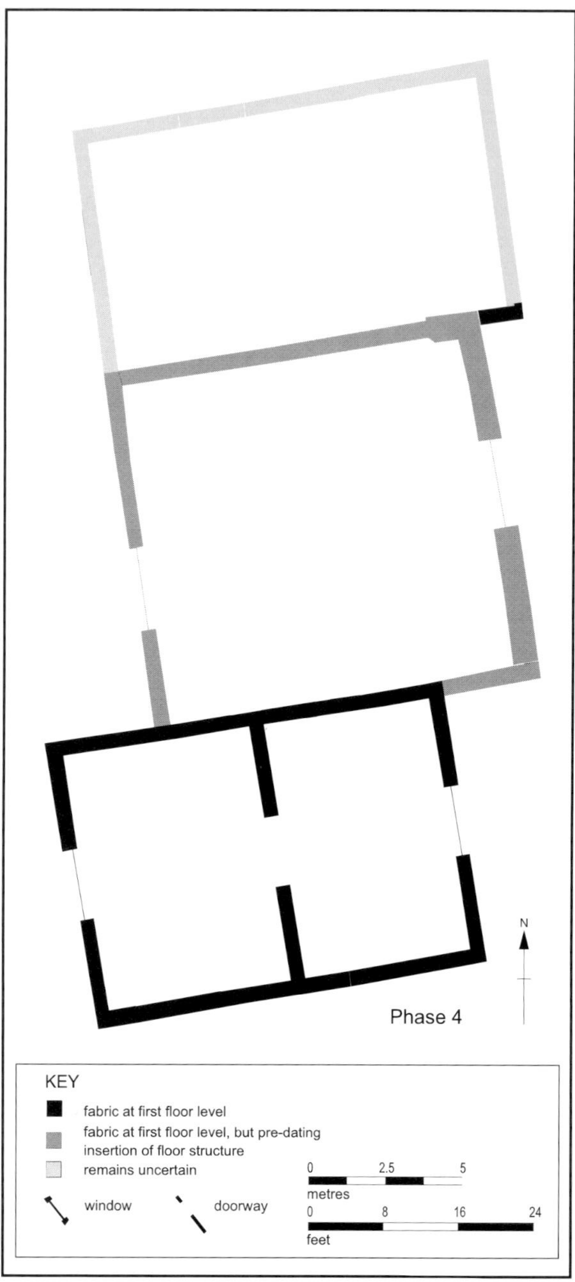

Figure 30: Suggested plan of the farmhouse first floor, Phase 4

ground for overlying floor surfaces, subsequently truncated. Two badly disturbed brick surfaces stratified above the northern clay layer may have been the remnants of a more extensive brick floor. The area between the brick surfaces had been made-up with deposits of rubble and clay. A further brick setting 0.5 m wide had been laid parallel with the west wall of the hall, within a shallow foundation cut. Its purpose is obscure, although it may have reinforced the floor of G1 along a corridor of heavy wear leading to the southern crosswing. This brick setting butted the west wall foundations, and can be said to post-date the west wall.

The west wall

Wall 2010 was substantially complete from foundations to eaves, although two areas of later walling bonded with mortar (2233 and 2806) were evident at first floor level. The bonding was irregular, with many half bats used in the outer skin. The Phase 4 wall had no stratigraphic relationship with the Phase 3 north wall of the central hall (2101) because of the presence of later brickwork (2233) at the point of intersection. However, the foundations did appear to butt those of 2101 and, to the south, the wall appeared to post-date stone block 4044 in the north wall of the crosswing, attributed to Phase 2. At ground level, courses of bricks laid in English Garden Wall bond were evident, with three courses of stretchers between each one of headers. However, higher in the elevation, the brickwork became extremely crude, irregularly bonded, and in places composed almost entirely of brick bats. Any evidence for a Phase 4 window had been removed by the insertion of later Yorkshire sash windows after the flooring over of the hall.

The west wall foundations

The west wall foundations were laid within a very shallow foundation trench (4706). The trench was 0.52 m wide but no deeper than 0.08 m, and appeared to have been truncated externally. The base was uneven, sloping down from east to west; this may have been the result of settling, and the foundations were correspondingly uneven. Foundations (4685) consisted of two courses of bricks bonded to no regular pattern, a maximum of two headers wide, 0.52 m. They were bonded with and surrounded by mortar (4695).

Above the foundations, two successive courses of brick were laid (4684), *c* 0.28 m wide. The courses were uneven and consisted of stretchers, headers, and half bricks.

Above 4684, a single course of large, roughly worked stone blocks had been laid (numbered 4084, 4085, 4086, 4680, 4681, 4682 and 4683). Most were of a red or yellow sandstone. The dimensions of the blocks ranged from 400 mm x 230 mm x 200 mm to 720 mm x 280 mm x 250 mm. Block 4046 also appeared to have served as the southern door-jamb for the main west entrance into the farmhouse.

Deposit 4615

Towards the south-east corner of Room G1, a very mixed layer of sandy clay (4615, Fig 33) overlaid cobbled surface 4616. It was 0.05 m thick, and contained frequent medium fragments of coal, and eight sherds of pottery (Fabric 4; including Fig 29.8), assigned to the mid to late seventeenth century, or slightly earlier.

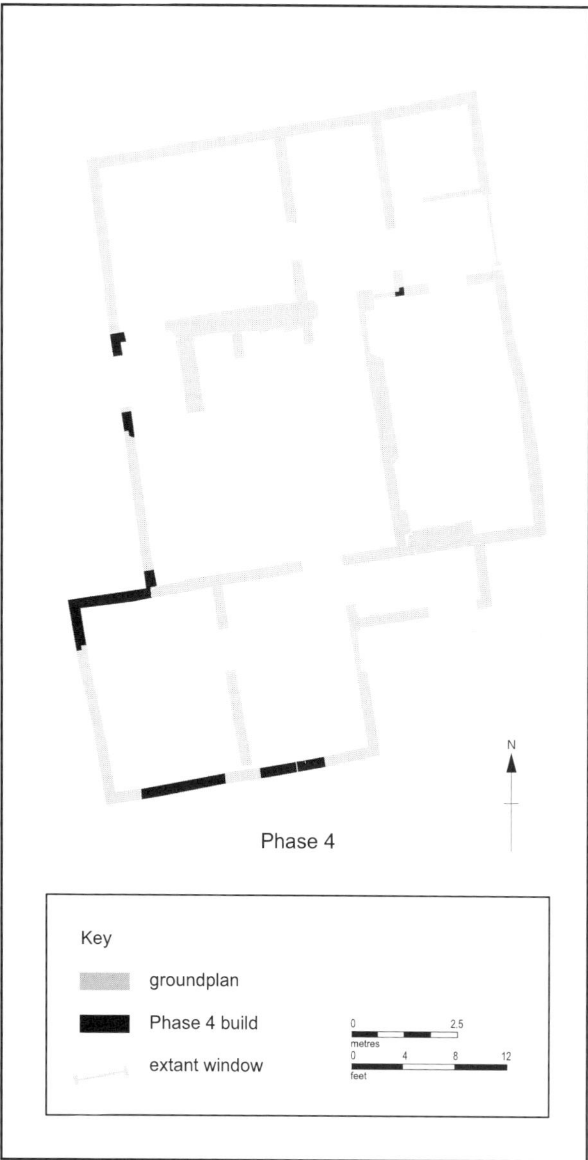

Figure 31: Plan of the farmhouse ground floor showing physical evidence, Phase 4

Floor/make-up 4266

Towards the north end of Room G1 (*see Ch 11*, Fig 69), a compact brown sandy clay layer was recorded (4266). It contained occasional brick flecks, and tipped into the hollow which remained after square cut 4582, a possible medieval hearth (Phase 1, *see Ch 3*), had been partially infilled. This deposit probably represents levelling for a floor surface, or part of a clay floor. It had no stratigraphic relationship with the walls of Room G1, but post-dated fill 4597 within 4582, which contained a sherd of late seventeenth century pottery (Fabric 4), and fragments of ceramic building material. It is thought to pre-date stone flags 4264 (Phase 5), as it was cut by pit 4549 which in turn was below firejamb 4296, probably contemporary with the flags.

Pits 4549

Two shallow pits, possibly postholes, were recorded, pre-dating the Phase 5 fireplace but cutting through deposit 4266. They were contiguous, and were together numbered 4549 (Fig 33). The cut of the eastern pit was very close to the north wall foundation of the central hall, but it was unclear whether the wall or pit was the earlier feature. The pits were subcircular in plan, *c* 0.25 m in diameter and 0.28 m deep, a single deposit filling both features. This was composed of brown clay and cinders, with lenses of dirty grey sand, occasional large fragments of brick, and three fragments of clay pipe. Two of the pipe fragments were unidentifiable, but the third was from a bowl, probably of the late seventeenth or eighteenth century (*Ch 10*). The pits' function is uncertain, but they may represent postholes for a fixture or fixtures relating to the inglenook fireplace. The finds within the fill may have been deposited when the possible fixture was removed, and may thus post-date the digging of these features.

Brick surfaces 4527 and 4529, and associated make-up

Two damaged areas of brickwork, each one course thick, were built on top of floor 4266. To the west, 4527 (Fig 33) measured *c* 0.8 m x 0.8 m. It was built of poor quality brick which had largely disintegrated to fragments. To the east *c* 1.2 m away, 4529 (Fig 33) measured *c* 1.0 m x 0.6 m. It was irregular in plan, and had been reduced to dust in places. It was unclear whether these brick features were remnants of a robbed-out floor, or merely areas of make-up. A deposit of stone and brick rubble (4528, Fig 33) had been dumped between the two brick surfaces, and this was covered with a layer of yellowish brown clay (4534). Together these deposits made up the ground surface to approximately the level of the extant top surface of the bricks.

Brick setting 4516

The base of a brick structure (4516, Fig 33) lay parallel with the west wall of Room G1, butting foundations 4685. The structure had dimensions of *c* 3.0 m x 0.5 m; it was mostly only a single course of bricks high, but survived to a height of two courses towards the north-east corner. It consisted mostly of bricks laid parallel with the west wall, but some half bricks were also used. Some of the bricks were spalled, and many had been crushed or were missing. It lay within cut 4713.

The Southern Crosswing

The survey of the building fabric demonstrated that the Phase 4 brickwork of the central hall's west wall continued round uninterrupted to the north-west gable of the crosswing (Figs 31, 32), suggesting that repairs to

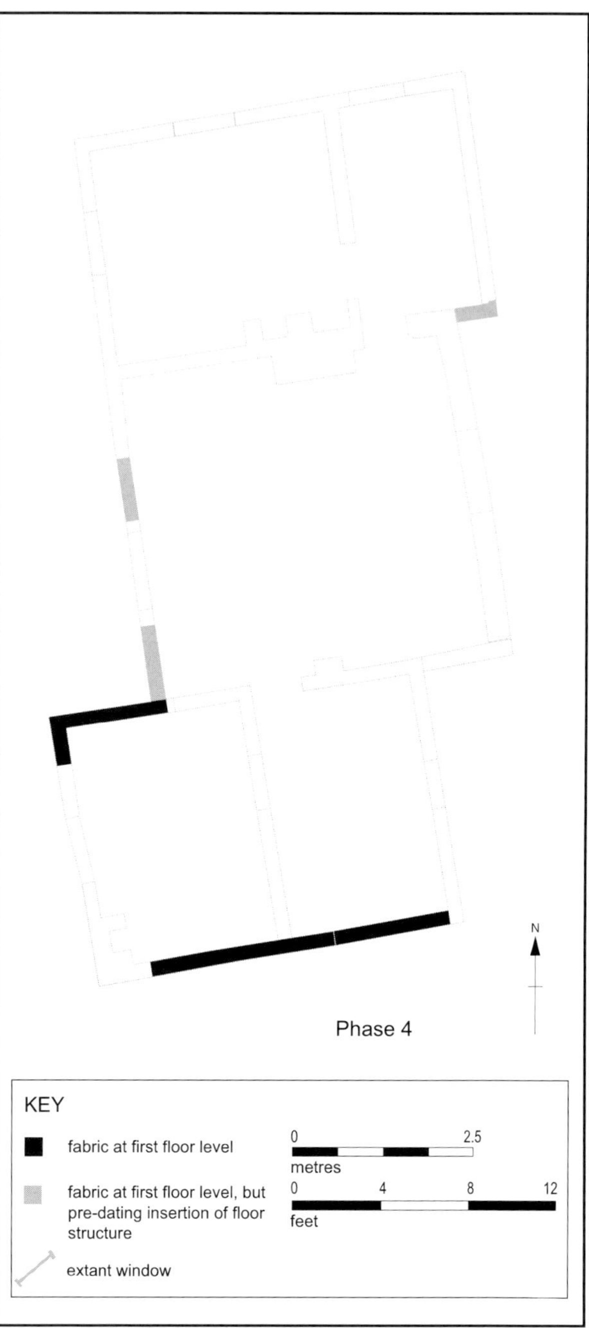

Figure 32: Plan of the farmhouse first floor showing physical evidence, Phase 4

the hall and crosswing were part of a single phase of activity. Phase 4 brickwork was also identified along most of the length of the crosswing's south wall. The purpose of the rebuilding was probably to underpin a failing timber frame. This may have related to decay of the fabric or to failure of the insubstantial stone footings on the western side, allowing the wing to tilt to the west. On the south wall, variations in the brickwork showed how the new wall was built up to an existing timber post. The walling was continued beyond the timber, the position of the post being demonstrated by later brick blocking present internally, inserted when the post was eventually removed in Phase 5.

It seems improbable that once rebuilding had begun, the timber-framed gable walls of the crosswing, including that facing west, would have been retained. The Phase 4 brickwork of both the northern return wall and the south wall extended a short distance along the face of the west gable. This appears incompatible with the survival of the timber frame of the gable, suggesting that the Phase 5 brick build of the gable was not the first brick wall in this location. The recording of the base of the gable during excavation gave a further indication that this might be the case. A course of headers set on edge close to the base of the west gable wall corresponded to a similar course of headers present towards the west end of the Phase 4 brickwork of the south wall. It may be that rebuilding of part of the gable in Phase 5 began above this distinctive course of headers. In contrast, there was no direct evidence that the extant east gable foundations might pre-date Phase 5, though this may be viewed as likely. The less exposed internal north wall of the crosswing, however, may have been retained until Phase 5.

Excavation of the base of the external north return wall of the crosswing suggested that a former doorway with a brick threshold probably deriving from Phase 3 had been blocked at the start of the Phase 4 rebuilding. Blocking of clay-bonded bricks and stone was recorded at the base of the Phase 4 brickwork of this wall.

This first phase of renewal of the crosswing walls seems not to have affected the internal plan of the wing. A single cell unit seems to have been retained on the ground floor, and may have continued to serve as the parlour.

The crosswing's north (external) and west walls

The Phase 4 brickwork of the central hall's west wall (2101) appeared to continue unbroken around to the corner of the western gable of the crosswing and for a short distance on the gable face; on the crosswing it was numbered 2009. The bond here was largely English Garden Wall, with three courses of stretchers to every one of headers, but many irregularities were evident. The bricks were bonded with clay.

It is thought possible that the base of the west gable wall, recorded during excavation and numbered 4050, was also derived from Phase 4. Four courses of bricks immediately above the plinth had been laid in an irregular form of English Garden Wall bond, with a course of headers laid on edge above. The latter corresponded to a course of headers on edge sealed below the Phase 4 brickwork of the south elevation, and the Phase 5 brickwork on the gable may have started above this course. The bonding material was recorded as a soft sandy yellowish brown mortar,

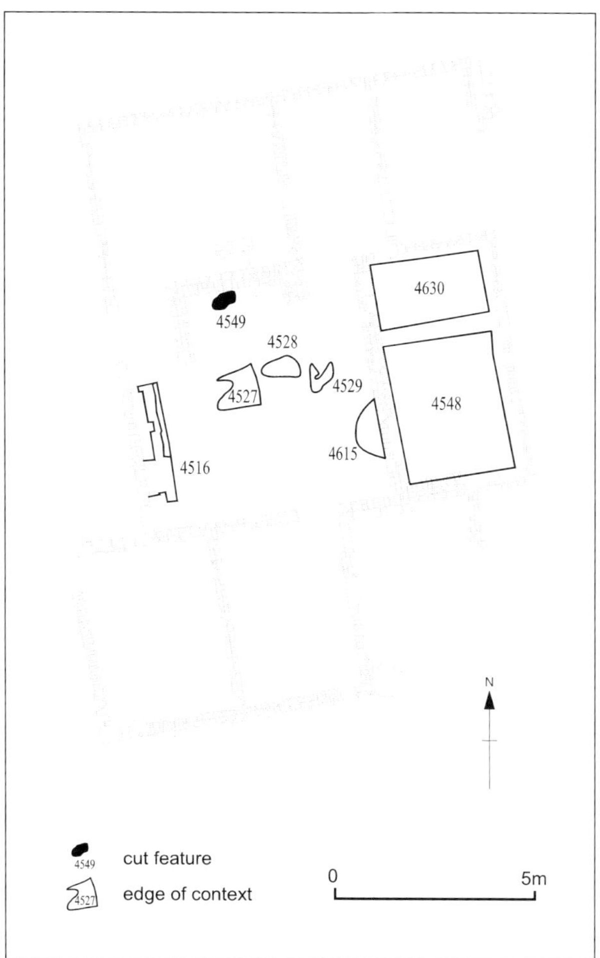

Figure 33: Excavation evidence, Phase 4

rather than the hard lime mortar characteristic of Phase 5. The surviving brick wall butted against the irregular remains of the Phase 2 plinth, consisting of stone block 4048 to the north, and other sandstone blocks within 4053 to the south. A fragment of glass representing the neck and rim of a small cylindrical bottle of late seventeenth or early eighteenth century date was found within the brickwork (*Catalogue 9*; Fig 62.9).

Excavation demonstrated that a blocked doorway lay at the base of the crosswing's northern return wall. A threshold of broken bricks, 4689, between stones 4044 and 4049, was attributed to Phase 3. However, the doorway above had subsequently been blocked with a layer of quarter bricks, 4088, above which was stone blocking 4687, loosely bonded with a silty clay matrix. A course of badly damaged half bricks was built over the top, bonded with clay. The blocking courses and walling post-dated the possible Phase 3 doorway, but were sealed by the Phase 4 walling above.

The crosswing's south wall

The survey revealed sections of clay-bonded walling similar to 2009, numbered 2023 and 2253, located along the southern wall of the crosswing, not quite reaching either of the two gables. A small window was included within 2023 on the ground floor, centrally placed on the south wall, and measuring c 0.76 m x 0.54 m. All the brickwork was one header thick, and was bonded with clay. The bond was again largely English Garden Wall, but with considerable irregularity, resulting in part from the use of broken bricks. The lower courses, numbered 4051 during excavation, were highly irregular, in effect filling in gaps between the sandstone blocks below, which were retained from the pre-existing plinth. Immediately above the sandstone, a course of headers laid on edge was present towards the west of the wall, at the same level as in the west gable. The more regular brickwork in English Garden Bond began above, though even here there were several instances of vertical joints being in line with those below.

Within the Phase 4 brickwork, two different episodes of construction could be discerned externally, meeting at a canted vertical butt joint. The earlier brickwork numbered 2023 to the west, almost certainly built up to a post, the position of which was confirmed by an empty mortise in the original wall-plate immediately above. Brickwork 2252 seems to have been built up to the east side of the post shortly afterwards. The post was replaced internally by blocking 3078, a single skin of bricks thick and 200-580 mm wide. However, blocking 3078 was bonded with a light brown mortar with frequent flecks of sandstone and lime, which may indicate that the wall-plate may have been supported by new brickwork some time before the old vertical post was removed and the void blocked. The composition of the mortar suggests that the removal of the post may finally have occurred in Phase 5.

Walling to the North-East of the Central Hall

Two further fragmentary sections of clay-bonded wall were found towards the north end of the building, on a small offset extending east from the north-east corner of the Phase 3 central hall (Figs 31, 32). When considered together, these fragments demonstrate that earlier brick walls stood on the site of the Phase 6 northern wing of the house. The northern wing appears to have been first constructed in brick after elements of the central hall were rebuilt in brick, but whilst clay bonding was still in use.

It seems likely that the new brick rooms to the north represented the rebuilding of an existing timber-framed northern service. The Phase 4 fragments described above projected up to 0.75 m east of the extant central hall. It is possible that the Phase 4 structure here followed the line of an earlier Phase 2 service area, in the form of a crosswing, which broke backwards from the main hall at the service end (Fig 29). If earlier footings were grubbed out and replaced, evidence for an earlier wall would have been removed.

Wall fragments 2900 and 2593

Brickwork 2900, the stub of a wall, was located at ground level, confined to the eastern corner of the offset, and was seated upon stone footings. It survived to a height of 0.95 m, and extended for only 0.23 m to the west, at which point it had been cut off to accommodate a repair in modern bricks (2109). It extended for an even shorter distance to the north, here being cut off when the brickwork around the northern part of the house (2107) was rebuilt during Phase 6. In all, 13 courses of bricks remained, with the clay bonding material evident around the bottom four courses.

The second fragment (2593) was located at a high elevation on the south face of the offset. It was physically separated from 2900 below, but appeared to be of the same construction, again of irregular hand-made bricks with soft brown clay bonding. The remaining portion was 1.41 m high by 0.73 m wide. It was keyed into wall 2103 to the west, the north wall of the Phase 3 central hall, and extended east to the corner of the offset. To the north it was butted by 2107, the Phase 6 build of the northern end of the house.

Raising of the Roof During Phase 4

The existence of blocked purlin holes within the fabric of the brick north wall of the central hall has been described as part of Phase 3 (*see Ch 5*). It is clear that at some stage these holes fell out of use and the whole roof of the central hall was raised, perhaps by c 0.35 m, thereafter being supported on top of the hall's north wall (Fig 27). There is evidence to suggest that this change occurred during Phase 4.

It is thought that the roof was raised towards the start of the Phase 4 improvements because the Phase 4 brickwork to the west of the hall reached right up to the height of the extant roof structure, whereas the older east wall was lower. It does not seem possible that the roof could have remained in a lower position once the west wall had been constructed. The lesser height of the east wall led to the use of a double set of wall-plates here once the roof had been raised, with the pre-existing wall-plates retained, but acting merely as blocking to give extra height, and new wall-plates added above. However, if this is accepted, it remains difficult to determine which elements of the extant roof structure date from this time, and which derive from further alteration during Phase 5. Given the evidence for the use of former A-frame rafters in the Phase 5 floor of the central hall, it may be that alteration of the roof structure was minimal until that time, with the roof raised but the timbers not replaced. An exception to this may have been the upper set of eastern wall-plates. These adjustments to the roof are not fully understood, because the discrepancy in height between the east wall and later walls was less than the distance between the blocked purlin holes and the extant purlins in the north wall.

Ancillary Structures

Deposits considered to represent two successive clay surfaces were recorded within the footprint of the Phase 6 eastern outshut. They were stratified above cobbled layer 4676 (Phase 2?, but containing a small assemblage of pottery, perhaps intrusive, of probable mid to late seventeenth century date), but below the walls of the Phase 6 outshut. Both layers were further truncated into two by the foundation cut (4450) for a later partition cut within G3. They were not identified beyond the walls of the later outshut.

Interpretation of the date of these layers is problematic because of uncertainty as to whether or not they butted or were truncated by the Phase 3 foundations for the west wall of the central hall. Although it is possible that the surfaces were first laid before Phase 3 and continued in use for a long period, accumulating later pottery, an origin in Phase 4 is preferred, as the late seventeenth century pottery assemblage recovered appears to suggest use during Phase 4. The surfaces probably represent floors within a lightly constructed lean-to or outshut for which no other evidence survived.

Surfaces 4630 and 4548

Layers 4630 and 4548 (Fig 33) were deposits of greyish brown redeposited clay, found to north and south respectively of 4450. Layer 4548 was 0.09 m thick, and contained small, medium, and large fragments of charcoal. Together they are seen to have represented part of a clay surface, the surviving area having dimensions of *c* 5.20 m high by 2.50 m wide. Twenty-four sherds of pottery (Fabric 4; including Fig 58.67) were recovered from 4548; the assemblage appears to date to the late seventeenth century. Surfaces 4461 and 4472 above appear to have been deposited during Phase 5.

Early Cobbling in Front of the Farmhouse

Evidence was recovered for a phase of cobbling in front of the farmhouse, pre-dating cobbles 4181 which were probably contemporary with the later construction and surfacing of a causeway (*see below, Ch 8*). The earlier layers contained probable mid to late seventeenth century pottery; this may give an indication of date, although the possibility of later contamination and the high likelihood of residuality during the construction process render the dating unreliable. The cobbling cannot be linked stratigraphically to the Phase 4 building activity. It can only be suggested that it may have been laid during roughly the same period.

Make-up layers for cobbling

Deposits of yellowish brown clay, dark brown clay silt, and two deposits of silt with charcoal, respectively 4586, 4592, 4640 and 4641, were thought to derive from an episode of dumping designed to make up the ground before the cobbles were laid. Deposit 4586 contained six sherds of pottery (Fabrics 4 and 5; including Figs 53.6, 53.12), together thought to date to the mid to late seventeenth century or slightly earlier, suggesting that the area was first cobbled at this time. A few cobbles remained, but most are thought to have been robbed-out and re-laid.

Fills Within the Moat

Three fills recorded in the moat at the western bridging point, close to the stone bridge, contained small late seventeenth century pottery assemblages. These, and a stratigraphically related fill, may have been deposited whilst the changes to the farmhouse attributed to Phase 4 were occurring. One lay directly over the cut, indicating that the moat had been thoroughly cleaned out at the start of this period. However, some of the fills now deposited were up to 0.6 m thick, demonstrating that regular cleaning out of the moat now came to an end. Failure to maintain the moat resulted eventually in its deliberate infilling, probably at the beginning of Phase 6 at the bridging point, and during Phases 6 and 7 elsewhere.

On the western side of the moat, a Phase 4 fill had formed against the vertical face of the west pier of the stone bridge; this appeared to be replicated to the east. Although Phase 4 fills were found to butt the face of the bridge piers, they did not seal the piers from above, and it is thus assumed that it was still maintained and continued to provide the main access to the platform.

General biological analysis samples from two of the fills attributed to Phase 4 underwent detailed investigation (Kenward *et al* 1998; *see Ch 10*). The plant and invertebrate macrofossil evidence showed remarkable similarity to that recovered from fills deposited in the late medieval period (*see Ch 3*). The immediate environment of the moat would appear to have changed little in the intervening years. It may be that the way of life of the occupants of the platform had altered very little, but the paucity of biological remains that can be linked directly to human occupation precludes a more confident judgement of the extent of economic continuity. Presumably cess was not finding its way into the moat, even if small numbers of artefacts were.

Fill 4719

A thin lens of greyish brown sandy clay with a maximum thickness of 0.10 m, 4719, was recorded coating part of the east edge of the moat immediately below the position of the bridge. It contained moderate small pebbles, fragments of decaying wood, very occasional fragments of sandstone, and a single sherd of pottery (Fabric 4) which can be attributed to the late seventeenth century.

Fills 4579, 4746, and 4720

Moat fills 4579 and 4746 (*see Ch 3, Fig 14*) had accumulated against the faces of stone piers 4568 and 4752 (Phase 2), to the east and west of the moat respectively. These were deposits of grey silty clay with a visibly high organic component, including wood fragments; they were thought to have formed whilst the moat was waterlogged, and were up to 0.58 m deep. Towards the top of both contexts a concentration of branch and twig debris was recorded. The two contexts are thought to correspond to 4720, present along the full length of the moat exposed in Area C. Five sherds of pottery were recovered from 4720 (Fabrics 4 and 5; including Fig 54.25), and a single sherd from 4746 (Fig 59.80). The pottery from both contexts was considered to be late seventeenth century in date. Analysis of two general biological samples from fills 4579 and 4746 suggested that the moat remained shaded and overgrown by trees, shrubs, and tall herbs, but few conclusions could be drawn about the wider environment, or the economy of the site at this time (*see Ch 10*).

7

PHASE 5 - REBUILDING IN BRICK, AND RE-ROOFING OF THE CENTRAL HALL

EARLY EIGHTEENTH CENTURY

Phase 5 involved a major remodelling of the interior of the hall, accompanied by further rebuilding of the gables of the crosswing and parts of the west face of the hall (Figs 34, 35). The brickwork was of hand-made bricks bonded with lime mortar. The central hall was also re-roofed using new materials. Dendrochronological analysis of a roof purlin suggests that this may have occurred soon after AD 1724.

Alterations to the Central Hall

The previously open hall was floored over, creating a first floor room which was accessed via the crosswing. A bridging beam and six of the joists within the floor structure were identified as re-used Phase 1 roof timbers, a tie-beam, and A-frame rafters respectively, from the original roof of the hall (Lee and Michelmore 1998). This suggests that changes were now made to the roof which involved major remodelling, liberating timbers for use elsewhere.

It seems likely that the extant roof truss located at the south end of the central hall was constructed at this time (Pl 13). It lay on the line of the probable former bay division between hall (room F1, *Ch 11*, Fig 70) and parlour, immediately adjacent to the north wall of the crosswing, the tie-beam of the truss being supported in the centre by a brick pillar, which was clearly part of the build of the Phase 5 south wall of the central hall. At either end the tie-beam was attached to lengths of wall-plate with a lap dovetail joint. These wall-plates, together with others jointed to them, may be contemporary with the truss, though it is possible that they were first installed in Phase 4, after the roof was raised slightly. New purlins seem to have been made from recently cut timbers; a purlin from the east pitch of the roof was dated by dendrochronology, and found to be from a tree felled in the spring or summer of 1724 (Pl 13). At its southern end, beyond the truss, the roof rested on the main structural timbers of the crosswing roof, the extant roof frame being covered by rafters, but these showed no coherent pattern in style or method of fixing. The rafters were pegged or nailed to the frame, and appeared to be a mixture of

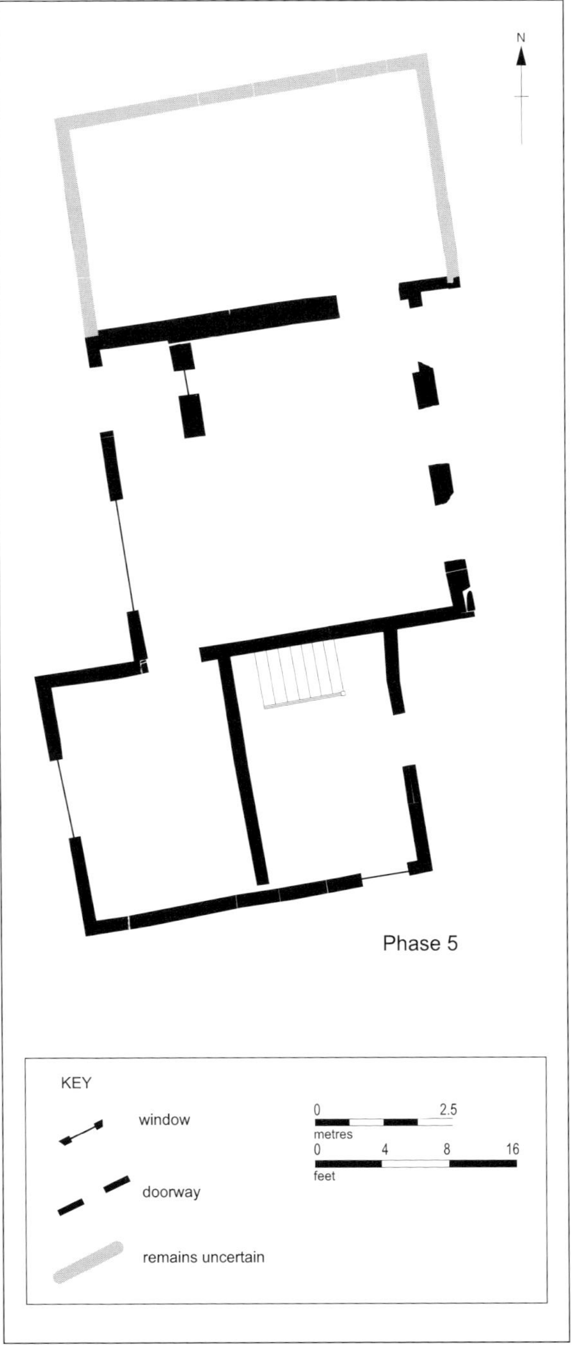

Figure 34: Suggested plan of the farmhouse ground floor, Phase 5

re-used and newly cut timbers. No discernible phasing was evident, suggesting a longevity of use of some rafters, coupled with constant maintenance and re-fixing since Phase 5.

The raising of the bressumer beam indicates that the smokehood installed in Phase 3 had now become redundant, and it appears to have been replaced by the first in a series of brick fireplaces contained within the former inglenook. The Phase 5 fireplace had been disturbed by several later modifications, but elements of the original chimney and chimney breast survived. Excavation revealed evidence of an ashbox and two firejambs, thought to be part of the same structure (Fig 36), with a surface of stone flags surrounding the fireplace, respecting the edge of the ashbox. A first floor fireplace was provided for the new upper chamber (Fig 37).

Alterations to the west wall were carried out to allow the insertion of two Yorkshire sash windows at ground and first floor level. This type of window, with an horizontally sliding light, was a feature of vernacular architecture from the mid seventeenth century to the mid eighteenth century (Brunskill 1981, 125), and might be fitted to a farmhouse where there was no space for a vertical sash, or used for the less visible side or rear elevations. A more comprehensive rebuilding of the south wall was carried out at the same time as rebuilding of the crosswing gables and the construction of a new crosswing partition. It is thought that the southern wall of the central hall had still been of timber-framed construction at the start of Phase 5. The new brick build contained a single doorway towards its western end, to give access to the western ground floor room of the crosswing.

The presence of a third doorway in the centre of the east wall of the hall is not easily understood. It appeared to post-date the construction of the wall in Phase 3, but may be explained by the arrangement of an outshut of unknown form standing during Phase 4 or 5. Although the mortar used for the blocking appeared similar to that used in the blocking of the northern doorway in Phase 6 or 7, the narrower bricks may imply that the doorway was actually closed in Phase 5.

Flooring over of the open hall

The bressumer beam which had formerly supported a smokehood was raised by 0.30 m, and was used as a bridging joist aligned east / west. The timber was 4.67 m long; its western end rested on Phase 3 heck wall 2102, whilst the eastern end had been cut into Phase 3 east wall 2103. At both ends, the beam lay above areas of blocking which indicated its former position, both consisting of hand-made bricks bonded with lime mortar. A second bridging joist (3169), *c* 6.0 m long, also aligned east / west, was inserted to the

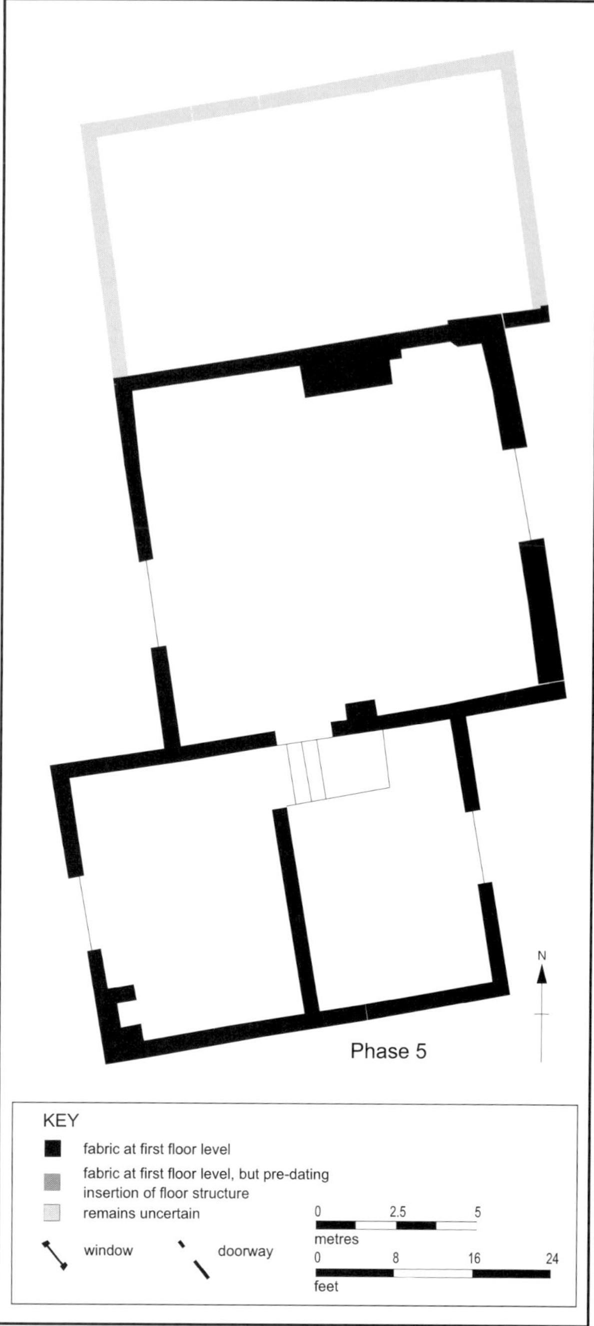

Figure 35: Suggested plan of the farmhouse first floor, Phase 5

south. This was supported on the west side by a stone mullion set within new window 2059 inserted into the west wall; the other end was let into the east wall.

Fourteen joists were used between bridging joist 3169 and the south wall of the hall. Several of these may have been replaced subsequently, but four of the extant joists were thought to be original timbers, 3166 A-D. They were jointed to the bridging joist by bare-faced soffit tenons, and three were cogged into the south wall. One, 3166 B, had chamfered sides, but redundant joints indicated that it was a re-used timber; it was tenoned rather than cogged into the south wall. The probable replacement joists, 3165 A-J, were mostly

Plate 13: The Phase 5 roof of farmhouse room F1, showing the southern truss and purlins 2734 and 2735

cogged into the bridging joist, but were often poor fits within the mortises.

All 14 joists jointed to the north of bridging joist 3169, 3167 A-N, were attached by bare-faced soffit tenons. The six furthest west were *c* 3.53 m long and extended right across to the north wall of the hall (2101), into which they were cogged. The remaining eight extended to bridging joist 3108, the re-used bressumer beam. They rested on the upper surface of the beam, and brick packing had been inserted between them. Ten further joists, 3168 A-J, spanned the remaining gap to the north. Of these, 3168 G-J appeared to be cut off lengths of the corresponding joists to the south, 3167 K-N. It is not clear why these joists should have been cut in line with the bridging joist, rather than allowed to continue over it, as to the west with 3167 A-F. The central joists at this northern end rested on a shelf within fireplace 3123; the three to the east were let into north wall 2101.

The earlier of two layers of floorboards recorded, 3145, also dates from Phase 5. A brick pillar (2151), clearly part of the build of the south wall of the central hall, rested on these boards, demonstrating their early date, but also being indicative of poor-quality workmanship. The presence of the pillar, which supported the tie-beam above, also shows that the

flooring over of the hall must have been complete by the time the new roof structure was erected. However, the two alterations may have been part of the same episode of construction, with the old roof dismantled before the floor was inserted.

The roof of the central hall

Along the east wall, four lengths of wall-plate had been jointed together, and installed on top of two underlying wall-plates, which had probably served as plates in Phase 3, but had been used as blocking when the roof was raised in Phase 4. The wall-plates comprised three main timbers, 2747, 2748, and 2749 respectively from north to south, attached by mortise and tenon joints. A further length of plate (2911) only 0.35 m long, was attached by a pegged lap joint to the southern end of 2749, and may have been cut at its southern edge. Of these wall-plates, 2747 was re-used, with peg holes indicating that it had been turned through 90°, but 2748 and 2749 showed no evidence of former use. Three wall-plates, 2787, 2788, and 2789 respectively from south to north, had been laid along the western wall, with a further thin timber attached to the top of 2787 being a later repair. Again, the plates were joined with pegged mortise and tenon joints, and showed some evidence of re-use. Although the functioning wall-plates to both the front and rear of the hall were jointed to a roof structure thought to have been assembled as part of the Phase 5 works, it remains possible that they had originally been placed in position in Phase 4.

A pair of principal rafters (2753 and 2780) were attached by pegged tenons to the tie-beam, and were thought to be contemporary with it. Both were of rectangular section, measuring 100 mm wide by 200 mm high and 110 mm wide by 170 mm high respectively. The eastern principal rafter (2753) was attached by pegged tenon to the western, with a ridge purlin (2736) again probably contemporary, supported in a birds mouth joint at the apex. The side purlins of the eastern pitch were trenched within halving joints but, to the west, the side purlins were separated from halving joints cut into the principal rafter by plaster (upper purlin) and a wooden pad (lower). It might be thought that the presence of these materials related to the raising of the roof but, in each instance, the elevation from the principal rafter was minimal; it is considered rather that the packing was the product of some more minor adjustment to the roof. Within the truss, a pair of braces had been inserted between the tie-beam and the principal rafters. A pair of vertical timbers was also present, in the position of queen posts, but measuring only c 40 mm wide by 80 mm high in section, and attached to the rafters by nailed lap joints. Additionally, a total of 22 staves set in peg holes formed a grill to which laths and daub could be attached.

The truss supported two pairs of purlins and a ridge purlin which carried the roof over the large central bay of the house to the north. These were of substantial dimensions, the largest measuring 180 mm wide by 270 mm high in section, and to the north they rested on the top of the north wall of the central hall. Some may have been re-used from an earlier phase of roof, but one timber (2735) was dated by dendrochronology, giving a felling date of AD 1724B (Sheffield, 1998). Clearly this purlin at least was installed in Phase 5, and was made from new timber.

The roof continued south from the truss to meet the northern pitch of the crosswing roof, leaving an attic space below. A short ridge purlin, probably re-used, was attached to the ridge purlin of the main roof to the north by a tenoned splayed scarf joint. It was raised on a post above the southern side purlin of the crosswing roof, but was unattached at the south end, possibly having been reduced in length. Side purlins rested on the principal rafters of the truss, or were jointed to the purlins of the main roof to the north. Their southern ends rested on the side purlin of the crosswing roof. A pair of valley rafters of substantial scantling, constructed from re-used timber, was placed diagonally against the north pitch of the crosswing roof, again resting on the north side purlin; that to the east appeared to rest additionally on the cut back end

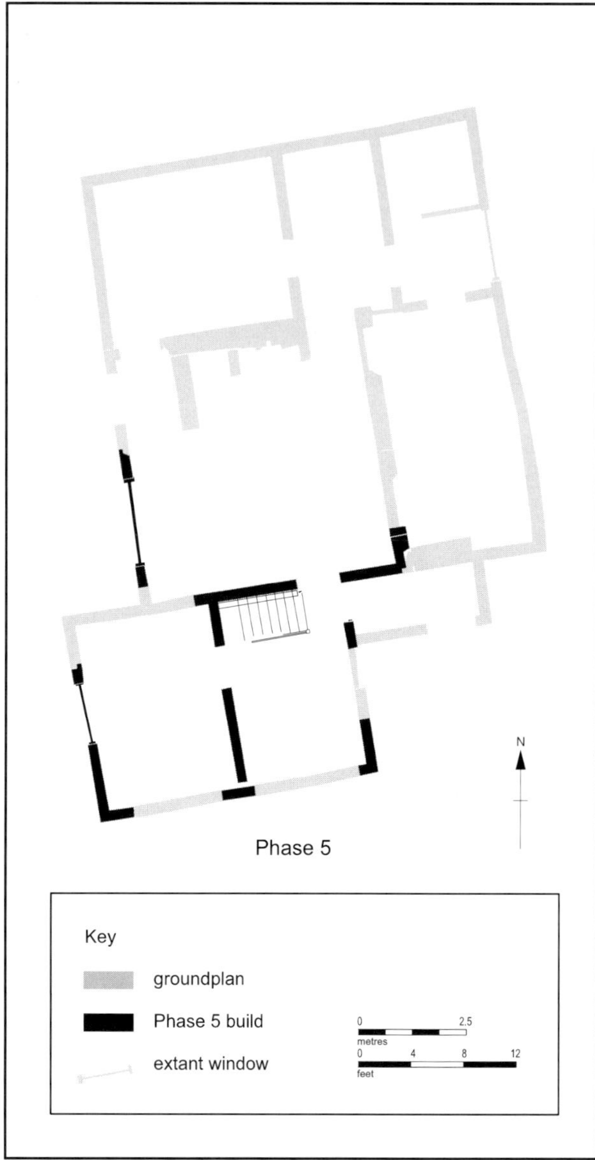

Figure 36: Plan of the farmhouse ground floor showing physical evidence, Phase 5

of the new ridge purlin. These valley rafters (2075 and 3120) were identified as cut down sections of wall-plate, probably derived from the Phase 2 wall-frame of the crosswing gables.

Two further timbers raised the possibility that the roof had formerly extended over the angle between the gable of the crosswing and the south-east corner of the central hall, above the later porch. An additional purlin only 0.47 m long had been jointed to the south end of the lower side purlin towards the south-east corner of the roof, extending the timber slightly south of the truss. Its short length suggested that it may have been cut off in line with the south wall of the central hall. This was replicated at the base of the roof, where the wall-plate had likewise been extended south by 0.35 m. Although the extensions may only have been intended to key the purlins into the new brick south wall, it is possible that the roof once

Plate 14: The Phase 5 ashbox associated with fireplace 3134

extended further south. This possibility is further reinforced by wide grooves in the lower purlin on the east side of the roof extending south of the truss to meet the crosswing. The grooves housed a series of rafters extending up the pitch of the roof, but seemed too wide for this function alone. The purlin had been pegged twice in each groove, the second peg probably relating to a second set of rafters that may have extended below the purlin, and out over a larger roof area. One possibility is that purlins and wall-plates supported the roof for a possible outshut or porch attached to the east gable of the crosswing.

Fireplaces in the central hall

The aperture of the earliest fireplace had been subject to later modification, but seven courses of brickwork remained above it, constructed of hand-made bricks bonded with lime mortar (3134). They showed the chimney breast to have been 1.50 m wide, projecting *c* 0.85 m from the north wall of the hall, with plaster containing animal hair applied to its east and west faces. This area of brickwork stopped at the level of the newly inserted ceiling. Above, the chimney breast for a first floor fireplace (2144) was built directly on top, but recessed back by *c* 90 mm to leave a ledge on which the adjacent first storey floor joists were supported. This upper section of chimney breast had a straight west side, but tapered inwards to the east, to a minimum width of *c* 1.0 m. An area of brickwork to the east (2583) appeared to be bonded into the chimney breast over the bottom seven courses, but

this may be later keying in. It can be suggested that this was later infill to fill the awkward gap between the chimney breast and doorway 2578, the latter probably built during Phase 6.

Other remains from the Phase 5 fireplace at ground floor level included an area of brickwork at the rear of the chimney (3192) and an area of blocking in the rear wall (3221). Three courses of bricks located low down to either side of the aperture (3184 and 3187) may derive from Phase 6.

At ground level, excavation showed that the earliest surviving elements of the first fireplace were an ashbox (4295, Fig 38, Pl 14), and two firejambs. The ashbox was rectangular and measured 0.71 m x 0.64 m by 0.35 m deep. It was constructed of three courses of brick set on edge, of average size 240 mm x 120 mm by 70 mm high, bonded with a very hard white mortar with fine grit inclusions. It was built flush against a construction cut, stepped in near the bottom to support the bricks, and with a gently rounded base.

The ashbox is thought to be contemporary with two brick firejambs to east and west, numbered 4296 (Fig 38). The jambs were two brick courses high, with the bottom course laid on edge. The bricks were an average of 240 mm x 120 mm by 50 mm high, and were bonded with a hard white mortar. The upper course showed traces of a brittle white plaster with fine inclusions of chalk or lime.

The basal fill of the ashbox was a black silty clay (4474) with frequent cinders, fragments of sandstone, and small fragments of stone flags. Above, the western part of the feature had been infilled with unbonded bricks (4302), laid loosely on top of one another, four bricks deep and two courses wide. This blocking may have been intended to reduce the size of the ashbox for later use. The remaining space had subsequently been filled with sandy silt with frequent large brick fragments and occasional stone fragments (4297). At some stage prior to the deposition of the overlying deposit, brick 4535 was mortared to the eastern firejamb and the top of the ashbox. It was bonded with a brownish white mortar, and probably represents a repair or provision of a support for a later grate.

To the west of the fireplace, a deposit of cinders and silt (4267) had been dumped. Deposits were also found directly underlying plinth 4081 associated with later fireplace 4185. Deposit 4267 may thus have been derived from use of fireplace 4317.

The upper floor fireplace (2766) had survived relatively intact. It was cut through the outer skin of wall 2101, and its aperture would originally have measured 0.79 m x 0.49 m by 0.14 m deep. A sandstone slab formed the hearth within the fireplace, with a second slab directly in front covered with a layer of lime plaster *c* 15 mm thick. This slab to the front was overlaid by a floorboard from the earliest extant set of floorboards (2934); the plaster butted the floorboard. A vertical flue which appeared to lead from the downstairs fireplace was also accommodated within the chimney breast; it was located to the east of fireplace 2766.

The west wall of the central hall

Alterations to the west wall were carried out to allow the insertion of two windows, 2059 and 2061, at ground and first floor level respectively (Figs 34 and 35). An area of the Phase 4 wall (2010), a maximum of 3 m wide, was demolished and rebuilt with apertures for the windows. The rebuilt section of walling (2806/2809) was identified by its bonding material, a hard cream mortar with frequent flecks of lime and occasional coal fragments; it was distinguished from adjacent areas of repointing by the absence of clay bonding material below the surface mortar. The bond was irregular.

The extant Yorkshire sash window frames of 2059 and 2061 are thought to have been contemporary with the window apertures. Yorkshire sash windows typically contain two lights, one fixed, the other a sliding sash moving horizontally, though the examples at Old Abbey Farm included more lights. The frame of 2059 consisted of a simply moulded window surround with four parallel lights divided into two pairs by a central stone mullion (3056). The mullion was unusually substantial, measuring 1.51 m x 0.22 m by

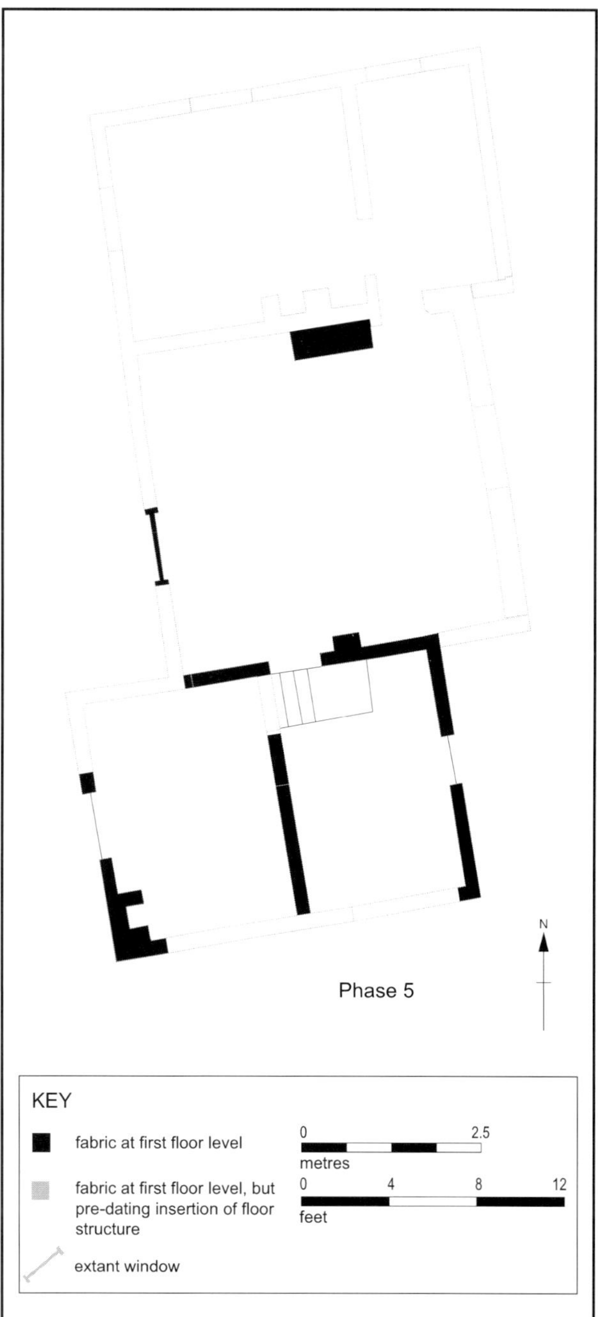

Figure 37: Plan of the farmhouse first floor showing physical evidence, Phase 5

0.31 m deep, and extended 0.54 m below the base of the window. No evidence for any earlier, lower window was observed, and the large size of the mullion can be accounted for by the fact that it also supported bridging joist 3169, the main east-west member for the newly inserted floor over the central hall. The window had an external lintel consisting of two blocks of sandstone, painted first yellow and then black. The brickwork of the wall was not cut through at either end of the lintel, suggesting that it was contemporary with the rebuilt wall and window aperture. Internally, a wooden lintel was recorded, again thought to be contemporary with the insertion of the window. An external sill was covered with cement: it was unclear whether this was covering a course of protruding bricks. The window aperture had overall dimensions of *c* 0.98 m high by 1.93 m wide, with the individual lights varying in size from 0.75 m high by 0.31 m wide to 0.87 m high by 0.34 m wide.

At first floor level, Yorkshire sash window 2061 originally consisted of three parallel sashes, each with two lights, two sashes being extant. The window aperture had overall dimensions of 1.31 m wide by 1.13 m high, the lights within the external sash measuring 0.42 m wide by 0.36 m high, and those of the internal sliding sash 0.38 m wide by 0.34 m high. The lintel was formed directly by the two jointed wall-plate timbers at the top of the west wall. Internally, the sill consisted of three thin stone slabs, with a course of facing bricks above, some near square in shape. The external sill (3076) consisted of a skin of 16 headers protruding from the wall, covered with cement. As with window 2059 below, the surrounding brickwork bonded with lime mortar was not cut through, suggesting that the creation of the aperture was contemporary with the rebuild of the wall. Eight courses of bricks above rebuild 2809 to the south side of the window were bonded with clay. Again, they were not cut through, and may relate to the south edge of an earlier window.

The south wall of the central hall and north wall of the crosswing

A wall of irregular hand-made bricks bonded with a white lime mortar was built, extending around the south-east corner of the central hall and along its southern end as far as the doorway (2188) close to the south-west corner. The portion lying east of the gable of the crosswing was numbered 2019; its bond was largely irregular, and the inner, north face was particularly roughly built, with many brick bats. The wall forming the division between the crosswing and the hall at ground floor level, 2859, was built in part using English Garden Wall bond, with five courses of stretchers to every one of headers. Again, many brick bats were used for the north face. Wall 2104 was built at first floor level above 2859 and to the west of 2019, probably immediately afterwards and as part of the same constructional episode. The brickwork was identical to 2859. A vertical join remained between the two sections of brickwork at first floor level, aligned with the east gable of the crosswing and with a mortise on the underside of the wall-plate extending along the top of wall 2790. It seems very probable that wall 2019 had been built up to a surviving post within an existing timber-framed wall, and that this timber was then removed and the brickwork to the west built. A brick pillar (2151) was tied into the north-facing side of wall 2104, and appeared to be contemporary. Its function was to support tie-beam

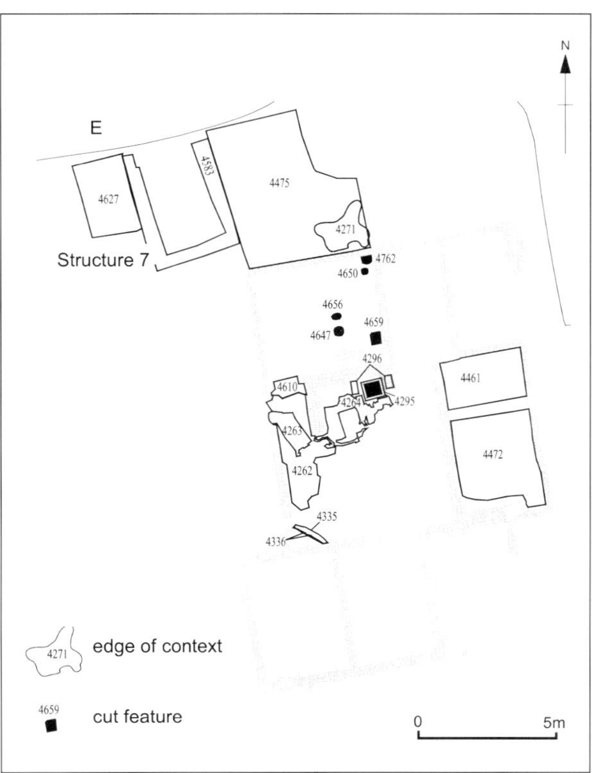

Figure 38: Excavation evidence, Phase 5

2752, which rested on a timber wedge inserted between the two. The pillar rested on floorboards 3154, and was probably built after the floor was constructed, but was butted by floorboards 2934, which were contemporary or later.

Doorway 2188 was contemporary with wall 2859 and it was positioned at the western end of the south wall to give access to the western ground floor room of the crosswing. The eastern side of the aperture was not cut through 2859, but the western edge truncated Phase 4 wall 2009. Brick blocking 3006, similar in character to 2859, probably represents repair of the jagged edge. The northern- and southern-facing timber lintels (3005 and 3001) were both thought to be contemporary with the aperture, although the positioning of 3005 displayed two irregularities. The aperture on the north side was higher than to the south, extending two courses above the lintel whilst, to the east of the doorway, the lintel was recessed 40 mm into wall 2859, and faced with two cut bricks. Southern lintel 3001 supported Phase 2 bridging joist 3008 and post 2791. The lintel is thought to have been inserted below these timbers when the timber-framing was replaced. Also probably contemporary with the aperture were a stone block (3003) to the east of the doorway, perhaps intended to support a door-jamb now removed, and a line of bricks (3004) at the foot of the doorway, considered to be the remains of a brick floor within the crosswing. Similar bricks also occurred in the south-west corner of the western room (G5/6), below flags 3227.

The foundations of the south wall (4389) were laid within a foundation trench (4594), *c* 0.5 m wide by 0.2 m deep. The foundations were 0.38 m wide by 0.26 m deep, and consisted of whole and broken bricks, with a firm yellowish brown silty clay (4593) used to backfill the trench. The foundation trench and foundations appeared to extend beneath doorway 2188 up to, but not beneath, western door-jamb 4044, in line with the west wall of Room G1, and it seems probable that they butted this door-jamb. Door-jambs 4043 and 4044 flanked the doorway to east and west. Jamb 4043 was sub-square in plan, measured *c* 200 mm x 200 mm by 180 mm deep, with roughly hewn faces, and was mortared to wall 4055. Jamb 4044 was larger, subrectangular in plan, and measured 430 mm x 260 mm by 250 mm deep; clay bonding material was visible on its upper surface. This door-jamb did not appear to overlie foundations 4389; it may represent part of an earlier wall plinth which had remained *in situ*. A layer of silty clay 0.02 m thick had been laid between the jambs on top of wall foundations 4389. Above this make-up, a layer of sand (4381) was laid, and survived to a maximum depth of 0.02 m. A brick threshold (4380) had been constructed over the sand, butting up against the door-jambs. It consisted of a double row of bricks a single course high, with stretchers to the south, and half and broken bricks to the north.

Access to the new first floor of the central hall was via the crosswing. Internal division wall 2104 was built with a doorway placed just to the east of the crosswing's first floor partition, at the top of the staircase, 3200 (*see below, p 73*). Doorway 2624 was constructed with two wooden jambs jointed into the wall-plate above, which served as a lintel. The doorway was clearly a secondary insertion below the wall-plate, as is indicated by the awkward cutting of the full mortise for the hanging stile. Moreover, the closing stile was unmortised, and merely nailed into a notch cut at the side of an existing brace. The crudeness of the cutting shows that this took place whilst the wall-plate was *in situ*.

Floor Surfaces and Structures within the Central Hall

Much of the hall was floored with beaten clay, but stone flags were laid around the fireplace. Additionally, brick surfaces covered the threshold of the main west doorway, and the area immediately within that doorway, presumably reinforcing the floor where it was liable to suffer heavy wear. A feature in the south-west corner of the room may have been a step up to the doorway into the crosswing.

Floors 4262, 4263, 4264, and 4610 (Fig 38)

A grey clay surface (4262) survived in two large patches within the hall. An area to the west of the room had maximum dimensions of *c* 4.2 m high by 2.2 m wide, and butted against the western wall, whilst a separate area to the east measured *c* 4.4 m high by 2.0 m wide, butting the eastern wall. The surface was compact, flat, and smooth, and several fine lenses of cinder were thought to indicate frequent repairs to the floor. The surface overlaid brick structures 4516 and 4527 in the west and north of the room, and layer 4615 to the east.

A stone flagged floor surface (4264) was recorded in the north of the hall, covering an area measuring *c* 2.9 m long by 1.6 m wide. The individual flags were subrectangular or irregular in shape, and varied considerably in size, up to a maximum of *c* 400 mm long by 260 mm wide. The flags were thought to be contemporary with clay floor surface 4262, and may never have covered the entire room, perhaps representing decoration or reinforcement around the fireplace.

Two brick surfaces were recorded lying within clay floor 4262. To the north-west, brick surface 4263 lay just inside the main doorway, aligned north-west / south-east and covering an area measuring *c* 1.5 m long by 0.7 m wide. It was one course deep, unbonded, and may represent reinforcement of the clay floor surface in an area of heavy wear. Immediately to the north and west, the threshold area itself was reinforced by brick surface 4610, again predominantly one course of bricks deep.

Stone setting 4336

In the south-west corner of the hall, a triangular shaped cut, 4335 (Fig 38), was recorded, located in the angle between the west and south walls and butting up to their foundations. The cut was deepest along the north-east edge, where it acted as a short foundation trench, *c* 1.15 m x 0.20 m by 0.26 m deep. Within this slot, two flagstones numbered 4336 (Fig 38) were set on edge to stand vertically, the south-eastern flagstone being additionally secured by insertion into a slot in the foundations of the south wall, 4399. The flagstones had dimensions of 490 mm x 260 mm by 40 mm deep and 600 mm x 280 mm by 50 mm deep. The remainder of the cut had been backfilled with yellowish brown sand (4334) from which four sherds of eighteenth century pottery were recovered (Fabric 10), as well as two copper alloy buttons of probable late seventeenth to early eighteenth century date (*Catalogue 1* and Fig 61.1; *Catalogue 2, see Ch 10*). The structure was of uncertain function: it was thought likely to represent a step up to doorway 4039, rather than the foundation for some form of corner cupboard. It pre-dated flagged floor 4069.

Both gables of the crosswing were rebuilt in brick bonded with a lime mortar (Figs 36, 37), redefined windows being added at ground and first floor level in the west gable, and at first floor level in the east gable. The first floor west gable window appeared to have been replaced subsequently by a vertical sliding sash, but otherwise the Yorkshire sash windows inserted had survived to the time of the building survey. At ground level, the east gable contained a centrally placed doorway. Characteristics such as irregular brick bonds, widespread use of brick bats, and asymmetrically placed lintels are all indicative of poor-quality workmanship.

It is thought unlikely that the gable walls had retained their timber-framing until Phase 5; it seems more probable that the Phase 5 brickwork represented a rebuild of brick gables first added during Phase 4. The jaggedness of the joins between the Phase 4 and Phase 5 brickwork in the west gable, and their locations, provide some evidence for this.

A brick partition wall was constructed to divide the ground floor of the crosswing into two rooms. During excavation, the base of the wall was thought to post-date the extant brick wall dividing the crosswing from the hall, but the building survey suggested that both were built in Phase 5. On the first floor, the existing wattle and daub room partition was retained, but the doorway was moved to the north end.

A re-modelling of the floor of the crosswing allowed for the emplacement of a staircase alongside the north wall, to gain access to both the newly floored upper storey of the hall and to the western upper room through the relocated partition wall doorway. Six bricks laid at the base of the north wall of Room G5 (*Ch 11*, Fig 69) suggest the former presence of a brick floor at ground floor level. This pre-dated the blocking of the doorway into G1, and may have been contemporary with the north wall of G5.

The east gable wall (Pl 15)

The new east gable consisted of a wall (2022) which was keyed into and contemporary with the south wall of the central hall (2019). It extended south around the south-east corner of the crosswing, to butt brick walling 2252 *c* 0.36 m along the south elevation. The overall bond of the brickwork was irregular, though some courses were laid in English Garden Wall, with headers separated by three, four, or five courses of stretchers; many brick bats had been used.

Plate 15: The east gable wall of the crosswing

A single stone block was recorded at the base of the southern end of the wall, perhaps representing part of a plinth for the Phase 2 gable wall, robbed-out further north when a brick foundation was constructed within a shallow trench (4715). A sample portion of 4715, 0.91 m long, was excavated; it was 0.39 m wide by 0.10 m deep, with vertical sides and a flat base. Within the trench, the foundation element of the wall was up to three courses high, and *c* 0.38 m (three stretchers) wide. The bottom courses of the wall above (4058/4060) were built using an irregular bond, with no attempt to prevent the vertical joints falling in line with those of courses above and below. A hard yellowish brown sandy mortar with lime fragments was used to bond the brickwork there, so that, in contrast to the west gable, there was no indication that lower courses might have originated in Phase 4.

Access to the eastern cell of the wing was via doorway 2224, 0.94 m wide, centrally located in the gable wall. Its north and south edges did not appear to be cut through, suggesting contemporaneity with the build of the gable. The top of the doorway was formed by a sandstone lintel 1.22 m long, and a stone slab was set at the base of the doorway externally as a doorstep. It measured 900 mm x 380 mm by 50 mm high, with two door frame plugs at either end, one square, one circular. Both these elements appeared to be contemporary with the creation of the entrance. Other features recorded in the wall in the vicinity relate to the subsequent conversion of the doorway into a window.

At first floor level a Yorkshire sash window (2842) was incorporated within the new wall above the central doorway, similar to the examples recorded in the western elevation of the central hall. The brickwork on either side of the aperture did not appear to have been cut through, indicating contemporaneity with the wall. The aperture had dimensions of *c* 0.88 m wide by 1.08 m high, and the frame contained two parallel sashes, each divided horizontally into two lights, these varying slightly in dimensions, from *c* 0.40 m high by 0.35 m wide to *c* 0.35 m high by 0.32 m wide. A thin wooden board formed an internal sill 0.17 m deep. At the top of the window, an internal timber lintel was laid on two stone pads, one at each end. An external timber lintel was positioned *c* 0.10 m higher, physically above the window frame, and bedded directly onto the brickwork. The internal lintel also projected further than the external one beyond the south side of the window aperture. These irregularities, together with a groove noted in the base of the internal lintel, might be thought to suggest that the internal timber was derived from an earlier window within the aperture. However, when this window is considered together with the other Yorkshire sashes, and the brickwork within which they are set, there seems insufficient evidence to suggest that some or all were replacements within existing apertures.

The west gable wall

The Phase 5 brickwork of the west gable of the crosswing (2008) extended from close to the north-west corner of the wing south to the south-west corner, and around to a point *c* 0.60 m along the south elevation. It was later than north and south walls 2009 and 2023, which it clearly butted. Internally, it could be seen that both joints were very jagged; 2023 clearly had had bricks removed, whilst some bricks within 2009 had been cut through. The fact that earlier wall 2009 extended part way around the north-west corner and along the gable wall further suggests that Phase 5 wall 2008 was a rebuild of earlier brickwork rather than the original brick build of the gable. Wall 2008 was largely built of very irregular re-used bricks, but occasional finer, thicker bricks were also recorded, further suggesting that it may have been a rebuild intended to allow the insertion of new windows. The bond was highly irregular, with many brick bats used internally, where vertical joints often corresponded over several courses. Some evidence was recovered to suggest that the lowest courses of the wall might have been retained from the Phase 4 build (*see Ch 6*).

At ground floor level, a Yorkshire sash window (2063) occupied an aperture with overall dimensions of *c* 1.38 m wide by 1.23 m high. On the exterior, a sandstone lintel 1.60 m long was topped by a brick soldier course, both appearing contemporary with the aperture. A timber lintel was present on the interior of the window, and four sockets on the underside found filled with plaster demonstrated that the timber had probably once held four mullions. Two gaps of about 70 mm separated the ends of the lintel from wall 2008. An external window sill was built of a course of protruding headers, found covered with cement, whilst four stretchers occupied a corresponding position on the inside of the window. Both skins of bricks had been laid on a line of thin stone slabs, visible both internally and externally. Outside, this extended for the full width of the window, but on the inside the damp course and stretchers above were less wide. The extant window had three parallel lights, varying in size from *c* 0.35 m wide by 0.63 m high to *c* 0.39 m wide by 0.71 m high. Whilst the frames of the sashes may be contemporary with the window aperture, the window surround and the internal sill were in a different style and appeared to have been nailed into position later.

As with the first floor window in the east gable, some features of this window might suggest that the Yorkshire sash recorded *in situ* was a secondary insertion. The gaps at the ends of the interior lintel and irregularity of the interior of the damp course and overlying bricks might suggest later modification of an earlier, narrower aperture. However, again the edges of the aperture showed no sign of having been cut through, and it seems most probable that the irregularities were a function simply of lack of attention to detail and poor-quality workmanship.

A vertically sliding sash window was recorded at first floor level in the west gable, within aperture 2064. Here, there was good evidence that the aperture and window were secondary insertions into the Phase 5 brickwork, and traces of an earlier window were observed. An area of brick blocking (3080) was identified below the extant window aperture. It measured 0.80 m high by 1.13 m wide, and was built of thicker bricks than wall 2008, and bonded with a different mortar. It was considered to represent the position of a window aperture, set lower in the wall than that for the sliding sash. To the south of the existing aperture, the bricks were uncut up to a height of *c* 0.89 m; above that point the brickwork had been cut through. This seems to suggest that the aperture shared the bottom part of this edge with an earlier, lower, window. Above the earlier window, the aperture had needed extending. To the north, the sequence was unclear because of repair of the wall with modern bricks. It seems probable that the original Phase 5 window in this gable occupied an aperture measuring *c* 1.87 m high by 1.13 m wide, though it is possible that some of the later blocking and repair work may have extended beyond the original aperture. The height of the early aperture relative to its width may suggest that it was not occupied by a Yorkshire sash, unlike other apertures dating to this phase.

The crosswing partition wall

A partition wall (2825), dividing the crosswing into two equally sized cells, appeared to have been built as part of the same rise as the south wall of the central hall. It was aligned north / south, and lay directly below the upper floor wattle partition. The bond was irregular; in places definable courses of headers were separated by three, four, or five courses of stretchers. The wall did not originally include a doorway.

Excavation showed that a foundation trench 0.43 m wide by 0.17 m deep was excavated prior to construction of the wall. It had vertical sides and a flat base, and was deepest towards the southern end. Brick foundations (4628) were tightly laid against the sides of the trench, but were not keyed into the north or south walls of Rooms G5/6/1. They were 0.43 m wide, and two courses deep, except at the southern end of the wall where they increased in depth to three courses. The foundations were bonded to an irregular pattern, built predominantly of stretchers and half bricks.

Alterations to the south wall

The insertion of the brick partition wall at ground floor level necessitated the closure of a former window mid way along the south wall. Its blocked aperture measured 0.76 m wide by 0.53 m high. The window was probably replaced by another further east along the south wall; a stone damp course and brick sill 0.74 m wide probably related to a window inserted at this time, and in turn subsequently replaced by a higher window in Phase 7. The sill of the earlier window was bonded with a lime mortar very similar to that of the other brickwork attributed to Phase 5.

The crosswing staircase and reflooring of the upper storey

The two strings of a new staircase were supported by recesses within partition wall 2825, and rested on a timber sill at the base of the stair. Wooden wedges were nailed to the strings, with treads and risers in turn nailed to the wedges. The stair was enclosed by vertical boards attached to the southern, outer string, and nailed to a further sill aligned east / west at their base. Brick floor 2961, ending just to the south of the sill, appeared to be a later insertion. It is thought most probable that the stair was contemporary with the

construction of partition wall 2825, and with the relocation to the north of the original central doorway through the first floor partition wall. The construction of the recesses in 2825 demonstrates that the stair did not post-date this wall, although there was clearly some later renovation, perhaps during the twentieth century, with new treads, risers, and an enclosing partition wall being added (*see Ch 9*).

It seems clear that the floor of the upper storey of the crosswing was comprehensively remodelled whilst the gables, ground floor partition wall, and stair were being built. A bridging joist (2997), aligned east / west, spanned the centre of the western ground floor room, supported by the gable wall and partition wall. It did not appear to have been cut through the gable wall, and was thus probably also contemporary with the partition. The bridging joist had been sawn off at its west end, and is thought originally to have spanned the wing from north to south: it may have been jointed to a post in the position of blocking 3078 in the south wall, and have been aligned across a bay division of the original timber-framed structure. Post and joist may have remained in this position until this Phase 5 remodelling, with the mortar of the blocking suggesting insertion at this time. Dendrochronological analysis of 2997 gave a felling date of AD 1534-72 (Sheffield, 1998; Hillam *et al* 1987 for 10-55 sapwood estimate), confirming that the timber was derived from the first build of the crosswing (*see Ch 4*).

A smaller bridging joist to the north, 3000, was aligned parallel with 2997. Its function was to support the north end of floor joists 2996 D-F where the stair passed up through the floor, and it in turn was jointed to rail 3178 resting on the partition wall to the west, and to joist 2996 C to the east.

Joists 2996 A-F supported the floor to the north of bridging joist 2997. All six joists appeared to be jointed to 2997 with bare-faced soffit tenons. The three eastern joists were set in joist holes in wall 2104, suggesting contemporaneity with the wall, whilst those to the west, 2996 D-F, were set into simple but well-fitting sockets in bridging joist 3000. The joist tenons were a poor fit in the sockets of 2997, perhaps suggesting that earlier mortises relating to the former use of the bridging joist were being re-used. The joists were not chamfered. A newspaper fragment dated 1909 was found in the gap of the joint between 2996 E and 2997. However, in view of the other evidence reviewed above, it is thought that the bridging joists and most of the floor joists were considerably older than this. Joist 2996 E was one of two re-used timbers among the northern floor joists and may have been replaced in the twentieth century, or the newspaper fragment may relate to packing of the loose joint to prevent movement. The date of extant floorboards 2932 is unknown.

South of 2997, chamfered floorboards 2995 A-F were again jointed to the bridging joist with ill-fitting bare-faced soffit tenons, again suggesting re-use of mortise holes in the re-aligned timber. At their southern end, the sockets in the Phase 4 walling had in some cases clearly been cut through the brickwork, demonstrating the later date of the floor.

To the west of the first floor partition, the north / south bridging joist (3008) and nine floor joists from the original Phase 2 floor survived. Other joists had been replaced with machine-cut timbers which may post-date Phase 5, 3027 A-F. A rectangular area of patching within the earliest surviving floorboards, 3159, may indicate that the aperture for a stair had been first opened then blocked up here. However, this aperture was cut through boards which must post-date underlying joists 3027 A-C, so any stair in this position must post-date those joists. With a probable Phase 5 stair already identified to the east of the crosswing, it seems unlikely that the patching of floorboards to the west relates to the former presence of a further stair.

The Northern Rooms

The rebuilding in brick of a northern service wing probably occurred during Phase 4 (*see Ch 6*), and this part of the house may have been re-roofed at the same time. There is no evidence of alteration of the fabric during Phase 5; the extant roof of the northern rooms appears to have dated largely to Phase 6, all the rafters being nailed rather than pegged to the wall-plates.

Five postholes were found within the footprint of the Phase 6 build of the northern rooms, at least two being truncated by the Phase 6 foundations. It is possible that all these postholes were contemporary, and formed the south-west corner of a rectangular timber structure. However, this seems unlikely given the alignment that this would suggest. The postholes all post-date a layer, 4759 (Phase 1), and by this time the pattern of north / south orientation shown by the later farmhouse had been adopted. The features also showed different shapes and fill characteristics. It thus seems probable that not all were related, and that they had different functions. Some may have supported internal fixtures within the northern rooms, or indeed scaffolding poles during episodes of construction. Although these postholes have been assigned to Phase 5, some may be earlier or indeed later in date.

Postholes 4762, 4650, 4659, 4647, and 4656 (Fig 38)

These shallow postholes lay within the footprint of the Room G2 (*Ch 11*, Fig 69). Posthole 4762 was cut into clay surface 4759 (Phase 1), and truncated by foundation trench 4613, thus pre-dating the Phase 6 build of the room. Posthole 4659 was cut into floor surface 4760, and truncated by foundation trench 4604, again pre-dating the brick build. Postholes 4650, 4647, and 4656 were sealed directly by Phase 6 floor 4177 (*see Ch 8*). Posthole 4650 was cut into clay surface 4759 (Phase 1), whilst the other two features cut clay floor 4760 (Phase 1 *see Ch 3*). Fragments of brick were found within 4659 and 4647, with 4762 containing mortar fragments.

Ancillary Structures

Two clay surfaces containing early to mid eighteenth century finds were recorded east of the central hall of the farmhouse, overlying earlier Phase 4 surfaces, suggesting that an external outshut structure was still in use there. Immediately north-west of the farmhouse, the base of a rectangular brick structure was recorded, extending north to the moat edge. The south-east corner survived relatively intact, but elsewhere the foundations were marked by brick fragments.

Surfaces 4461 and 4472 (Fig 38)

These yellowish brown silty clay floor surfaces, 4461 and 4472, *c* 0.05 m thick, overlaid Phase 4 surfaces 4630 and 4548. Of the two, 4461 was thought to be the more compact. Seven sherds of pottery were recovered from 4461 (Fabrics 4 and 5), and 21 sherds from 4472 (Fabrics 4, 5, 6, 7, 10, and 19; including Figs 57. 61, 58. 75, and 60.100), the two assemblages being assigned to the early to mid eighteenth century, and early eighteenth century respectively. Three fragments of green 'forest glass' probably derived from a beaker of seventeenth century date (*Catalogue 1*, Fig 62.1). Surface 4461 in turn was truncated by cut 4634, containing a black fill with high charcoal content, which was stratified below the Phase 6 outshut partition wall, 4330 / 4451 (*see Ch 8*).

Structure 7 (Fig 38, Pl 16)

Evidence for a structure to the north-west of the farmhouse consisted of brick fragments forming three sides of a rectangle, 4583. More complete brickwork survived in the south-east corner of the structure only, but no evidence of a foundation trench was recorded. A pottery assemblage (Fabrics 4, 5, 6, 7, 9, 10, and 11; including Fig 57.62) was recovered which, although mixed, was composed mainly of late seventeenth or early eighteenth century sherds. This

Plate 16: Structure 7, facing north

suggested that nineteenth and twentieth century sherds present might be intrusive, perhaps being introduced at the demolition of the structure.

Deposits Recorded to the North of the Farmhouse

Three deposits recorded between the north wall of the farmhouse and the moat appeared to date to Phase 5. These consisted of thin layers at the upper interface of the clay surface of the platform, sealed by later surfaces and dumps probably deposited during Phase 6.

Layers 4271, 4475, and 4627 (Fig 38)

Three deposits (4271, 4475, and 4627) appeared to have formed at the interface between undisturbed clay and the dumps above. Deposit 4271 was a layer of brown silt truncated by the foundations of the farmhouse's north-west room, G2. To the north, 4475 was a patchy layer of brownish yellow silty clay mottled with dark brown silt; 4627, identified to the west of 4475, probably represented part of the same deposit. Both layers were less than 50 mm thick, and produced small assemblages of pottery dating from the late seventeenth to early eighteenth centuries (4475, Fabrics 1, 4, 5, and 8; including Figs 54.20, 59.89; 4627, Fabrics 4 and 5). These layers were identified by selective cleaning, so that their full extents are not known.

Deposition within the Western Arm of the Moat

Three concentrations of twigs and branches were recorded at the bridging point, above the moat fills attributed to Phase 4. They are considered to represent accumulations of organic debris, perhaps having collected around the bridging point at a time of low water level. These deposits were stratified above fills containing small late seventeenth century pottery assemblages, and two sherds of early eighteenth century pottery were found in association with the branches. These deposits of branches have been attributed to Phase 5 because they appear to be broadly contemporary with the changes made to the farmhouse in *c* 1724. However, it should be noted that the artefactual dating is too imprecise to allow deposition within the moat to be related with confidence to a particular phase of building work. Thus, deposition within the moat may have occurred before, or indeed after, the Phase 5 farmhouse alterations.

Thirteen stakes were first revealed at the same depth as the concentrations of branches, but the level from which they had been driven could not be established, and there was no indication that they were contemporary with the branches. The fact that the stakes survived to a maximum length of *c* 1 m may suggest that they had in fact been driven from a lower level. They formed a linear alignment *c* 3.25 m long, traversing the deepest part of the moat immediately to the south of the bridging point. Although they remain unexplained, it may be possible that they had formed part of a crude temporary coffer dam erected whilst work to the stone bridge was being carried out.

In the centre of the moat, the deposition of mottled silty clay continued around and above the branches and wood debris, suggesting that the feature had held still or sluggish water, at least periodically. A fill up to 0.80 m in thickness was recorded here. Eight sherds of mixed nineteenth and twentieth century pottery were thought to be derived from this deposit when it was excavated by machine, but the sherds must now be regarded as intrusive, perhaps dragged by the machine, because of clear cartographic evidence that the overlying causeway was in place by 1757 (LRO DDRf 11 / 54 (1)), and because of early eighteenth century pottery which dates the roadway associated with the causeway to the east of the moat (*see Ch 8*). A general biological analysis sample from the fill was subject to detailed investigation (Kenward *et al* 1998; *see Ch 10*). This confirmed that the filling of the moat was still by waterlain deposition, at least in the area from which the sample was taken, and suggested that the immediate environment of the moat had changed very little since deposition of the Phase 1 and Phase 4 fills. However, once more, little information could be gained about the human economy.

Several additional fills were recorded tipping into the moat from the west. These deposits could not be related stratigraphically to the stakes and branches identified towards the east of the moat, but they clearly sealed the top of the western stone bridge pier. Together, these silty clay fills were up to 0.4 m deep, and they again appeared to be the product of waterlain deposition. Their presence above a stone bridge pier may indicate that there was an interval of some years between dismantling of the bridge, and creation of a causeway. The only alternative explanation is that these silty clays had originally been waterlain, but were redeposited as the first stage in the establishment of a causeway. Even if the bridge was disused for a period of some years, it remains possible that the platform could have been reached via a bridge or causeway in another location where the moat was not excavated. However, the uncertainty over the continued use of the stone bridge means that the possibility of a break in occupation of the platform must be considered.

A single sherd of eighteenth or nineteenth century pottery was recovered from the lowest fill sealing the bridge pier, with early eighteenth century pottery and probable seventeenth century window glass being found in an overlying fill, which was possibly associated with the branches lying to the east. These fills in turn were sealed by the causeway built in the mid eighteenth century at the latest. It thus appears that disuse of the stone bridge, and possible abandonment of the site, may have occurred in the earlier eighteenth century, immediately before or sometime after the Phase 5 farmhouse improvements.

Deposits 4570, 4741, and 4718

A cluster of branches (4570) lay towards the east of the moat, *c* 0.9 m west of eastern pier 4568. The wood appeared to be intertwined, but was not thought to represent wattlework; two sherds of pottery (Fabric 4; Figs 53.14, 60.99) found in association were thought to be of early eighteenth century date. Deposit 4741, more centrally located within the moat, but probably derived from the same period as 4570, consisted of dark grey silty clay together with a concentration of small branches and twigs. Deposit 4718 was a further concentration of small branches.

Stakes 4723-35

Thirteen stakes, collectively numbered 4722, were first revealed at the same level as 4570, 4718, and 4741. They ranged in diameter from 0.04 m to 0.08 m, and were individually numbered from 4723 to 4735, forming an east / west alignment across the moat, on the same line as the timber and stone bridge foundations (Phases 1 and 4). The stakes survived to a maximum length of *c* 1 m (4734, Fig 15), but the level from which they had been driven was not established.

Fills 4569 and 4721

Fill 4569 (Fig 15) was deposited over the concentrations of branches and the top of the stakes. It consisted of dark grey mottled silty clay, a maximum of 0.80 m deep, and contained nineteenth and twentieth century pottery (Fabrics 3 and 5; including Fig 53.13), as well as a shoe sole, almost complete, with part of the upper still attached (*Catalogue 3,* Fig 64.3). The sole is late medieval in date (*see Ch 10*), and must be considered residual to the context in which it was found; it was probably at least 300 years old when deposited within fill 4569. Analysis of a general biological sample from this deposit allowed the environment immediately around the moat to be reconstructed (*see Ch 10*).

Fill 4721 may be an equivalent deposit. A single sherd of seventeenth to eighteenth century pottery (Fabric 4; Fig 54.23) and a fragment of probable seventeenth century window glass were recovered, together with several wooden items. These included two joining fragments of a probable wooden bowl or dish (*Catalogue 1, see Ch 10*), as well as three fragments of wooden pegs, (catalogues *5, 6,* and *7*). There was also a large wooden post (*10*), and wood-working debris consisting of a broken wedge (*11*), a wooden block (*12*), and a fragment of waste from notch and chop conversion of a large timber (*13*). The wedge may have been used for splitting timber, whilst the block may be an off-cut from the cutting of a lap-joint. Together, these fills show the resumption of silty clay deposition within the moat, the fine sediment and mottled colour again suggesting a wet environment.

Fills 4745, 4156, 4520, 4736, 4744, and 4554

Fill 4745 (Fig 15) covered the western stone pier and part of the moat's edge. It was a greyish brown silty clay up to 0.40 m thick, from which a single sherd of eighteenth to nineteenth century pottery was recovered (Fabric 5). The position and composition of 4156 (recorded to the north of the bridging point) suggested that it was probably part of the same deposit. Fills 4736, 4744, 4520, and 4554 were overlying grey and greyish brown clay, the former containing large lenses of organic material and tree branches, and probably representing an extension to the west of the clusters of wood described above. A single sherd of probable early eighteenth century pottery (Fabric 5; Fig 55.37) was recovered from 4736, and a very worn iron knife of uncertain date was recovered from 4520 (*Catalogue 1, see Ch 10*). Fills 4736 / 4744 were truncated by a cut immediately south of the causeway, and only partly revealed in the moat sondage. This may have been a pit or pond.

Features Pre-dating the Construction of the Barn

A few features were identified in Trench J which appeared to pre-date the remains of the Phase 6 barn. The features, however, were difficult to interpret with certainty because of the small size of Trench J, exacerbated by the fact that some contexts were only recorded within a small hand-dug sondage towards the west of the trench.

Evidence was recovered for two probable drainage ditches on different alignments. In addition, a length of brick walling was recorded *c* 0.6 m to the west of the barn, but parallel with it, perhaps indicating that an earlier brick structure had stood on the site. A probable make-up layer had been laid after the construction of the wall, building up the ground surface on either side. Two clay layers to the east are thought to have been internal floor surfaces, whilst a layer incorporating broken brick to the west may have been external hard-standing.

Ditches 4413 and 4565, and peat deposit 4407

Two linear features were found truncating the undisturbed boulder clay at the base of Trench J. Cut 4413 (Fig 39) was revealed in a hand-dug sondage excavated at the western end of the trench. It was linear in plan and had a wide 'U'-shaped profile *c* 0.20 m deep; it appears to be a truncated ditch. It was aligned east / west, a slightly different orientation to the later barn,

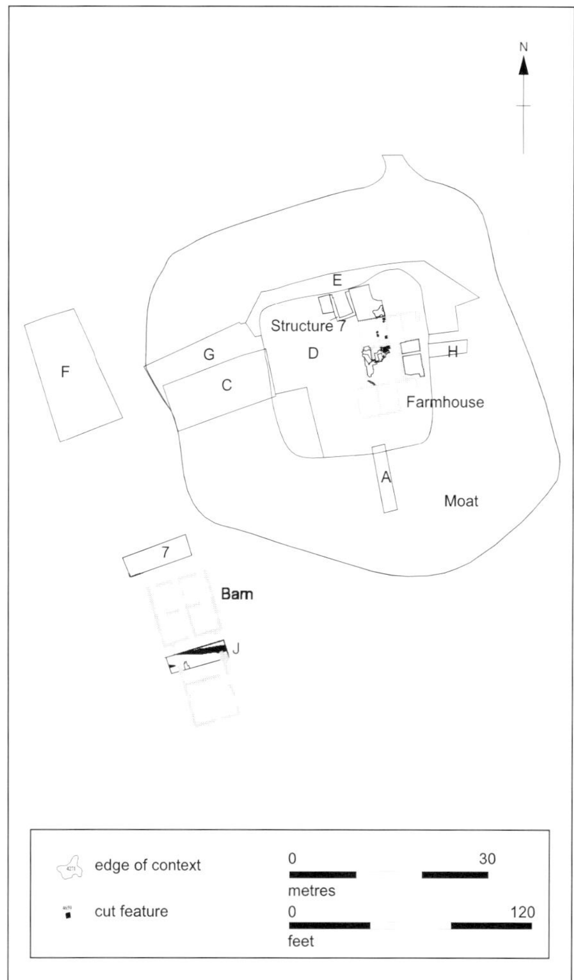

Figure 39: Excavation evidence for Phase 5 features, including those in the area of the Phase 6 barn

and the silty clay fill contained occasional brick and charcoal fragments, but no finds.

To the north, a second linear feature, (4565, Fig 39) was recorded on a slightly different alignment, oriented west-south-west / east-north-east, and narrowed from *c* 0.9 m wide in the east to *c* 0.4 m wide in the west. It was 0.24 m deep where excavated, with a wide 'U'-shaped profile, and a grey silty clay fill. Its function remained uncertain.

Cut 4413 was sealed by a layer of brown peat (4407), *c* 0.08 m thick, which appeared to be sloping down gently towards the west. The peat also sealed several broken bricks (4456) which had been pushed into the surface of the natural clay.

Wall 4364

A length of brick walling built directly on to the natural clay was recorded to the south of the peat (4407, Fig 39). It was aligned north-north-west / south-south-east, and was a maximum of 0.64 m wide, narrowing towards the northern end, and was two courses deep. It was parallel with the foundations of the west wall of the barn which lay *c* 0.6 m to the west, its northern end being in line with the doorway in the west wall. It seems probable that this walling, 4364, was part of the foundation for a brick structure which preceded the barn.

Layers 4404, 4363, 4395, and 4456

A deposit of mottled light grey silty clay 0.12 m thick, 4404, butted wall 4364. It was revealed in the sondage at the western end of Trench J and thus its full extent was not established, but it extended from a line east of wall 4364 to the western limit of excavation. It is uncertain whether it was deposited as make-up, or itself formed an early surface. There was no indication from its location that it was internal to any structure.

A layer of light brown silty clay, 4363, had been deposited above 4404. It was up to 0.10 m thick, and probably represents a clay floor surface. It extended eastwards from the line of wall 4364 for a maximum of 3.4 m, having a diffuse interface with layer 4395 beyond. The latter was a very thin layer of yellow clay also thought to be a floor surface. It was at least 4.4 m long, being truncated to the east. Both of these deposits extended beyond Trench J to north and south.

West of layer 4363 and beyond the line of wall 4364, a mottled yellow and grey clay deposit was recorded, 4456. It may have been part of the same deposit as 4363, but was thicker and contained a high proportion of broken bricks. It was uncertain whether this represented a surface, or make-up for overlying layers. It sealed peat 4407.

8

PHASE 6 - ADAPTATION OF THE FARMHOUSE, AND CONSTRUCTION OF A NEW BARN
MID EIGHTEENTH TO NINETEENTH CENTURY

The northern wing of the farmhouse was rebuilt in brick, and seems to have been adapted for agricultural use; stock may have been kept downstairs, with a possible hayloft and workroom above (Figs 40, 41). An eastern outshut was built in brick (equipped with a fireplace with oven, suggesting use for food preparation), possibly replacing a more ephemeral structure. Buttery functions may have been moved from the north wing to the southern crosswing. A Lancashire-type barn was built off the island to the west, providing accommodation for cattle, a threshing floor, and stabling for horses, under one roof. Two of its roof timbers were from trees probably felled in 1735 and 1753. The moat was probably also backfilled at the former bridging point to provide access via a causeway. An estate map of 1757 suggests that the barn and causeway had been constructed by that year; the works to the farmhouse may have been carried out at the same time.

The Northern Rooms

The extant fabric of the northern rooms of the farmhouse (G2, G2A (*Ch 11*, Fig 69), F2, and F2A (Fig 70)) dates almost exclusively from Phase 6. The walls were built to eaves level in lime-mortared brick, but the brickwork, especially of the lower courses, was so poor that it was difficult to believe that a two-storey building could ever have been supported. A partition wall was built as part of the same rise, dividing the ground floor into two unconnected cells, accessed from the east and west, lit by windows in the northern gable and west wall. The rooms were floored over to give an upper storey, there being some indication that timbers forming parts of the floor structure may have been re-used from an earlier build of the wing. The upper floor was initially a single room, but was later subdivided, probably still during Phase 6.

It is suggested that the alterations to the farmhouse at this time may have been primarily concerned with conversion of the northern end of the house to agricultural usage. The upper storey of the newly built northern wing was accessed by an external stair

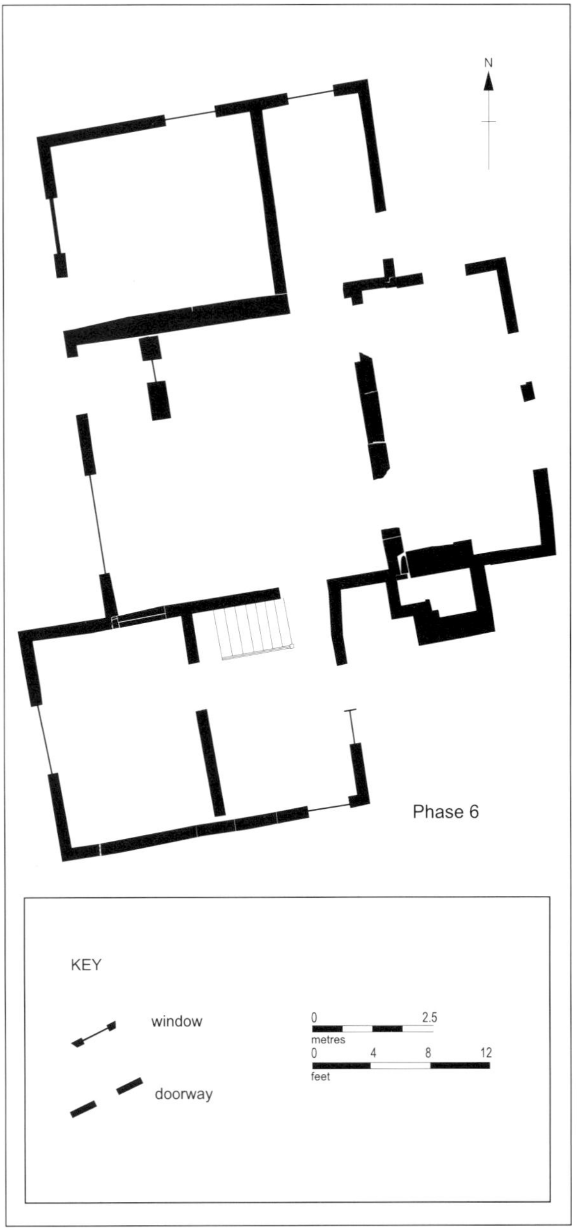

Figure 40: Suggested plan of the farmhouse ground floor, Phase 6

leading to an entrance at first floor level, which appeared to be a taking-in door. This suggests that the upper storey functioned primarily as a hay loft, although it is not impossible that seasonal labour or servants were also accommodated there at various times. The function of the ground floor rooms is less clear. However, the west doorway into Room G2 was slightly wider than others in the northern wing of the farmhouse, and it is possible that this room housed small livestock.

There are several indications that this Phase 6 structure replaced earlier rooms in the same location, which had probably accommodated service facilities. It has been suggested that a northern service bay existed from Phase 1 and, in the south-east corner of the wing, the new east wall butted a stub of brickwork at ground and first floor level which has been attributed to Phase 4. The presence of the latter demonstrates that a brick structure north of the hall incorporating an offset to the east existed by Phase 4, perhaps representing the rebuilding of a Phase 2 lower crosswing (*see Ch 6*). Excavation evidence demonstrated that the foundations of the Phase 6 north wall differed to the east and west of the line of the internal partition wall, with those to the west probably being earlier (Fig 42). It is uncertain whether this reflects merely the sequence of building during the Phase 6 improvements, or whether the foundation to the west had survived from a previous structure. Other evidence which was visible for a possible earlier build, in the north wall at first floor level, was a bridging joist in the north-west corner of Room F2 containing a redundant mortise on the line of the Phase 6 north wall (Fig 43).

Two layers were recorded within the eastern room, stratified above the Phase 6 foundations. They appeared to be the product of the patching and making-up of the floor surface, with the finds suggesting deposition and use within Phase 6. Within Room G2 to the west, a clay floor survived, perhaps laid some time after the construction of the walls, and containing pottery thought to have been deposited in the early nineteenth century. Its presence may suggest that, if stock had formerly been kept here, the use of the room had now changed. The earliest evidence for a fireplace in this room post-dated the clay floor. It is uncertain whether the fireplace was first installed late in Phase 6, or during Phase 7, but it certainly post-dated the early nineteenth century.

The walls

The northern rooms were bounded by wall 2233 to the west, wall 2011 to the north, and wall 2107 to the east. The walling appears to be all of a single phase, although the arrangement of doors and windows was subsequently altered, giving rise to areas of later blocking. All the walls, including the internal partition, wall 2100, shared the characteristic of being built using poor quality hand-made brick for the bottom eight to eleven courses, with larger, more regular bricks above, suggesting that all four walls were the

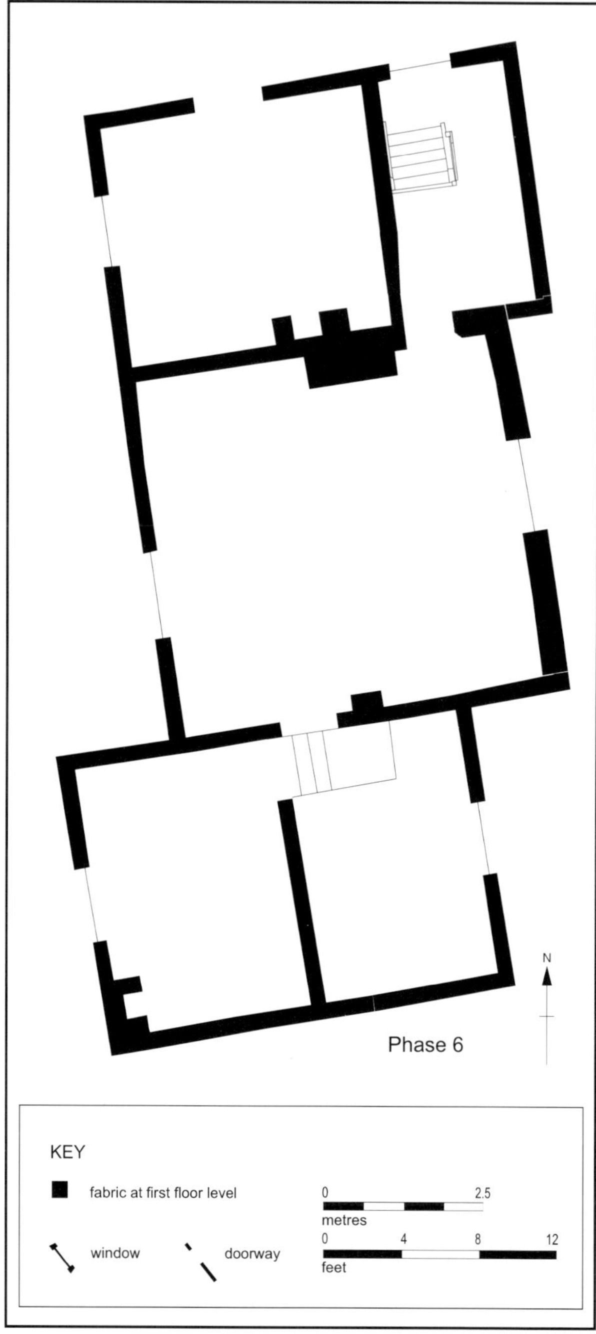

Figure 41: Suggested plan of the farmhouse first floor, Phase 6

product of a single build. The lime mortar with occasional small coal fragments was uniform for the full height of the walls, demonstrating that the bricks towards the base were re-used rather than part of an earlier phase of walling. The dimensions of the upper bricks (235 mm x 120 mm by 70 mm high) suggest a date of construction during or after the later eighteenth century. These walls were of very poor construction, weakly bonded with minimal mortar, and generally constructed with an irregular bond. In places a variant of English Garden Wall bond was used, but with several courses of stretchers to every one of headers (five courses of stretchers in the east wall, four or five in the west wall). The brickwork of the west wall was continued south above the main doorway of the farmhouse, replacing earlier Phase 4 walling in this location.

At ground floor level the internal dividing wall created two unconnected spaces with separate access from the west and east, and windows to the gable and west wall. The doorway in the west wall (2234) had an aperture width of 1.09 m, wider than other doorways in the northern wing of the farmhouse, and thus may have been constructed to allow access by stock. No trace of it remained at foundation level. Access to the eastern room was via a doorway at the southern end of the east wall. Door-jambs 4096 and 4097 were formed of stone blocks measuring 360 mm x 240 mm by 200 mm high, and 360 mm x 180 mm by 200 mm high respectively. Both were faced on at least four sides, had a socket on the upper surface, and may have been re-used. Subsequently, concrete threshold 4098 had been laid between the jambs (possibly associated with concrete 4008/9 in Room G7, laid in Phase 7).

It is probable that a further doorway (2169) gave access to the eastern room from the main hall of the farmhouse to the south. There was no evidence that the north and east wall of the hall had ever been joined, and there is a possibility that a doorway had always existed here. The extant door aperture was faced to the west by chamfered bricks (3130) bonded with lime mortar indicating construction during Phase 5 or later; it cannot be attributed with confidence to a particular phase. All the windows were of similar proportions, being slightly wider than their height. Those in the gable had subsequently been blocked, a small recess one skin of bricks thick surviving immediately below the western of the two. A simple wooden frame containing two lights survived within the window in the west wall.

Wall foundations

The foundation trench for the north and west walls of Room G2 cut through floor deposit 4760 (Phase 1) and an undated posthole, 4762. Foundation trench 4613 was up to 0.6 m wide and 0.35 m deep, with vertical sides and a flat base. It extended for 4.8 m east to west for the full length of room's northern wall, but for only 3.1 m north to south, thus not reaching to the southern end of the west wall. Shallow foundations 4717 consisted of two courses of brick two headers wide, and were surrounded by sandy clay fill 4612.

Two unexcavated deposits of reddish brown silty clay with brick rubble (4621, 4622) were recorded to the south of the butt end of foundation trench 4613. They were truncated by a vent (4614) and overlaid by west wall 4090. The deposits probably represent the fill of a linear feature, possibly a narrow foundation

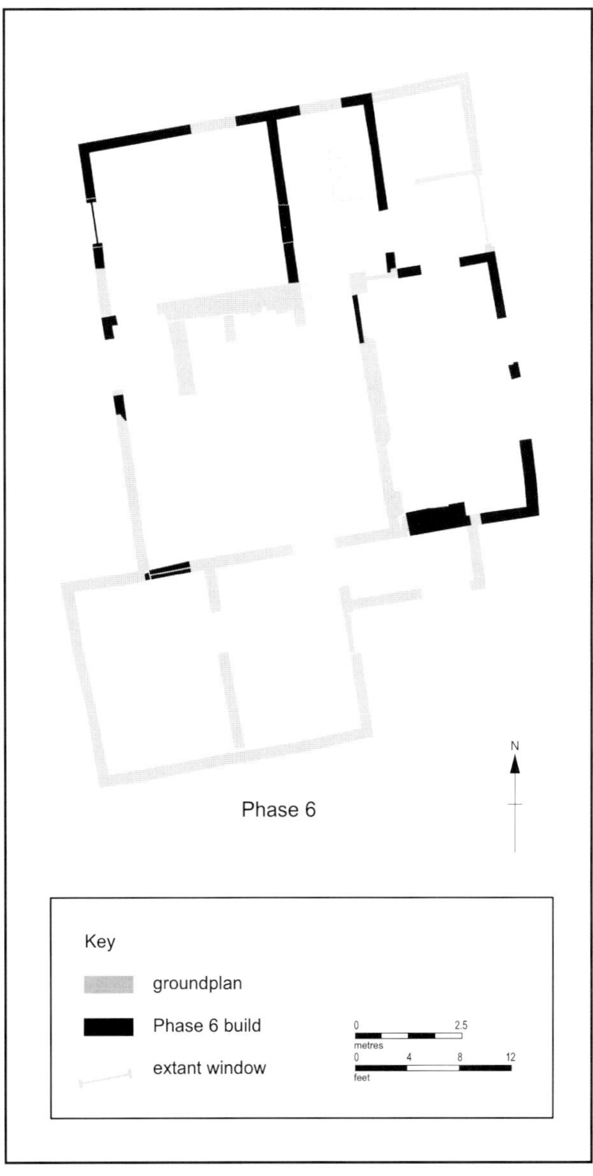

Figure 42: Plan of farmhouse ground floor showing physical evidence, Phase 6

trench which continued beyond the southern terminus of 4613.

The foundation trench for the northern and eastern walls of north-eastern room G2A, 4281/4283, was deeper, and appeared to be a later feature. It was a maximum of 0.6 m wide and 0.6 m deep, with vertical sides and a flat base. Foundations 4301 were five courses deep and roughly two headers wide, but were made up of whole, half, and third bricks, tightly packed against the sides of the foundation trench. The bottom course was surrounded by sand (4651); subsequent courses were bonded by sandy clay 4612. Fills 4282 and 4284 surrounded the foundations at the top of the trench.

At the south-west corner of the eastern room, a large stone block measuring 0.5 m x 0.3 m (4100) had been used as a corner stone. The foundations for the east wall of Room G2A did not extend west to the junction with 4126. Corner stone 4100 probably served as a surface-laid foundation for the courses of brick above, and may have been derived from an earlier Phase 2 stone plinth, and perhaps retained *in situ*.

A shallow foundation trench was dug for partition wall 2100. Cut 4604, 0.35 m wide, but only 0.08 m deep, had vertical sides with a flat base. The wall above was built onto the base of the trench, with two courses of headers on edge and one of headers laid flat acting as foundations. Sandy clay (4603) filled the remainder of the trench.

Layers 4280 and 4255, and scoop 4285

Two layers and a shallow scoop were located within the east room of the north wing. Layer 4280 contained frequent brick, mortar, and coal fragments, nineteenth century pottery and modern plastic; it may represent a dump of hard-core. Layer 4255, stratified above, was a deposit of quite compacted sandy clay, probably again laid as make-up. It contained six sherds of pottery (Fabrics 4 and 5; including Fig 54.24), regarded as a small nineteenth century assemblage, as well as a fragment of, perhaps, sixteenth or seventeenth century English-made *crystallo* glass, apparently residual to its context (*Catalogue 6, see Ch 10*). Shallow scoop 4285 may just be the result of animal disturbance.

Clay floor 4177 (Pl 17)

Clay floor 4177 covered most of the floor area of Room G2, with the exception of the south-east corner. It was 0.01-0.09 m thick, and was composed of dirty mottled brown silty clay; an assemblage of pottery (Fabrics 3, 4, and 5) assigned to the early nineteenth century was recovered from the floor. Four fragments of dark olive green wine bottle were also recovered, probably dating to the late eighteenth century (4177/7127, *Ch 10*), as well as small quantities of oyster shell and a bone and ivory domino piece, the latter probably from the late nineteenth century. The floor sealed several postholes of unknown date, and pre-dated the first fireplace in Room G2, but appeared to butt up to concrete threshold 4094, inserted into the central partition wall. In view of the other dating evidence, it is thought that the stratigraphic relationship with the threshold may not be reliable.

Fireplace 4482

A fireplace (4482) was constructed in the north-western room, G2, built against the southern wall and back-to-back with the earlier inglenook in the central hall (*see Ch 5*). This was the first of several fireplaces in this location. Its date is uncertain, but it is possible that, given the number of subsequent modifications, it was inserted towards the end of Phase 6 rather than during Phase 7. The remains of the fireplace at ground level were revealed by excavation.

Plate 17: Clay floor 4177, within room G2, looking east

The first floor rooms

The upper floor seems also to have been divided into two unconnected cells; if not initially built this way, it seems to have been subdivided at least before the end of this phase. This is because the doorway (2348) between the two rooms appeared to have been cut through after the construction of partition wall 2100, yet it seems unlikely that a partition without an access door would have been built in Phase 7. The western room, F2, had a doorway in the gable face, accessed by an external stair. Two windows, one in the gable wall of eastern room F2A, one in the western wall of F2, had similar proportions to those downstairs, but again showed some variation in size. Access to the eastern room may have been available via an internal door in the south wall, or by open ladder. The date of the insertion of doorway 2578 in the south wall is difficult to establish. The door aperture was edged with chamfered bricks to the east (2769) and broken bricks to the west, and appeared to be later than the Phase 3 walls of the central hall. It seems likely that the doorway was created in Phase 6, as there is further evidence that it post-dated Phase 5. Brick infill 2583, located between the doorway and the Phase 5 chimney breast on the south side of the wall, appears to have been built to fill an awkward gap between the chimney breast and doorway; the presence of this gap may imply that the doorway post-dated the chimney breast. The west room of the upper storey, F2, is thought to have been used as a hay loft in Phase 6; a function as a workroom is possible for the eastern room, F2A, after subdivision.

The floor structure

The floor of the upper storey was carried by two bridging joists aligned north / south (3031 and 2415), each c 3.8 m long and measuring c 0.20 m wide by 0.20 m deep, supported by the north and south walls. Eight floor joists were jointed to the western bridging joist using bare-faced soffit tenons with spurred shoulders; at the other end they were supported by joist holes in the west wall. A further joist was recorded resting on the north wall (3096), not attached to the bridging joist, although the west end was secured within a joist hole. An empty mortise in the bridging joist suggested that the floor joist had originally been positioned c 120 mm further north, aligned with the centre of the present north wall. The joists supported floorboards 2935, and at the north edge of the floor it was noted that the north wall rested on the boards, as did the central partition wall.

Seven floor joists (3033 A-G) in the centre of the floor extended between the bridging joists, joined to them by bare-faced soffit tenons which were housed to the west, but not to the east. At the north end of the floor, an additional joist (3093) again rested on the north

Figure 43: Plan of farmhouse first floor showing physical evidence, Phase 6

wall, attached to the eastern bridging joist by a halving joint. Two short joists at the south end of the floor lay on either side of the later chimney breast, built into it, and may be replacements of a single earlier joist.

Five floor joists (3162 A-E) lay beyond the eastern bridging joist, with empty mortise holes in the joist, and socket holes in the wall, showing that four more had been subsequently removed on the erection of a northern staircase. The joints to the bridging joist were by a mixture of housed and spurred bare-faced soffit tenons.

The roof over the northern rooms

Although the Phase 6 brickwork seems to have replaced earlier walls in the same position, the uniform nailing of all the rafters to the roof structure here suggests that these rooms may have been re-roofed. Each pitch of the roof was supported by two tiers of rafters, carried by three side purlins on the deeper east pitch, and two to the west. The purlins appeared to have been incorporated into the build of the Phase 6 north wall of the farmhouse, but in some cases were clearly cut into the internal wall to the south, 2101.

The External Stair to the Northern Wing

At some date after the construction of north wall foundations of north-west room G2 (*Ch 11*, Fig 69), an external stair was constructed against the north wall. The stair would have given access to first floor room F2 (Fig 70), via the blocked doorway recorded in the first floor gable. Only the foundations of the stair remained. Without the stair, and with stock possibly housed in the north-western ground floor room, easy access could only have been gained to the upper floor by ladder from the north-eastern room. If the upper floor functioned as a hayloft, such access would clearly have been inadequate.

Stair foundations

A large sandstone block (4298, Fig 44), and a length of brick walling (4269, Fig 44), were laid parallel with wall foundations 4717, displaced to the north by *c* 0.6 m. The wall was three courses wide, and was built within a foundation trench 0.38 m wide and 0.13 m deep. The west end of the wall showed signs of a disturbed return towards 4717. Brick wall 4300 (Fig 44) extended from the centre of 4269 back to 4717, butting against both. It survived to a height of 0.13 m, and was two courses wide. To the east, crushed brick 4636 (Fig 44) appeared to define the east of the structure. It was also thought to butt 4269, and lay parallel with 4300. Together, these features formed an 'E'-shaped foundation, attached to those of the north wall, 4717.

A deposit of firm clay silt with brick and stone fragments (4270) formed a rubbly infill between brick foundations 4269, 4300, and 4717. Three sherds of pottery (Fabrics 4, 5, and 13), together thought to date to the earlier eighteenth century, were recovered from the deposit. It was overlaid to the north by 4299, a layer of crushed brick and stone in a silty matrix, from which a sherd of pottery of nineteenth to twentieth century date was recovered (Fabric 3). These deposits may represent hard-core dumped before construction of the stairway above. Crushed brick layers 4299 and 4636 were partially sealed by a double line of half bricks (4635) butting the north wall of the house.

The Eastern Outshut

A substantial outshut structure was constructed against the eastern wall of the hall. It probably replaced earlier timber lean-to storage facilities, for which no evidence remained other than the presence of two doors in the Phase 3 west wall of the central hall and, to the east, successive clay floor surfaces containing pottery of Phase 5 date (early eighteenth century). It can be suggested that this outshut housed kitchen and service facilities that may have formerly been provided by the putative northern wing of the house.

The new brick walling was built out from the stub of the Phase 4 wall at the south-east corner of the northern rooms, which were also being rebuilt at this time. The wall turned south, parallel with the east wall of the hall, returning to meet the hall's south-east corner. As was the case for the rooms to the north, the bricks used were thicker than many of those within the earlier walls, being typically 70 mm thick (*see Ch 10*), but were still hand-made. The bond was irregular, with stretchers, headers, and cut bricks used seemingly at random. The brickwork was bonded with lime mortar. No evidence for any subdivision of this first phase of outshut was found during the building survey, but subsequent excavation showed the former presence of a brick partition wall aligned east / west. The presence of the partition wall suggests that the small northern cell may still have functioned as a wood store, with direct access to the central hall retained through the northern of the three doors in the east wall of the central hall. Detailed recording of paintwork demonstrated that the southern of the three doors in the east / west wall of Room G1 was the last to be blocked, and this doorway appears to have given access into the southern cell of the outshut. An additional doorway was provided on the external eastern face of the southern cell of the outshut, presumably giving access to the outside toilet and water facilities; an undated well was recorded a short distance to the south-east. The location of any original windows is uncertain; they may have been in the position occupied by later doorways inserted into the north and east walls. A fireplace was built against the outshut's southern wall, with a large external chimney stack apparently added subsequently. The presence of what are probably the remains of a bread oven in the chimney breast to the west of the fireplace appears to confirm that this was the new location for the kitchen, and the size of the aperture within the external chimney stack suggests that this room may also have

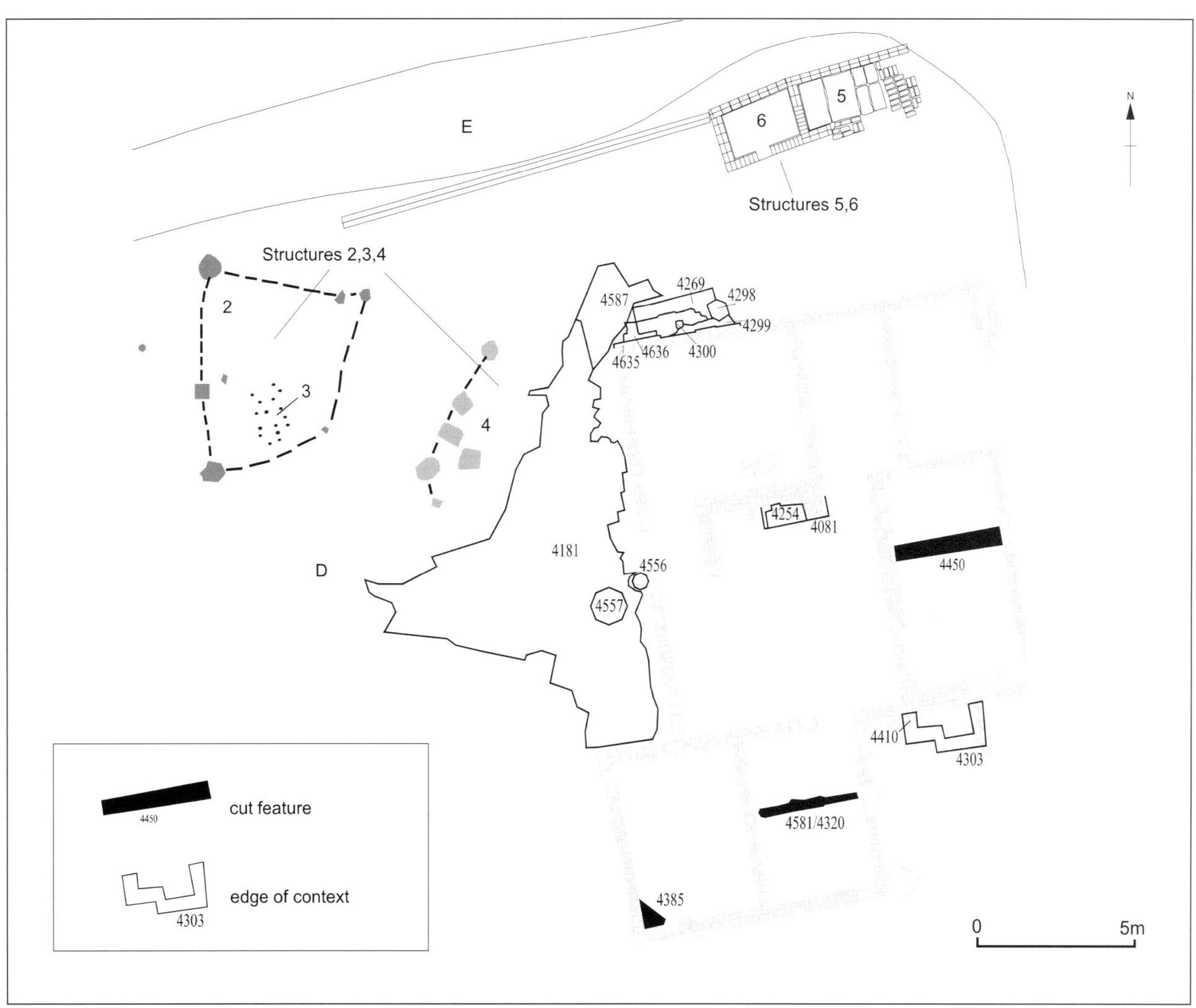

Figure 44: Excavation evidence, Phase 6

housed a boiler. The buttery functions may have been transferred from the putative northern wing to the lower west storey of the crosswing.

The wall foundations and walls

The wall foundations were built within a cut (4471) *c* 0.05 m wide by 0.35 m deep. This butted the eastern wall of Room G1 to the south, but to the north ended *c* 0.6 m short of the south-east corner of Room G2A. The base of the trench was filled with brick rubble (4601) 0.22 m deep; above, foundations 4600 consisted of one or two courses of brick, roughly laid with a highly irregular bond. The foundation trenches for the north and east walls had been backfilled with a silt deposit containing *c* 50% charcoal fragments.

After the construction of the outer walls, a partition was inserted dividing the structure into northern and southern cells. The northern area measured *c* 2.8 m high by 1.6 m wide, and that to the south *c* 3.2 m high by 2.8 m wide. The partition wall was built within a foundation trench (4450) 0.40 m wide by 0.30 m deep (Fig 44). This was infilled with a layer of brick rubble, on which wall 4330/4451 was constructed.

Doorways

Two doorways were evident in the east wall, almost adjacent to one another. The northern doorway (2232) had an aperture which appeared integral with the original build of the west wall (2014) to the north, and which appeared to have been rebuilt to the south. The doorway lay at the eastern end of the east / west partition wall; it is possible that it was blocked when the partition was erected, but was subsequently re-opened and repaired.

Immediately to the south, a doorway, 2895, lay between jambs 4107 and 4110. These were both of red sandstone, and 4107 to the north had a square notch at its south-west corner. In between, ten bricks laid as headers, 4109, were built over a levelling layer of clay 0.03 m thick, 4400. The lower part of the aperture had subsequently been blocked, and the upper part converted into a window, with the southern aperture edge being re-used. It is possible that 2895 was converted into a window when 2232 to the north was reopened. However, the original relationship between the doorways remains problematic, as both apertures contained elements which appeared contemporary with the original early to mid seventeenth century build of the west wall.

Floor surfaces

A layer of compacted brown silt (4328) covered the whole of the interior of outshut G3. It was interpreted as an earthen floor, which must have been laid after the removal of east / west partition wall 4330/4451. Brick rubble, coal, and clinker fragments were intermittently pressed into it, especially towards the northern end of the room. This was thought to represent make-up deposited before the laying of a later concrete floor. The finds recovered from floor 4328 were of mixed date, but deposition in the late nineteenth century appears likely. They included pottery (Fabrics 2, 4, 5, and 9; including Figs 54.27, 54.31), metalwork, and glass.

Nine flagstones of irregular size and shape (4112) survived towards the south end of the room, overlying 4328. They probably represent the remains of a more extensive floor, and were found in association with a mixed assemblage of pottery dating from the seventeenth to nineteenth centuries (Fabrics 3, 5, 7, and 10). Elements of the southern doorway (2898) with the central hall post-dated probable earthen floor 4328. Bedding sand 4314 was deposited over 4328, and the five stone slabs forming the threshold were set into it. These threshold flags may be contemporary with flagged floor 4112.

The fireplace

The fireplace in Room G3 (4115) had an aperture measuring 0.95 m x 0.69 m by 0.29 m deep. An oven had been constructed along the chimney breast to the west, partially cut into the wall of the hall, with an aperture measuring *c* 0.43 m high by 0.51 m wide. The bricks at the sides of the oven had been cut off at the rear, perhaps indicating that the oven had originally extended further south: fragments of a brick arch surviving here suggest that the oven had been vaulted. An aperture connected a cavity at the base of the oven to the fireplace, but the oven also had its own flue. A brick repair to the eastern side of the chimney breast may be in the position of a second oven or, perhaps more probably, a water boiler.

The base of the fireplace structure was recorded during excavation. The fireplace was found to lie within a foundation cut (4465) up to 0.16 m deep. This cut extended *c* 0.9 m further east than the structure above, suggesting that the latter had been partially removed and shortened at some stage after its construction.

To the west of the fireplace, areas of brick and stone slab flooring and of more regular brick flooring were recorded, 4261 and 4111, measuring 0.92 m long by 0.45 m wide and 0.95 m long by 0.75 m wide respectively. The sequence in which they were laid is uncertain. In front of the fireplace was another area of flooring which was probably contemporary with it; floor 4314 was composed of bricks and stones, and was present over an area of *c* 1.4 m long by 0.3 m wide. Above the level of this floor, small amounts of wall plaster (4353), 0.02 m thick, remained adhering to fireplace base 4115.

The south wall chimney

After the construction of the southern wall, an external brick chimney stack was erected, opposite the fireplace (Fig 44). Its remains were uncovered by excavation, set within a shallow foundation cut 0.18 m deep, demonstrating that it was *c* 1.3 m wide and 1.1 m thick, built of stretchers, the bricks being generally very strongly cemented together. The inside of the chimney was filled by deposits 4467 and 4485, respectively clay with coal inclusions, and sand and brick rubble.

At some stage subsequently, it became necessary to buttress the chimney to the south. Wall 4304 was constructed, set within a cut of maximum depth 0.10 m. It was of very irregular construction, mostly of half bricks, but with some stretchers, and survived to a height of four courses, including foundation course 4458 on the southern side.

The roof

The roof was of machine-cut timbers. Thirteen rafters were nailed to the wall-plate, a purlin half way up the pitch of the roof, and one at the apex, the purlins and wall-plate supported by the brickwork. Fifteen joists for a ceiling were also nailed to the middle purlin, and extended to the east wall of the central hall.

The Central Hall

Alterations to the fireplace show that this room was used for cooking at least during the early part of Phase 6, and remained central to life in the house. The chimney breast was underpinned by the construction of a new fireplace structure, with a segmental arch of bricks laid as a soldier course above. The aperture measured 1.40 m wide by 1.48 m high, a size appropriate for housing a cooking range. The interior of the aperture, however, may have been adapted twice during this period. A stone hearth may have initially occupied the fireplace, whilst disturbed fragments of brickwork to the rear, bonded with a hard grey ash mortar, may have been part of the housing for a range inserted subsequently. A length of iron pipe protruding from the rear wall suggested the position of a water boiler within such a range. The cooking function may, however, have moved to a proper kitchen within the eastern outshut during the course of Phase 6, since the two rooms both have fireplaces with evidence for ovens which must be attributed to this phase.

The position of the doorways out of the central hall was altered, probably reflecting the changing use of the central hall, crosswing rooms, and outshut. The doorway through to the western room of the crosswing was blocked, whilst a new doorway was cut through the south wall of the central hall to give direct access to the eastern crosswing room. The northern doorway from the central hall to the outshut was blocked, probably at the same time as the outshut partition wall was removed.

Changes to the position of doorways

A doorway to the eastern room of the crosswing was inserted after the rebuilding in brick of the south wall of the central hall, probably during Phase 6. The door-jambs were of yellow sandstone, measuring 350 mm x 250 mm by 140 mm high and 550 m x 240 mm by 160 mm high respectively. Jamb 4057 to the east was roughly hewn with chisel marks visible on its top surface, and it appeared to have been re-used, possibly having been part of a window sill. Jamb 4056 to the west was worked on three faces, and a notch had been cut into its east face to accommodate a door frame.

The doorway to the west leading to Room G5 was blocked by a double row of stretchers (4039) built to form a wall 0.26 m wide. The bricks used had dimensions of 230 mm x 120 mm by 70 mm high. It seems probable the blocking of this doorway accompanied the opening of the new doorway to the east. The northern doorway in the east wall was blocked with bricks with similar dimensions, which were bonded with lime mortar.

Alterations to the fireplace

The fireplace had undergone considerable adaptation, with the large number of small alterations making it difficult to relate the survey evidence gathered above ground to the features revealed by excavation. However, it was clear that the Phase 5 ashbox, 4295 (*see Ch 7*), had gone out of use. Roughly bonded brick infill (4253) had been laid over the top, and then covered with a very dark brown silty sand (4252), a maximum of 0.05 m thick. Above, two flagstones, 4254 (Fig 44), appeared to form the base of a new hearth, the western flag having been cut to fit around the western brick firejamb. A brick setting to the east of the flagstones, 4081 (Fig 44), overlaid the firejamb of the earlier fireplace (4296). It measured 0.49 m x 0.43 m by 0.12 m high, and consisted of a course of bricks set on edge laid over a flagstone, and bonded to it with thick white mortar. It is suggested that this structure corresponds to bricks 3187 recorded during the building survey; it may represent the seating for a boiler or oven.

It seems that this fireplace may have been used whilst floor 4264 remained in use; if this was not the case, a subsequent floor must have been robbed-out. Flags 4254 at the base of the fireplace do not appear to have been originally associated with flagged floor 4069, which must be later. This is because 4081 was built on a flag thought to relate to flags 4054, and was butted by the bedding sand for floor 4069.

The range, suggested by brickwork bonded with grey mortar, is thought to have been a later insertion. The evidence for its presence was recorded during building survey, and it was not represented below ground level.

Postholes 4483 and 4484

Two postholes were identified to the south and east of baffle wall 4080, within *c* 0.1 m of the wall. To the south, 4483 was 0.30 m deep, and to the west, 4484 was 0.37 m deep. Both contained postpipes measuring 0.10 m high by 0.10 m wide and 0.11 m high by 0.12 m wide respectively, and were filled with sand 4190. It is suggested that the postholes may have supported some insubstantial fittings associated with the baffle wall.

The Southern Crosswing

A beamslot showed that the eastern room of the crosswing had itself been subdivided to north and south, probably by a light wooden partition (Fig 44). To the north of the new partition, a clay floor was laid, and this was cut in turn by two postholes, which probably supported a further wooden fixture. After this had gone out of use and the posts had been removed, a layer of black silt, probable occupation debris, was allowed to accumulate over the floor. It could not be dated, but seems to indicate that the room was not being kept clean.

At some stage after the dismantling of the structure set within the beamslot, the doorway between the western ground floor room of the crosswing and the central hall was blocked, and a new doorway was knocked through the partition wall giving access from the eastern room. The jambs of the new doorway were tenoned into the lintel and pegged, suggesting that these alterations were undertaken before the twentieth century. Also at this time, a small window appears to have been cut through the eastern gable wall, immediately to the south of the existing external doorway. This window was subsequently blocked in two stages. Firstly, an outer skin of blocking bricks was inserted to create a shallow cupboard or recess internally, using lime mortar similar to that for the external chimney of the outshut, but narrower bricks. Later, probably in Phase 7, the recess was also blocked.

At first floor level, a brick fireplace was installed in the south-west corner of the western room, G6, clearly post-dating the Phase 5 gable wall. The base of a triangular brick structure was found immediately below at ground floor level. This was probably the remains of a brick pillar which had formerly supported the fireplace and chimney above. The brick structure lay below a machine-cut timber tie which supported the fireplace at the time of the building survey; the brickwork may have been removed down to ground level when the tie was inserted.

Beamslot 4581

A beamslot (4581) subdivided the eastern crosswing room into northern and southern cells. The slot was 2.46 m long, and extended from the eastern wall to a butt end *c* 0.08 m east of north / south partition wall 4040. It was steep sided, with the base being flat at the two ends but with a 'V'-shaped profile in the centre. The feature was partially backfilled with clay which appeared identical to overlying clay floor 4251. The clay did not completely fill the slot; along the south side of the cut, an area of brown silty sand (4320), 0.08 m wide and 0.15 m deep, probably indicated the position of an upright timber structure (4321), which had been removed from the foundation trench after the period of its use.

The similarity of the backfill to floor 4251 appears to indicate that the structure within the beamslot was contemporary with this clay floor of Room G4. Structure 4321 was probably an internal wooden screen or other light partition wall. The brown silty sand (4320) which seems to have filled the void on the removal of the partition, was itself identical to the sand bedding layer, 4256, for a later floor. The partition structure would appear to have been removed when the floor of the room was resurfaced.

Floor 4251

A clay floor (4251) was laid in the eastern crosswing room, G4, north of internal partition slot 4581. Floor 4251 was composed of compact mottled brown silty clay with occasional small rounded stones. It covered an area measuring *c* 2.74 m long by 1.8 m wide, and varied in thickness from 0.03 m to 0.07 m.

Postholes 4591 and 4525

Two square postholes had been dug in the north-east of the eastern crosswing room, G4, cutting through clay floor surface 4251. Cut 4591 contained a postpipe (4523) surrounded by clay packing, the postpipe containing decayed remnants of a square wooden post 0.14 m wide and 0.35 m deep. Cut 4525 was only 0.13 m deep, a large stone below the feature probably having prevented further depth. It also contained

remnants of a square post, 0.14 m thick. The two postholes may relate to an unknown internal fitting or structure within the room.

Occupation debris 4311

A small spread of black silt, 4311, overlying clay floor 4251 in the north-west corner of Room G4, probably represents an accumulation of occupation debris, or debris associated with the disuse of the floor. It measured 1.12 m x 0.76 m by 0.03 m thick, and is thought to have formed over the clay floor after the disuse of the structure supported by postholes 4525 and 4591.

First floor fireplace

The fireplace aperture (2836) in Room F4 measured 0.41 m wide by 0.84 m high. Subsequent partial infilling of the structure may have been intended to narrow the chimney and improve the draw of the fire. The lower floorboards in the room, 3159, had been cut through in order to insert the fireplace, whilst upper floorboards 2399 had been laid around it.

Brick footing 4384 and posthole 4399

A triangular-shaped cut (4385) was revealed by excavation at the south-west corner of the crosswing, below the first floor fireplace. It was 1.15 m long and 0.24 m deep, with the eastern side angled at a gradient of *c* 45° to the vertical. The cut was filled with a dark yellowish brown clay silt (4385) with frequent brick, plaster, and mortar fragments. Two courses of unbonded red bricks (4384) had been laid above the clay silt, and appeared to butt the foundation element of western brick wall 4050. Modern rubbish appeared to have fallen down into the structure, as fragments of polystyrene were found, along with sherds of seventeenth to eighteenth century glass, and three sherds of nineteenth century pottery (Fabrics 3, 5, and 8).

The foundation cut for this structure truncated an earlier rectangular posthole (4399). The posthole was cut through Phase 1 clay layer 4766, but the feature contained no dating evidence, and there was no indication that it pre-dated the brick structure by any significant time period. It measured 0.33 m x 0.28 m by 0.20 m deep, and had steep sides and a flat base. The position of the feature suggests that it may have held a prop or post providing support at the corner of room, indicating that a structural problem had occurred there.

Surfaces, Drains, and Postholes North and East of the Farmhouse

---

A layer of cobbles was laid north-west of the farmhouse, providing hard standing at the base of the external stair, and overlapping the more extensive area of cobbling at the front of the house (*see below p 90*). It was partially overlaid by a deposit of sandy clay and coal fragments, which sealed two undated postholes of uncertain association. A 'V'-shaped ditch immediately beyond the western wall of the north wing of the farmhouse was sample-excavated. It was probably an open drain dug to collect eaves-drip water from the adjacent roof and was sealed by a deposit of silty clay which butted the farmhouse wall.

To the north of the farmhouse, a yellowish clay surface was laid, butting the farmhouse wall. Two postholes, one of which cut through this clay, may be contemporary, suggesting the presence of a light structure such as a fence. To the east, a succession of dumps of cinders and a brick surface had been laid. These were found underlying the foundations of a further room to the farmhouse which was added during Phase 7.

Cobbled surface 4587/4632, layer 4585, and postholes 4588 and 4589

A layer of small cobbles and brick fragments had been deposited, 4587/4632 (Fig 44), butting against the foundations of the external stair. It was partially covered by a layer of sandy clay and coal fragments (4585) which extended north and east from the edges of cobbles 4181, petering out to the east. Layer 4585 sealed two undated postholes (4588 and 4589) of uncertain association, and contained a pottery assemblage which has been assigned to the mid eighteenth century or later (Fabrics 1, 3, 4, 5, 7, 9, 10; including Figs 58.72, 58.79). Glass fragments from a late seventeenth or early eighteenth century olive green wine bottle were also found (*Catalogue 12, see Ch 10*).

Ditch 4768 and layer 4779

Immediately beyond the western wall of farmhouse Room G2, a ditch 0.55 m deep, with a relatively steep 'V'-shaped profile (4768), was sample-excavated. It contained three fills (4780, 4781, and 4782), was cut into clay which may have been undisturbed, and was sealed by clay silt deposit 4779 which butted the farmhouse wall. The feature was revealed by a sondage across the adjacent wall foundations, and its full extent was not established.

Surface 4278, and postholes 4272 and 4276

A yellowish clay layer immediately north of the farmhouse, 4278, overlaid Phase 5 deposit 4271 (*see Ch 7*). It was probably laid as a surface. The clay partly covered a scatter of sandstone blocks (4279) which was not fully revealed.

A posthole (4276) had been cut into this clay. It may have been associated with a second posthole (4272) *c* 1 m to the south-west, cut directly through Phase 5 layer 4271 (*see Ch 7*).

Deposits 4175/4326 and 4248, and brick surface 4221

A compact dump of coal and cinders (4175/4326) lay to the north of the Phase 7 extension, being cut by its foundation trench. Deposit 4326 contained a mixed assemblage of seventeenth, eighteenth, and nineteenth century pottery (Fabrics 1, 3, 4, 5, and 10). The earliest deposit to the south was a layer of black cinders and silt (4248) containing eighteenth and nineteenth century pottery (Fabrics 1 and 3), and seventeenth to eighteenth century glass. This had dimensions of *c* 3.0 m long by 2.75 m wide, and also pre-dated the construction of the Phase 7 extension. It probably represents a further episode of ground consolidation.

Above 4248, an external brick surface had been laid, 4221. It was an irregular shape in plan, and covered an area measuring 5.4 m north / south by 2.1 m east / west. It was constructed of whole and half bricks on edge, randomly laid except at the edges of this structure. The bricks were unbonded, but sat in a silty matrix containing a mix of seventeenth to nineteenth century pottery (Fabrics 1, 3, 4, and 5; including Fig 59.87). Open brick drain 4223 was constructed within the surface, and provided drainage down towards the moat. The drain had originated west of the surface; there the bricks had been robbed-out, but staining showed that it had begun at slot 4247, running along the east wall of the Phase 6 north wing. The latter was 0.04 m deep with a flat east side and vertical base.

The Causeway, Access Road, and Cobbled Surfaces West of the Farmhouse

A large deposit of firm clay up to 1.4 m thick was dumped over the organic moat fills where they covered the remains of the stone bridge piers. The clay effectively capped the soft, wet, moat fills, providing a crossing point onto the platform on the line of the former bridges. A deposit of cinders recorded in one section above the clay may have been associated with a drain to the south, but this was covered by a layer of sand which had been laid as bedding for a cobbled roadway. The cobbled surface itself appeared to have been largely worn away, or had perhaps been lifted before later surfaces were laid. However, two patches of cobbling survived on the causeway, delimited by a kerb of larger cobbles. One lay towards the west of the causeway, and was bounded to the north by a brick drain. The other area of cobbling lay to the east, and appeared to be continuous with a cobbled roadway on the platform beyond, leading to the front of the house.

East of the causeway, this cobbled roadway extended east-north-east for *c* 10 m to a cobbled apron providing an extensive area of hard standing in front of the main west door of the house. Several decorative features had been included within this area of cobbling, suggesting that when the cobbled surface was laid, it was intended that it should be kept visible and free of mud, giving the area in front of the farmhouse a decorative as well as practical function. One implication may be that the moated platform remained a purely domestic space, perhaps challenging the suggestion made above that the rebuilt north wing of the farmhouse may have been partly intended to accommodate stock.

Excavation of a sample of the cobbled apron revealed a levelling deposit below, overlying the fragmentary remains of Phase 4 cobbling. Further west, deposits underlying the road were investigated in a sondage; here a central dump of redeposited clay make-up was flanked to north and south by two possible drainage features containing cobbles and broken brick. The latter were not excavated, but several sherds of probable earlier eighteenth century pottery were recovered from the surface. The cobbled surface of the road had suffered heavy wear.

The causeway, road, and cobbled apron appeared to derive from the same episode of construction, with finds of pottery suggesting an origin in the early to mid eighteenth century. A late seventeenth or early eighteenth century pottery assemblage was recovered from the levelling deposit below the cobbled hard-standing, whilst the make-up for the roadway contained predominantly earlier eighteenth century pottery. The earliest extant estate map of Pesfurlong certainly suggests that, by 1757, the farmhouse was accessed by a causeway rather than a bridge (LRO DDRf 11/54 (1)). This estate map also shows a barn with a large double door centrally placed along the western elevation, suggesting that the Phase 6 improvements, including construction of a Lancashire-type barn, had also been completed by this date. It can thus be suggested that the construction of the causeway was part of a scheme of large-scale improvements to the farm, also including works to the farmhouse and provision of a more modern barn.

Clay 4521

A deposit of clay (4521) was dumped in the moat at the former bridging point to form a causeway (Fig 15). The clay was up to 1.4 m thick, mottled yellowish brown in colour, and contained occasional rounded pebbles and fragments of coal. Deposits 4750 and 4739 (Fig 15) sealed the possible pond to the south of the crossing point, and were probably contemporary. The clay also extended a short distance north of the bridging point, where fills 4137 and 4157 were recorded.

Deposit 4553, and brick drains 4228, 4230, and 4229

Above the capping clay, an area of mixed deposits was recorded in section, 4553 (Fig 15), consisting of clay, cinders, charcoal, and brick. This may represent infilling of an area of slumping, possibly related to a drain lying immediately to the south. Along the northern edge of the causeway west of the moat, a concave brick surface formed a shallow open drain (4228) sloping downwards into the moat. It was *c* 0.65 m long, and survived for a length of greater than 7.4 m, with the bricks at the east end being jumbled and disturbed (4230). It was bounded to the north by a further brick surface (4229).

Bedding sand 4552, and fragments of cobbled surface 4226

Bedding sand 4552 (Fig 15) was recorded extending for *c* 15 m over the eastern end of the causeway and onto the platform. Fragments of cobbled surface 4226 were less extensive, but survived south of drain 4228 at the west end of the causeway, and close to the causeway's eastern end. The cobbles were rounded, 40-100 mm in diameter, and tightly packed; they appeared quite well worn. Cobbles along the edges were carefully set to a regular pattern, all the cobbles being laid on bedding sand. The cobbling appeared to form the surface of a metalled road across the causeway.

Cobbled roadway 4046 and related deposits

East of the causeway, the cobbled surface was numbered 4046 (Pl 18), and was investigated by the excavation of a sondage. A layer of yellowish brown redeposited clay (4699) 1.6 m wide, had been laid as make-up on top of the undisturbed clay, and an assemblage of pottery thought to date from the eighteenth century was recovered from this (Fabrics 3, 4, 5, and 7). It was flanked to north and south by narrow deposits of brick and cobbles, 4702 and 4701, not excavated but possibly roadside drainage features. Immediately to the south, a band of cobbles and cinders 1.1 m wide, 4700, may represent an addition to the make-up, or the remains of an early surface. These three contexts all contained assemblages of pottery thought most probably to derive from the first half of the eighteenth century (4700, Fabrics 1, 3, 4, 5, 7, 9, 10, 11, 18; including Figs 53.10, 56.43, 57. 54, 58.69, 59.82, and 59.90; 4701, Fabrics 4 and 5; 4702, Fabrics 4 and 5). Additionally, two fragments of a very dark purple glass vessel of probable early seventeenth century date were recovered from 4700 (*Catalogue 10* and Fig 62.10). Above these deposits, a layer of bedding sand (4333) had been laid, into which cobbles 4046 were set. This cobbled surface was cambered, and widened at its east end to north and south to form cobbled area 4181 described below. To the west, it

Plate 18: Cobbling 4046 at the western end of the causeway

appeared to be continuous with cobbled surface 4226, a remnant of the surface of the causeway.

Levelling layers 4584 and 4742, and cobbled surface 4181

A layer of dark greyish brown sandy silt, a maximum of 0.07 m thick, 4584, was stratified above the remains of a supposed Phase 4 cobbled surface (4586, 4592, 4640, and 4641, *see Ch 6*) in front of the house. It probably represents further levelling before the laying of a new cobbled surface, 4181; layer 4742 to the north may have had a similar origin. A mixed assemblage of pottery was recovered from 4584 (Fabrics 1, 4, 6, 7, 9, 10, 18, and 19; including Figs 53. 7, 53.17, 54.19, 54.21, 54.29, 54.34, 55.35, 56.48, 56.49, 57.55, 57.59, 59.81, 60.97, and 60.102); the material was mostly of late seventeenth and early eighteenth century date, with later material thought probably to be intrusive. Likewise, a small but mixed assemblage from layer 4742 appeared mostly to date from the early eighteenth century (Fabrics 4, 5, and 10); a single twentieth century sherd should be regarded as intrusive (Fabric 17). A small loop of thick copper alloy wire recovered from 4584 was probably of late medieval origin (*Catalogue 7* and Fig 61.7), and two fragments of green 'forest' glass probably dated from the seventeenth century; one is thought to be from a beaker (Figs 62.2, 62.3).

As the roadway approached the farmhouse from the causeway, it broadened to form a roughly triangular surface, 4181 (Fig 44), measuring *c* 10 m north to south by *c* 6 m east to west. The surface was subdivided by a double row of elongated cobbles (4559) forming a border or decorative feature around a rectangular area immediately north of the crosswing and west of the central hall, measuring *c* 6.5 m long by 1.4 m wide. Cobbles had been robbed or lost through heavy wear immediately outside the main entrance to the house, and an area of soil immediately between the cobbles and the farmhouse walls probably derived from a later flowerbed. Within the decorative border, cobbles 4558 (Pl 19) lay south of the front door, and 4560 to the north, the latter showing evidence of greater wear. A whetstone and a grindstone, 4556 and 4557 (Fig 44), had been incorporated within 4558, and several sherds of seventeenth to late eighteenth century pottery (Fabrics 3, 4, 6, 7, and 8; including Figs 54.38, 54.39, 57.53, 59.86, and 59.88) were found among these cobbles. Cobbling beyond the decorative border was numbered 4564. With the exception of the decorative border, the cobbles were generally rounded and measured *c* 70 mm by 100 mm wide; within the border, they were up to 190 mm in length.

A drainage feature composed of larger cobbles (4555) was located at the north-west corner of Room G5/6. It contained sherds of nineteenth century glass.

Ancillary Structures and Related Deposits North and North-west of the Farmhouse

Evidence for three small wooden structures was recovered on the platform north-west of the farmhouse (Fig 44). Structure 2 was represented by a cluster of postholes, perhaps suggesting the presence of an irregular building measuring *c* 4 m long by 4 m wide. Structure 3, immediately adjacent, was indicated by a cluster of stakeholes with overall dimensions of *c* 1.45 m long by 0.70 m wide. It may have been a small freestanding structure, a part of Structure 2 immediately to the north-west, or may simply have been the product of horticultural activity. Structure 4 was represented by an alignment of postholes. The absence of further related features suggests that this may have been a fenceline rather than a building, although further postholes may have been removed by truncation.

The cuts forming Structures 2 and 3 truncated deposits of silty clay which covered the underlying boulder clay of the platform in this area. These features were

Plate 19: Cobbling 4558 west of the farmhouse, showing grindstone 4557

in turn sealed by a very similar layer of silty clay. The deposits contained fragments of coal and may be the product of dumping, perhaps reworked by horticultural activity.

Two brick ancillary structures were constructed to the north of the farmhouse, on the moat edge. They were adjacent to one another, and the sequence of construction of the walls demonstrated that they had been built at the same time. Structure 6 had a sunken floor, and deposits of coke covering the base demonstrated that it had last been used as a coal bunker. Structure 5 was a small outhouse immediately adjacent to the east. These interrelated brick structures may be the remains of the 'necessary houses' known from documentary evidence (J Lewis pers comm), with the sunken floor of Structure 6 perhaps functioning as a cess-pit. Later walls were built along the moat edge to the east and west of Structures 5 and 6.

Structure 2
This consisted of eight postholes (Fig 44), 4427, 4428, 4429, 4439, 4441, 4442, 4443, and 4445, typically angular in plan, and extending up to c 0.5 m in diameter. They may indicate the groundplan of a wooden structure,

with irregularly placed posts, but measuring c 4 m long by 4 m wide. Posthole 4445 was excavated, and two sherds of late eighteenth or nineteenth century pottery (Fabrics 3 and 5) were recovered from its fill (4674), perhaps suggesting that the feature had been dismantled in the nineteenth century.

Structure 3
A subrectangular cluster of stakeholes (Fig 44), numbered 4430-4438 and 4489-4497, was identified c 8 m west of the farmhouse, and at the south-eastern end of Structure 2. The cluster had dimensions of c 1.45 m long by 0.70 m wide.

Structure 4
A cluster of six closely-spaced subrectangular postholes (Fig 44) lay c 4 m west of the farmhouse, no more than 0.9 m apart and aligned roughly south-west / north-east. Posthole 4134, 0.38 m deep, contained two clay packing fills which surrounded a square postpipe with dimensions of 0.20 m x 0.20 m by 0.36 m deep. Posthole 4132 also contained clay packing surrounding a postpipe with dimensions 0.28 m x 0.20 m by 0.34 m deep. The pipe sloped down at an angle of c 1:2 (x:y) towards the north-east, suggesting that the original post was angled towards 4134 to the south-west. A sherd of black-glazed redware pottery of no clear date was found within the clay packing fill, with a sherd in a yellow bodied fabric of possible eighteenth century date within the postpipe. Posthole 4712 had a mixed fill and was truncated by 4679, perhaps suggesting repair. The latter again had redeposited clay packing, and a postpipe measuring 0.46 m x 0.36 m by 0.36 m deep with brick and coal inclusions. Postholes 4145 and 4136 were not excavated. With the exception of 4136, the postholes were roughly parallel with the north-western edge of cobbled surface 4181.

Layers 4324, 4670, and 4323
Patches of light yellowish brown silty clay with coal fragments (4324 and 4670) overlaid the natural clay in the north-west corner of the platform. Layer 4324 was truncated by the cut features forming Structures 2 and 3, but also by an isolated posthole (4666) and a tree bole (4444) containing five sherds of pottery (Fabrics 3 and 4) dating to the late eighteenth century or later. Both the layers contained mixed assemblages of pottery. The assemblage from 4670 (Fabrics 5, 7, 13, and 18; including Figs 58.73, 59.85) appeared to date to the late seventeenth or eighteenth centuries, but that from 4324 (Fabrics 1, 3, 4, and 5; including Fig 54.32) also contained nineteenth and twentieth century sherds as well as modern glass and plastic. It may be that the later finds had become incorporated after post-deposition mixing of the layers, perhaps by horticulture, though it is also possible that Structures 1 and 2 were in fact of later date than is suggested above.

Deposit 4323, overlying 4324, consisted of brown silty clay very similar to the underlying layer. It contained frequent fragments of coal and occasional fragments of brick, as well as a mixed assemblage of seventeenth to nineteenth century pottery (Fabrics 1, 3, 4, 5, 6, 7, 8, 9, 10, and 13; including Figs 54.26, 54.28, 56.47, 58.65, 60.93, and 60.94). It was sealed by Phase 7 road surfaces 4227 (Fig 15) and 4146 extending east from the causeway.

Structures 5 and 6

The earliest element was a wall (4027) forming the west and south sides of Structure 5 (Fig 44). No trace of an eastern wall was found. A brick threshold (4028) butted the surviving part of the south wall, and stone flags (4030) were laid over what is thought to be the internal floor of the structure, giving internal dimensions of 2.0 m long by 1.05 m wide. Plaster 4032 covered the probable internal face of wall 4027, and to the west, bricks butting the flagged floor were interpreted as representing the remains of a garden feature at the north-east corner of the platform.

A section of walling 2.2 m long (4025) was constructed then along the moat edge, its east end butting the north terminal of wall 4027. The angle between these walls was then excavated to a depth of *c* 1.3 m, and enclosed by a further wall (4026) to form a sunken floored building, Structure 6. The building had a doorway in the south wall, and overall dimensions of *c* 2.2 m high by 1.35 m wide. The foundation cut was backfilled using compact clay with brick and slate fragments (4518) and the internal walls were covered with a hard cement-like plaster (4031). A deposit of coke and cinders 0.1 m deep (4505) covered the floor of the bunker. Twenty-two sherds of pottery, thought to date to the early nineteenth century, were recovered from 4518 (Fabrics 1, 3, 5, and 20).

After the construction of wall 4025, further lengths of brick walling were added to the east and west along the moat edge, 4029 and 4024 respectively, 4029 forming the north wall of Structure 5. These walls survived to a maximum height of four courses of machine-made bricks, although additional courses had tumbled down-slope into the moat. The walls were built directly onto topsoil without a foundation cut, and had straight joints with 4025. Wall 4029 continued east for 3.4 m; 4024 extended west for 9.4 m, ending at a vertical timber post, a probable fence or gate post.

The Well, and Features to the South-east of the Farmhouse

To the south-east of the farmhouse, a brick-lined well and the opening of a ceramic drain were recorded, 4139 and 4290. Additionally, two very small undated postholes, 4315 and 4318, were excavated close to the south-east corner of farmhouse Room G3. No obvious dating evidence was recovered, but it seems probable that these features date from the eighteenth or nineteenth centuries.

The Barn

The barn, to the south-west of the farmhouse and beyond the moat, was largely of single phase construction; later alterations were limited to relatively minor internal remodelling and the addition of modern lean-to structures, reflecting changing agricultural emphasis (Pl 20).

The Phase 6 structure was built entirely from hand-made brick with some localised stone footings, and is representative of a Lancashire-type barn. These buildings are typically five bays long and consist of a hand-flail threshing barn, with a cow house and loft attached at one end, the latter occupying two bays (Brunskill 1982, 111). The cow house was generally wider than the barn, and was served by three doors in the gable end, allowing access to a central feeding passage and side manure passages. A variation on the type was sometimes built, with the addition of a stable and loft at the other end of the threshing floor.

The barn at Old Abbey Farm generally conformed to this latter configuration, with provision of stalling for stock at the north end, the threshing floor centrally located, and stabling for plough horses to the south (Figs 45, 46). The structure was built in four bays, the northern two bays being given over to the cow house, but the roof was markedly different and was built in five bays. All the external walls derived from the original build, the hand-made bricks being bonded with a pale brown sandy lime mortar. The bond was predominantly irregular, although a variant of English Garden Wall was employed in some areas, notably the west wall of the cow house, with courses of headers separated by five courses of stretchers. The brick partition wall between the first two bays of the cow house, extending up for the full height of the roof, and the lower partition wall between the cow house and threshing floor, were also integral to the first build.

A mixture of new and re-used timbers was used in assembling the wall-plates and roof structure of the barn. The wall-plates were an assorted mix of timbers (Lee and Michelmore 1998), seemingly indicating that materials were re-used from what may have been a collection of ramshackle smaller structures, as well as a larger building. Some of the timbers contained joints, such as bare-faced tenoned lapped-joints for braces, which indicate an origin in structures of medieval date, even allowing for conservative

Plate 20: The barn from the south, with appended lean-to structures

carpentry design. It is feasible that some timbers came from the house, as in times of rebuilding or demolition there must have been considerable quantities of large old timbers to hand. However, the difference in section, size, and spacings of mortises and infill staves imply that timber for the wall-plates was derived from different phases of work, and probably different structures.

In the roof superstructure above the wall-plates, re-used timber had mainly been employed for the purlins. The size and look of these indicate that they were not from a house, but rather from a barn of some type. Such a structure may have been cruck-framed, though there was no evidence amongst the re-used timbers for cruck principal rafters, cut down or re-used as tie-beams. The quality of the conversion of the purlins was quite good, suggesting that they derived from a building constructed before 1600 at the very latest.

Specialist analysis of the re-used wall-plates and purlins indicates the presence of at least two other large structures on the site, in addition to the house, which may have superseded each other: another early aisled structure and a later barn, possibly cruck-framed and dating from the late sixteenth or early seventeenth century (Lee and Michelmore 1998). No direct excavation evidence was found for such buildings, although a short length of wall found in Area J to the west of the barn indicated the possibility of an earlier brick-founded structure in a similar location (*see Ch 7*). It may be that when it was found desirable to erect a new barn in the mid eighteenth

century, it was possible to re-use much of the roof frame of an earlier barn. Dendrochronological analysis of two of the purlins made from new timber suggested that they were derived from trees felled in AD 1735 and AD 1753.

The cow house

The cow house was wider than the rest of the barn, measuring 9.40 m across externally as opposed to 7.05 m (Fig 45). As it was served by the same roof structure, this meant that the external side walls, 207 and 209, were *c* 0.52 m lower than those of the rest of the structure, with a height of 3.65 m (Figs 45, 47). Longditudinally, it was divided into two bays each of *c* 4 m, separated by an internal wall which extended for the full height of the barn, supporting the purlins of the roof. Its original plan comprised three enclosed stock pens, two to the west, the third to the north-east, separated by a central feeding passage (Fig 45). This passage was in fact displaced slightly to the west of centre, so that the pen to the east was slightly larger than those to the west. A fourth stock pen to the south-east appeared originally to have been open to the central passage, and was possibly used for storage. The pens were bounded by low walls *c* 1 m in height, constructed of hand-made bricks bonded with a pale brown sandy lime mortar.

Access to the stock pens was through one of three doors in the northern gable, the central door opening onto the feeding passage which continued through to the threshing floor (Figs 45, 47). The three doors (234, 235, and 236) were of regular size, each measuring

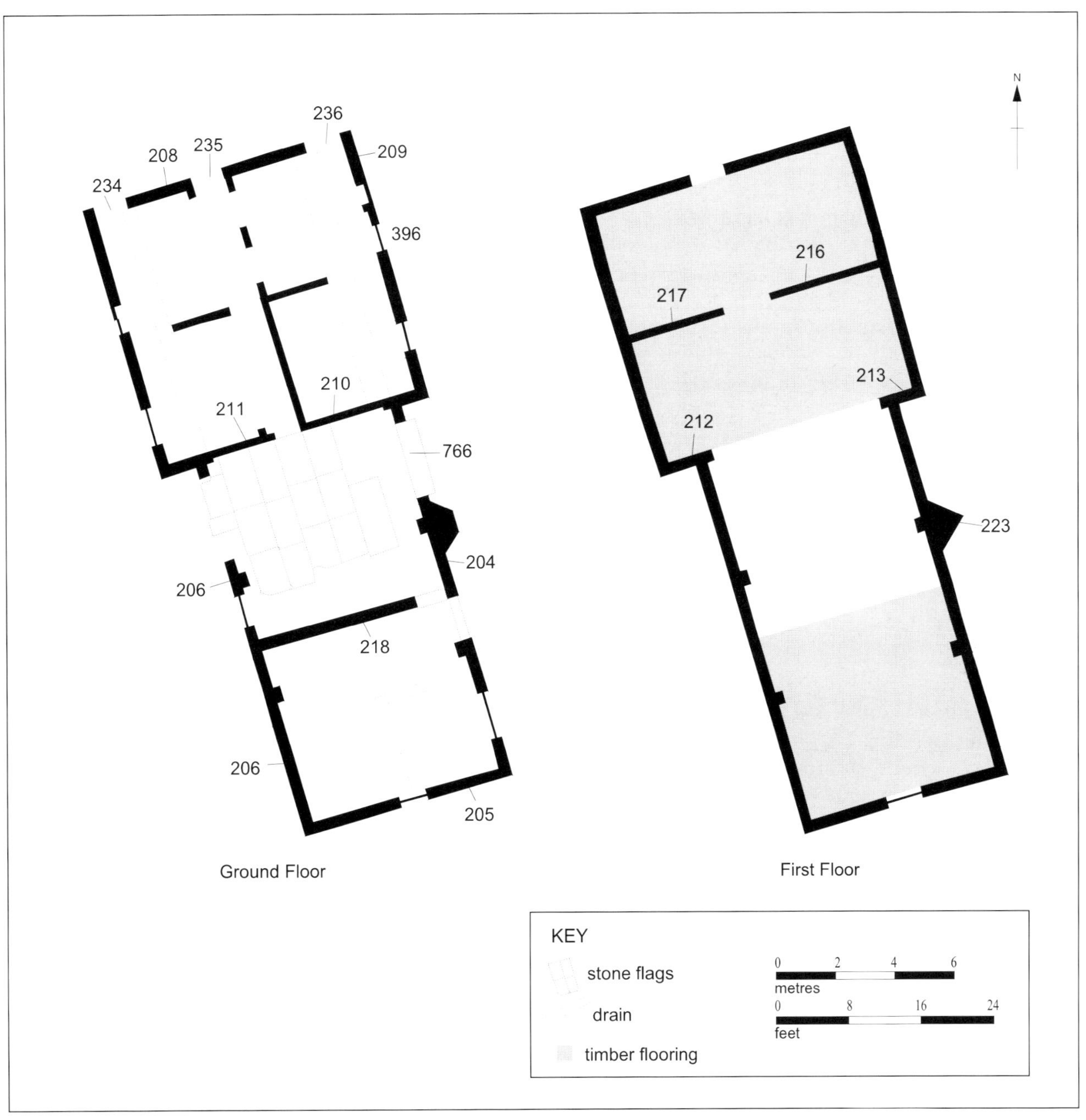

Figure 45: Ground and first floor plans of barn

2.00 m high by 1.00 m wide, and were constructed with a stone pad at the base on either side of the aperture, with the exception of the outside edges of the east and west doors. These stone blocks acted not as pads for door-jambs, but as foundation stones for the wall itself.

The northern gable wall (208) also contained a window and four air vents, two of nine-holes and two of fifteen (Fig 48). The window (237) was centrally located within the upper storey, and measured 1.00 m square; it appeared to be too high above floor level to have functioned as a pitching hole, and was constructed of large timber jambs which contained hinges, indicating that it was shuttered rather that glazed. The jambs were thought to be possibly contemporary with the build of the wall, although the lintel and sill had been

replaced. Above, an owl hole was present close to the apex of the wall.

The eastern external wall, 204 (Fig 46), had undergone extensive modification, and was the most complicated part of the fabric. Nevertheless, it seemed clear that the original build of the wall, constructed of dark red hand-made bricks bonded with coarse lime mortar, had contained two doorways giving alternative access to the eastern pens. The reason for this multiplicity of access arrangements is not fully understood. However, if the south-eastern stock pen had originally been for grain storage, it might have been desirable to have direct access to this room.

The position of northern doorway 396 was visible in the interior brickwork, this area being complicated by an extensive re-build of the outer skin of the wall. The door's location was marked by a low column of brickwork, 910, which was all that remained of the original northern edge of the aperture, by the rebuilt southern edge of the aperture, and by subsequent brick blocking in between. Brickwork 910 was found to have a ragged northern edge and was butted by rebuild 811 to the north, but had a smooth reveal on its southern side where the original doorway had been. The original fabric survived for a height of only 1.00 m, with the brickwork above having been rebuilt. The two sides of the aperture and an original timber lintel above it defined a door space measuring approximately 1.5 m wide by 2.10 m high.

Parts of both the eastern and western edges of door aperture 248 were subsequently rebuilt. This is thought to have occurred during Phase 6, although the dating is problematic and the mortar used was very similar to that employed for the subsequent blocking of the doorway in Phase 7. Firstly, the upper part of the northern edge of the door aperture (813) was rebuilt. This brickwork probably also formed the southern jamb for a new window or recess (248) inserted immediately to the north. The rebuilt outer skin of the wall, 858 (Phase 7), makes it difficult to determine whether this aperture had originally pierced both skins, and what its function had been. An area of wall (811) was also rebuilt below the newly inserted aperture. Further north, a large lintel (903) within the fabric of the wall may be associated with extensive rebuilding here, and may have acted as a support whilst work was carried out below. The southern edge of the original door aperture may also have been remodelled at the same time, although some of the bricks within re-build 858 may have been factory-made, and the pinkish brown mortar appeared to differ slightly to that used to the north.

Door 405 was 2.06 m further south along the eastern wall of the cow house, once giving access to the open south-eastern pen. The north edge of the original aperture was indicated by a stone pad, 954, below the vertical join between wall 209 and a later pier, 734. The southern extent of the doorway was obscured by later alterations, but it cannot have been wider than 1.50 m, whilst a further stone pad below subsequent rebuilding suggested a possible width of *c* 1.3 m. The full height of the doorway was also impossible to gauge because of extensive modification.

The second discernible phase of construction here was the insertion of a brick pier (734) itself placed on a stone pad (892). The pier reduced the width of the door space, or shifted it southwards, and was keyed into wall 209 to the north. The straight edge to wall 209 to the south may mark the other end of the original aperture, re-used for a later doorway to give a width of *c* 1.20 m. The cuts for the insertion of this second doorway appeared to extend above the lintel, the space above the new door being filled with re-used hand-made brick bonded with harder grey mortar. The period of use of this second doorway remains uncertain.

The western wall of the cow house (Fig 48) is thought originally to have contained one window, and one recess to the north, rather than two windows. The southern feature (232) retained an original jamb *in situ* on the south side, extending for the full depth of the wall, and probably represents a window contemporary with the wall's construction. The north edge of the aperture had been disturbed by later remodelling. The feature to the north (233) appeared to have originated as a recess or shelf space one skin of bricks deep, the southern part of which was subsequently cut through to form a small window. Four nine-hole vents were provided at first floor level, with two further nine-hole vents located to the north of the ground floor window, and to the north of the recess. Six vents in the same configuration had also been built into the east wall.

The cow house had originally been constructed with a loft above, but the level of the loft floor had subsequently been raised in Phase 7 (*see Ch 9*). The only remaining element of the earlier floor was a bridging joist (461). This timber contained trenches along its top surface for floor joists, and a corresponding series of joist holes was present in the east and west walls of the cow house. The bricks around the joist holes were cut, but with considerable precision, suggesting that they were cut during construction of the wall. The brick partition wall between the two bays of the cow house continued up to the top of the roof space, and contained two apertures, one at floor level acting as a communicating doorway between the bays, the other immediately above the lintel of the doorway. The doorway measured 1.62 m wide by 1.82 m high, and the aperture above 0.95 m wide by 1.04 m high. The function of the upper aperture is uncertain. It may have acted as a pitching hole, possibly to be used if the loft was full of hay or straw.

The threshing floor

South of the cow house, the barn narrowed to a width of 7.05 m (Fig 45). The east and west walls, 204 and 206 respectively, continued on the same alignment to the southern gable, with the interior space divided between central threshing floor and stable, the two probably being separated by a wooden partition wall.

The threshing floor was served by two opposing double doors (224 and 231, Fig 46), and was paved with heavy flagstones. The door aperture in the east wall measured 2.60 m wide by 3.40 m high, large enough to allow the access of laden carts to the

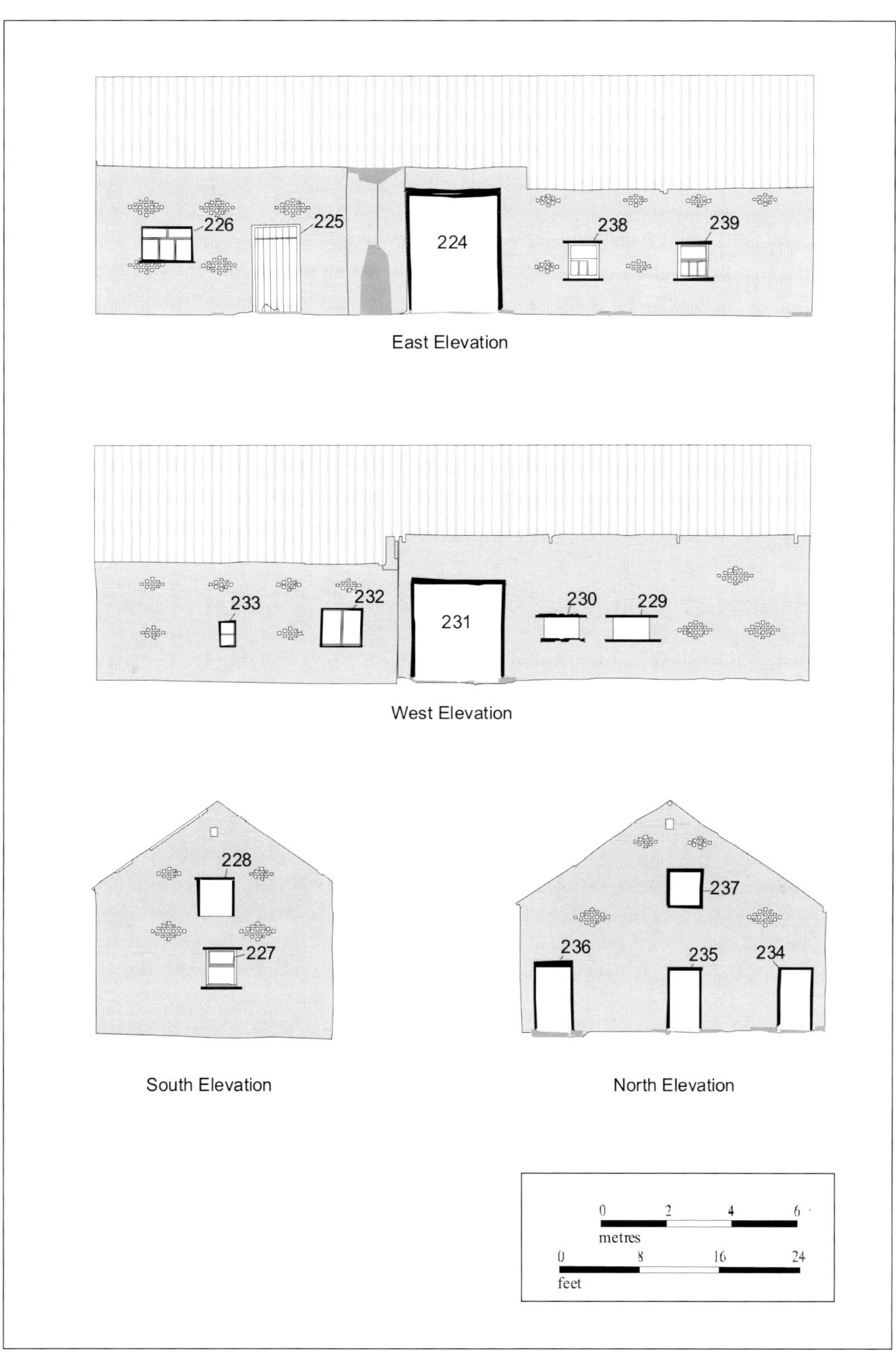

Figure 46: Barn elevations

threshing floor. The doorway, although contemporary with the construction of the barn, contained re-used timbers from an earlier structure. The lintel (744) visible on the inner face, contained mortises and a trench, which possibly indicate that a former wall-plate or tie-beam had been incorporated into the door's construction. The remaining elements, the jambs and top frame of the door, were purpose built. The door-jambs were thought to display evidence for a change in doors, in the form of blocked holes which may have been used to accommodate a different door. However, a timber from the extant door produced a dendrochronological felling date of AD 1734-79 (Sheffield, 1998; Hillam *et al* 1987 for 10-55 sapwood estimate). The jambs were connected to the wall through a pair of pegs/blocks which were mortised out from the side of the door-jamb and accommodated into the wall fabric on either side, emphasising the contemporaneity of the door.

A triangular brick buttress (223) was situated on the external face of the barn to the south of the eastern doors. It is a common feature of early brick barns in the area and provided support for an extended canopy to protect the weather side of the threshing floor. The buttress and this canopy in this location may have housed threshing machinery, or provided protection for laden carts.

The large western doorway (231) to the threshing floor partnered that to the east, but was lower, measuring 2.56 m wide by 2.81 m high. Its construction was otherwise identical, with re-used timber again employed for the lintel. There was no adjacent buttress, but a window (230), 1.18 m to the south, illuminated the threshing floor. The aperture measured *c* 1.02 m wide by 0.60 m high. An external timber lintel and sill were contemporary with the build of the wall, but there was no window furniture.

Excavation below the threshing floor (Area J)

The brick foundation of the barn's west wall was recorded, 4365/4423 (Fig 47), one and a half stretchers wide (0.36 m). The wall was visible before excavation within Trench J, and ended within the excavation trench at the south side of an entrance (the western doorway to the central threshing floor, Fig 45). A sandstone door-jamb measuring 0.50 m x 0.36 m by 0.32 m high, 4379 (Fig 47), had been laid on the brick foundation to the south of the entrance. An additional, irregularly bonded brick wall one stretcher wide, 4367 (Fig 47), had been built at right angles to the wall foundation, butting it on the west side. It was greater than 1.24 m long, continuing west beyond the limit of excavation, perhaps representing the wall of a small lean-to structure built along the side of the barn. To the east of the wall foundation, and almost opposite

4367, a brick buttress had been built, 4366. It was two stretchers wide and extended out for the length of one stretcher (0.47 m wide by 0.24 m high).

Wall 4365 was butted by a deposit of black cinders (4362) to the east. Deposit 4362 extended from the west wall of the barn as far as threshold stones 4371 (Fig 47) and 4376, identified as belonging to the east wall. It extended beyond the limit of excavation to north and south, and was found to be up to 0.07 m thick. The cinders are thought to be part of the make-up dumped to level the ground surface so that stone flags could be laid above, and they raised the floor level within the barn to a height equal to that of the top of earlier brick wall 4364 (Phase 5), so that the floor for the new brick barn could be laid over the top. A bedding layer of sand, 4360 (Fig 47), and patches of brown sandy silt (4386) were intermittently present above the cinders, and a stone flagged floor had been laid above. The latter (4359) had been removed from the barn before excavation began. The stone flags extended from the west wall of the barn for *c* 5.6 m as far as a brick surface laid close to the east wall. They ranged in size from 1290 mm x 850 mm by 90 mm deep to 2270 mm x 1000 mm by 110 mm deep, and were thought to have formed a threshing floor. The flags had been re-laid in the twentieth century (Phase 7), or finds had fallen down between them, since the bedding sand below contained fragments of twentieth century plastic, metalwork, and pottery (Fabric 16).

A deposit of cinders very similar to 4362, 4422, was laid to the west of wall 4365. It contained six sherds of nineteenth century pottery (Fabric 3). This deposit continued beyond the limit of excavation to the north and west, and was covered by a deposit of cinders with brick and stone fragments (4368) which probably formed a rough external surface. The top of this deposit lay at roughly the same height as the surface of the threshing floor within the barn. Four unbonded bricks (4369), laid within 4368, may represent part of a robbed-out threshold, or simply be part of the make-up.

Towards the eastern wall of the barn, bedding sand 4360 had been covered with a layer of light grey mortar *c* 0.1 m thick, which had been laid as bedding for a brick surface, 4370 (Fig 45). The surface was *c* 1.06 m wide, extending to *c* 2.04 m near the north edge of Trench J.

To the east, the brick surface butted up against a stone block (4371) and a setting of mortared bricks which extended beyond the limit of excavation. These were probably part of the east wall of the barn, perhaps serving as a door-jamb. The surface also butted a very long stone flag, 4372 (Fig 47), measuring 2500 mm long by 720 mm wide, which may have been the threshold stone for an eastern entrance opposed to that identified to the west. These elements of an eastern wall were butted to the east by a probable brick buttress, 4375 (Fig 49), an adjacent stone setting (4377) a cobbled surface extending beyond the limit of excavation (4373) and two blocks of sandstone, 4374 (Fig 47), perhaps part of a surface associated with the cobbles. It seems probable that the cobbles and stone surface were part of an area of external hard standing east of the barn.

The stable

The stable at the southern end of the barn provided accommodation for up to four horses, with the location of stone pads and channels suggesting that the stalls were contemporary with the cobbled floor. They were of high quality craftsmanship, with chamfered sides.

Access was gained through a large door (225) in the eastern wall, or from the threshing floor (Figs 47, 48). The eastern doorway was relatively large, measuring 1.20 m wide by 2.00 m high, and was clearly intended to accommodate stock. Although the reveals of the doorway were constructed by using part bricks rather than finishing off in a regular bond, the mortar was uniform throughout the wall, suggesting that the doorway was contemporary with the original wall construction rather than a later insert.

Five vent holes allowed ventilation of the stable through wall 204, three on the upper storey and two at ground floor level. These had all been partially blocked. They were all the typical reclining diamond pattern constructed through the omission of alternate headers, and comprised nine or fifteen voids. The southernmost void, which had been exceptionally well blocked, rendering it almost invisible from the outside, was largely cut through by the insertion of window 226.

Window 226 (Fig 46), cut through air vent 641, must therefore be later stratigraphically than the air vent, and a secondary insertion in the east wall of the stable, although, in other respects, the window might have been thought to be an original feature. Its reveals were very similar to those of the adjacent door, 225, being constructed from partial bricks, giving the impression of contemporaneity with the build of the wall. It may thus be an addition made shortly after construction, and dating to Phase 6. A small cut above the window, 275, was thought to be associated with the construction of the floor above, and was much larger on the inside face than the outside.

A further window, 229 (Fig 46), was originally situated in the west wall of the stable. It was of the same size and construction as window 230, which illuminated the threshing floor to the north. Three air vents of 17 holes were also built into the wall, two at ground floor level and one opening to the first storey.

The southern gable wall of the barn contained two windows. The upper window, 228 (Fig 46), was contemporary with the construction of the wall, whereas the lower was possibly a later addition. Window 228 mirrored an identical window in the northern gable, 237 (Fig 48). The square frame was modern, but the lintel (926) may have been an original timber, and showed possible signs of re-use. The window would have been shuttered and did not contain a window casement.

The gable wall also contained a series of vent holes, tiered in pairs on either side of the gable. Those on the ground floor were of six-hole construction, whilst the pair immediately above were of 16 holes. The uppermost vents had remained completely open and were of nine holes. At the apex of the southern gable

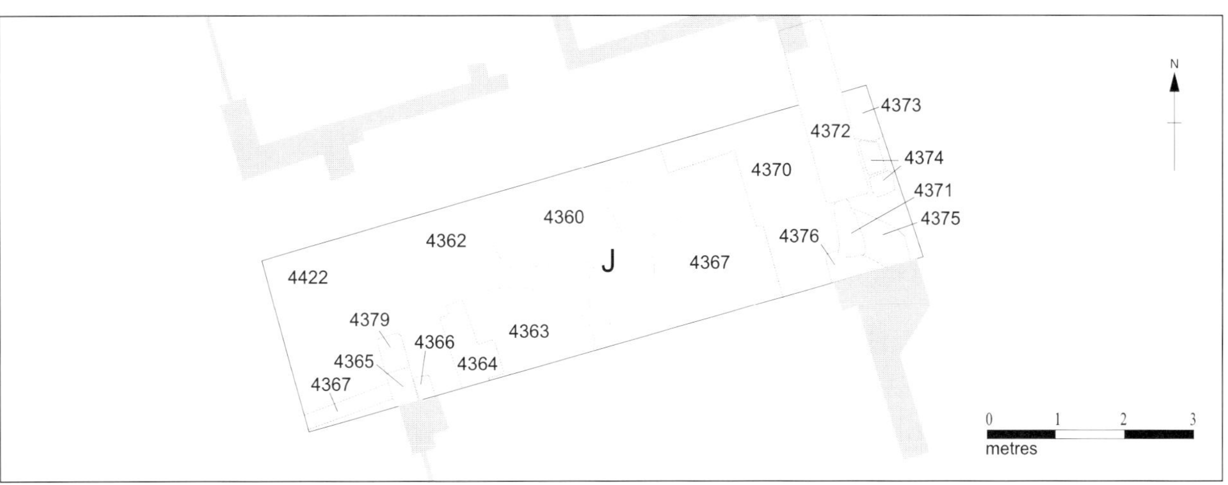

Figure 47: Area J - Excavation below the threshing floor of the barn

was an original and deliberate rectangular hole for owl access.

The extant brick wall (218) dividing the stable from the threshing floor (Fig 45) was a later construction, clearly butting the east and west external walls of the barn. No trace of the original partition survived, and it was probably built of timber, but a division with through access at the eastern end clearly had existed there, as a large stone step *in situ* indicates the position of an original entrance.

The first floor in this area is difficult to date in relation to the walls as the floor joists were contained in cuts within the walls. It is not clear whether these were created at the same time as the construction of the wall by using broken bricks, or whether they were cut through later. It seems most probable that the floor was original. Although the northern ends of the two bridging joists were found to be accommodated within recesses within the Phase 7 partition wall at the north of the stable, they may previously have rested on a precursor to this wall, whether brick built or timber supported and open. The surface of the loft floor was 2.70 m above the stalls below.

The structure of the roof, and evidence for re-use of earlier timbers

The roof configuration was markedly different from the bay structure of the walls below, since the roof was divided into five bay divisions and employed three timber roof trusses. The northernmost bay was defined by the northern gable and the nearest internal east / west wall, the internal wall, 216/217, acting as an internal gable with the purlins resting on each wall. The remaining bays were defined by king post trusses and the southern gable wall. The northern truss effectively rested upon the east / west returns of walls 207 and 209, which divided the cow house from the threshing floor, whilst the central and southern trusses rested on purpose-built internal buttresses, contemporary with the original phase of construction.

The king post trusses were through-tenoned, constructed with angled braces to either side of the king posts. The trusses were well finished, having run out chamfered edges to the braces and king posts, and appear to have been made specifically for this barn. A

timber from the northern truss was sampled for dendrochronological analysis, and a felling date obtained of AD 1750-?1795 ((Sheffield, 1998; Hillam *et al* 1987 for 10-55 sapwood estimate); although a labelling error occurred during sampling, nevertheless the sample is thought to relate to the king post, 107, rather than to the principal rafter, 103). The date of the timber shows that, in the eighteenth century, a barn might still be made employing high-quality timbers and skilled carpenters. Some assembly marks were visible on the upper faces of the trusses.

The massive purlins were trenched within the principal rafters. Purlins 74, 86, and 101 were successfully dated by dendrochronology, producing felling dates of AD 1747-86, AD 1735, and AD 1753 (Sheffield, 1998; Hillam *et al* 1987 for 10-55 sapwood estimate), suggesting that recently felled timber had been used for these three purlins at least. However, many of the remaining purlins showed obvious sign of prior use, seatings being present on 76, 77, 78, and 98, and evidence of former usage was also preserved on many of the wall-plates; several of these timbers appeared to be medieval or sixteenth century in date, and they have been described in more detail in *Chapters 3 and 4* above. Other timbers had also been re-used, but their appearance was more recent. The infill and stud spacings on timber 744, a lintel, suggested a former use earlier in the eighteenth century.

Deposits in front of the north gable of the barn

Evaluation Trench 7 was opened immediately north of the barn in order to test the survival of archaeological deposits in a possible area of early farm buildings. A surface of large cobbles was revealed, part of an area of hard-standing visible in places on the surface outside the barn. Beyond the western of the three doorways (234) were the remains of a roughly-laid path of small cobbles covering an area of *c* 2 m long by 2 m wide; this was partly overlain by a dump of iron-working slag. Below, a dump of clinker and rubble covered much of the base of the trench. These dumps were not securely dated, but may have been deposited in Phase 6, although no conclusive evidence for any older deposits was recovered. The underlying natural clay was revealed at less than 0.5 m below the present surface.

9

PHASE 7 - TWENTIETH CENTURY ALTERATIONS

Work carried out during the final phase provided extra domestic rooms in the farmhouse, presumably for an enlarged family group (Figs 48, 49). This involved a major internal reorganisation without recourse to radical structural alterations. According to oral reports, the render covering the external brickwork of the south, west, and north elevations was applied during this phase. Minor alterations were also made to the barn.

The Central Hall

At the time of dismantling, a stone flagged floor survived within the central hall of the farmhouse. It was bedded on a layer of orange brown silty sand, which extended north through the doorway from crosswing Room G4 (*Ch 11*, Fig 69), and contained mixed assemblages of pottery, metalwork, and glass. Each assemblage included twentieth century artefacts, but a copper alloy pin of possible seventeenth century origin was also found (*Catalogue 9*, Fig 61.9). The floor was badly damaged, subject to subsidence, and incomplete, the deterioration necessitating repairs using concrete, culminating in the laying of a concrete floor, typically 0.35 m thick.

Alterations were made to the southern door between Room G1 and the eastern outshut (Fig 50). Initially the doorway was re-built, with re-used door-jambs laid on top of a concrete floor repair. Traces of red plaster on the door-jambs appeared to be the same as that adhering to the blocking wall in the northern doorway, demonstrating use of the remodelled southern doorway after that to the north had been blocked. Subsequently, the southern doorway itself was blocked with a wall of modern machine-made bricks.

The range within the central hall was removed and replaced by a smaller fireplace for a coal fire, its aperture measuring 0.40 m wide by 0.80 m high. The tiled hearth was laid over a concrete slab, suggesting that this alteration occurred during Phase 7, and its removal indicates that the room no longer had any cooking function, and served as a reception room.

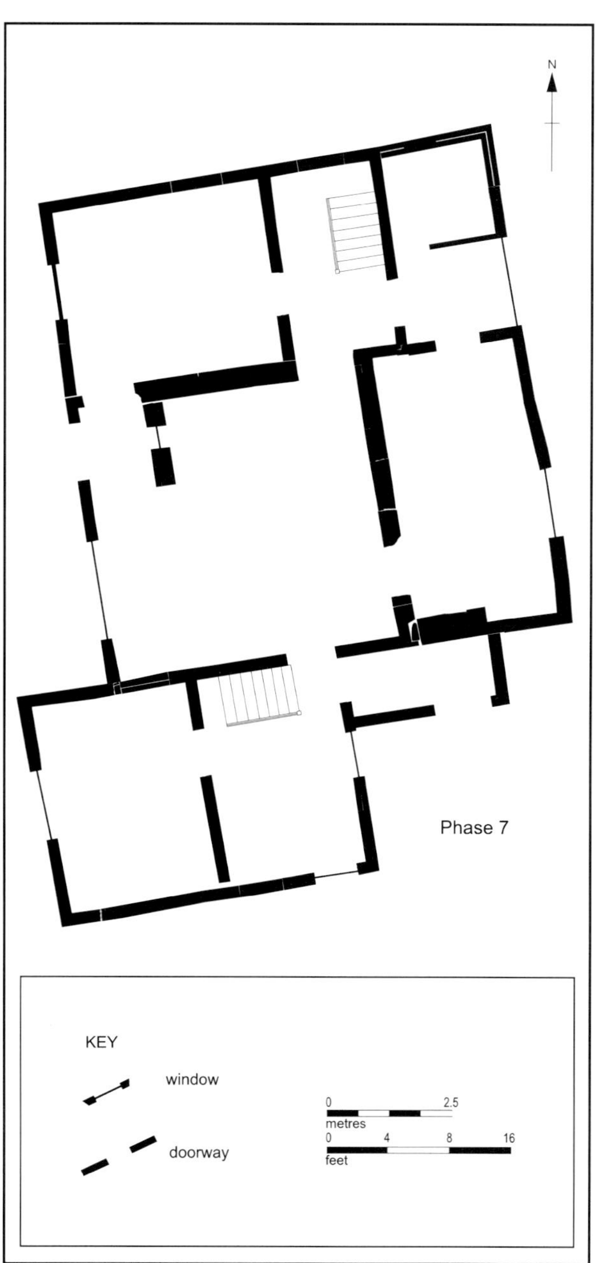

Figure 48: Suggested plan of the farmhouse ground floor, Phase 7

Oral reports suggest that the western wall of the farmhouse, together with the northern and southern walls, was rendered during the twentieth century (LUAU 1990).

The Southern Crosswing

Local people remembered that in the 1940s the eastern cell of the crosswing was a general utility room, whilst that to the west was a pantry/dairy, where milk was served. A bench along the north wall carried barrels of beer for workmen at harvest time.

Later in Phase 7, probably during the 1950s, the kitchen was moved from the outshut to the eastern ground floor of the crosswing. The external chimney stack to the south of the outshut was probably demolished at the same time. The staircase to the crosswing was upgraded by covering the older unit with modern materials, and two small bedrooms were created on the upper floors. The central doorway in the eastern gable was partially blocked and converted into a window, and a new doorway was knocked through to the north. A porch was also built giving access to the new doorway. Both the porch and the blocking in the old doorway were constructed mainly of modern machine-made bricks bonded with hard grey cement though, at the base of the east wall of the porch, several courses of brickwork from the former external chimney appeared to have been re-used. Two further modifications probably also date to this time: a casement window slot was inserted into the aperture towards the east of the south wall, and the western cell of the wing was divided by a partition and converted into a toilet and bathroom.

Elements of flagged floors surviving within the ground floor crosswing rooms were revealed by excavation, and were thought to date to the earlier twentieth century use of the wing. In Room G5/6, six flagstones represented the remains of a flagged floor which probably once covered the whole floor area of the room. Traces of three sheets of lino, in different colours, remained on the upper surface of the floor slabs.

Within the eastern room, G4, two flagstones remained apparently *in situ* in the south-east and south-west corners, deriving from a robbed-out floor, probably contemporary with those in Rooms G1 and G5/6. In the north-western part of G4, a brick surface was constructed of a single course of unbonded bricks, and was found to contain twentieth century pottery and plastic, as well as a small copper alloy thimble of eighteenth century or later date (*Catalogue 8*, Fig 61.8). It measured *c* 1.2 m long by 0.8 m wide, and appeared to be revetted to the south and east by two horizontal timbers, serving as the base of the staircase giving access to the first floor. The staircase itself was first constructed in Phase 5, but the new brick footings are thought to have been inserted underneath during the

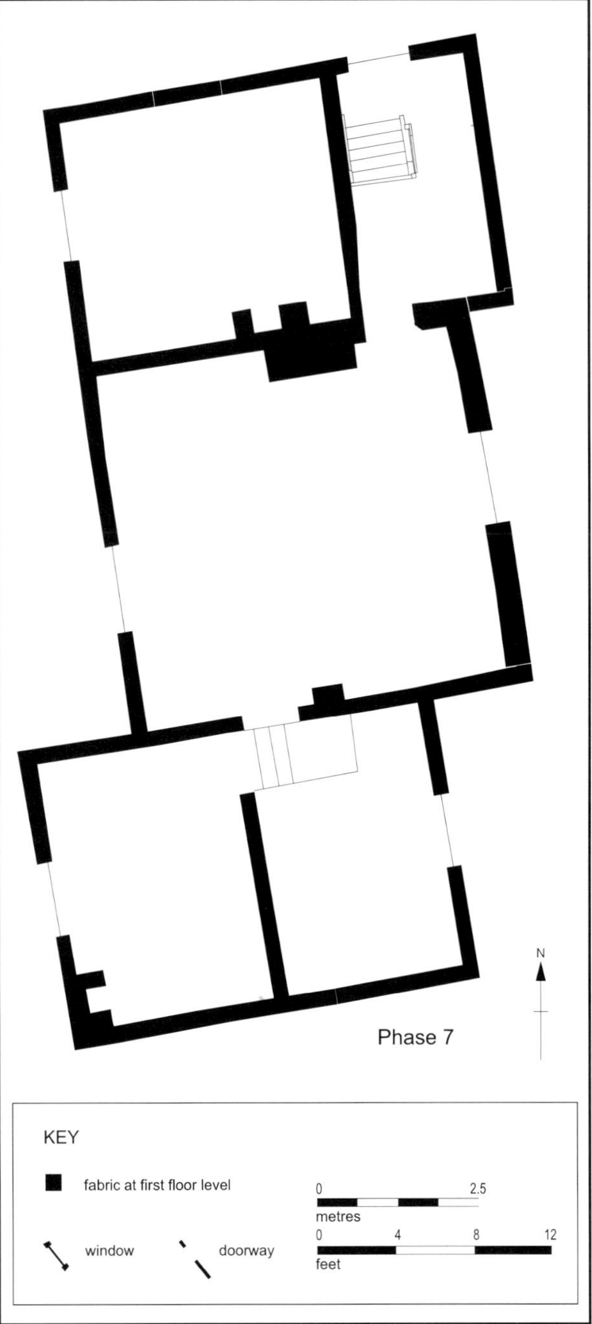

Figure 49: Suggested plan of the farmhouse first floor, Phase 7

twentieth century, probably when the staircase was overhauled and new risers and treaders installed. A further brick surface to the south extended right across the room. The floor and brick structures were probably contemporary, though the presence of patches of probable make-up above the bedding sand in some places suggested that repairs to the flagged surface had been necessary. In addition, four broken flagstones were sealed by the bedding sand, suggesting the former existence of a flagged floor in a previous phase.

The Northern Rooms

A four-celled domestic unit was created in the northern part of the house by providing doorways through the brick partition wall at ground and first floor levels. First floor access was via a staircase which cut through the floor in the north-east corner of the eastern room. The first floor taking-in door and ground floor gable windows were blocked, and an additional doorway was knocked through from the western ground floor room to the entrance vestibule at the main west doorway into the house. Fireplaces were installed in both lower and upper storeys (Figs 50, 51), within Rooms G2 and F2 (*Ch 11*, Fig 70), backing onto the existing fireplaces to the south in Rooms G1 and F1. The ground floor fireplace had undergone four phases of development, probably all during Phase 7. An initial chimney breast and fireplace aperture had been built, and a lintel inserted subsequently, perhaps for the attachment of a slate fire surround, neo-classical in style, which was found stored under the staircase. The aperture was later partially blocked and narrowed, and a quarry fire surround constructed, which was finally covered by a modern slate fireplace.

Within the eastern room, excavation revealed evidence for a rough trampled surface of mortar, plaster, brick, ash, and coal, producing very modern dating material, as well as fragments of oyster shell. To the north of the room, a layer of clean, loose orange sand a maximum of 0.12 m thick had probably been deposited to produce a level surface prior to the laying of a later stone flagged floor. Eighteen flagstones survived. To the west, in Room G2, five brick 'joists', aligned north to south, suggested the former presence of a floor of wooden boards. This had been removed, and a concrete floor laid on top of a deposit of hardcore.

The New Toilet and Utility Room

An inside toilet and utility room were built in the angle between the northern rooms and the outshut, with access from both these parts of the house. This occurred some years after the conversion of the northern rooms to domestic use, probably in the mid to late twentieth century. The brickwork consisted of modern bricks bonded with a hard grey cement, and the east window of the utility room was fitted with an aluminium frame probably datable to the 1970s. This toilet may have been added to supplement the bathroom installed in the western cell of the southern crosswing in the mid twentieth century, though the sequence is not firmly established. Earlier in the century, the household must have continued to use

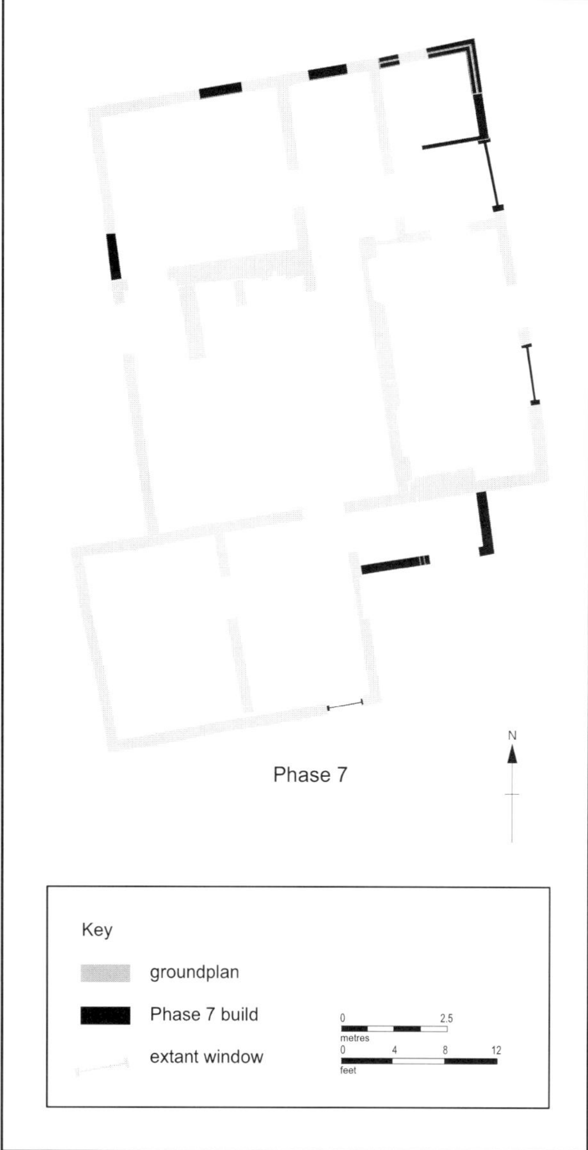

Figure 50: Plan of farmhouse ground floor showing physical evidence, Phase 7

an external privy, for which Structures 5 and 6 represent the only possibly evidence found. The north wall of the toilet was subsequently demolished, and the toilet extended a further 1 m northwards, so that the new north wall was in line with that of the adjacent rooms to the west.

The Eastern Outshut

The outshut's eastern doorway was converted to a window, with a new east doorway inserted to the north in the position formerly occupied by the brick partition, now demolished. Once the new utility room and toilet to the north had been built, access to the outshut from the rest of the house was created through a new north door, and the southern doorway from the central hall through the west wall was blocked. The fireplace and oven were blocked, and a wood burner is thought to have been inserted in front of the fireplace, free-standing but using the flue of the chimney. Two irregular areas of concrete were laid to fill gaps left by broken flags. The outshut seems now to have been used as a wash house.

Exterior Surfaces and Features on the Platform

The causeway and access road were covered with a layer of hardcore, consisting of cinders, crushed brick, and stone, and subsequently surfaced with a red deposit of burnt, crushed siltstone. Three small knife-cut fragments of leather, originally joined, were recovered from the former deposit (*Catalogue 5,* Fig 64.5). The causeway had finally been covered by topsoil and turf, which also extended over the platform to the east, and south of the roadway, the old cobbled surface being overlaid by an extensive area of mixed garden soil. This appeared to have formed after the laying of drainage pipes and an electricity cable, which all entered the house at the north-west corner of the crosswing.

To the south of the outshut, the disused outshut chimney and adjacent areas of dumping were floored over with concrete and stone flags. Beyond, a path of reinforced concrete slabs had been laid out to the south of the crosswing. Between the path and the south wall was a flowerbed, *c* 1.05 m wide, and bounded by bricks. The bed had been cultivated down to the surface of the underlying clay, removing all stratigraphic relationships between the southern farmhouse walls and other deposits to the south.

To the north-east of the house, the brick surface probably laid during Phase 6 was truncated by a pit, possibly wooden lined, and by several service trenches dug for pipes providing sewerage and mains water to the toilet in the new north-west room.

The Moat

The moat had survived to 1994 as a pronounced hollow holding water to the north of the farmhouse, and as a shallow depression to the south-west, being completely in-filled elsewhere. However, wherever the feature was investigated, evidence for twentieth century deposition was present, often in the form of dumps of building rubble. A context for this dumping was provided by oral reports from local people that the moat had been partially cleaned out soon after World War Two, and subsequently infilled in the 1950s with material from the demolished brick works on Silver

Figure 51: Plan of the farmhouse first floor showing physical evidence, Phase 7

Lane. Several of the windows of the farmhouse appeared to have been replaced in the 1960s, and iron glazing bars and twisted fragments of leaded window lights had been dumped in the moat. A mixture of seventeenth to eighteenth century, and more recent, glass quarries remained within some sections of milled lead kame, the kame itself being probably of nineteenth century date (*see Ch 10,* Fig 65).

In Area G, deposits of rubble and whole bricks had been dumped into the moat immediately north of the causeway. Beyond, further dumps of building rubble were encountered, together with fills of silty sand or clayey sand. These deposits had completely filled the upper 1.5 m of the moat which had still been open at the time of construction of the causeway.

Within Area E, to the north of the farmhouse, the moat had never been completely infilled, and had survived as a deep depression. The top of the moat was revealed by machine-excavation on its southern side, where it had been truncated by construction of a brick retaining wall along its southern margin (*see Ch 8*). A layer of redeposited clay had been dumped immediately in front of the wall, and was overlaid by a shallow silty clay fill, in turn covered with topsoil.

A sondage was excavated across the moat to the east of the farmhouse (Area H), but excavation did not continue to the base of the moat. The lowest fill recorded was a thin layer of brown silty clay adhering to its western edge, and containing a mixed assemblage of seventeenth, eighteenth, and nineteenth century pottery. Above, four fills, consisting of clays, silts and sands, appeared to be the product of modern backfilling of the moat. The shallow depression which survived was covered with topsoil.

Trench A was excavated across the moat to the south of the farmhouse, where the feature had again been almost completely infilled. A deposit of black organic silt with occasional brick and charcoal fragments occupied its base and was found to be up to 1.6 m thick. Modern finds were present throughout the deposit. The upper part of the cut was filled with mixed modern rubble and refuse, and was clearly the product of recent levelling of the area. A similar range of deposits, again predominantly modern, was revealed in Evaluation Trenches 1, 2, 5, and 6.

Area F

Two parallel rows of postholes were found immediately below the topsoil within Area F to the west of the island (Fig 52). They do not appear to correspond to the lightly constructed farm buildings present here in the late twentieth century, and may represent two earlier twentieth century fence lines. A small number of other unassociated postholes and stakeholes also appeared to derive from Phase 7; all were sealed by a considerable depth of topsoil, 0.3-0.4 m deep, reflecting probable horticultural land-use.

The Barn

Several minor alterations were made to the barn. At the northern end, where the cow house was situated, the placing of doors and windows was changed, internal space was re-arranged to increase the number

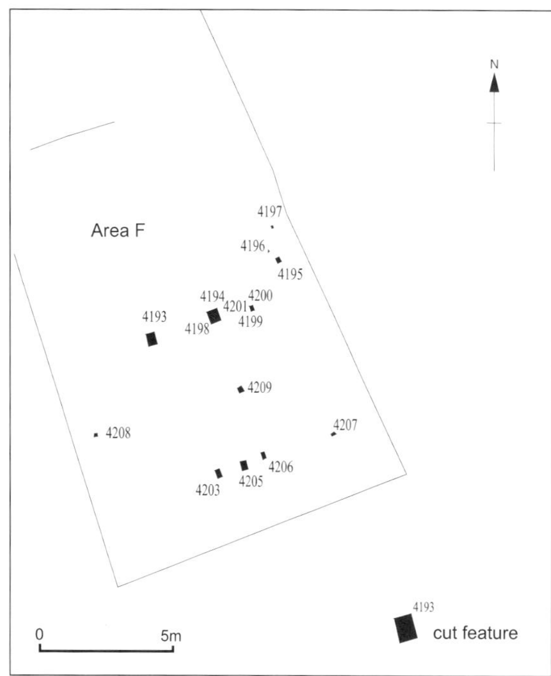

Figure 52: Excavation evidence, Phase 7

of stock pens, and the roof was raised. To the south, a new brick partition wall was added between the threshing floor and the stable, with further changes to the placement of windows. Some roof purlins were replaced, probably when the roof was covered with asbestos sheeting, and scars showed that a western outshut was removed.

Many of the small-scale changes made to the fabric of the barn are difficult to date, although they seem certain to reflect a process of continuous alteration, rather than a second discrete phase of building work, and may date to the late nineteenth as well as twentieth centuries. Hand-made bricks, sometimes clearly re-used, were employed in many of the modifications, sometimes bonded with pale brown lime mortar that was difficult to distinguish from that used earlier.

The cow house

Subsequent alterations to the cow house included the closing of the eastern doorways (*see Ch 8*), enclosure of the storage cell for conversion to stock accommodation, and the flooring of all stalls with modern concrete. The loft floor was raised by approximately 0.30 m.

The reconstructed northern door in the east wall of the cow house underwent further modification. The doorway was blocked with hand-made bricks, perhaps after a collapse, and an extensive area of the outer skin of the wall was also re-built, having the effect of blocking the aperture to the north (248), although it is not certain that this had originally penetrated the full depth of the wall. A recess was retained on the inner side of the wall there, creating a shelf. In addition, a new window (239) was incorporated towards the southern side of the blocked doorway. The brickwork constructed at this time was bonded with mortar lighter than that used for earlier rebuilds 811 and 813.

The southern doorway through the east wall of the cow house was also partially blocked, and a window aperture (238) created. The blocking was bonded with a very coarse pale brown lime mortar, perhaps suggesting contemporaneity with the insertion of the window within the former northern door. The wooden casement seems to have been inserted subsequently, by means of a further cut filled in places by modern bricks.

A cut was made around the original southern window (232) in the west wall of the cow house. This was most extensive immediately above the window, suggesting that the lintel may have collapsed. The cut was filled with modern factory-made brick, which supported the lintel, further suggesting that replacement of the lintel had been necessary, and a new frame had also been fitted. To the north, a window (233) was inserted into the southern part of the original recess, and the extent of the modern brick fill also suggested that this recess was re-lintelled at this time.

Slight modification to the lintel areas of all three doors in the northern gable appeared to represent repointing rather than rebuilding. However, the central first floor window (237) had been re-lintelled and re-silled, since the rebuilt brickwork was concentrated at the top and bottom of the window, and the lintel and sill were modern machine-cut timbers. A further area of brickwork had been rebuilt at the apex of the gable in order to accommodate a new ridge purlin, 73, a re-used telegraph pole. Repair work here was otherwise limited to the application of a coarse render to weathered areas of the wall, and the rebuilding of a small area in the western corner.

Internally, the south-eastern pen was separated from the central corridor for the first time by the construction of a brick wall *c* 1.0 m high. This itself showed evidence of having been repaired on several occasions. The raising of the roof was achieved by retaining an original bridging joist (461) and adding a series of props along its top surface, allowing the joists to be supported at a higher level. Ten additional bridging joists were installed, spanning the two bays of the cow house from north to south, carried by the gable wall and internal partition walls. The bridging joist holes from the earlier floor were expanded at the top and re-used, the timbers being propped up on modern bricks, but it is not clear why the floor was raised. The bridging joists carried joists aligned east / west. Relatively modern timbers

appeared to have been used for the floorboards, the surface of which lay 2.28 m above the pens below, and 2.46 m above the central feeding passage.

The threshing floor
The brick east / west dividing wall between the threshing floor and stable at the south end of the barn was a secondary addition, replacing the postulated Phase 6 wooden partition wall (*see above Ch 8*). The new wall was probably coincident with the alteration of windows, provision of a manger, and remodelling of the loft floor within the stable.

The stable
A window (227) was inserted into the southern gable wall at ground floor level, its late date being demonstrated by the substantial cut filled with blocking of modern brick which surrounded the modern casement. The existing window at first floor level (228) was also remodelled, with the insertion of a square frame constructed wholly of modern timber. The areas of removal associated with the insertion of this frame were sealed by a coarse cement render. An inscription on the internal sill read '*MW 1972*', suggesting that some of the alterations may have been the work of Michael Wareing, son of the owner Peter, who would have been aged 18 at the time. The date corresponds to works carried out to the farmhouse in 1972-3. Further work to the gable wall included repair of both corners, and the application of render to eroded brickwork.

A window originally present in the south wall of the stable was partially blocked. The inner side of the window was filled with a single skin of bricks, leaving a recess on the outer, western side.

The manger along the stable's western wall was probably installed after the construction of the brick partition wall to the north. Its front board appeared to be cut through the partition, whilst the back board was cut through the internal buttress of the west wall. The manger was of more workmanlike construction than the stalls, which are thought to date to the construction of the barn.

The roof
Generally the primary roof structure remained much as it was when originally built, although all of the rafters had been removed at some stage, probably when the roof covering of stone flags was replaced by corrugated asbestos sheeting. Some former GPO pressure-creosoted telegraph poles were used to replace presumably decayed purlins at this stage. Peg holes in the upper surfaces of the purlins bear witness to the former rafter positions.

Removal of the outshut

Two large vertical scars were present in the external face of the west wall of the threshing area and stable, 4.22 m apart. The scars appeared to have derived from alternated keyed butt joints. They extended up to eaves level, and to within *c* 0.5-0.7 m of the ground surface. A smaller mortar scar and three missing bricks at the extreme south end of the stable wall appeared to derive from the partial keying in of a further wall. The scars demonstrated the existence of a western outshut, now removed, probably originally of two cells, and in this, they partially confirm the evidence of map sources, which depict lean-to additions present to east and west of the barn since at least 1907.

10

THE FINDS

Christine Howard-Davis

Introduction

Following the completion of fieldwork at Old Abbey Farm in 1995, the whole material archive was subject to assessment in the manner advocated by English Heritage (English Heritage 1991b). Many of the finds from the 1995 excavation, together with some of the general biological samples, were considered to merit further analysis, and the results of that study are presented in this chapter. The archive also contained a wide range of materials and samples collected during the recording of the standing structures in 1994. The assessment demonstrated that the structural timbers were worthy of detailed specialist study; this was undertaken, and the results have been incorporated within *Chapters 3-9* above. Further analysis of other categories of material could not be justified, but their evaluation nevertheless produced several informative assessment reports. Consequently, the assessment studies of the brick, building stone, mortar, and daub samples have also been included within this chapter.

All finds and samples (including modern material) were collected by stratigraphic unit, and the location of each artefact was recorded. Finds are referred to within the discussion by a catalogue number only, a fuller identification comprising context number, object record number and, if necessary in related groups, a fragment number being listed in the catalogues. If, for any reason, an object is mentioned in the text but does not appear in the published catalogue, the fuller identification is given. This is also the identification used for the samples.

Pottery

In total, 2940 fragments of pottery vessels were recovered from the site. A policy of total collection of material of all dates was followed during the excavation, in this instance resulting in the large majority of the assemblage being of late nineteenth and twentieth century date. A fabric series was drawn up, but, with regard to the later

material from the site, the parameters were left deliberately broad since detailed analysis of late pottery was not considered appropriate to the revised scope of the project at the assessment stage. More detailed notes on the material are available in the archive.

No detailed microscopic examination or thin-sectioning of fabrics was undertaken, as in the North West this has been shown to be fruitless (Philpott 1982-83, 28) with regard to even early post-medieval fabrics, as most of the local producers used clay from the local coal measures, which are homogeneous. Later mass-produced fabrics are impossible to source in this fashion.

So little medieval pottery was recovered from the site (seven sherds) that any attempt to identify its source would not have been worthwhile. Similarly, there is little evidence from the site for a wide network of trade during the very early post-medieval period. The few fragments of Cistercian-type wares are likely to have been imported from Yorkshire and, although it is not impossible that they might have been produced locally, the fragment of an ornamental salt (Fig 53.6) is so closely paralleled at Wrenthorpe, near Wakefield (Moorhouse and Roberts 1992, fig 58.158), that it seems reasonable to suggest that it was made there.

Comparison of the forms of early black-glazed wares with those known to have been produced in the region suggests relatively local production with numerous parallels amongst material produced at Rainford and Prescot to the west (Davey 1991). Certainly, by the earlier part of the eighteenth century, it seems likely that most material on the site was derived from the same general area, with, perhaps, tin-glazed wares and fine stonewares coming in small quantities from Liverpool, and slip-trailed wares from the Midlands, although, again, these could have been produced locally. Whilst none of the few fragments of porcelain from the site derive from secure contexts, one or two may be of eighteenth century date, reflecting the widespread fashion for imported Chinese tea wares at that time.

After the end of the eighteenth century, whilst the redwares are likely to have continued to be obtained from relatively local sources, the finer, mass-produced

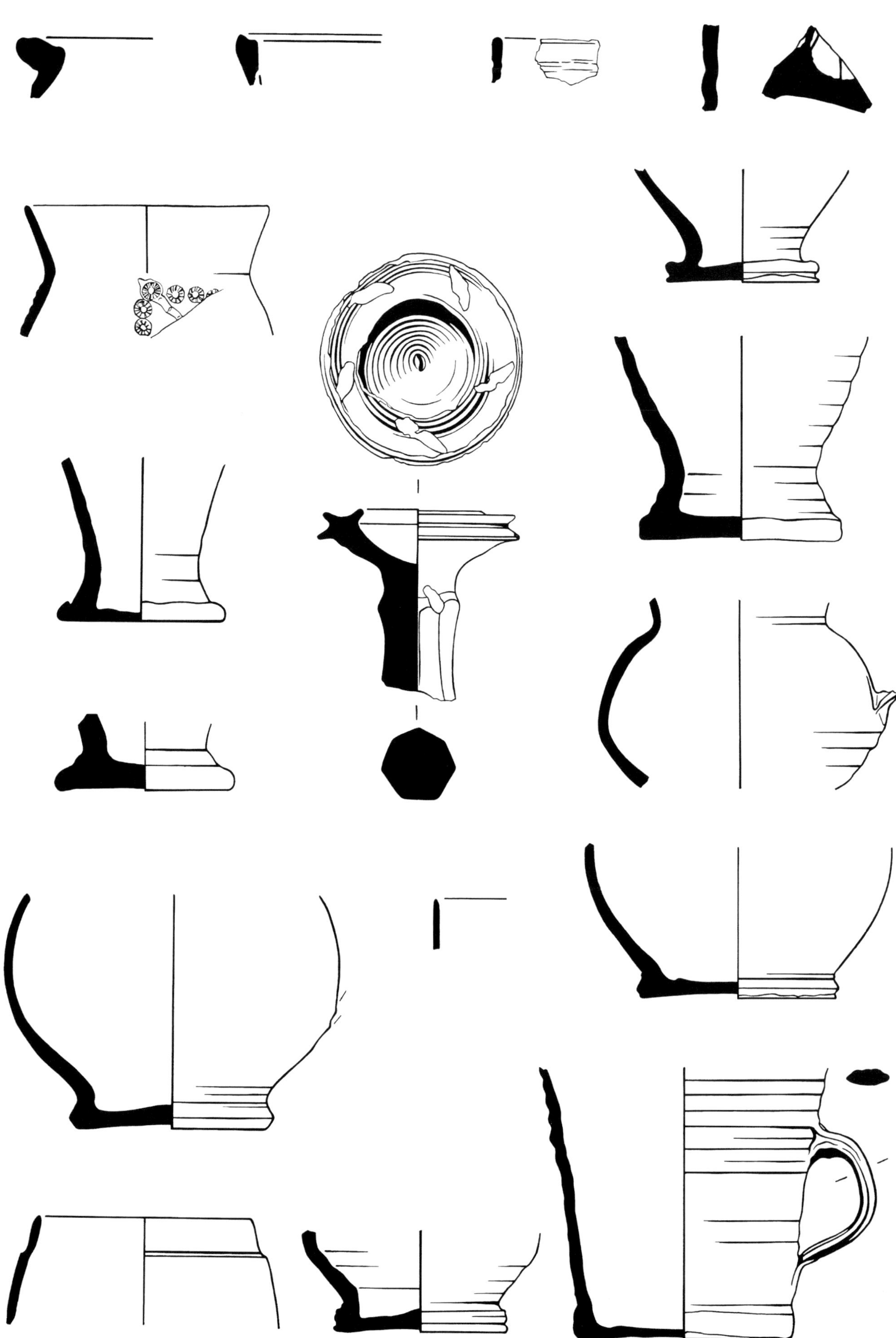

Figure 53: Pottery (scale 1:2)

white-glazed table and kitchen wares, and the stoneware kitchen wares will have been obtained indirectly from a far wider range of sources, including the Midlands.

The assemblage

It is, perhaps, surprising that the site produced so little medieval pottery, especially in view of the presence of medieval timbers within the structures, and evidence from the waterlogged timbers of the bridge of a mid fifteenth century date for that structure. It is, however, not uncommon in some areas for moated sites to be peculiarly devoid of medieval artefacts (Davey 1991, 124, with regard to Merseyside), as if the platform had been thoroughly cleared before reconstruction of the house. Little can be said of the few fragments recovered, except that the fabrics seem typical of the region.

The earliest pottery that appears in any significant quantities on the site can be dated to the later part of the seventeenth century, although a few fragments of Cistercian-type wares are likely to be marginally earlier. The salt from 4586, a make-up deposit beneath cobbling in front of the farmhouse (Phase 4), would seem to be a product of the Wrenthorpe potteries near Wakefield, paralleled by vessels made towards the end of the life of Wrenthorpe Site 1, dating from the late sixteenth to mid seventeenth centuries (Moorhouse and Roberts 1992, 90). As has been noted at Wrenthorpe and many other sites, when dealing with small or undecorated fragments it is difficult to differentiate between Cistercian-type wares and the generally hard-fired black-glazed wares which effectively developed from them (*op cit*, 97; Davey 1991, 127), especially as they share forms in common. The range of forms present at Old Abbey Farm includes the pedestalled cup, a type restricted in its distribution to Cheshire and South Lancashire, and certainly in production at Rainford by the mid seventeenth century (Davey 1991, 127), and a slightly flaring tankard, again seen in a seventeenth century context at Rainford. Yellow ware plates and dishes from the site, whilst in the Staffordshire tradition, could well have been produced locally.

Unless there was a break in the occupation of the site around the beginning of the eighteenth century, it seems likely that the same range of blackwares must have remained in use, locally available and presumably preferred by the inhabitants, as there is little admixture of the more diagnostic early to mid eighteenth century fabrics: only a few sherds of manganese speckled wares, a few tin glazed wares, a few stonewares (both white and brown), but nothing in any great quantity. The tankard is a form that appears to continue through into the next century, with fragments of similar looking vessels appearing in several of the characteristically eighteenth century fabrics. Slip-trailed wares are again poorly represented on the site, with only a few fragments of press-moulded dishes and a single probable posset cup rim present, almost all bearing the same 'feathered' decoration.

Black-glazed redwares and yellow wares remained in production well into the eighteenth century and, although there was a general trend towards confining their use to the larger domestic vessels such as storage jars and pancheons, and a general trend towards softer fabrics, they remain abundantly represented in this assemblage, alongside a range of brown-glazed vessels in similar forms, occasionally decorated with simple slip-trails.

There appears to be a significant lack of later eighteenth century tablewares, with little, if any, diagnostic material obvious amongst the assemblage. After this point, however, white-glazed tea and tablewares, especially the ubiquitous blue and white under-glaze transfer-printed cups and plates, become abundant, and it is clear that the deposition of pottery in and around the dwelling did not cease until the house was abandoned, shortly before these excavations.

The Fabric Series

Fabric 1: late stonewares

This is represented predominantly by brown and grey stonewares produced for domestic use. The forms are dominated by deep dishes, pie dishes, stew pots, jam jars, ink pots *etc*, which can be dated to the later nineteenth and early twentieth centuries.

Fabric 2: unglazed terracotta

These are generally garden wares although it is not impossible that some unglazed fragments of the softer late redwares have been included in this category in error. These forms are dominated by small flower pots, and can be dated to the later nineteenth and twentieth centuries.

Fabric 3: white-glazed earthenwares

This forms a catch-all category for all white-bodied, and predominantly white-glazed, earthenwares. The group is dominated by blue underglaze transfer-printed vessels, but transfer-printed designs in green, black, pink, and purple were noted. Some hand-painted vessels were also noted, but not in great quantity. Forms represent the complete range of tea and dinner wares. Under-glaze transfer-printing was introduced as a mass-market decorative technique in the late eighteenth century, but it is unlikely that much (if any) of the material recovered from the site can be dated earlier than the mid nineteenth century. The range of material represented continues more or less to the present day. Late (nineteenth century and later) slip-decorated white-bodied wares were also included within this group.

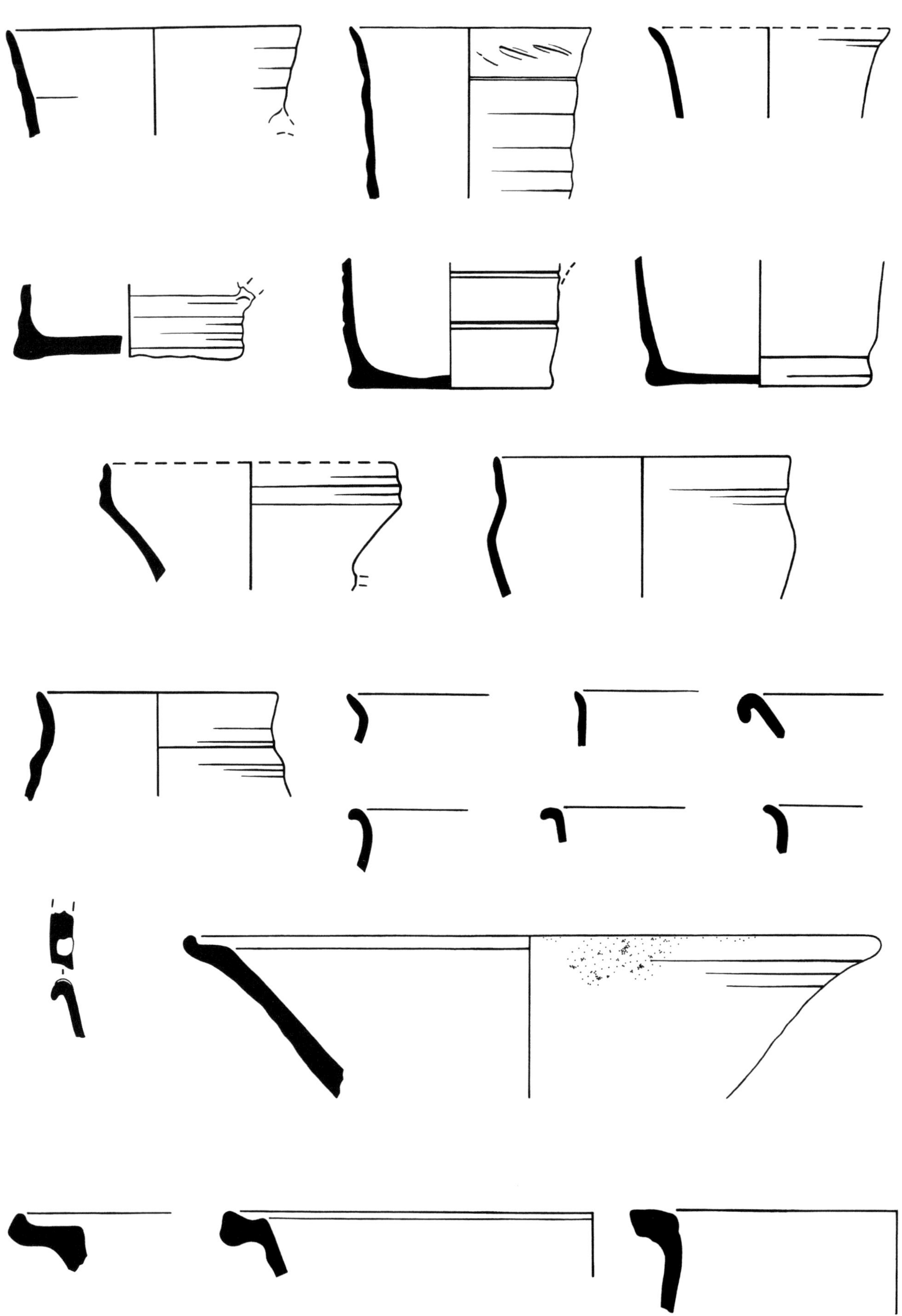

Figure 54: Pottery (scale 1:2)

Fabric 4: hard-fired black-glazed redwares (Figs 53.4-17, 54.18-27)

If the few fragments of Cistercian-type wares are included within this group, the early black-glazed wares form by far the largest group of later seventeenth and early eighteenth century material from the site, some 446 fragments. Many of the fragments are admittedly very small, but when considered alongside the 17 fragments of slipwares, 11 of early stonewares, *etc*, the assemblage displays an almost complete reliance on hard-fired black-glazed pottery at this point. Only three fragments (Fig 53.4-6) were considered to be indisputably Cistercian-type wares, but, as the local tradition effectively presents a continuum, with extremely hard-fired purplish fabrics and metallic black glazes extensively produced, it is not unlikely that one pottery type replaced the other smoothly without any significant interruption, and probably without notice by its users. A range of forms is represented in the assemblage, with upright (Figs 53.7-53.10) and globular (Figs 53.12-53.16) drinking vessels, straight-sided and slightly flaring tankards (Figs 53.17, 54.18-54.23), small vessels with a tightly hooked rim (Figs 54.28-54.31), narrow-bodied jugs (Figs 58.64-58.65), jars (including the so-called butter jar) (Figs 57.57-57.58), and other storage vessels (*eg* Figs 56.50, 57.63), along with one or two shallow dishes (Figs 54.34, 55.36). Decoration is scarce, applied cordons and incised lines on one jug only (Fig 58.64), and incised decoration on another (Fig 58.67). These black-glazed wares are hard to date with precision; there is ample evidence to suggest that Cistercian-type wares remained in production to the third quarter of the seventeenth century, and that black-glazed wares overlapped that late production considerably (Barker 1986a; 1986b). There are some similarities of form between this assemblage and a relatively tightly-dated group of sixteenth century material from Speke Hall (Higgins 1988-89), but the material seems to furnish more and closer parallels with that from Civil War and later seventeenth century deposits at Beeston Castle, Cheshire (Noake 1993, 191-210), and other later seventeenth century deposits in Liverpool (Davey and McNeill 1980-81), Rainford (Davey 1991), and Prescot (Philpott 1982-83) and such a date is reinforced by the other finds, especially glassware.

Fabric 5: soft-fired black-glazed redwares

These are in essence very similar in origin to the hard-fired fabric discussed above. It is clear, however, that the production of large domestic vessels continued well into the nineteenth, and even into the twentieth, century. As the forms remained largely unchanged such material is relatively difficult to assign to a specific date and in consequence this material has been dated broadly to the eighteenth and nineteenth centuries. It is normally thought that large coarseware vessels such as these were not disseminated widely from their place of production, and thus these are all likely to have been made relatively locally.

Fabric 6: slip decorated wares (Fig 58.71-58.79)

Only 17 small fragments of slip-decorated wares were recovered. Three small and abraded fragments appear to be of Metropolitan-ware-type (Fig 58.75-58.79), but the majority are from cream- or red-bodied press-moulded plates with embossed (Fig 58.72) or feathered (Fig 58.73-58.74) decoration. A single fragment of a thrown plate in a red fabric was recovered (Fig 58.71). Hollow wares are represented by a single posset? pot rim (Fig 58.76) and three small fragments of other vessels. Whilst the Metropolitan-type fabric may date to the relatively early seventeenth century, and the hand-thrown vessels would fit comfortably into the later part of that century, there is little doubt that the press-moulded wares are of early eighteenth century date.

Fabric 7: yellow-bodied wares (Fig 59.80-59.85)

In total, 29 fragments of yellow-bodied and self-glazed fabrics were recorded. Although a small group, they are distinctive and, with the exception of a single jar and the large base of a storage vessel, all derive from shallow dishes and bowls, forms commonly produced in this fabric. Like the blackwares, it seems likely that they were produced locally, and again parallels can be seen in a seventeenth century context at Rainford (Davey 1991). Production of yellow wares seems to have persisted throughout the eighteenth and nineteenth centuries, but it is thought that the majority of fragments from Old Abbey Farm belong to the earlier period of production.

Fabric 8: early stonewares (Figs 59.86-59.89)

Very few fragments of early stonewares were recovered. Nine were small body fragments: seven of speckled salt-glazed wares (one from a globular-bodied jug perhaps as early as the seventeenth century in date but without diagnostic features); one with impressed decoration within a ferruginous-slipped brown band, possibly a straight-sided tankard (Fig 59.86); such vessels were widely made, perhaps imported from Staffordshire, although Liverpool potters were technically capable of such products (Davey 1991, 136); and one dark brown with deeply incised parallel lines (Fig 59.88). The latter two are probably early eighteenth century in date. A single rim fragment, of a delicate two-handled vessel (Fig 59.89), with a pale, silvery-brown glaze over a greyish body, from deposit 4475, a layer which formed above the natural clay of the platform and has been attributed to Phase 5, has not been dated with certainty, but seems most likely to be of eighteenth century date.

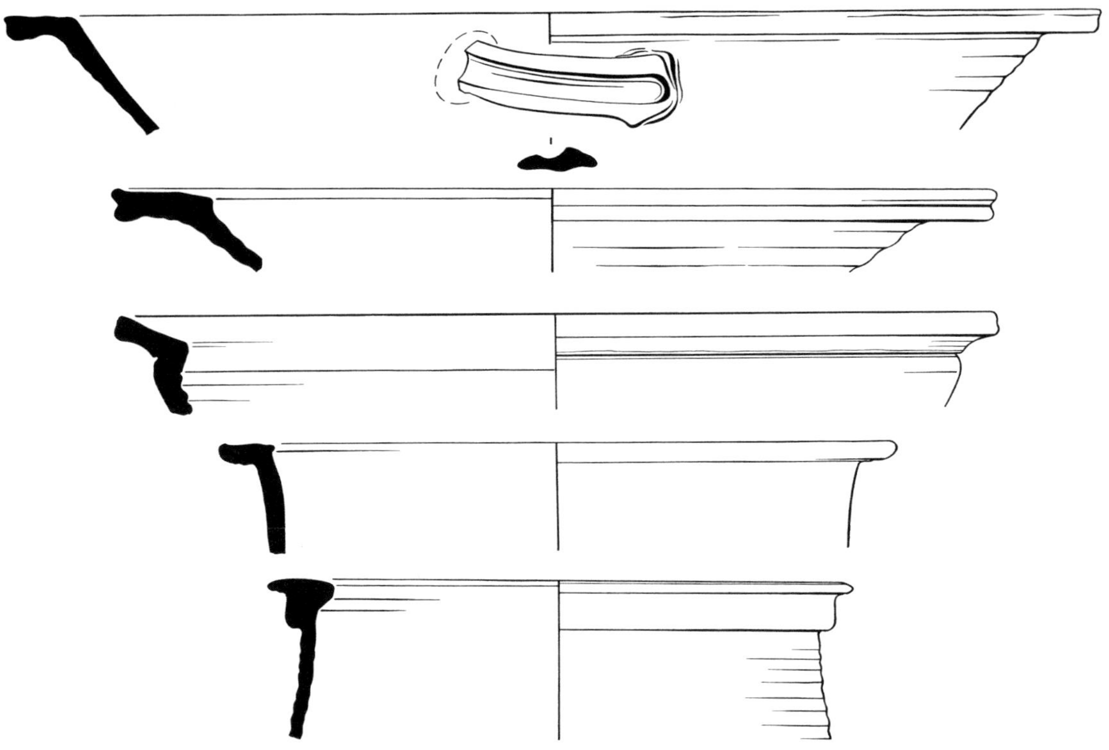

Figure 55: Pottery (scale 1:4)

Fabric 9: black-glazed cream wares (Fig 58.68-58.70)
Some 41 fragments fall into this category; all are in a relatively fine, hard cream fabric with few obvious inclusions apart from a fine black speckle, with an often thick and lustrous black glaze. Forms include a straight-sided tankard, and fragments of strap handles of various sizes. The tankards would seem to suggest an eighteenth century date although the fact that many of the contexts from which they derive are mixed must allow the possibility that some, at least, are more recent.

Fabric 10: manganese-speckled (mottled) wares (Figs 59.90-60.97)
A total of 65 fragments was recognised, 48 of them relatively undiagnostic body sherds. Most derived from medium to thin walled vessels, predominantly dishes (Figs 59.90, 60.91-60.92) and tankards (Fig 60.94), but with several small hook rims (Fig 60.97) from small vessels, the form of which was not identified. These wares are first seen in the very late seventeenth century, but are rather more characteristic of the eighteenth century, continuing in production at Prescot until at least 1780 (Philpott 1980-81, 52).

Fabric 11: white salt-glazed stonewares (Fig 60.98)
Of the eight fragments recovered, five are relatively undiagnostic body sherds, although two (both very small) from 4583, the foundation of Structure 7 (Phase 5), have a band of blue slip. Two unstratified fragments from 4697, derived from a sondage excavated through the cobbled road leading to the farmhouse, would appear to come from the rim of a tall vessel, possibly a chamber pot. Finally, there is part of the base of an engine-turned tankard (Fig 60.98); such technology was introduced *c* 1720 (Gooder 1984) or slightly later (Davey and McNeill 1980-81, 78).

Fabric 12: all medieval fabrics (Figs 53.1-53.3)
Only seven abraded fragments of medieval pottery were recovered, all but one (4759/8000; Phase 1) from very mixed deposits. None were large enough to attribute confidently to any local fabric series, although all were oxidised gritty fabrics with splashes of green glaze, most likely to be of mid twelfth to mid fourteenth century date. Although small, two fragments of cooking pot-type rims (Figs 53.1-53.2) could be recognised. A single small fragment of dark green copper-glazed ware ('Tudor Green' type) was also recovered (Fig 53.3); it was the upright rim of a narrow vessel, presumably a cup or beaker, and can be considered to be of fifteenth to sixteenth century date.

Fabric 13: bone china and porcelain of all dates
Some 36 fragments were recovered. Few were of significance, for the most part being bone china tea wares typical of the late nineteenth and twentieth centuries. The few fragments of porcelain, however, are likely to be Chinese exports, some possibly eighteenth century, whilst others, including part of an egg cup, were of the type seen commonly today.

Fabric 14: fine oxidised orange/salmon yellow fabric

A single fragment, significantly different to the rest of the assemblage, was recorded. It was thought to be late in date.

Fabric 15: metallic copper-glazed redware

Again, only a single fragment was recovered. Its provenance was not sought, but there is little doubt that it is of recent date.

Fabric 16: Pyrex and other heat-resistant glass

Only a few fragments were recovered, and they are included here on the basis that they are similar in function and form to the late stoneware and earthenware kitchen vessels noted above. These fragments can be dated to the mid to late years of the twentieth century.

Fabric 17: clear-glazed blue fabric

A single fragment was recovered. Such coloured fabrics were in vogue for cheap tea and dinner wares in the middle years of the twentieth century.

Fabric 18: very coarse and crudely made earthenwares

Some 26 fragments were recovered in unusually coarse oxidised red and yellow fabrics. Of these, only two were diagnostic, both rims and, as both derived from 4584, a levelling layer in front of the farmhouse (Phase 6), probably datable to the late seventeenth to early eighteenth century, there seems little reason not to date them similarly. There is, however, a strong chance that individual vessels in such a fabric could have been produced at any time.

Fabric 19: tin-glazed wares (Fig 60.99-60.103)

Only seven fragments were recovered. Three derived from relatively small hand-painted plates of a type seen at South Castle Street, Liverpool (Morgan 1980-81, 63-72, figs 123, 128, 129 1710-30) (Fig 60.99-60.101); one was similar but appeared to be green-glazed on the underside (possibly an early trait); two were fragments of handle (one with stabbed decoration, Fig 60.102); and one was a relatively large fragment of a delicate bowl, decorated in the Chinese manner (Fig 60.103), which has been tentatively identified as a Liverpool product of the eighteenth century.

Fabric 20: black basalt-type ware

A single fragment of a lid in this fabric was noted. It is of late eighteenth century or later date.

Catalogue of illustrated vessels

The catalogue is presented in chronological order, and illustrated in Figures 53-60.

	Context	Phase	Description
1.	4289/7268	7	Cooking pot rim, diameter unknown (fabric 12)
2.	4759/8000	1	Cooking pot rim, diameter unknown (fabric 12)
3.	4710/8359	1	Small cup rim? 'Tudor Green' ware, diameter unknown (fabric 12)
4.	4242/7191	7	Cup, Cistercian-type ware (fabric 4)
5.	4143/8448	7	Cup with flaring rim, Cistercian-type ware? (fabric 4)
6.	4586/7634	4	Salt, Cistercian-type ware (fabric 4)
7.	4584/7504	6	Pedestalled cup base, purplish hard-fired (fabric 4)
8.	4615/7901	4	Pedestalled cup base, purplish hard-fired (fabric 4)
9.	4616/8106	2	Pedestalled cup base, purplish hard-fired (fabric 4)
10.	4700/7310	6	Pedestalled cup base, purplish hard-fired (fabric 4)
11.	us/7817	-	Insubstantial upright rim, purplish hard-fired (fabric 4)
12.	4586/7714	4	Globular-bodied cup; body only but with flaring rim, purplish hard-fired (fabric 4)
13.	4569/7576	7	Globular-bodied cup base, purplish hard-fired (fabric 4)
14.	4570/7594	5	Globular-bodied cup base, purplish hard-fired (fabric 4)
15.	4188/8446	7	Globular-bodied cup, upright or in-turned rim, purplish hard-fired (fabric 4)
16.	4663/8107	2	Globular-bodied cup base, purplish hard-fired (fabric 4)
17.	4584/7618	6	Slightly flaring tankard, purplish hard-fired (fabric 4)
18.	4143/8448/1	7	Slightly flaring tankard, purplish hard-fired (fabric 4)
19.	4584/7647	6	Slightly flaring tankard, purplish hard-fired (fabric 4)

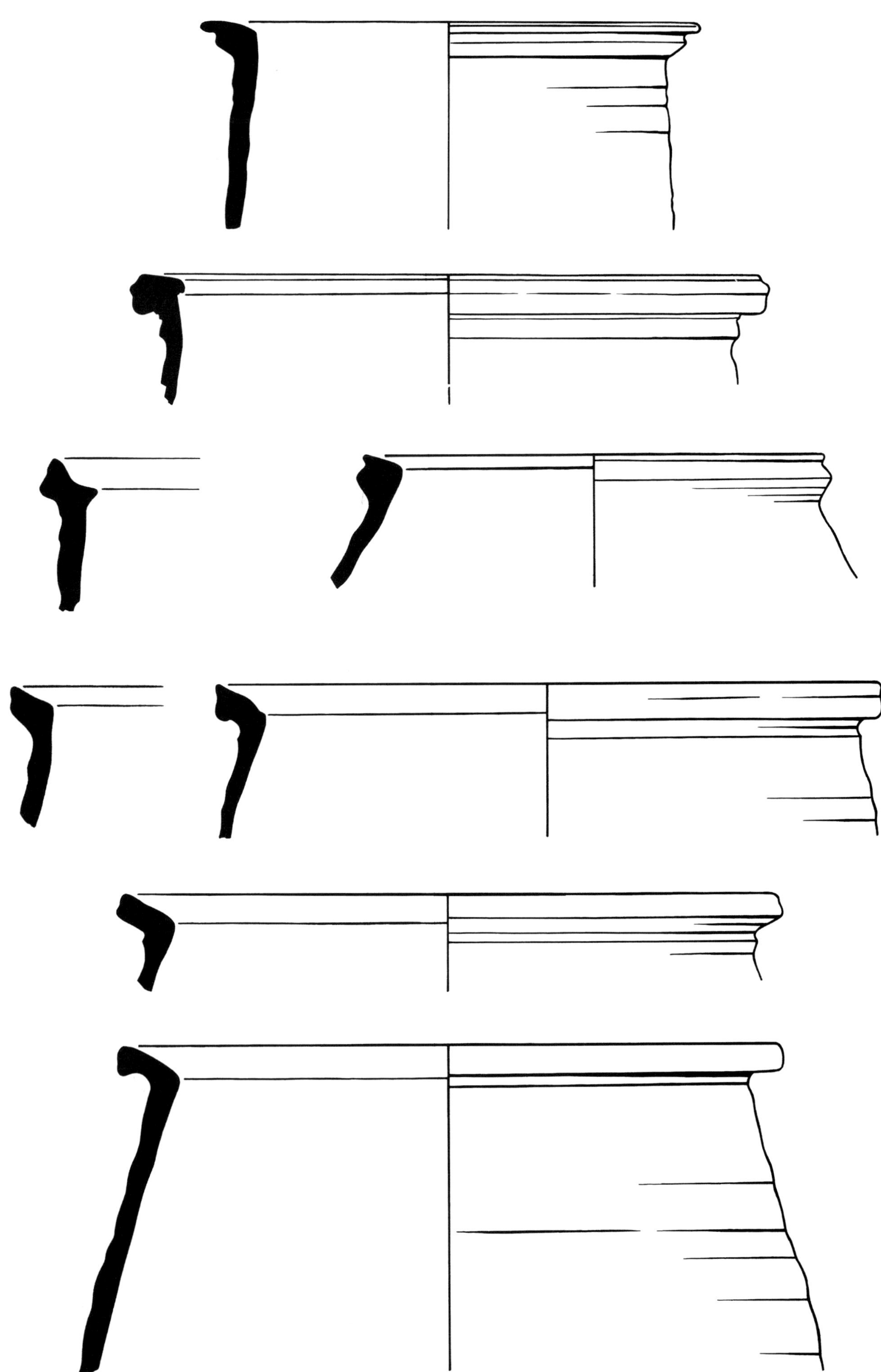

Figure 56: Pottery (scale 1:2)

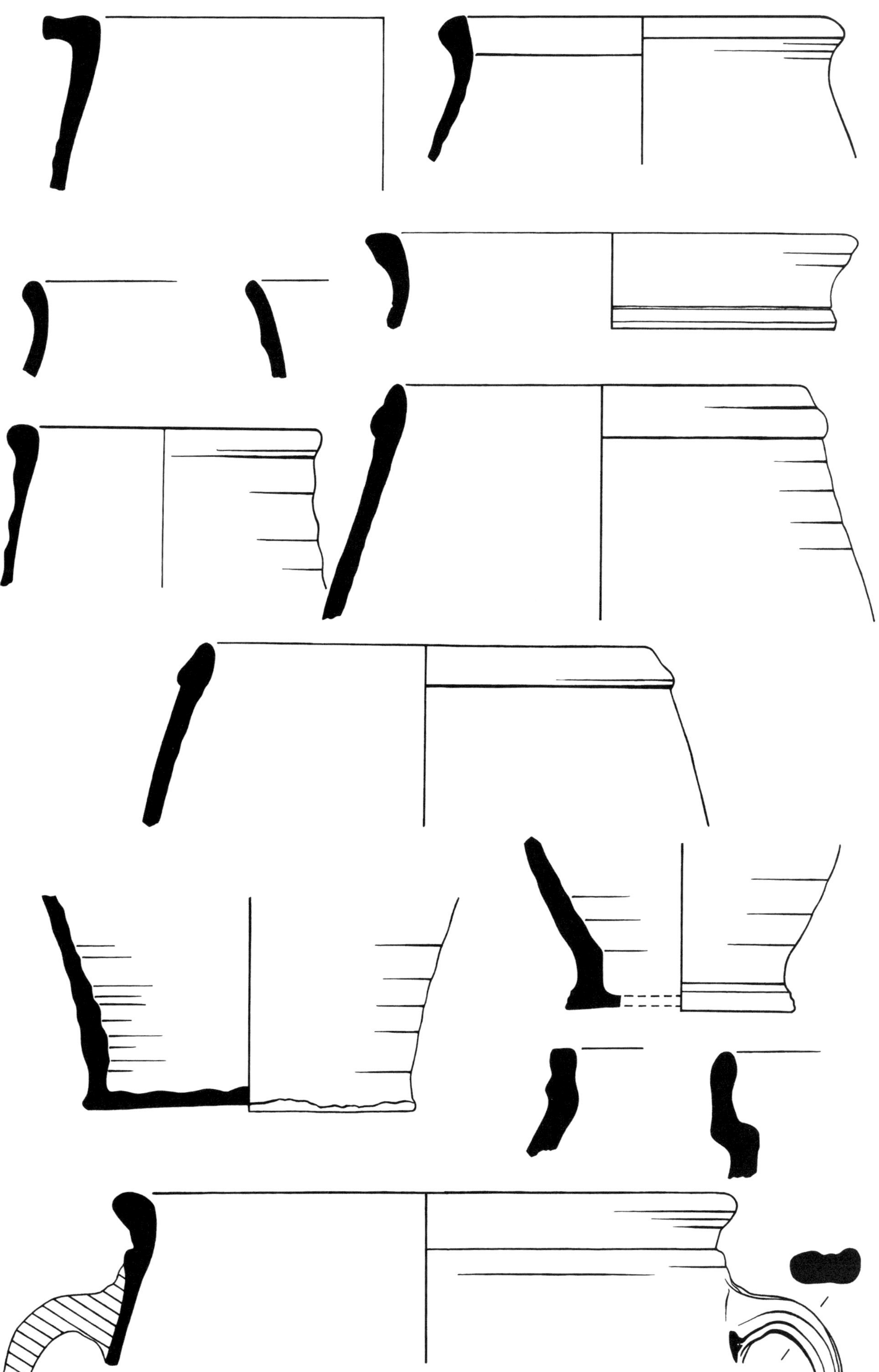

Figure 57: Pottery (scale 1:2)

117

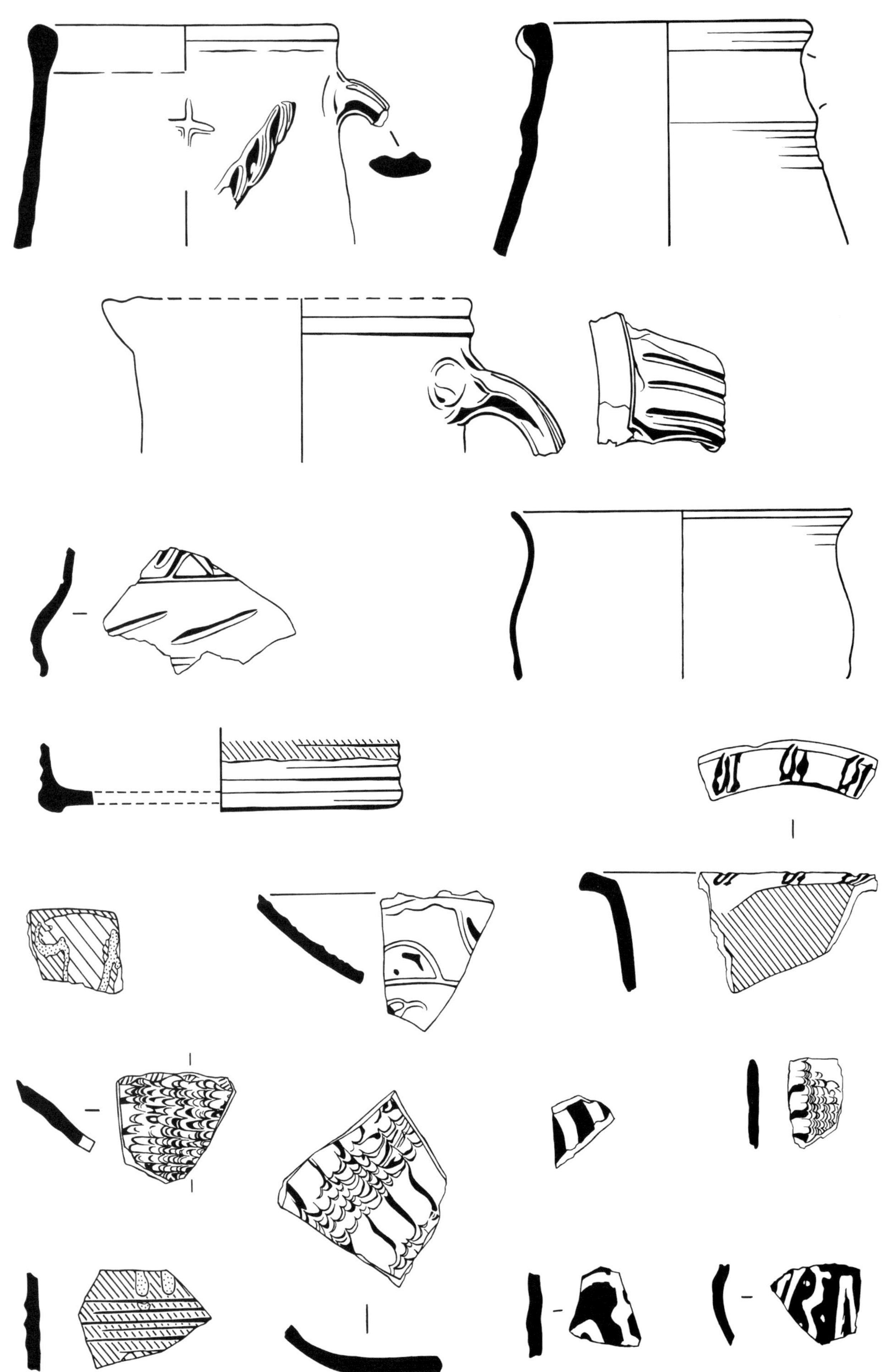

Figure 58: Pottery (scale 1:2)

118

	Context	Phase	Description
20.	4289/7250/1	7	Insubstantial out-turned rim, purplish hard-fired (fabric 4)
21.	4584/762/1	6	Tankard, base only, purplish hard-fired (fabric 4)
22.	4143/7084	7	Tankard, base only, purplish hard-fired (fabric 4)
23.	4721/8363	7	Tankard, base only, purplish hard-fired (fabric 4)
24.	4255/7911	6	Cup with flaring rim (fabric 4)
25.	4720/8384	4	Cup with almost upright rim (fabric 4)
26.	4323/8116/2	6	Cup with slightly flaring rim (fabric 4)
27.	4328/8315/2	6	Cup with slightly flaring rim (fabric 4)
28.	4323/8134/1	6	Cup with slightly out-turned rim (fabric 4/5)
29.	4584/7700	6	Slightly out-turned rim (fabric 4/5)
30.	4475/7444	5	Down-turned or hooked rim (fabric 4/5)
31.	4328/8315/1	6	Down-turned or hooked rim (fabric 4/5)
32.	4324/7277	6	Slightly flaring rim (fabric 4/5)
33.	4260/7807/1	6	Deep bowl rim (fabric 4/5)
34	4584/7625	6	Blackware dish (fabric 4/5)
35	4584/7612/1	6	Blackware large bowl or pancheon rim (fabric 5)
36	4146/7133	7	Blackware large dish rim (fabric 5)
37.	4736/8387	5	Blackware large dish or storage vessel rim (fabric 5)
38.	4558/7656/4	6	Blackware dish rim (fabric 5)
39.	4558/7656/1	6	Blackware dish rim (fabric 5)
40.	4143/7112	7	Blackware storage vessel rim (fabric 4/5)
41.	4122/7673	7	Blackware storage vessel rim (fabric 4/5)
42.	4142/8105	7	Blackware storage vessel rim (fabric 4/5)
43.	4700/7322	6	Blackware storage vessel rim (fabric 4/5)
44.	4119/7400	7	Blackware storage vessel rim (fabric 4/5)
45.	4119/7025	7	Blackware storage vessel rim (fabric 4/5)
46.	4710/8457	1	Blackware storage vessel rim (fabric 4/5)
47.	4323/8116/3	6	Blackware storage vessel rim (fabric 4/5)
48.	4584/7615	6	Blackware storage vessel rim (fabric 4/5)
49.	4584/7625/1	6	Blackware storage vessel rim (fabric 4/5)
50.	4143/7082	7	Blackware storage vessel rim (fabric 4/5)
51.	4142/8015/2	7	Blackware storage vessel rim (fabric 4/5)
52.	4743/8390	5	Blackware storage vessel rim (fabric 4/5)
53.	4558/7656/2	6	Blackware storage vessel rim (fabric 4/5)
54.	4700/7308	6	Blackware storage vessel rim (fabric 4/5)
55.	4584/7641	6	Blackware storage vessel rim (fabric 4/5)
56.	4143/7110	7	Blackware storage vessel rim (fabric 4/5)
57.	4119/7031	7	Blackware storage vessel rim (fabric 4/5)
58.	4119/7022	7	Blackware storage vessel rim (fabric 4/5)
59.	4584/7616/2	6	Blackware storage vessel base (fabric 4/5)
60.	4118/8327	7	Blackware storage vessel base (fabric 4/5)
6.1	4472/7736	5	Blackware rim (fabric 4/5)
62.	4583/7637	5	Blackware rim, seated for lid (fabric 4/5)
63.	4143/7094	7	Blackware two-handled storage vessel rim (fabric 4/5) 64.

Context	Phase	Description
64. 4751/8440/1	5	Blackware jug with applied decoration (fabric 4/5)
65. 4323/8116/1	6	Blackware jug with simple pinched rim (fabric 4/5)
66. 4289/7250	7	Blackware jug, incised decoration on handle (fabric 4/5)
67. 4548/7505	4	Blackware jug? fragment, decorated (fabric 4)
68. 4289/7250/2	7	Blackware (cream body) rim (fabric 9)
69. 4700/7308	6	Blackware (cream body) tankard? base (fabric 9)
70. 4289/7917	7	Blackware (cream body) rim with trailed slip decoration (fabric 9)
71. 4289/8129	7	Slip decorated plate (fabric 6)
72. 4585/7779	6	Impressed and slip decorated plate rim (fabric 6)
73. 4670/8301	6	Slip decorated plate rim (fabric 6)
74. us/8025	-	Slip decorated base fragment (fabric 6)
75. 4472/7730	5	Metropolitan ware? fragment (included within fabric 6)
76. 4180/7142	7	Slip decorated, upright rim of cup (fabric 6)
77. 4289/7294	7	Slip decorated fragment (fabric 6)
78. us/7816	-	Slip decorated fragment (fabric 6)
79. 4585/7661	6	Slip decorated fragment (fabric 6)
80. 4746 and 4747/8424	4	Yellow ware bowl (fabric 7)
81. 4584/7622/2	6	Yellow ware bowl (fabric 7)
82. 4700//7320	6	Yellow ware bowl (fabric 7)
83. 4698/7303	6	Yellow ware deep bowl (fabric 7)
84. 4119/7032	7	Yellow ware jar? (fabric 7)
85. 4670/8300	6	Yellow ware base of storage vessel? (fabric 7)
86. 4558/7658	6	Stoneware decorated tankard? fragment (fabric 8)
87. 4221/7937	6	Stoneware decorated handle fragment (fabric 8)
88. 4558/7656/3	6	Stoneware decorated fragment (fabric 8)
89. 4475/7556	5	Stoneware, two handled cup? (fabric 8)
90. 4700/7330	6	Manganese ware dish (fabric 10)
91. 4190/7997	7	Manganese ware dish (fabric 10)
92. 4180/7139	7	Manganese ware dish (fabric 10)
93. 4323/8134/3	6	Manganese ware upright rim (fabric 10)
94. 4323/8134/2	6	Manganese ware tankard base (fabric 10)
95. 4289/7968	7	Manganese ware storage vessel rim (fabric 10)
96. 4289/7263	7	Manganese ware storage vessel rim (fabric 10)
97. 4584/7225/2	6	Manganese ware rim (fabric 10)
98. 4119/8187	7	White stoneware tankard base (fabric 11)
99. 4570/7593	5	Tin-glaze plate rim (fabric 19)
100. 4472/7781	5	Tin-glaze plate rim (fabric 19)
101. (u/s) 4697/7439	-	Tin-glaze plate rim (fabric 19)
102. 4584/7688	6	Tin-glaze handle (fabric 19)
103. 4332/7883	7	Tin-glaze bowl, possibly Liverpool in origin (fabric 19)
104. 4166/8071	6	Chamber pot, blue painted design (fabric not determined)

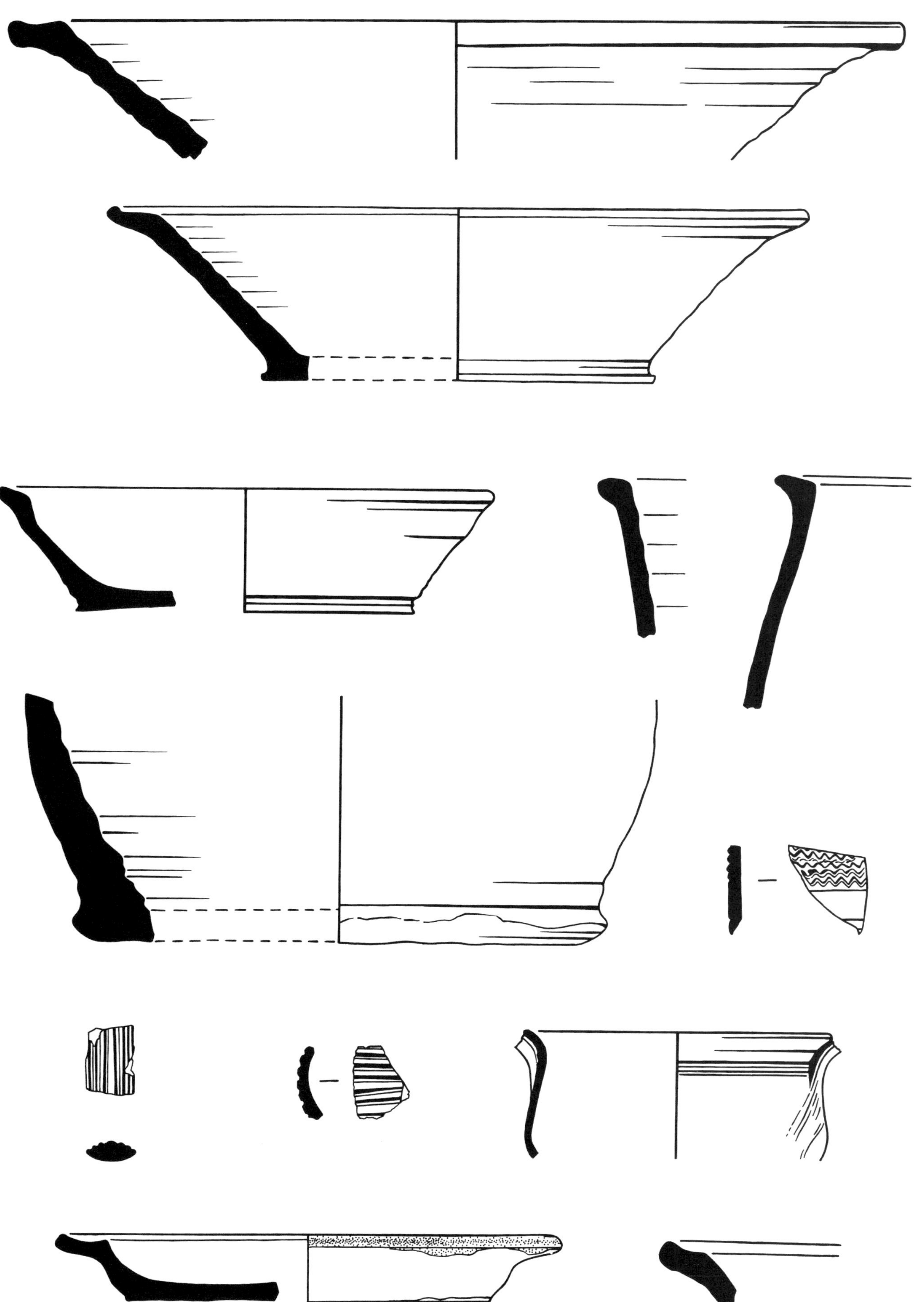

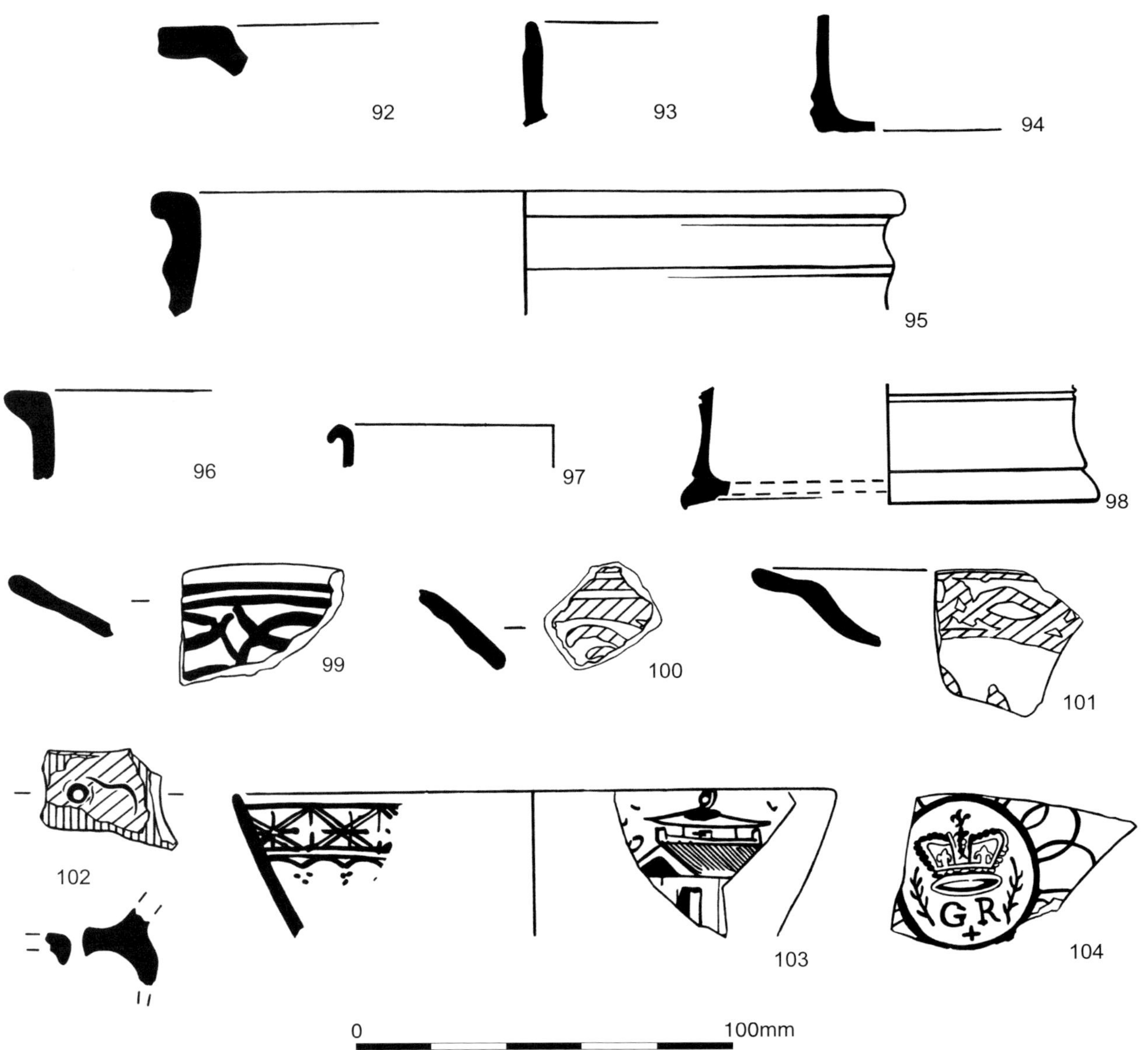

Figure 60: Pottery (scale 1:2)

Clay Tobacco Pipes

Caron Newman

In total, 123 clay tobacco pipe fragments were recovered from the excavation. Of these, one was a decorated stem, one a mouthpiece, six were heel fragments, and there were 12 complete or partial bowls, making a total of 20 identifiable fragments.

The mouthpiece (4328/8314) comprises two adjoining pieces and has a partial lead-glaze at the tip, whilst the stem fragment (4221/7939) has part of a relief decoration around the circumference. The design is unclear but may include a fleur-de-lis pattern.

Of the six heel fragments, three are of unknown type (4670/8302, 4221/7939, 4250/7991) and one is an oval heel (4122/7048), probably dated to *c* 1700-40 (Oswald 1975, fig 30). The final two are unmarked spurs, the first of which is a narrow, straight spur, and dates to *c* 1810-40 (*op cit*, fig 40). The second (4227/7566) is a truncated spur, which has a fragment of moulded ribbed decoration surviving at the very base of the bowl. This style belongs to the nineteenth century, and is similar to other moulded pipes from Manchester (Ayto 1979, 26).

Four of the bowl fragments (4378/8149, 4530/7549, 4585/7752, and 4700/8373) were too small to provenance or date accurately, but are probably of the late seventeenth or eighteenth century. The remainder of the bowls, eight in all, range in date from *c* 1600 to

Context	Phase	Marks	Description	Date	Reference
4584/7712	6	None	Small bulbous bowl with pedestal sub-circular heel, rouletted rim	1600-40	Oswald 1975, 37
4122/7046	7	1B	Short, small bulbous bowl with rouletted rim and small round heel, with stamp in relief on base of heel. Maker unknown, but there are documented London makers of that period	1630-50	Rutter and Davey 1980, 58-9
4670/8302	6	None	Small slightly bulbous bowl in a fine fabric, with small oval heel	1640-60	Rutter and Davey 1980, 61
4518/7668	6	None	Straight-sided bowl with short straight spur	1640-80	Rutter and Davey 1980, 65
4122/7041	7	None	Straight-sided bowl in fine fabric with short straight spur	1690-1710	Oswald 1975, fig 40
4627/7749	5	None	Straight-sided bowl in fine micaceous fabric with short straight spur	1690-1710	Oswald 1975, fig 40
4743/8391	5	None	Long bowl with curved front face and a slightly forward-projecting spur	1720-*c*1740	Rutter and Davey 1980, 88
4122/7045	7	None	Bowl fragment decorated with moulded, ribbed design	1800-1900	Ayto 1979, 12

Table 1: Dated clay pipe bowl fragments

the nineteenth century. Details are given in Table 1 above.

Conclusion

There are too few clay tobacco pipes from the excavated material to make any conclusions about their sources; indeed, the total is remarkably small. The bowl types are generally similar to examples from Chester (Rutter and Davey 1980), which is unsurprising given the site's location near to that production centre. Other sources would have been Manchester and Liverpool. However, only one pipe has a maker's mark, IB, and although local makers with those initials are known, none are of the same period as the bowl type.

Other Ceramic Objects

A small collection of ceramic objects was recovered in addition to the large assemblage of pottery vessels. Two were black-glazed redware door knobs from 4242 (Phase 7) and 4166 (Phase 7). Two small deliberately-made cubes of stoneware were also recovered, one white (4289, Phase 7), the other glazed dark green (4146, Phase 7). No obvious function can be assigned to these. The base of a glazed but unpainted porcelain statuette was recovered from 4248 (Phase 6), but it appeared to be of no great antiquity, and would accord with the mid eighteenth to nineteenth century date of Phase 6.

Coins

Six coins of nineteenth and twentieth century date were recovered, as well as three other discs, at least two of which appeared to be tokens. A catalogue is available in the project archive.

Copper alloy

Twenty-three objects of copper alloy were recovered during the excavation, many of very recent date (these are only listed here and fuller notes will be found in the project archive). The items discussed below form no significant or diagnostic groups, and simply represent a narrow range of the kind of personal and domestic items which were likely to be lost or discarded in and around a household of reasonably elevated, but not high, status.

Seven buttons were recovered; of these, four (4092/ 8296, 4122/8254, 4328/8150, 4334/7325) were modern in date. The remaining three illustrate changing fashions and manufacturing techniques over an extended period. The first (*Catalogue 1*, Fig 61.1) is a bun-shaped, probably solid-cast, button, a type known in London from the late thirteenth century (Egan and Pritchard 1991, 279) and continued more or less unchanged to at least the later seventeenth century (Noël Hume 1970, 89). The second (*Catalogue 2*) is a small composite button which derived from the same context (4334, farmhouse Room G1, Phase 5). Although its original appearance is not clear, it is suggested that it might have held a cut-steel insert, a form which became increasingly popular in the mid eighteenth century (White 1977, 68). Whilst neither button can be dated with precision, the context also produced pottery with a manganese-speckled glaze, which was in vogue from the late seventeenth to the mid eighteenth century. Button *3* (Fig 61.3) is a long-lived post-medieval type.

The three buckles again reflect a relatively long time-span. Object *4* (Fig 61.4) is of a common form, and this particular example is rather crudely made, a thin casting only cursorily tidied by filing. Parallels are numerous, for example at Beeston Castle (Ellis 1993, fig 100.12), and Norwich (Margeson 1993, fig 16.172), and two relatively closely-dated examples from Basing House (Moorhouse 1971, fig 25.169-70) point to a seventeenth century date. Object *5* (Fig 61.5) is a simple, light-weight buckle of common form, again closely paralleled at Beeston Castle (*op cit*, fig 100.6). Object *6* (Fig 61.6), a shoe buckle, is later in date, such large rectangular-framed buckles being in vogue from the 1760s (Davis 1997, 42 and fig 9).

The function of Object *7* is not clear (Fig 61.7). It comprised a carefully made loop, tightly wound with thin wire or thread, and it seems likely that it forms part of a fastening hook or, perhaps, a more complex piece of wire-wound hair or clothes' decoration. Such objects seem to be confined to the mid late sixteenth to early seventeenth centuries (Egan and Forsyth 1997), suggesting that it might be marginally residual in its context (probably late seventeenth to early eighteenth century; Phase 6).

The small thimble (Fig 61.8) is likely to be of eighteenth century or later date. It bears a strong resemblance to one from excavations at Furness Abbey (Howard-Davis 1985, find 3/27) and machine-made examples such as this are known from numerous sites. Machine-made thimbles were introduced from the Netherlands in the seventeenth century, and manufactured in this country from 1693 (Margeson 1993, 187). A single small dress pin (Fig 61.9) seems most likely to be of

seventeenth or earlier eighteenth century date. It falls into Caple's type C (Caple 1985) which was noted at St Peter's Street, Northampton (Williams 1979, 260, type H2) as predominating in late sixteenth and seventeenth century contexts.

Object *10* (Fig 61.10) cannot be identified with confidence but may be a tuning peg or similar.

Catalogue
Buttons
1)   Hemispherical button, probably solid-cast, with the shank and loop soldered in place (Fig 61.1). The top appears plain, but has a beaded line around the outer edge. The button is in poor condition and incomplete, with the loop missing.
Diam: 11 mm; Ht: 3-4 mmOAF95, 4334/7327,
Phase 5, late seventeenth-early eighteenth century?

2)   Flat-topped composite button, the top (now badly corroded) apparently of iron, and the back comprises a thin cover of sheet copper alloy, which barely laps over the outer edge of the top (not illus). The wire shank passes through the back and was presumably held in place by the front insert. The original appearance of this button is not now clear, but it may originally have held a cut steel insert, or may have been cloth-covered, although presumably an iron backing would have soon discoloured any fabric stretched over it. The button is in poor condition, complete but the shank distorted.
Diam: 11.5 mm; Ht: 3 mm
OAF95, 4334/7326, Phase 5, late seventeenth-early eighteenth century?

3)   Flat round button, top and shank cast as one (Fig 61.3). The top is undecorated; fair condition, and complete.
Diam 14 mm; Ht: 6 mm
OAF95, 4166/8285, Phase 7, not closely dated

Buckles
4)   Double-oval buckle frame, slightly asymmetrical (Fig 61.4). Flat cast. Fair condition and complete, except for the pin.
L: 48 mm; W: 25 mm; Th: 1.5 mm
OAF95, 4488/7473, Phase 5, ?seventeenth century

5)   Sub-rectangular buckle frame with extremely insubstantial central bar (now missing but probably iron) (Fig 61.5). A single groove runs around the outside of the buckle. Good condition but very incomplete, only one side surviving.
L: 36 mm; W: 7 mm; Th: 4 mm
OAF95, 4122/8144, Phase 7, not closely dated

6)   Rectangular shoe-buckle frame, decorated by a symmetrical pattern of rectangular perforations (Fig 61.6). The surface is not greyish in colour, suggesting that it was originally tinned. Fair condition, incomplete.
L: 70 mm; W: 54 mm; Th: 3 mm

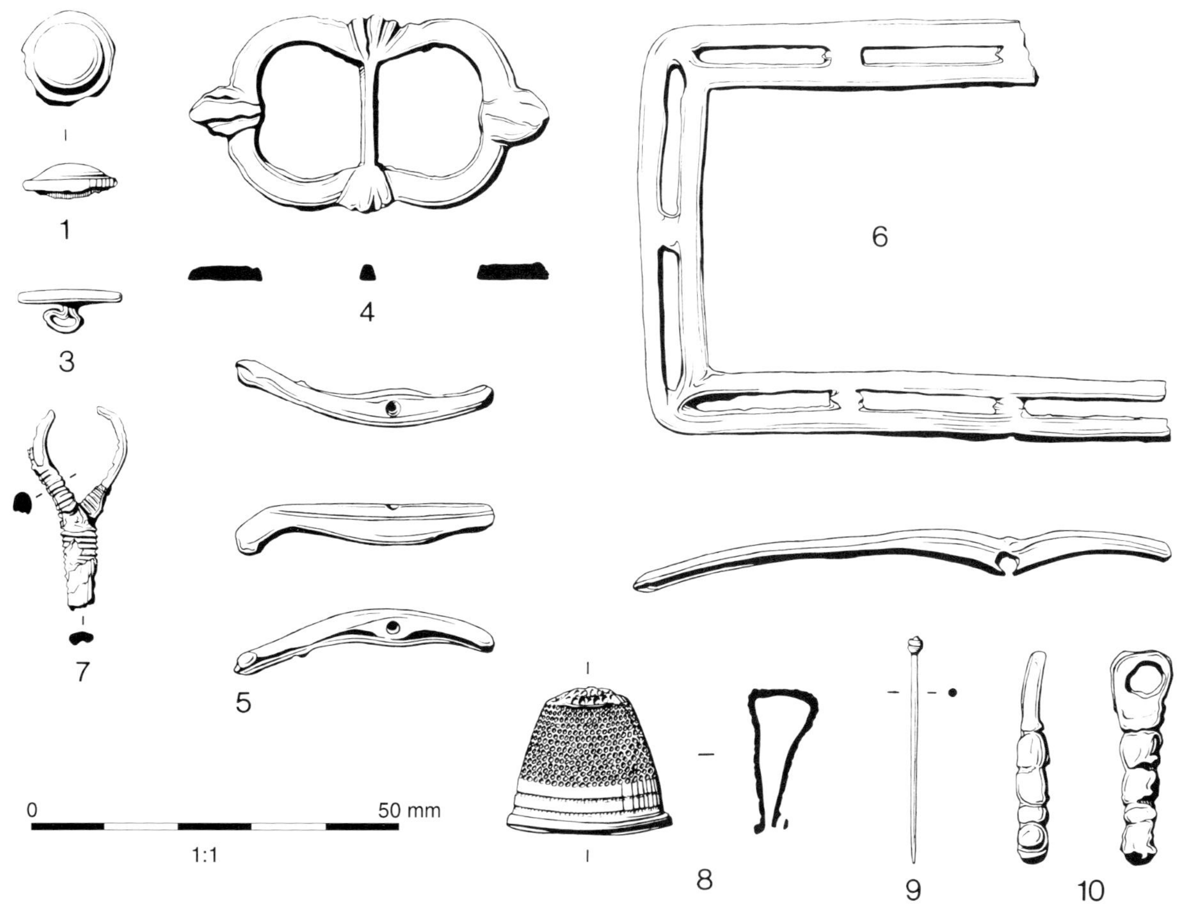

Figure 61: Copper alloy (scale 1:1)

OAF95, 4425/7462, Phase 7, later eighteenth century

Other

7)   Small loop of thick copper alloy wire, tightly bound by thin wire or mineral-replaced thread (Fig 61.7).
L: 27 mm; W: 13 mm; Th: 4 mm
OAF95, 4584/7628, Phase 6, late medieval?

8)   Thimble of relatively small size, stamped from a single piece of sheet with the rim rolled back (Fig 61.8). Although distorted, it is likely to have been tall and more-or-less straight-sided. There is a plain band *c* 5 mm wide above the rim, decorated by two widely-spaced lines of tiny punched dots; the remainder of the thimble has 14 lines of small punched depressions in quincunx covering the sides, and six concentric lines of larger depressions covering the slightly domed top. Good condition and complete, but crushed.
L: 20 mm; W: 22 mm
OAF95, 4061/7206, Phase 7, eighteenth century or later

9)   Pin (now in two) (Fig 61.9). Short shank with head formed from a single turn of wire, crimped into a sphere. Fair condition, complete.

L: 30 mm, Diam shaft: 0.5 mm; Diam head: 1 mm
OAF95, 4190/8034, Phase 7, possibly seventeenth century

10)   Unknown object, possibly a tuning peg (Fig 61.10). A short tapering peg, with a flattened rectangular sectioned head, pierced with a round hole at the widest end; three beads of diminishing size divide the shaft, and it ends with a short cylindrical extension. Fair condition, ?complete.
L: 28 mm; W head: 8 mm; Min diam: 3.5 mm
OAF95, 4711/8372, Phase 6.

Lead Objects

Apart from a lead kame (discussed below in conjunction with the window glass, Fig 63), only three fragments of lead were recovered. Two were round-headed nails, both from the modern access road across the platform (4146, Phase 7); the third, a small curling twist, possibly cut from sheet, derives from a levelling deposit laid below a cobble surface in front of the farmhouse (4584, Phase 6). The objects are fully described in the project archive.

Ironwork

The only items of interest recovered from the site were the iron glazing bars which remained attached to fragmentary leaded lights and were recovered from a mixed modern context recorded within the moat, and a small knife of uncertain date. This scale-tang blade was very worn indeed, effectively nothing more than a fine tapering point, presumably the result of frequent sharpening. Plain wooden scales forming the hand grip suggest that the knife was not of any particular value, and the integral bolster suggests it to be of post-medieval origin. Three iron rivets secured the wooden scales to the blade tang.

Other ironwork from the site (described in the project archive) comprised obviously very modern artefacts, or nails. Galvanised, wire-drawn and sheet-cut nails are also likely to be modern in provenance. Hand-forged nails may be earlier in date, but cannot be dated with any precision, as their form is largely dictated by the method of manufacture, which has effectively remained unchanged since the Roman period.

Catalogue
1)   Small-scale tang knife with narrow iron blade and wooden hand grip secured by three iron rivets (not illus). The individual scales of the hand grip have bevelled edges, giving the grip an overall oval section.
L: *c* 195 mm; Max width blade: *c* 20 mm; Min width blade: *c* 4 mm
OAF95, 4520/7546, Phase 5

White Metal Objects

A few demonstrably modern objects in a range of white base metals, including aluminium, were recovered from late contexts. The objects are described within the project archive, and have been discarded.

Vessel Glass

Despite the collection of a relatively large assemblage of glass from the site (some 171 fragments and complete vessels), only 42 fragments are relevant to its earlier history. The remainder is late in date, produced in the last quarter of the nineteenth and the twentieth centuries; this material is described in project archive and has been discarded.

Five fragments (representing four vessels) are from vessels in natural green 'forest glass' dating to the late sixteenth or (more likely) seventeenth century. This may well have been produced locally, and several parallels for the beaker rims can be seen in material from the glass-house at Haughton Green, Denton (Hurst Vose 1994). Both of the rims (Figs 62.1, 62.2) are likely to be from typical tall-sided beakers with a slightly in-curved rim which appear in the second half of the sixteenth century (Charleston 1993, 171, fig 116, 13-15, 17), whilst the base (4) is probably that of a cylindrical 'case bottle', a form associated with the late seventeenth century. The small out-turned rim (Fig 62.5) presumably comes from a similar vessel.

A small body fragment of yellowish-colourless glass (6) may be English-made *crystallo* glass, made in imitation of Venetian glass in the sixteenth century, and perhaps residual in its context. A base (Fig 62.7) and wine glass fragment (Fig 62.8) both appear to be in fine quality lead glass, patented by George Ravenscroft around 1675 (Charleston 1975, 214). Although little of the vessel remains, the base probably derives from a small ribbed vessel and the teared knop is almost certainly from a wineglass of late seventeenth or early eighteenth century date (Crompton 1982, 91).

Purple glass was certainly made in England before the end of the seventeenth century (Charleston 1993, 171) and 'black' glass was produced relatively locally at Haughton Green (Hurst Vose 1994); thus the heavy and abraded base in dark manganese purple glass (Fig 62.10) may be local.

Finally, there is a small group of fragments from dark olive green wine bottles which, where recognisable, appear to be of late eighteenth century form. It is perhaps surprising that this normally ubiquitous type is not better represented on site, possibly reflecting local conditions or habits. The base of a thick and heavy mould-blown bottle in dark olive green glass is presumably contemporary with the majority of the wine bottles, and can thus also be dated to the mid to late eighteenth century.

Catalogue
Green 'forest glass'
1)   Small fragment of a simple upright, fire-rounded rim (Fig 62.1). Also two small body fragments. Fair condition, surfaces dulled, Beaker?
Th: 1-2.5 mm
OAF95, 4472/7728, Phase 5, seventeenth century?

2)   Small fragment of a simple upright rim, turned in and slightly fire-rounded (Fig 62.2). Fair condition, surfaces dulled. Beaker?
Th: 1-2 mm
OAF95, 4584/7686, Phase 6, seventeenth century?

3)   Part of a small diameter pushed-in base (Fig 62.3). Fair condition, surfaces dulled and abraded.
Diam: *c* 68 mm; Th: 1.4 mm
OAF95, 4584/7655, Phase 6, seventeenth century?

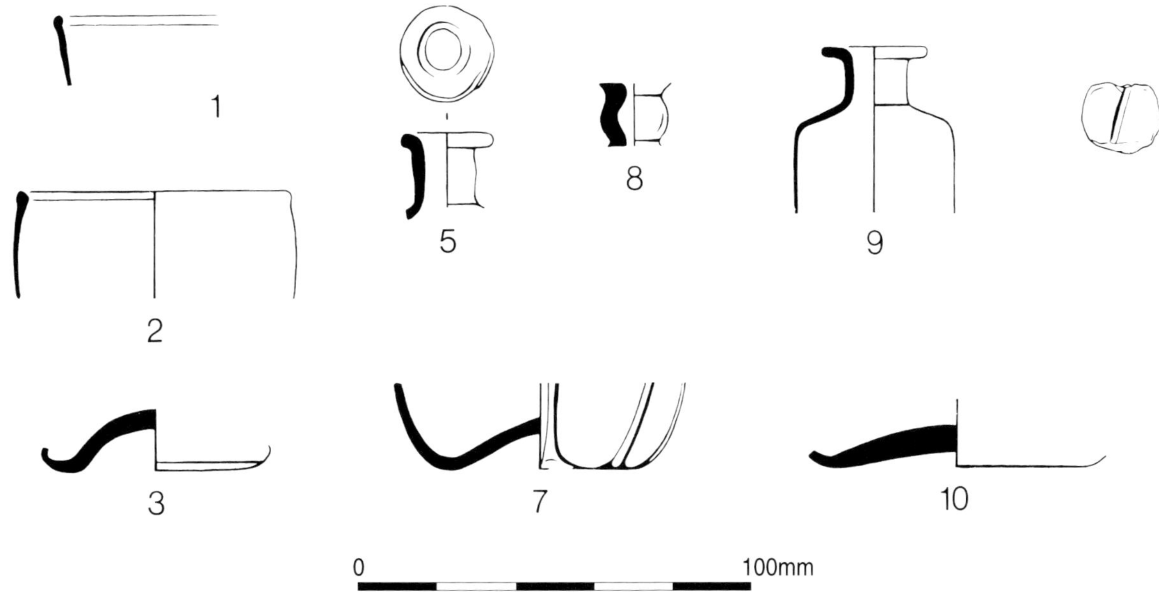

Figure 62: Vessel glass (scale 1:2)

4)   One small base or body fragment (not illus). Fair condition, surface dulled and abraded.
Th: 1.5 mm
OAF95, 4539/7554, Phase 6, seventeenth century?

5)   Neck and out-turned rim of a small ?pharmaceutical bottle (Fig 62.5).
Diam rim: 21 mm, Th: *c* 2 mm; Ht: 19 mm
OAF95, 4677/8267, Phase 6, seventeenth century?

Colourless glass
6)   One small yellowish-colourless body fragment (not illus). Fair condition, slight iridescence. Possibly *crystallo*.
Th: *c* 8 mm
OAF95, 4255/7913, Phase 5, seventeenth century or earlier?

7)   Part of a small diameter pushed-in base in good quality ?leaded glass (Fig 62.7). Pontil clearly visible, as is the beginning of 'wrythen' decoration. Excellent condition.
Diam: *c* 70 mm; Th: 1-4 mm
OAF95, 4289/7248, Phase 7, seventeenth century?

8)   Hollow knop from wine glass in good-quality ?leaded glass (Fig 62.8). Good condition.
Diam: 18 mm
OAF95, 4602/7651, Unstratified, late seventeenth century or early eighteenth century

9)   Neck and turned-out rim of small ?mould-blown cylindrical bottle (Fig 62.9). Fair condition.
Diam rim: 21.5 mm; Diam body: 41 mm; Th: 1-1.5 mm; Ht: 40 mm
OAF95, 4696;4050/8456, Phase 4, late seventeenth century or early eighteenth century

Other coloured glass
10)   Two joining fragments of a slightly pushed-in base, blown vessel (Fig 62.10). Very dark manganese purple. Fair condition, dulled and abraded.
Diam: *c* 80 mm; Th: 2-5 mm
OAF95, 4700/7295, Phase 6, early seventeenth century?

11)   Base of rectangular or hexagonal bottle. Mould-blown vessel (not illus). Dark olive green. Good condition, slight abrasion.
Th: 6-18 mm
OAF95, 4289/7966, Phase 7, late eighteenth century?

Dark olive green wine bottles
12)   Body fragment (not illus). Fair condition.
Th: 6 mm
OAF95, 4585/7781, Phase 6, late seventeenth century or early eighteenth century?

13)   Four fragments base and kick (not illus). Fair condition, slight surface dulling.
Th: 4-7 mm
OAF95, 4177/7127, Phase 6, late eighteenth century

14)   Two non-joining fragments of thick, squat base with relatively low kick (not illus). Good condition, slightly abraded.
Th: *c* 7 mm
OAF95, 4014/8211, Phase 7, late eighteenth century

15)   Three joining fragments of thick, narrow-diameter base, with five non-joining body fragments (not illus). Fair condition, abraded.
Th: 4-7 mm
OAF95, 4166/8449, Phase 7, late eighteenth century

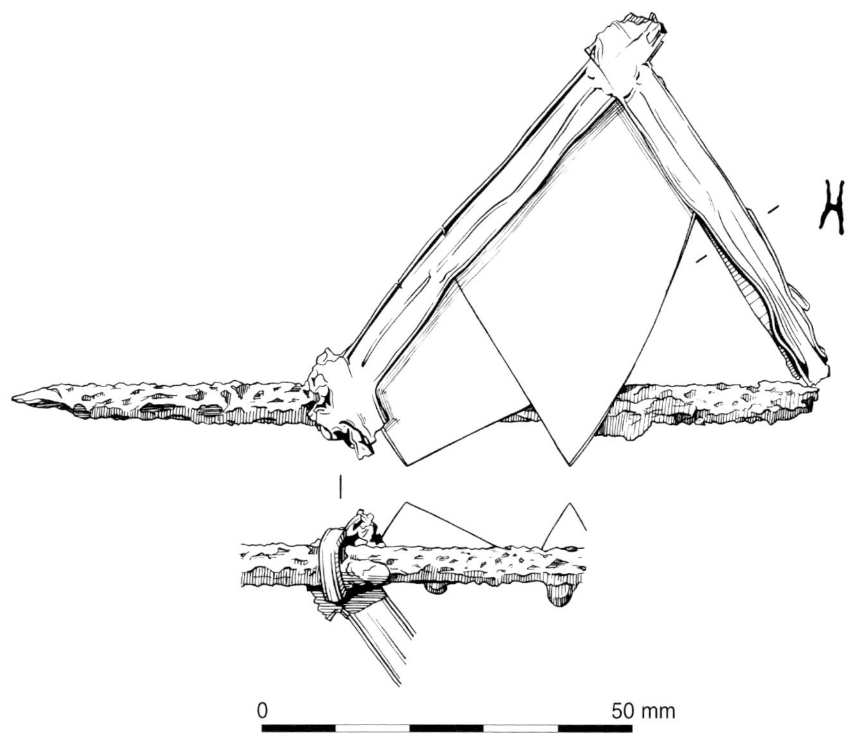

Figure 63: Window glass (scale 1:1)

Window Glass

Like the vessel glass, the majority of the window glass recovered from the site was modern, mainly colourless sheet glass; these fragments have been described in the project archive and discarded. However, there were also 71 fragments of thin greenish glass, often with grozed edges, which formed parts of diamond-shaped quarries from leaded window lights. The glass for these quarries had, for the most part, been diamond-cut, although irregular breaks were tidied by grozing. Many of the quarries showed differential preservation caused by the lead kame into which they were set, allowing the depth of the kame to be certain at around 5 mm. In no instance was a full quarry preserved and thus the dimensions cannot be ascertained, although they seem unlikely to have been more than *c* 70 mm long. In some instances, quarries were found still within twisted fragments of the discarded leaded window lights, for example within moat fill 4117 (Phase 7; Fig 63). Interestingly, both seventeenth / eighteenth century and much more modern quarries were set in ?nineteenth century milled lead kame, indicating frequent renewal and repair before the lights were removed and dumped in the moat at some time in the 1960s.

Other Glass Objects

Several glass stoppers were recovered, some cast and ground, some tooled from molten gathers of colourless glass. All are of recent date and are described in the project archive. Four glass 'marbles' were also recovered, again modern. There was also a light bulb.

Ten beads were recovered; most are likely to be of recent date, and some (*eg* 4061 / 8089, Phase 7) had probably been imported. Bead 4334 / 7312 is from a context attributed to Phase 5, but cannot be closely dated.

Leather

Only five fragments of leather were recovered, all of which were conserved. Four of the fragments derive from shoes; of these one (Fragment 4) is probably nineteenth or twentieth century in date and may be part of the quarters of a laced ankle boot of common type.

Although of slightly differing styles, the two almost complete soles are of later medieval type, both coming from shoes of turnsole construction, a method of production favoured throughout the medieval period (Grew and de Neergaard 1988, 46-8). Fragment *1* (Fig 64.1) is the sole of a relatively restrained poulaine-type shoe with an exaggerated pointed toe. The sole shows clear evidence for a clumsy repair at the narrow waist, and again the small fragment of upper that survives suggests that a sole patch was sewn to the upper rather than to the sole itself. The long narrow toe was stuffed with moss in order to retain its shape. This form of shoe was in fashion in the later part of the fourteenth century and survived into the earlier part of the fifteenth before dying out. The other (Fragment *3*, Fig 64.3) is similar, although not with a particularly exaggerated toe. In this case part of the upper survives, but in poor condition. The vamp was apparently undecorated.

Fragment *2* (Fig 64.2) appears to be a repair patch of the kind that might have been used on Fragment *1*, although the two cannot be firmly linked. The uneven and clumsy stitching suggests repair by an inexperienced hand, with the repair covering the worn tread of the shoe and running-stitched to the upper just above its join with the sole.

A small rectangular fragment (Fragment *5*, Fig 64.5) comprised three separate elements neatly sewn in a complex seam. They appear to have been cut from a much larger composite object but there is no indication of its original appearance.

Catalogue

1)   A complete left shoe sole, with associated small fragment of upper (Fig 64.1). The sole indicates a well-made poulaine-type shoe of turnsole construction, with neat and even stitching all round. Slight irregularities towards the point might indicate that because of the narrowness of the shoe at the front the poulaine was joined after the shoe had been turned right way out. A small amount of moss surviving in the toe indicates that, as was usual, it was stuffed. The small fragment of upper may be a welt, but the appearance of the stitching makes this unlikely; rather, it represents the original upper, cut or torn away. Apart from the expected row of stitching by which it was joined to the sole, there is a second row of widely spaced tunnel stitching, with thread impressions suggesting a long running stitch, presumably indicating the unskilled attachment of a repair. Large and irregular stitches across the waist of the shoe also indicate repair. The sole was worn, but not severely on the outside, and a clear impression of the wearer's big toe was left on the inside, indicating a foot constricted by the narrow form of the shoe.
L: 304 mm; W: 7.8 mm, Th: 2 mm
OAF95, 4576/7597, Phase 1b, late fourteenth - early fifteenth century

2)   Part of a repair piece for a worn sole (Fig 64.2). The surviving original edges seems to suggest a roughly cut and irregular-shaped patch to the sole of a pointed-toed shoe, as the stitches appear to converge at one end. The large and irregular stitches are similar to, but do not match, those seen around the edge of Shoe *1*, suggesting that this repair piece may have been attached to a similar or at least broadly contemporary sole. The leather is worn and torn, suggesting that the repair piece had itself worn through before it and/or the shoe were discarded.
L: *c* 122 mm; W: *c* 82 mm; Th: 2 mm
OAF95, 4602/7648, Phase 1b, late medieval?

3)   Almost complete right shoe sole with part of the upper (vamp) surviving but in very a fragile condition (Fig 64.3). The shoe is of turnsole construction, with a pointed toe, though not exaggeratedly so. Several small detached fragments of upper and a possible welt could not be reassembled. The sole appears worn, especially at the back, but does not appear to have been repaired. The upper is plain.
L: 239 mm; W: *c* 103 mm; Th sole: 2 mm; Th upper: *c* 1 mm
OAF95, 4569/7674, Phase 5, late medieval

4)   Small fragment of leather shoe upper with a row of ?brass eye-holes along one edge (not illus). The leather appears to be a double layer, with a stiffener between (probably cardboard or paper – J Jones pers comm). Thread survives in the stitch holes but cannot be identified. Probably part of a relatively modern ankle boot.
L: 62 mm; W: 19 mm; Th: 2 mm
OAF95, 4117/7756, Phase 7, modern?

5)   Three small knife cut fragments, originally joined by sewing (Fig 64.5). The three have clearly been cut from a much larger composite object. The stitches are small, evenly-spaced and neat, suggesting relatively high-quality work.
L: 36 mm; W: 34 mm: Th: 1-2 mm
OAF95, 4227/7275, Phase 7, not closely dated

Wood

Several fragments of waterlogged wood were recovered from the moat in the later stages of the excavation. Many of them were simple roundwood stakes and other large fragments of timber associated with the construction of the bridge across the moat; these suffered insect infestation during storage and all surface detail was obliterated. The wood was therefore discarded.

A few artefacts were also recovered from waterlogged deposits within the moat. None warranted conservation, but they have been maintained in stable conditions sufficient to halt further decay; line drawings are available in the project archive.

Only two of the fragments appear to represent domestic items. Although clearly damaged and

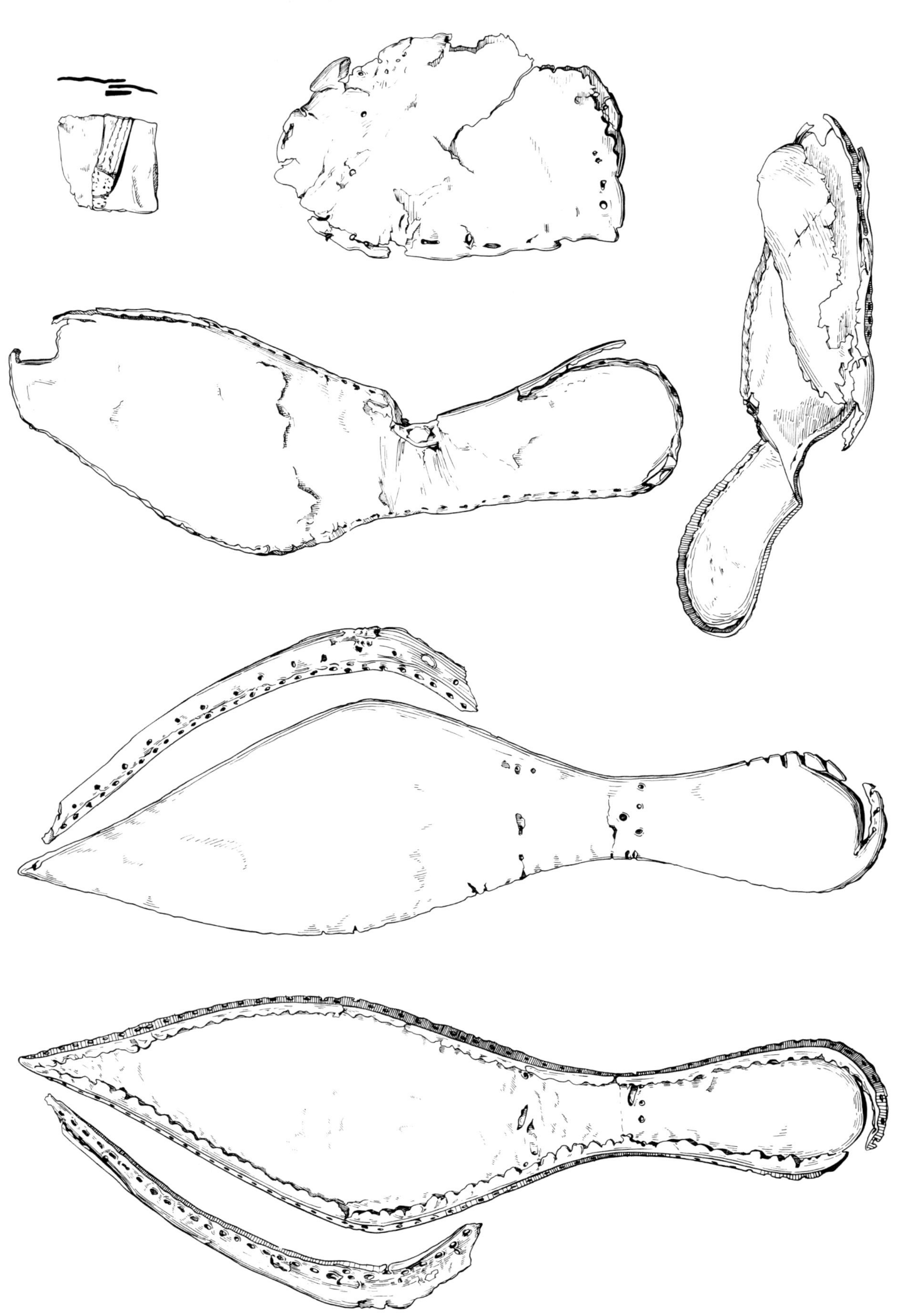

Figure 64: Leather (scale 1:2)

incomplete, Fragment *1* appears to derive from a turned bowl or dish. Object *2* seems likely to be of relatively modern date. It is a shallow turned cup of the kind used in the late nineteenth and twentieth centuries to protect carpets and floors from damage from heavy items of furniture.

The remainder of the wooden objects recovered were all connected with wood-working and carpentry. Pegs *3 - 9* are all small and carefully fashioned; these could have served several purposes, but it would seem likely that some at least derive from the construction of the pegged timber bridge across the moat. Pegs *5* and *8*, both complete, carefully fashioned slender examples, might well be unused trenails. Post *10* is too small to be part of a building or similar structure and presumably derives from a fence nearby.

Objects *11* to *13* all derive from the on-site conversion of timber. Wedge *11* bears some indication of having been used to split timber, being forced or driven into a narrow split in a timber in order to divide it along the grain. Fragment *13* is a 'notch and chop' waste offcut, typical of the primary conversion of timber, when the round trunk is trimmed to produce a box conversion. Both indicated the production of major construction timbers on site. Fragment *12* is typical of the small blocks removed in the creation of lap joints, again suggesting carpentry on site and presumably dating to one of the periods of construction or reconstruction of the main house or the timber bridge across the moat.

Catalogue (not illus)
Vessel
1)   Two small joining fragments of what appears to be a shallow turned bowl or dish. It is, however, unclear whether the rim of the vessel actually survives or the upper part of the fragment is merely abraded, mimicking a rim. Fair condition, very incomplete.
Diam vessel: +140 mm; Th: 6 mm; Ht vessel: +24 mm
OAF95, 4721/8386, Phase 5

Other domestic items
2)   Shallowly dished turned object in a distinctive dark red wood, possibly mahogany. Probably a relatively modern 'cup' of the kind intended to protect carpets from damage from furniture legs. Fair condition, complete.
Diam: 76 mm; Th: 24 mm
OAF95, 4240/7858, Phase 7

Small pegs
3)   Broken tip of a multi-facet point (possibly seven facets). The point is cut down from a large ?radial split, although the grain showing is very fine, perhaps indicating that the original timber was not of any great age. Fair condition (some decay on one surface), incomplete.
L: 98 mm; W: 18 mm; Th: 14 mm
OAF95, 4747/8407, Phase 1b

4)   Broken tip of a four-facet point. The point is cut from a tangential split, with facets cut from each of the four original sides giving a chisel-shaped end. Shallow, irregularly-placed tool marks indicate some trimming of the original split. Fair condition, incomplete.
L: 78 mm; W: 22 mm; Th: 16 mm
OAF95, 4748/8427, Phase 1b

5)   Complete peg, possibly a discarded and apparently unused trenail. The point is cut down from a tangential split and appears to have originally been cut to a fine multi-facet point and then abraded to give an approximately round section. The grain showing is very fine, perhaps indicating that the original timber was not of any great age. Fair condition (some encrustation on parts of the surface), complete.
L: 267 mm; W: 22 mm; Th: 20 mm
OAF95, 4721/8362, Phase 5

6)   Tip of a multi-facet point cut from roundwood. Fair condition, incomplete.
L: 72 mm; Diam: 24 mm
OAF95, 4721/8366/3, Phase 5

7)   Small chisel-ended peg or off-cut, cut from a tangentially split lath. Fair condition, complete.
L: 80 mm; W: 26 mm; Th: 21 mm
OAF95, 4721/8366/4, Phase 5

8)   Complete peg, possibly a discarded and apparently unused trenail. The point is cut down from a tangential split with an almost square section. The top is significantly wider than the rest of the peg, tapering rapidly to a carefully trimmed square section with bevelled corners and giving the peg a nail-like appearance. The three-facet point is slightly damaged. The wood from which the peg is made is knotty and has a slight curve to the grain. Good condition (slight damage to the tip of the point), complete.
L: 268 mm; W: 30 mm; Th: 33 mm
OAF95, 4602/8287, Unstratified

9)   Small roundwood peg. Made from an unstripped pole, one end of which has been cut neatly across and the other cut and pulled to a single-facet point. Fair condition, complete.
L: 108 mm; Diam: 23 mm
OAF95, 4751/8356, Unstratified

Post
10)   Broken fragment of a large roundwood post. No bark remains on the post and the surfaces are water-worn. Both ends are broken but it appears the post was originally cut to a multi-facet point.
L: 242 mm; Diam: *c* 67 mm
OAF95, 4721/8366/6, Phase 5

Wood-working debris
11)   Broken wedge. Originally an almost complete radial wedge, now with the heartwood broken away. The pattern of compression and damage on one of the flat surfaces suggests that it may have been used for splitting larger timbers, although there is no apparent damage from hammering to drive it into the timber. Fair condition (some decay on one edge), incomplete.

L: 127 mm; W: 61 mm; Th: 14 mm
OAF95, 4721/8366/1, Phase 5

12)   Small block of oak. There is evidence of sawing on
many of the surfaces, and on one surface the block has
clearly been levered away from the main baulk of timber,
leaving rough torn fibres. Wood-working offcut, probably
from cutting a lap-joint. Fair condition, incomplete.
L: 71 mm; W: 60 mm; Th: 11-27 mm
OAF95, 4721/8366/2, Phase 5

13)   Fragment of wood-working waste, probably from
'notch and chop' conversion of a large timber. Fair, complete
but slightly decayed.
L: 113 mm; W: 57 mm; Th: 21 mm
OAF95, 4721/8366/5, Phase 5

Other Materials

Some items in other, mainly modern, materials were
collected in the course of the excavation, in part to aid
in the dating of certain features. Items included toys,
hair slides and containers in plastic, modern synthetic
textiles, and modern organic objects such as peach
stones. Few were of further significance to the site
beyond establishing very late disturbance or
deposition. The small size and variable preservation
of the animal bone assemblage, and the very few
identifiable and measurable fragments present,
rendered this material of limited potential. All of the
material has been described briefly in the project
archive, and most has been discarded.

Oyster shell was recovered in small quantities from
4177 (Phase 6; a clay floor surface within Room G2 of the
farmhouse), 4239 (Phase 7; a layer of trample within
Room G4), and 4289 (Phase 7; a garden soil). A single
example of the common garden snail (*H aspersa*) was
also collected from 4177. Fragments of slate pencils
were recovered from contexts 4306 (Phase 7; a layer of
bedding sand within Room G4) and 4166 (Phase 7; an
external rubbish dump). A bone or ivory button of mid
to late nineteenth century date was recovered from 4190
(Phase 7; a deposit of bedding sand within Room G4), and
a bone and ivory domino piece was also recovered from
4177; the latter is probably contemporary.

Plant and Invertebrate Macrofossils

Harry Kenward, Paul Hughes, and Alan Hall

Introduction
A series of General Biological Analysis samples
('GBAs' *sensu* Dobney *et al* 1992) was submitted for an
assessment of their biological remains. This
demonstrated that further investigation of samples
taken from the moat had the potential to contribute to
the project's research objectives, although samples
taken from other parts of the site were effectively
barren. In view of these results, the Environmental
Archaeology Unit (EAU) was commissioned to carry
out detailed analysis on five samples from the moat
fills. The results of that analysis are presented here,
although a fuller version of this report, containing full
lists of species, can be found in the project archive
(Kenward *et al* 1998).

Methods
The five GBA samples were inspected in the laboratory
and a description of their lithology recorded using a
standard *pro forma*. All of the available sediment was
processed for each sample; three samples had a mass
of 5 kg and the remaining two were both of 4.3 kg. The
extraction of plant and invertebrate macrofossil
remains followed the procedures of Kenward *et al*
(1980; 1986); the sediment was sieved to 300 microns
and invertebrate remains extracted using paraffin
flotation, while the plant remains were recorded in a
series of sieved fractions (2 mm, 1 mm, 0.3 mm) from
the residue. Plant remains were recorded on a semi-
quantitative four-point scale of abundance (from 1:
one or a few individuals or fragments, or a minor
component of the sample, to 4: abundant individuals
or fragments, or a major component of the sample).
For plant material, a three-point scale was used ('few',
'some', 'many'). Material was identified using
reference collections in the EAU and standard
reference works. For recent accounts of interpretative
methods employed in the EAU for plant macrofossil
assemblages, see Hall and Kenward (1990) and
Kenward and Hall (1995).

The flots were sorted under a binocular microscope
and invertebrate remains picked out onto damp filter
paper. The flots were large and difficult to sort, and
meticulous checking was necessary. Remains were
identified using the collection at the EAU and standard
identification works. Recording was nominally at the
'scan' level of Kenward (1992), although an attempt
was made to identify all remains as far as was feasible
within project restraints.

Results
The results are presented below in stratigraphic order,
although in view of their uniformity, most of the
invertebrate material is considered together. All of
the samples produced abundant and well-preserved
plant remains ranging from fruits and seeds to bud
scales, moss and large wood fragments. For the
invertebrates the interpretation given below is based
primarily on adult beetles and bugs (other than aphids
and scale insects). All the samples produced useful
numbers of these insects, although the concentration
of remains varied considerably, from 18 per kilogram
in the subsample from 4579/7692, to 104 per kilogram

in that from 4746/8394. Preservation varied, but was generally good and sometimes quite exceptionally good - this being reflected in the identifications of very fragile insects such as the capsid bug *Heterotoma planicornis*. Sample 4746/8394 gave quite superb preservation, while the assemblage from 4579/7692 was a little poorer, but still good. Both 4576/7588 and 4747/8397 gave rather good preservation, but in the latest layer in the sequence, 4569/7581, preservation was rather poor, the fossils being brownish to orangish in colour. Only in the last did the level of preservation place substantial limits on identification of insects, although the plant remains were in a similar state to those from the remaining samples.

Phase 1b

4576/7588/T (4.3 kg; flot and washover)

The sediment was moist, pinkish mid grey brown, slightly plastic and locally sticky to crumbly (working soft and rubbing brown) sandy and clayey silt. Some of the sediment contained patches of oxidation/reduction indicated by variable amounts of orange colouration. Stones in the size ranges 2-6 mm and 6-20 mm were noted; rootlets and pieces of leather were also present.

The small washover (10% of the processed subsample by volume) was rich in degraded wood fragments, amongst which there were some apparently wood chips, natural twists of bark, and occasional twigs. Dicotyledon leaf fragments were common and several unidentifiable bud scales were also noted, together with seeds of blackberry and raspberry *(Rubus fruticosus* aggregate and *R idaeus)*, blackberry or rose prickles, plum stones *(Prunus domestica* ssp *insititia)*, crab apple *(Malus sylvestris)* endocarp, and hazel *(Corylus avellana)* nutshell. These, and the fruitstones and hazel nutshell fragments, may have been food waste, but seem rather more likely to have originated from wild scrub vegetation growing in the vicinity of the moat. Leaf fragments, prickles, and bud scales demonstrate that trees and bushes were growing very close to the moat's margin.

Other species represented by fruits and seeds included a wide range of weed taxa of open disturbed/waste or cultivated ground; fat hen *(Chenopodium album)* and red goosefoot or a relative *(C* sect *Pseudoblitum)* were recorded within this group, the latter being indicative of substrates containing organic-rich rubbish or manure. The strong representation of waste and disturbed ground species may be a consequence of the proximity of the farmyard contained within the moated area. Species indicative of taller growing wayside/rough grassland/field margin habitats (nipplewort, *Lapsana communis*; thistles, *Carduus/Cirsium*; and burdock, *Arctium* sp), were also present. These species may well represent the field layer at the margins of the scrub or hedge that fringed the moat.

Several taxa identified in the weed assemblage are characteristic of shorter grassland habitats or hedge banks at field margins (selfheal, *Prunella vulgaris*; buttercup, *Ranunculus* sect *Ranunculus*; blinks, *Montia fontana* ssp *chondrosperma*). These species may have originated from areas fringing the scrub or (less probably in view of the evidence from the insects) they could represent the hay component of manure.

The principal wetland taxa were pond weed *(Potamogeton* sp(p)) and water pepper *(Polygonum hydropiper)*, both of which indicate shallow standing water. The presence of *P hydropiper* suggests that the water was slow moving or stagnant. Traces of the bog moss *Sphagnum palustre* and white beak-sedge *(Rhynchospora alba)* would, if *in situ*, suggest a degree of acidification; however, it is quite likely that both of these species were transported to the site in peat used for building materials, flooring or fuel and subsequently redeposited in the moat. The moderately large residue from the washover (30% of the sample by volume) was dominated by coarse quartz sand and accompanied by occasional well-rotted wood fragments, further hazel nutshell fragments, and a limited amount of unidentifiable charcoal.

The insect assemblage from 4576/7588 was of modest size (124 individuals of 81 taxa of adult Coleoptera and Hemiptera). Like the remaining groups from the site it included an appreciable component of aquatics, numerous plant-feeders, a range of species associated with decaying matter, and a modest proportion of insects favoured by, or requiring, habitats created by human occupation.

4747/8397/T (5 kg; flot and washover)

The sediment was wet, light to mid/dark grey, soft (working soft and slightly sticky), sandy clay with 2-6 mm calibre stones present. Very well rotted wood and twigs, and seeds, were also present.

The washover produced a large quantity of well-preserved plant material (40% of the original subsample by volume), mainly composed of wood fragments together with a few worked chips (produced on the spot or dumped occupation waste?), bark, twigs, and numerous dicotyledon leaf fragments. The main macrofossil groupings were very similar to those recognised for 4576/7588, to an extent supporting the interpretation of 4576/7588 and 4747/8397 as broadly contemporaneous (but *all* of the plant assemblages from the site were surprisingly similar).

The scrub/hedge/bankside assemblage included elder *(Sambucus nigra)* and willow *(Salix* sp(p)), and there were several additional weed species indicative of arable fields (corncockle, *Agrostemma githago*; corn spurrey, *Spergula arvensis*). In common with 4576/7588 there were few food remains, although seeds of flax (*Linum usitatissum*) and wild strawberry (*Fragaria vesca*) were both present, as were blackberry seeds and apple endocarp fragments. Among these, flax is the only plant likely to have been cultivated. Conceivably, retting was occasionally carried out in the moat.

A slightly wider range of wetland taxa was recorded (in comparison with 4576/7588), including water-dropwort (*Oenanthe fluviatilis*), lesser spearwort (*Ranunculus flammula*), water crowfoots (*R* subgenus *Batrachium*), celery-leaved crowfoot (*R sceleratus*), and gipsywort (*Lycopus europaeus*), providing evidence for a well-developed aquatic flora (albeit of a rather limited kind), with a few waterside or swamp species. Coarse quartz sand dominated the moderate-sized residue from the washover (20% of the original sample by volume), accompanied by frequent rounded pebbles (to 35 mm), and pieces of coal. Traces of brick/tile and charcoal were also noted.

The subsample from 4747/8397 yielded a substantial assemblage of beetles and bugs (267 individuals of 140 taxa), including a large group of aquatics (36 individuals), even though the proportion of water beetles and bugs was the lowest for the site. This was probably a result of dilution by the component from decaying matter, which was the largest for the site (although less than half of the individuals were formally coded as decomposers). This assemblage also included the largest proportion of synanthropic forms, offering a clue as to the origin of the decomposers - in the debris of human occupation.

Phase 4
4746/8394/T (4.3 kg; flot and washover)
The sediment was moist, mid brown, sticky (working soft and sticky), humic silty clay with fine, coarse and woody herbaceous detritus and orange, 1 mm to 10 mm scale patches of reduction/oxidation. Some of the sediment was slightly layered, with patches that were black internally (probably very rotted organic matter). Coal (5-6 mm), leaves, very rotted wood, and monocotyledon stems were also present.

The moderate-sized washover (20% of the original sample by volume) consisted mainly of wood fragments, twigs, dicotyledon leaf fragments and fine herbaceous detritus. Other remains of woody plants included oak bud scales, elder seeds, willow fruits, hawthorn pyrenes, and crab apple endocarp. These species, together with blackberry, raspberry, and rose, provide further evidence for the tangled scrub/hedgerow habitat identified from 4576/7588 and 4747/8397.

A wide range of weed taxa was present, many of which inhabit tall, rough grassland or wayside habitats such as those found on scrub or hedge margins and headlands. Members of this group included woody nightshade (*Solanum dulcamara*), common mallow (*Malva sylvestris*), hogweed (*Heracleum sphondylium*), sow thistle (*Sonchus oleraceus*), true thistles, cow parsley (*Anthriscus sylvestris*), burdock, and nipplewort. Other weed species present in the sample were indicative of disturbed places (including cultivated soils) and damp grassland or fen. Achenes of a buttercup (*Ranunculus* subgenus *Ranunculus*) and stinging nettle (*Urtica dioica*) were abundant although many were poorly preserved.

The sample contained species indicative of a range of wetland habitats including open water (pond weed; *Glyceria* sp(p), sweet grasses), fen or waterbank habitats (meadow-sweet, *Filipendula ulmaria*; willow; gipsywort) and acidic peatland (ling, *Calluna vulgaris*; hare's tail cotton grass, *Eriophorum vaginatum*; and *Hypnum cupressifome*), though the open water species were much more common than the other two groups. The acidic bog taxa were almost certainly transported to the site as cut peat. The occurrence of these remains in the moat therefore represents minor dumping or accidental redeposition of occupation waste.

The small residue (5% of the original sample by volume), which consisted mainly of coarse quartz sand, contained additional evidence of minor dumping in the form of traces of clinker, wood chips and occasional fragments of coal. Dicotyledon leaf fragments and further twigs/wood fragments were present, amounting to approximately 2% of the original sample.

A very large group of beetles and bugs was recovered: 197 taxa and 446 individuals. 'Outdoor' forms were very abundant (62% of the assemblage) and aquatics numerous (71 individuals of 33 taxa; there were also abundant cladocerans and caddis fly larval cases). Plant feeders accounted for another third of the assemblage. Decomposers were numerous, but contributed less than a third of the assemblage, with only a modest proportion of synanthropes. It seems that the rate of input of insects from around human occupation may have reduced at this stage. This sample provided the only heath/moor insect recognised at the site - *Lochmaea suturalis*, a leaf beetle which feeds on heather.

4579/7692/T (5 kg; flot and washover)
The sediment was moist mid brown (internally greyer) crumbly, and in places layered, slightly sandy clay silt. Patches of the sediment were slightly sticky (working soft and rubbing brown). Fragments of brick/tile, stones with a size range of 2-6 mm, leaves, wood, twigs, and herbaceous rootlets were visible.

Large twigs and fine through to coarse wood fragments dominated the moderately large washover (30% of the original sample by volume), which also contained occasional dicotyledon leaf fragments, bark scrolls, oak bud scales, and further unidentified bud scales. Other remains from woody plants included the elder seeds and hawthorn (*Crataegus monogyna*) pyrenes, together with hawthorn/sloe thorns and blackberry seeds. This assemblage represents a very similar scrub/hedge habitat to that seen in the other samples.

The sample contained a similar, although slightly more restricted, group of weed seeds compared with 4746/8394. The main habitat types represented included open disturbed ground, and a slight hint of damp acid grassland; however, there was little evidence of arable weed species and the range of tall hedge/field margin weed species was also more restricted. With the exception of the edible fruits of hedgerow trees and bushes, the only 'useful' plant was flax (seeds and pods). In common with 4746/8394 there were wetland species from acidic raised mire (hare's tail cotton grass; *Sphagnum*), indicating the presence of cut peat, and fen/bank fringe habitats (greater spearwort, *Ranunculus lingua*; meadow-sweet, sedges, *Sphagnum palustre*). Species indicative of open or standing water included pond weed and bulrush (*Scirpus lacustris*). The latter species is common in lakes and ponds where there is abundant silt.

The main constituents of the moderately small residue from washover (10% of the original sample by volume) were coarse quartz sand, coal fragments (to 6 mm), mineralised twigs (to 7 mm), and rounded pebbles (to 20 mm). Occasional dicotyledon leaf fragments, rare pieces of brick/tile, and a single large wood fragment (?stake; to 225 mm) were also present.

Although this context gave the smallest group of insects from the site (69 taxa, 91 individuals), there was a strong similarity to the assemblage from 4746/8394, although the proportion of decomposer insects was even lower (25%) and synanthropes even less well represented. Aquatics were particularly important (almost a quarter of the individuals).

Phase 5
4569/7581/T (5 kg; flot and washover)
The sediment was moist, light grey to mid dark grey and light brown, crumbly to unconsolidated, clay sand, with some patches more sandy or more clayey. Twigs, and stones in the size range 2-20 mm, rootlets, and some white mould, were also present.

The moderate-sized flot and washover (the latter being 15% of the sample by volume) was rich in fine herbaceous detritus, amongst which there were many achenes of stinging nettle (*Urtica dioica*), stinking mayweed (*Anthemis cotula*) and corn marigold (*Chrysanthemum segetum*), nutlets of sedges (*Carex* sp(p)), mericarps of cow parsley, willow bud scales, and unidentified bud scales similar to those from

4746/8394. Preservation of plant remains was mostly very good though the concentration of identifiable material was fairly low.

Macrofossils from this deposit demonstrated that it was clearly waterlain. Leaf epidermis and stem fragments of pond weed (*Potamogeton* sp(p)) were common together with achenes of pond weed, frequent resting egg cases (ephippia) of water fleas (*Daphnia* and at least one other type), occasional fruits of water pepper, and ostracods. Several fen, damp grassland, or waterside species were also present, including meadow-sweet, toad rush (*Juncus bufonius*), and saw sedge (*Cladium mariscus*), though none of the species in this group were well represented.

Most taxa were weeds in the broad sense, though there were some hints of the presence of grassland in the vicinity (or of the deposition into the moat of cut grassland vegetation, such as hay, possibly via herbivore dung). 'Useful' plants were restricted to traces of flax seed fragments and a single fig seed. Besides the bud scales already mentioned, a few of the woody plants noted from 4746/8394 were present here, too.

An assemblage of beetles and bugs of quite large size was recovered (263 individuals of 143 taxa). Preservation was substantially less good than in the rest of the deposits examined. The fauna was broadly similar to that from the other samples in the sequence, with proportions of the main groups more like those of Phase 1b than of Phase 4.

Discussion
The plant assemblages were remarkably consistent through the whole sequence of moat fills. The main ecological groups were a range of trees and shrubs representing scrub, a rich variety of tall and short herbs indicative of hedge-banks, rough pasture and disturbed (including cultivated) ground, a limited range of aquatics, and a few waterside forms. Some peatland taxa were noted, probably introduced in cut peat rather than turf. Remains of edible plants (other than from species likely to have grown wild along the moat edges) were only present in traces.

The underlying nature of the insect assemblages was also consistent, with a predominance of 'outdoor' forms of various kinds, but a clear component of species favoured by buildings and intensive human activity (synanthropes). Subtle variations were evident, but their significance was generally hard to determine. In view of this, and despite the long time span represented, the assemblages are considered together. Variations on the theme are considered below.

The entire sequence of contexts from which insects were examined was clearly waterlain; aquatics were both relatively numerous and diverse, the assemblages including between 13 and 33 species of water beetles and bugs, contributing between 13% and 24% of the individuals of these groups. The aquatic bugs included *Velia* and *Gerris* species (pondskaters), *Notonecta* (backswimmers), and Corixidae (water boatmen). The water beetles included a range of Haliplidae, Dytiscidae, Hydrophilidae and Hydraenidae, all the species recorded being able to exploit fairly small pools of still, but not too polluted, water; as a community they would be rather typical of shallow ditches. In contrast to this rich and moderately (but not extremely) abundant fauna, waterside insects were not very common, the assemblages including 2-16 individuals in this category, contributing 2-6% of the assemblages. Species associated with emergent and waterside vegetation were not at all common.

While aquatic plants were present, apart from pondweeds they were not abundant and were represented by only a limited range of species. Several aquatic *Ranunculus* species (crowfoots, particularly *R sceleratus*), and the water pepper (*Polygonum hydropiper*) were consistently present. These plants are tolerant of shallow, muddy water. Together, the insects and plants indicate that the moat did not present habitats like those in a large pond or deep dyke; however, it probably held water for most of the time, the bottom remaining permanently wet. The *Daphnia* and other cladoceran resting eggs may have been formed at times when the level dropped.

The rarity of marginal plants and waterside insects requires explanation. The two principal hypotheses are either disturbance or deep shading by overhanging vegetation: there may have been a combination of both of these. The second cause is well supported by the botanical evidence, since there were thorns of sloe or hawthorn and prickles of rose or blackberry. Unlike leaf debris, these dense objects seem likely to have originated very close to the moat. Further choking of the aquatics may have been caused by dense stands of tall herbs on the banks.

Two beetle species associated with clean flowing water were present, the 'riffle beetles' *Esolus parallelopipedus* and *Oulimnius* sp (probably *O troglodytes*). These may have been introduced in a stream inflow, or have arrived as 'background fauna', presumably in flight. Flowing water cannot be suggested to have been important, and there is no reason to suspect the moat to have had more than a sluggish flow.

The main component of the diverse terrestrial flora was a range of scrub plants and trees, insects from which were also present. It seems likely that there was a loose, perhaps fragmented, hedge-like tangle of scrub, perhaps with a few taller tree stems. This was

probably surrounded by a mosaic of tall and short herbs, including species typical of hedgebanks such as woody nightshade and tall umbellifers (hedge parsley and hogweed). Shorter vegetation was represented to a limited extent by plants such as buttercup, daisy, blinks, and self-heal.

A rich fauna of terrestrial plant-feeding insects reflected the flora. The number of beetle and bug species in this category ranged from 23 to 60 in the assemblages, and they contributed 14-35% of the individuals. A very diverse vegetation was indicated. There were several species from grasses (*eg* the capsid bug, *Capsus ?ater*, and the froghopper, *Aphrodes flavostriatus*), a range of nettle feeders (*eg* the pollen beetle, *Brachypterus* sp, and the weevils, *Apion urticarium*, *Cidnorhinus quadrimaculatus*, *Ceutorhynchus pollinarius*), several weevils associated with clovers and their relatives (*Sitona* spp), and smaller numbers of species found on *Juncus* (*Conomelus anceps*), *Polygonum* spp (*?Gastrophysa polygoni*), *Rumex* (*Apion miniatum*), figworts and mullein (*Cionus* sp), *Matricaria* or *Anthemis* (*Ceutorhynchus ?rugulosus*), apple and pear (*Anthonomus ?pomorum*) and other Rosaceae (*A rubi*), and willows (*Rhynchaenus foliorum*). Some of these plants are notably absent from the list of botanical remains, perhaps through preservational characteristics, or because the mobile insects originated at some distance. A further plant indicated by the insects is ash (*Fraxinus*), in the small branches of which the bark beetle, *Leperisinus orni*, bores.

There was not much evidence of extensive bare ground, and few ground beetles (Carabidae) were noted other than those typical of waterside habitats. Overall, the terrestrial component associated with natural or semi-natural (*sensu* Kenward and Allison 1994) habitats, like the aquatics, seem to have originated along or very close to the moat and so can be used to reconstruct its surroundings.

These 'outdoor' insects, like the plants, conjure a picture of a stagnant ditch with limited marginal vegetation, but adjacent to an area of rich and varied herbaceous and woody vegetation, most probably scrub, perhaps a hedge, edged by tall and short herbs, on the margin of the moat. The flowers of tall herbs and shrubs may have overhung the ditch, so that insects visiting them fell off and drowned in the water below, since several of the beetles are commonly found on flowers.

Whether marginal plants were limited by overhanging trees, or by some other factor, is not certain (*see above p 136*). One limit on development of marginal vegetation would be grazing. True dung beetles (*Aphodius* spp, mostly *A prodromus*) were not especially abundant, except for the record of 18 *A prodromus* (and single individuals of two other species) from 4746/8394. It seems possible that livestock were present, but there is no evidence for grazing at the water margins from most of the assemblages. The richness of the terrestrial flora might at first be taken as a counter-indication to cutting of vegetation, but if the plants were cut back only infrequently, or only on one (the inner?) side, abundant and varied insects would still have been able to exist. The evidence of short and tall herbs, and shrubs and/or trees, perhaps supports the hypothesis that vegetation was subject to more than one regime at any time, and localised cutting (or trampling) seems a likely cause.

Beetles associated with dead wood (or moribund areas of live trees) were not very abundant (2-4% of the assemblages, 3-12 individuals per assemblage), and the woodworm (or furniture) beetle *Anobium punctatum* was very much the most numerous. It may have originated with the synanthropes (*see below, this page*), living in structural timber, including fences and the like, but it also occurs in dead branches and trunks of standing trees and large shrubs. *Grynobius planus* and *Lyctus linearis* may similarly have 'human' or 'natural' origins. The remaining dead wood insects seem most likely to have come from trees near the moat. The records of *Leperisinus orni* are notable; its congener *L varius* is common in occupation deposits, at least sometimes probably having been introduced in firewood. *L orni* is associated with ash trees (*Fraxinus*). It is worth noting that the samples contained large quantities of wood fragments, as well as a range of other remains of trees and shrubs.

Insects from decaying matter were well represented (totalling 25-49% of the individuals, with 16-46 taxa, in each assemblage). This component of the fauna at Old Abbey Farm is not easy to interpret, and it may have had complex origins. However, the manner in which the proportions of 'outdoor' and decomposer insects reciprocate suggests that one group diluted the other. Since the insects from semi-natural habitats seem likely to have been fairly constant, changes in the rate of input of insects from rotting matter around human occupation is the likely causal factor.

The 'dung' beetles have been discussed (*see above, this page*); other species associated with very foul matter were rare (single individuals except for *Cryptopleurum minutum* (two) and *Platystethus arenarius* (three)) in the assemblage from 4746/8394, the context which produced numerous dung beetles, and with which they probably originated.

Many of the decomposer beetles found at Old Abbey Farm are synanthropic, that is to a greater or lesser extent associated with the artificial habitats created by human occupation. However, the decomposers typically found in rather dry decaying matter (usually plant litter) are particularly problematic at this site, for they include species which seem as likely to have lived in plant litter as to have come from the artificial habitats with which they are more usually associated in archaeological assemblages. Both origins seem likely, in fact, and the classification of many of these 'dry decomposers' as facultative synanthropes reflects this.

Some of the synanthropic species seem almost certainly to have come from nearby buildings, notably *Laemostenus ?terricola*, *Tipnus unicolor*, *Ptinus fur*, *Mycetaea hirta*, and *Typhaea stercorea*; to argue otherwise would be to ask for too many coincidences. A range of other insects probably came with them. The rather small numbers of individuals involved provide no clear evidence for deliberate dumping of waste into the moat, and these insects seem likely to have travelled accidentally, flying, walking or wind-blown, as 'background fauna', in drainage water, or in scatter. In particular, although pasture plants were present in small amounts, there is no evidence of the stable manure 'indicator group' discussed by Kenward and Hall (1997) and Hall and Kenward (1998).

Kenward (1997) has discussed the value of synanthropes from isolated occupation sites as indicators of the nature of such sites. The range of synanthropes recorded at Old Abbey Farm was rather limited, some typical denizens of archaeological sites (such as *Aglenus brunneus*, *Blaps* and *Tenebrio* species, and *Trox scaber*) being notable absentees. No grain pests were found, which seems particularly surprising at what was presumably at some stages at least a site of considerable status. Taken at face value this suggests a site which, despite existing for some hundreds of years, did not accrete much synanthropic fauna, and was thus isolated (with limited exchange of materials with other settlements), or only intermittently occupied. However, the way in which fauna become incorporated in the fills of peripheral ditches and moats at sites such as this is poorly understood, so these observations must be treated with due caution. The rarity of 'useful' plants (other than species likely to have grown along the moat edges) in these fills perhaps emphasises the low rate of transfer of debris from nearby occupation; only flax can be seen of a near-certain human origin.

Were the slight variations in flora and fauna seen through the succession at all significant? For the insects, there was little system in the variations. The values for PNOB (the percentage of outdoor individuals) was strikingly higher in 4579/7692 and 4746/8394, from Phase 4, matching the lower proportion of decomposers and synanthropes in these assemblages; perhaps transfer of insects from artificial habitats was reduced at the time these layers were forming. Sample 4579/7692, and to a lesser extent 4746/8394, yielded significantly less weeds of cultivated ground than the other layers, too. However, variations in most parameters can hardly be seen as significant, and the constancy of the assemblages over perhaps as much as 400 years is quite surprising; if the chronology is not over-extended, this seems to have been an establishment with a rather unchanging, and perhaps limited, way of life.

Assessment of the Brick Samples

W John Smith

Twenty-nine samples were examined, 17 from the farmhouse and 12 from the barn. No further study of the bricks was made during the analysis phase of the project. Details are given in Tables 2 and 3 below.

Methods
All the samples were visually examined, noting colour, texture and the presence of other material in the clay, the effects of firing *ie* warping, burnt areas, and the effect on the brick of the unequal expansion of pebbles and stone chippings. The samples were all measured to a tolerance of 1 mm, measuring each main axis of each brick. On bricks where the sides were not parallel, edge measurements were taken, although this process was not applied to damaged bricks. Measurements were initially taken in imperial units, but for this report metric units have been used.

General comments on sampled farmhouse bricks
There are differences of up to 60 mm in the general dimensions of the bricks, which could be accountable by variations in the dimensions of the wooden moulds used. These would have been very basic and without the use of a stock for the frog. Variations in thickness between bricks and even in an individual brick are probably accountable to the limited skills employed.

All the bricks examined had a good proportion of pebbles and stone chippings in the clay. Some pebbles were as big as an index finger joint. From this it can be argued that a pug mill was not used in the preparation of the clay: the stones would have damaged the blades in the pug mill. In all probability the brick clay, plus its stones, would have been mixed by treading the mixture, perhaps by animals. If workers were employed, they could have used clogs. The lack of evidence for a pug mill would suggest a temporary brick-making site, together with a place to set up a clamp for firing, sufficient for the modest number of bricks required.

From the samples examined, the brick clay would have been quite stiff before being put into the moulds. Many bricks showed signs of the clay being 'folded' into the mould. The filled moulds would then have been carried to an area for drying, where there was a mat of chopped straw to allow air to reach the lower face of each brick, so help by the drying out of the 'green' brick. Most of the bricks had clear impressions of this straw matting. There were no signs on the examples of the use of a wire or a flat stick being used to scrape off any surplus clay and smooth the surface. On the contrary, many top surfaces were uneven, pitted with dents and finger impressions. These errors would not have been seen once the wall was built, the mortar filling any cavities/hollows.

Dating of the farmhouse bricks
The crudeness of the bricks and the manner in which they were laid obstructs a positive date or period for their manufacture and use being ascertained. Their relative positions prior to dismantling add more problems to interpretation. Excavation of the foundations and footings demonstrated that the brickwork and bricklaying was of very poor quality, with no consistency in bonding. Poor bricks and brickbats had been used indiscriminately.

Different sizes of bricks in the context of the building can be attributed more to the variety of wooden brick moulds used than to different periods of manufacture. If the hypothesis is accepted that the bricks had been made by unskilled workers, using what brick moulds were available to them, with others being made (see Sample 6298, observations) to a regular size, then trying to use such measurements as dating criteria becomes unacceptable.

The presence of coal fragments and dust within some bricks may give a rough indication of date, since coal particles might be related to mining activities in the district, to dust deposits from transporting coal, or to its use as a fuel for the brickclamps and/or kilns. Sample 6462 had evidence of coal lumps in the mortar plus coal dust, suggesting the use of coal for firing the brick, and most samples of mortar from the site had traces of coal dust. An early reference to making 7000 bricks is given in the diary of Nicholas Blundell of Crosby in 1708, one disbursement being for 'sods at 4 d per hundred' (LiRO 920 MD 74-5). This suggests use of dried turf (sods) as a fuel for brick kilns in the early eighteenth century. The number of coal mines in south Lancashire increased after the mid eighteenth century (Ashmore 1982, 8), and the price of coal fell relative to other fuels. However, such considerations again do not allow accurate dating of the bricks from Old Abbey Farm.

A further approach is to consider improved technology in brick production. Brick clay from the pug mill,

Context/ Sample	Phase	Room	Dimensions in mm	Colour	Observations
2103/6625	3	G1	242 x 120 x 64	Cherry	Fine texture - soft. Straw impressions. Lime wash on one side
2009/6460	4	G5	242 x 120 x 58	Orange	Straw impressions
2010/6605	4	G1	255 x 115 x 70	Cherry	Straw impressions on lower surface
2008/6459	5	G4	242 x 115 x 64	Orange	Lime wash on one side
2022/6467	5	G4	245 x 115 x 70	Cherry/ orange	Hard, some cracking, splitting during firing - visible signs of small stones in brick. Lime washed on outer face; this had covered the early pointing in which there is surface dirt, later sealed in by the lime wash coating
2859/6608	5	G4	242 x 108 x 64	Cherry	Split in firing. Straw marks
2011/6462	6	G2	235 x 120 x 70	Cherry	Sample consisted of three bricks, all with the same dimensions. Good, firm fine-grained bricks with only small solid materials - no serious cracking. The mortar on one face was very friable, easily disintegrating with only light rubbing pressure. Mixture was mainly coarse sand containing coal dust and some lumps 5 mm square
2014/6252	6	G3	241 x 108 x 70	Dark red with burnt areas	Well shaped with good corners. Sandy mortar with no additions or intrusions. This brick had been subject to greater heat in the kiln which caused some splitting/fracturing through unequal expansions of clay and solid materials. One face had been fully blackened by firing. There are traces of lime wash
2100/6298	6	G2	242 x 120 x 76	Cherry	Well shaped with flat faces and sharp corners. The stretcher faces carry the impressions of saw marks from the wooden brick moulds. The mortar used on this sample has more sand in the mixture and is much softer and more friable than other examples
2107/6297	6	G2a	235 x 108 x 75-63	Orange	From external leaf of wall. Well moulded. Thickness varied. Coal dust in mortar. Whitewashed on one side: three layers counted

Table 2: Brick samples taken from the farmhouse

Context/ Sample	Phase	Room	Dimensions in mm	Colour	Observations
2107/6297	6	G2a	235 x 108 x 63	Orange	From internal leaf of wall. Cracked and warped - a badly shaped brick. The state of this brick is not unusual for the inner leaf of a brick wall. The mortar is strong and more resistant to abrasion than that in the outer leaf of the wall. Different mix during construction?
2119/6653	6	G3	235 x 100 x 70	Cherry/ orange	Outer face of this brick had three layers of whitewash, layers of dust identifying the layers. Soft mortar with few additions or intrusions
2256/6626	6 *re-used	G2	235 x 109 x 64	Orange	Sample consisted of three bricks, all cracked. Quantities of small pebbles and stone chippings noted. The mortar is quite hard, requiring some thumb pressure to break it down. Building survey suggested these three bricks were re-used
			228 x 108 x 64	Orange	
			242 x 108 x 70	Cherry	

Table 2: Brick samples taken from the farmhouse (contd)

from which it emerged like sausage meat, was not preformed but taken to a moulder. In 1838 a successful machine was invented which cut a column of preformed plastic clay from a pug mill into batches of brick by a series of stretched wires in a frame, and by 1860 its use was nationwide in a growing number of brickyards (Lynch 1994, 15). None of the bricks at Old Abbey Farm were made in this way except for some in a twentieth century outbuilding, suggesting manufacture prior to the mid nineteenth century.

Brick samples from the barn

The same conclusions can be drawn from the brick samples from the barn as those from the farmhouse (*see Table 3*).

Assessment of the Building Stone Samples

Shaun Rainford

During the structural survey 29 items of stone were retained as samples, including lintels, packing pieces, stone roof slates, and a single window mullion. Additionally, during the excavation, some further samples were taken of stone building dressings, jambs, threshold stones, flags, and roof slates. As part of the assessment, the samples were catalogued, and a possible provenance and age for each item was provided, following a consideration of the geology of the surrounding area.

With very few exceptions, the building stones examined were sandstones of the Triassic age (Bunter and Keuper), most of which subcrop within a short distance of the site, and are commonly used in all types and sizes of buildings.

The combination of thin superficial cover and the sheer extent of subcrop has promoted the use of Triassic sandstones for building materials over an extensive area. Small quarries appear to have been common as late as the mid nineteenth century (Ordnance Survey 1849) with larger quarries being a relatively modern occurrence. Because of the many different locations from which the stone could have been worked, additional study of the geology was considered unlikely to yield any significant further information. No further study was made during the analysis phase of the project.

Assessment of the Daub Samples

Wendy Carruthers

Eleven samples of daub were taken from ten individual contexts within the farmhouse during the building survey, and three of these were selected for plant macrofossil evaluation as part of the assessment. No further study of the samples was undertaken during the analysis phase of the project.

Samples 2528/6214 and 2147/6213 were taken from the north and south faces respectively of wall 2101, which formed the rear of the brick inglenook fireplace inserted into the central hall of the farmhouse during the

Context	Phase	Location	Dimensions in mm	Colour	Observations
6168	6	S Gable	a: 216 x 102 x 58-64	Orange/-red	Warped. Surface indents - fingers
			b: 216 x107 x67		Outside burnt. Hard mortar where it survives
			c: 235 x 121 x 63	Orange/-red	Warped. Surface undulates. did the brick warp in drying or firing?
6169	6	W Wall	a: 235 x 114 x 57-64	Orange/-red	Slight warping. Straw impressions on slightly concave uderside
			b: 228 x 107 x 64	Orange/-red	Slight warping. Fracturing due to expansion of pebbles and stone fragments in clay
			c: 228 x 109-119 x 63	Orange/-red	Slight warping. Similar groove down upper(?) surface edge to 6171D
6171	6	N Gable	a: 242 x 114 x 64-70	Cherry	Slightly warped. Hard mortar with coal dust
			b: 235 x 114 x 64-73		
			c: 228 x 114 x 64		Part damaged/ warped
			d: 228 x 118 x 58		Indented ridge on one side as if made by a brick placed above it having slipped in the kiln

Table 3: Brick samples taken from the barn

seventeenth century (Phase 3); its southern face was internal, but clear evidence has not survived to indicate whether further rooms existed to the north in Phase 3. In addition to the information daub analysis would provide on the biological constituents and their likely sources and treatment, it was hoped that comparisons between samples would provide some degree of similarity in areas of similar usage. To these ends the third sample examined was 2547/6667, taken from wall 2105, which was known to be a first floor internal partition integral with the construction of the southern crosswing in the mid sixteenth century (Phase 2).

Methods

Each 500 ml sample of daub was left to soak in hot water overnight and gently stirred to disaggregate the clay matrix. The resulting slurry was washed through a graded stack of sieves (four sieves ranging in mesh size from 4 mm down to 250 microns) with clean water, and each of the fractions was rapidly scanned by eye (4 mm fraction only) and/or microscopically sorted (plant remains picked out of the 4 mm fraction, and a proportion of each of the smaller fractions) in order to characterise the plant assemblages present. The 4 mm fraction was also roughly measured in volume for comparative purposes. The plant remains, having been removed from their protective clay matrix, were stored in 75% alcohol.

Results
Sample 2528/6214
Large quantities of straw/hay were visible prior to disaggregation, and an unpleasant smell was emitted on mixing with hot water. The straw fragments were very roughly chopped, up to 120 mm in length, but very variable and not always well preserved.

Two-row barley (*Hordeum distichum* L), represented by a few rachis fragments and occasional grains, was the main cereal present. In some cases large fragments of ear were preserved (*ie* several rachis fragments still adjoined). A few cultivated oat grains (*Avena sativa* gp) were present, still enclosed in their chaff (florets). There were also a few fragments of wheat ear and grains (hexaploid-free threshing wheats *eg* bread wheat, *Triticum aestivum*).

Lots of small grass seeds (Gramineae), some buttercup (*Ranunculus* sp), self-heal (*Prunella vulgaris*), sedges (*Carex* sp), knotgrass (*Polygonum aviculare*), and orache

(*Atriplex* sp) were also present. These species represent weeds of grassland, waste, and cultivated land.

Sample 2147/6213

Much less straw was present than within 2528/6214 (*c* 100 ml of 4 mm fraction), and it was more thoroughly chopped, to *c* 10-20 mm lengths (maximum = 45 mm).

Fewer grains and ear fragments (rachis segments) of cereals were present. Again, two-row barley grains and rachis predominated, with a few oat grains.

Weed seeds were dominated by common hemp-nettle (*Galeopsis tetrahit*), with lesser numbers of pale persicaria (*Polygonum lapathifolium*) and redshank (*P persicaria*) seeds. Several other weeds of grassland were also present, as well as weeds from cultivated and waste ground, *eg* cleavers (*Galium aparine*) and chickweed (*Stellaria media*). There were few small grass seeds.

Sample 2547/6667

As with 2147/6213, there was a lower proportion of straw than for 2528/6214 (*c*100 ml of 4 mm fraction), and it was well preserved, being more carefully chopped than in 6214, to primarily *c* 15 mm lengths.

Few cereals were observed, there being only a few barley grains and oat grains present, and very few rachis fragments. Weed seeds were not very frequent, generally. A few non-specific weeds of grassland were present, as well as weeds of cultivated and waste areas, *eg* chickweed, knotgrass, self-heal, and docks.

Interpretation

The organic material used to temper all three daub samples consisted primarily of cereal processing waste - mostly straw fragments with very little of the light chaff (rachis fragments, glumes). However, despite the fact that the plant macrofossil assemblages were only rapidly scanned, each of the three samples showed some differences in character. Sample 2528/6214 was the most distinctive, containing large quantities of very roughly chopped straw fragments, many of which were long. The large numbers of grass seeds present in this sample, and the presence of thin Gramineae culm (stem) fragments, suggest that hay was also present. This was probably the source of several of the other weed seeds. It is possible that the unpleasant smell and less well-preserved nature of the remains were due to the presence of dung, and both hay and some of the cereal remains could have been added in this form.

Samples 2147/6213 and 2547/6667 were similar in character, containing more thoroughly chopped straw in smaller quantities, and fewer cereal ear fragments, grains, and weed seeds. These samples did produce some weed seeds that may have been growing in grassland, but the much lower occurrence of grass seeds and thin Gramineae culms (stems) indicated that hay and/or dung may not have been present. Differences between these two samples were primarily in the occurrence of different weed taxa.

Relatively few samples of daub have been examined in this way to date (see Carruthers 1990), so that the amount of variation to be expected between samples is not yet known, within a single building phase, or from county to county, or in different periods. The significance of differences found between the samples, therefore, requires further research, but some suggestions can be made. The reason for taking the time to chop the crop-processing waste more carefully, and perhaps using a 'cleaner' straw sample with fewer ears, grains and weed seeds, might be to obtain a smoother finish to the daub prior to plastering. Such care is more likely to have been taken over internal walls than external ones, where weatherproofing would be the main priority. The significance of adding dung may be to produce a more adhesive coat less liable to cracking on drying out. A search of documentary sources might elucidate this point.

Two-row barley appears to have been the predominant crop used in the three daub samples from Old Abbey Farm, which is perhaps unexpected, since the straw has some value as fodder. Barley straw is a superior bedding straw, being softer and more absorbent than wheat, so some of these remains may have been introduced as dung and/or stable waste. The extent of cultivation of two-row barley in Britain has been difficult to trace from the archaeobotanical record, because archaeological remains are usually so poorly preserved. From the scant evidence recorded to date it was probably grown from the Late Saxon period onwards (Moffett 1987), and it is now the preferred type of barley grown because it produces a superior quality of malt to six-row barley (six-row barley was grown from the Neolithic to present day). It would be interesting to see if there are documentary records for brewing having taken place locally.

This study has shown that well-preserved plant macrofossils survived in large quantities within the daub samples taken at Old Abbey Farm, and clear differences between the three samples investigated were observed. Clearly, useful archaeological and archaeobotanical information can be preserved within assemblages such as these. The plant remains cannot provide direct evidence of dating, as most of the taxa likely to be found have been present in Britain at least from the medieval period, but comparison of several samples around a building may assist in relating phases of rebuilding, providing that some links are made with dendrochronological dates, however loose these may be.

The archaeobotanical value of these samples is outstanding because of the unique nature of the preservation. Desiccated crop-processing waste is invaluable in understanding the cultivation of different cereals, as important identifiable characters are often lost in archaeologically preserved material. The post-medieval period is one that has, up to now, been neglected, but current research on smoke-blackened thatch (J Letts pers comm) is producing information which will be useful to the study of cereal cultivars, and to the study of daub. In addition to cereal remains, evidence of other local industries such as flax processing can be obtained from daub (Carruthers 1990). Weed seeds may provide information on where and how crops were being cultivated, and the identification of grassland taxa will provide information on hay meadows and pastures (if introduced in dung).

Assessment of the Mortar Samples

Colin Peacock

During the structural survey, mortar samples were systematically collected from all walls and identifiable repairs or rebuilds in both the farmhouse and the barn. Samples were judged as representative of the context on visual and textural examination in the field. This resulted in a total of 143 samples of clay, lime or cement-based mortars being available for analysis. For assessment purposes, six lime/cement-based and two clay-based mortars were chosen to determine their potential for providing corroborative comparisons or distinctions between suspected phase similarities or changes, where stratigraphical relationships were truncated or indistinct. Two plaster samples were also analysed (*see Table 4, below*). Following the recommendations detailed in the English Heritage *Technical Handbook on Practical Building Conservation* Volume 2 (Ashurst and Ashurst 1988), it was acknowledged that mortar samples by themselves are unlikely to give much indication of the dates when a mortar was prepared. Following assessment, no further study of the samples was undertaken.

Samples 208/6195 and 205/6184, from the north and south gable walls of the barn respectively, were included to test the variation within mortars from a single phase (Phase 6), and to allow comparison with mortars from the farmhouse thought to be from the same period. Samples 2023/6422 and 2103/6479, from the south wall of the farmhouse southern crosswing (Phase 4) and east wall of the central hall (Phase 3) respectively, were from physically separate walls, both clay bonded, but attributed to different phases. Samples 2008/6321 and 2256/6395, from the west and east gables of the farmhouse southern crosswing

respectively, were from physically separate walls thought to be from the same phase (Phase 5).

Samples 2011/6259 and 2256/6395, from different positions in the north wall of the farmhouse (*ie* from Rooms F2 and G2 respectively), were from a single wall with two visibly distinct sections, both of which shared a similar bonding material and were thought to be from the same date (Phase 6). The plaster samples, 3119/6494 and 2308/6045, were both considered to derive from Phases 3-4.

Methods
Each sample was subject to an initial visual inspection and a description was given. This is normally followed by sieve analysis, but unfortunately the sample components were too soft to isolate the particles of interest. Accordingly a representative oven-dried sample was ground down and a determination of calcium content and acid insoluble residue was made. Additionally, using thermogravimetry, weight losses on heating for each of the samples was established.

Results
All the samples except 2023/6422 and 2103/6479 had a basic fine sand which was mixed with lime, clay and sometimes charcoal. There were very few stones of size above 1 mm except in 3119/6494. The samples are arranged here in order of Thermo Gravimetric Analysis (TGA) weight loss from 650 - 850°C, which seemed to give a reasonable classification.

The first TGA weight loss is normally loosely bound water from clay minerals. The second is generally loss of carbon dioxide from carbonates, particularly calcium carbonate. In pure calcium carbonate this weight loss should be 10% greater than the calcium content. Anything less than this suggests that calcium is present as lime - calcium hydroxide - rather than as the carbonate. In a normal exposed environment calcium hydroxide is slowly carbonated by carbon dioxide in the atmosphere. Hence samples where the calcium level is significantly higher than the TGA weight loss are likely to be fairly recent.

The samples split into one group of four: 2308/6045, 2008/6321, 2256/6395, and 2011/6259. Some details from the TGA suggested that the first two might be very similar, as are the second two, but the degree of significance is uncertain.

Samples 2308/6045 was used as a plaster and 2008/6321 as a mortar but the basic composition was the same, although the former had some hair rather roughly mixed into it. The four samples seem otherwise to be very similar - a relatively crude mixture of sand and a not very well ground up lime which contains some charcoal left over from the burning. Although the last two came from the same part of the building the first two did not, and

Context/ Sample	TGA to 650° C	weight loss % (650-850° C)	Insoluble residue %	Ca %	Visual appearance
3119 / 6494	1.5	23.2	9.8	26.2	Sand / lime plaster on hair base
205 / 6184	0.3	14.8	52.6	18.4	Sandy mortar with lime pieces up to 10mm plus pieces of clay / brick
208 / 6195	2.7	15.7	46.0	16.8	Very soft with lime pieces up to 5 mm and some charcoal
2308 / 6045	0.5	12.8	61.9	11.5	Sandy mortar with lime up to 5 mm and some charcoal plus some hair
2022 / 6438	0.7	14.4	48.4	21.3	Like 205 / 6184
2256 / 6395	2.0	10.6	64.5	10.0	Like 2008 / 6321
2008 / 6321	0.3	12.7	63.0	10.8	Like 2308 / 6045 but with no hair
2023 / 6422	0.3	2.4	85.1	0.9	Brown clay with little other admixtures
2011 / 6259	1.6	9.2	62.8	10.7	Like 2008 / 6321
2103 / 6479	0.3	1.3	82.8	0.4	Like 2023 / 6422

Table 4: Results of the analysis of selected mortar samples

the stratigraphy suggests dates from the seventeenth to nineteenth centuries for the four samples. The carbonation of the last two was slightly less than that of the first two. This may suggest that they wereyounger but that the same method of preparing mortar was used over a long period of time.

Samples 205 / 6184 and 2022 / 6438 formed another group, this time where clay lumps also had been mixed into a relatively crude lime / sand mortar. The calcium contents of these samples were high compared with the TGA weight loss suggesting low carbonation, so that the samples were either relatively young or placed somewhere protected from attack by carbon dioxide. Samples 2023 / 6422 and 2103 / 6479 were quite different from the rest, being clay with very little admixture of lime or sand. The lack of lime in the samples precluded any carbonation determination. Sample 208 / 6195 looked like those in the set of four but had a higher calcium content and lower insoluble residue, suggesting a very different sort of mix using rather different sources of raw materials.

Finally 3119 / 6494 was a lime / sand plaster with a much higher lime content than any of the other samples. It seems to have been more sophisticated than the other materials with well ground lime and a somewhat different sand with more coarse granules. From the quality of the lime and the relatively low carbonation, a relatively young age was at first suggested for this plaster, but on examining the specific contexts it became apparent that this represented a much higher quality product that had been protected from carbonation by being used in the 'inglenook' fireplace.

Theassessment picked out certain patterns amongst the samples' carbonation values that appear to provide a broad dating capacity although various external factors may be introducing undefined bias. Further analysis might have refined the ability of this method to provide more quantifiable broad dating from a group of samples, but supporting evidence from other sources would still have been needed before any firm reliance could be placed on the results.

11

SYNTHESIS

Multi-disciplinary analysis of the results of the building survey and excavation, and a programme of dendrochronological sampling, has allowed an account of the chronology and development of the site to be constructed (Figs 65, 66). Specialist study of re-used timbers dated by dendrochronology has suggested that a late thirteenth or early fourteenth century open hall formerly stood on the site of Old Abbey Farm. The hall is thought to have been fully aisled, with a steeply pitched roof, but all the timbers from this phase were found re-used in secondary positions, so many aspects of the building's form and appearance remain uncertain. In the late medieval period it is probable that the aisles were removed, with new timber-framing built below the arcade plates. A clay floor found by excavation relates to the modified hall, or to an earlier structure. The medieval hall stood on a moated platform; the moat and platform could not be independently dated, but appear to be at least as old as the re-used timbers. A crosswing was added to the medieval hall in the mid sixteenth century; elements of the timber frame were found within the farmhouse, and represent the earliest *in situ* remains found within the standing structure (Figs 67, 68). Subsequently, the house was subject to piecemeal underpinning and rebuilding in brick, beginning in the early to mid seventeenth century, and was extended in the mid eighteenth century, with the final floor plan being achieved in the early twentieth century (Figs 69, 70). The brick Lancashire-type barn was also built at the time of the extensions to the house.

The Origins of Old Abbey Farm

The excavation and building survey revealed a body of evidence for the medieval origins of Old Abbey Farm, consisting of a group of re-used timbers, derived from a substantial structure or structures, found within the post-medieval farmhouse; a clay floor with three associated padstones; and a moat and moated platform. Of these elements, only the re-used timbers could be specifically dated. The successful dendrochronological analysis of samples from four timbers has produced a cluster of mid thirteenth century *terminus post quem* felling dates, ranging from AD 1240 to AD 1268. However, no sapwood was present on any sample, so in each case the cited earliest possible felling date has been calculated by adding ten years to the date of the latest tree ring, because it is currently accepted that British oaks have between 10 and 55 sapwood rings (Hillam *et al* 1987). When possible missing heartwood rings and additional sapwood rings are considered, it is clear that the actual date of felling may have been rather later, although the clustering of all the dates, and likelihood that wastage of heartwood was avoided, suggests that the number of missing rings was not great. As a consequence, it can be suggested that the timbers derive from a structure or structures of late thirteenth, or possibly early fourteenth, century date. The lack of any indication of earlier activity may indicate building on a previously unoccupied site, but it is difficult to draw conclusions as the paucity of medieval features on the platform suggests considerable disturbance of deposits in later centuries. This evidence must be set against the documentary references for the subdivision of the manorial estate of Gilbert de Culcheth following his murder in 1246, and indications that Old Abbey Farm was the homestead at the centre of the new estate of Pesfurlong (*see Ch 2*).

The main building suggested by the re-used timbers was an open, aisled hall. This could not definitely be fixed in space; indeed, it is conceivable that the timbers could have been imported to the site from elsewhere. However, the pattern of re-use of the timbers strongly suggests that some at least had been salvaged from an earlier build of the same house. For example, re-used rafters were employed in the flooring over of the formerly open hall during Phase 5, the same phase of construction in which the roof timbers of the existing building are known to have been replaced. The implication is that the former rafters were derived from the earlier building, and not from elsewhere. The width of the hall plus its side aisles, as suggested by a probable tie-beam, was greater than any subsequent build of the central hall of the farmhouse. It thus seems probable that, later in the medieval period, the aisles were dismantled, and new wall-

Figure 65: Suggested farmhouse ground floor development plan

frames erected in line with the aisle posts, creating the building plan which was to form the basis for subsequent modifications.

There was no direct archaeological evidence to indicate the chronological relationship between the clay floor and the aisled hall inferred from re-used timbers. Clearly there was no possibility of a stratigraphic relationship between the two, whilst the very limited artefactual evidence was of little value in clarifying the date of the floor; the two sherds of late seventeenth century pottery recovered are thought to be intrusive and derived from post-medieval layers deposited immediately above. Stratigraphic relationships do, however, show that the floor must post-date the consolidation of the eastern end of the moated platform, and pre-date the erection of the southern crosswing in the mid sixteenth century. Its width, narrower than the full width of the aisled hall but roughly equivalent to the span of the nave, suggests that the floor must pre-date the aisled hall, or derive from a time after the removal of the side aisles.

Despite the ambiguity, it can be argued that the clay floor may derive from a building which stood before the erection of the aisled hall. The presence of three possible padstones at the floor's eastern edge suggest a construction technique consistent with a thirteenth century date rather than a fourteenth or fifteenth century one, when a stone plinth or dwarf wall might be expected. The padstones imply a wall of several posts in contact with the ground, whereas a dwarf wall would have suggested the presence of a sill beam and fully-framed wall. Posts are known to have been placed on padstones in the early thirteenth century, as for example at Long Barn, Whiston Hall, South Yorkshire (Grenville 1997, 34), whilst uninterrupted sill beams were just coming into use in London at this time (*op cit*). By the time the early fourteenth century hall at Baguley Hall was erected, further east along the valley of the Mersey, the fully framed walls were jointed into sill beams carried on dwarf stone walls (Dixon *et al* 1989, 395). Although the evidence is not conclusive, the padstones recorded appear to suggest a thirteenth century structure pre-dating the aisled hall rather than a structure erected after the dismantling of side aisles in the fourteenth or fifteenth century.

The position of the clay floor further suggested that it might not relate directly to the aisled hall which slowly evolved into the post-medieval farmhouse extant on the site in 1994. The floor was displaced *c* 1 m to the west of the footprint of the later house. For the floor to have corresponded to the nave of the aisled hall, the entire structure of the hall would have had to be moved *c* 1 m to the east, probably prior to the construction of the southern crosswing in the sixteenth

century. Because of the way in which timber-framed buildings were framed and erected (Harris 1978), moving the structure would probably not just have been a matter of supporting the roof and shifting the walls; rather it would have been necessary to dismantle the roof, in order to move and re-assemble the cross frames which included the roof trusses. This would not have been impossible; in the Wakefield area, for example, there are many references made to medieval peasants who from time to time moved and re-erected their houses, by implication structures of some worth and permanence (Wrathmell 1989, 252; Grenville 1997, 127). Nevertheless, in this instance, it is difficult to find a possible motive for moving the hall 1 m nearer to the moat, and any move would surely have caused considerable inconvenience.

There are further reasons for supposing that the clay floor does not represent the footprint of the aisled hall, one of which is size. If the two were associated, the implication is that the whole hall structure, including any partitions for service and solar, would have been no more than 11 m long. This would be rather smaller than any published examples of contemporary buildings of comparable status (*see p151*). Instead, it could be suggested that the floor related to a building erected on the site immediately after the laying out of the moat and platform. An interval of a minimum of 23 years is known to have elapsed between the death of Gilbert de Culcheth in 1246 (Farrer and Brownbill 1911, 159) and the earliest possible date for the construction of the aisled hall, 1269. This represents roughly a generation. It may be that Gilbert's estate was divided soon after his death, and the site at Pesfurlong moated, but with the new manor administered from a relatively temporary building until Adam de Hindley and Elizabeth de Culcheth, apparently children in 1246, were ready to build the high-quality aisled hall, elements of which survived to the late twentieth century. It could even be suggested that the timber hall was built in the early fourteenth century, when Pesfurlong passed by marriage to the de Radclyffe family.

These suggestions are largely speculative, but although it might seem inconvenient to build a new hall over an earlier building, there is good evidence for medieval structures being constructed at least partly over the footprints of their predecessors. At Baguley Hall, the fourteenth century build of the hall overlaid the earlier aisled building (Dixon *et al* 1989, 408), whilst, lower down the social spectrum, it has been observed that peasant houses were almost always reconstructed on the same spot within their toft (Astill and Grant 1988, 59), to the extent that it has been suggested that there may have been some symbolic necessity for behaviour which appears to leave the household without good site-based shelter during re-

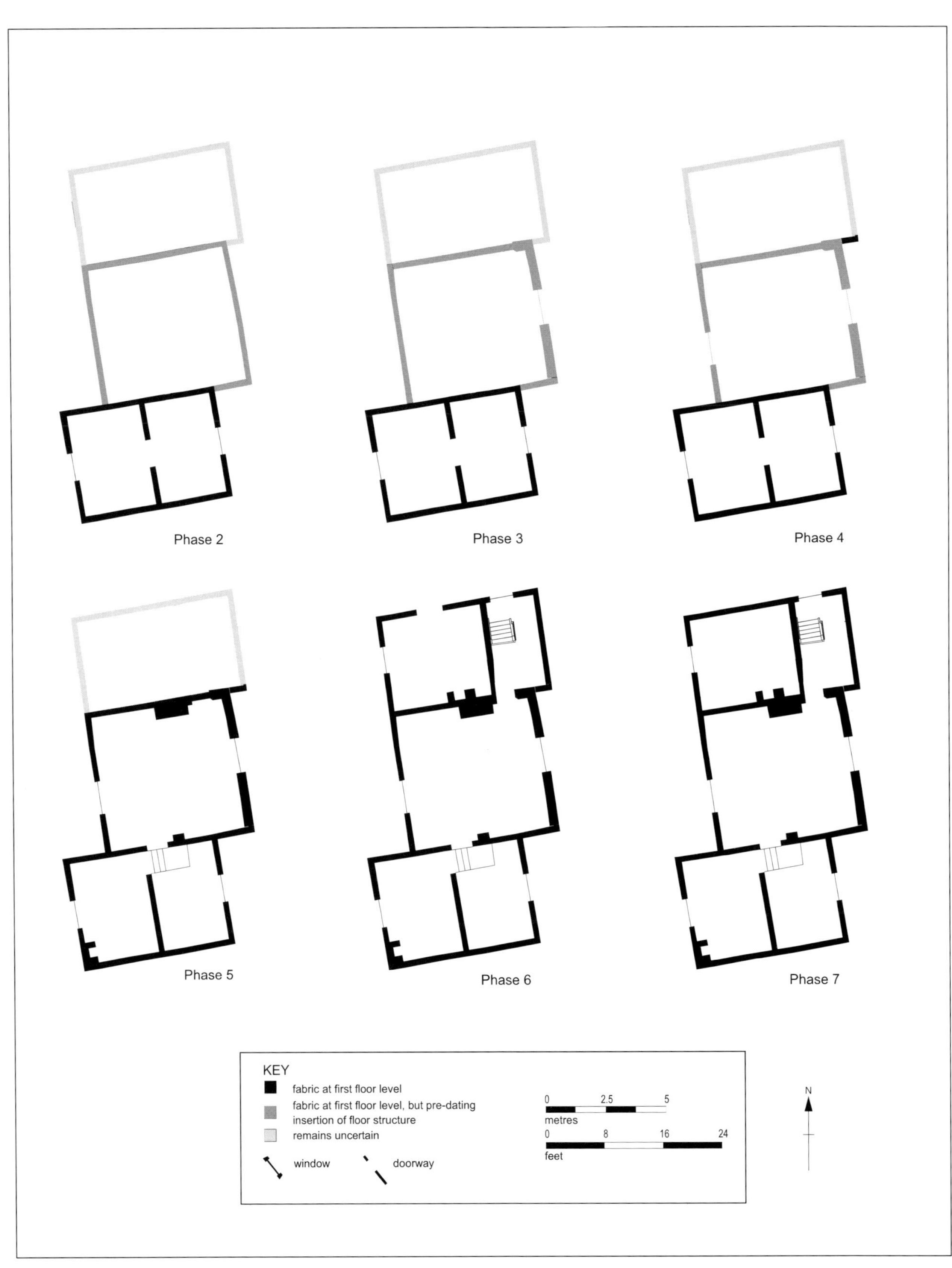

Figure 66: Suggested farmhouse first floor room development plan

building (Grenville 1997, 132). In the case of Old Abbey Farm, it is possible that the family may have occupied the homestead of the de Hindley family, or stayed with sisters and brothers-in-law elsewhere in Culcheth, during building work.

The lack of firm evidence for the sequence of construction of elements of a medieval building is not unusual. Despite a programme of building recording and relatively large-scale excavation at Baguley Hall, no clear archaeological evidence was recovered for the chronological relationship between the fourteenth century hall and *camera* to the south. As at Old Abbey Farm, it was dendrochronological analysis that allowed the dating of elements of the extant structure, with some aspects of the excavation evidence proving difficult to date, in relative or absolute terms. Again, few finds were recovered from surviving clay floors, and it was observed that the finds assemblage did 'little to clarify the date or the constructional detail of the hall' (Dixon *et al* 1989, 407).

Despite the uncertainty over the constructional sequence at Old Abbey Farm, both aisled hall and clay floor seem to have post-dated the consolidation of the eastern part of the moated platform, and by implication the moat. This contrasts with the nearby site at Tanners Farm, where a medieval house was found to have been truncated by creation of the moat in the fifteenth century (Freke 1982). There is no independent archaeological evidence for the date of the construction of moat or platform at Old Abbey Farm, but given the lack of documentary or archaeological evidence for settlement of the site prior to the division of the manor of Culcheth after 1246, a date in the range 1246-1315 can be suggested. This falls within the period when moat digging was most prevalent nationally, but may be relatively early for construction of a moat in this part of north-west England (Tindall 1985a, 15; *see p 159*). As stated above, no evidence for any form of activity on the site prior to the digging of the moat was found, but any evidence for pre-moat activity may have been destroyed by later disturbance, as was undoubtedly the case with many medieval features (for example, the lack of evidence for ancillary structures, ovens, and indeed the walls of the aisled hall). Nationally, evidence for activity pre-dating the digging of moats appears to survive best where spoil from the moat was heaped onto the platform, protecting earlier features (for example, at Wood Hall; Metcalfe 1993). At Old Abbey Farm there is evidence only for limited building up of the platform, at its eastern edge.

The moat and platform may have been constructed in the late thirteenth or early fourteenth century, but the timber bridge, elements of which survived, was clearly made from timbers felled in the mid fifteenth century (*see Ch 2*). It seems most probable that this bridge replaced an earlier timber structure, probably spanning the moat in the same place, though no evidence for such a structure was noted.

The Aisled Hall

Specialist analysis of re-used timbers has demonstrated that several were derived from an open hall with at least one aisle, built from substantial timbers after AD 1269. The hall was constructed using complex carpentry techniques, with mortise and tenon joints used to join posts and wall-plates, braces and wall-plates, and collars and rafters. It appears to have had a common rafter roof.

Other characteristics can be inferred with less certainty from the surviving evidence, and from parallels drawn with other buildings. It is suggested that the hall had a hipped roof with end aisles, being similar to slightly older aisled halls at Sandal Castle, West Yorkshire (Michelmore 1983, 73-5), and Lime Tree House, Harwell, in Berkshire (Fletcher and Currie 1980, 173-92). The central nave may have been *c* 5.8 m wide, if a particular re-used timber was in fact a tie-beam from this structure. This span is within 0.20 m of the external width of the later hall of the post-medieval farmhouse, which was 6.0 m wide. The form of the roof is uncertain. The hall might be expected to have had a crown post roof, a form used at Morleys Hall, Astley, a mile or so from Old Abbey Farm (surveyed by Nigel Morgan, J Lewis pers comm), and an early fourteenth century example is known from Til House, Clifton, Nottinghamshire (Grenville 1997, 130). However, no obvious evidence for crown post trusses was found at Old Abbey Farm, and the building may have been too early for such a roof. Crown post roofs appear to have been adopted in the mid thirteenth century, but their early distribution lies predominantly in the south-east of England (*op cit*, 48, 50). An older roof form seems probable, and indeed two fragments of tie-beams which may derive from this building contained empty joints suggesting the presence of passing braces or parallel rafters, a method of bracing employed in the eleventh to twelfth century carpentry tradition sometimes known as *romanesque* (*op cit*, 47). The roof is not fully understood, as the surviving collar did not appear to show evidence for passing braces towards the top of the roof. Nevertheless, there are indications that the hall was built during a time of architectural transition in the north-west of England, with elements of an older roof form occurring in a building constructed using complex and more recent carpentry joints.

It is suggested that the house was constructed with a cross-passage to the north of an open truss demarcating the lower, northern, end of the open hall, since the later seventeenth and eighteenth century plan form of the hall suggested that a baffle entry had been constructed in a former cross-passage linking opposed doorways. Although the truss could not definitely be located relative to the supposed cross-passage, the length of the surviving re-used wall-plate (4.2 m) corresponded to the distance from the south end of the post-medieval hall to the baffle entry and inglenook. This indicated the possibility that the main central bay of the open hall corresponded exactly to the hall of the later house, with a cross-passage to the north, in the position later occupied by the inglenook, and a service beyond.

Some aspects of the hall's structure could not be satisfactorily resolved. One of the most significant was the length of the building. It is possible to reconstruct the hall as being of a single bay in length, with two trusses carried by pairs of aisle posts defining the open hall. The main roof would be carried slightly beyond the trusses by oversailing arcade-plates, with end aisles beyond; the oversailing arcade-plates are paralleled at Lime Tree House in Berkshire (D Michelmore pers comm). This arrangement is suggested in part because only a single arcade-plate survived, but primarily because it would allow the aisled hall to fit the footprint, *c* 11 m long, suggested by the clay floor recovered by excavation; this 11 m length has been used for the reconstruction drawing and artist's impression of the Phase 1 building (Fig 12 and Pl 4). However, acceptance of this length might be thought problematic, partly because there is no decisive evidence that the clay floor related to this structure, partly because the building would be very short to have functioned as the hall from which an estate was administered. Indeed a length of 11 m would not have been excessive for many medieval thirteenth/fourteenth century peasant houses, with typical houses in late thirteenth century south Wales being 10 m in length (R Newman pers comm). Structurally such a length is problematic; given that the cross-passage is thought to be located beyond the northern truss, there would be little room for a pantry and buttery. Whilst it is possible that the cross-passage lay within the central bay, or that the service rooms were housed within a separate structure (*see p 157*), it seems safest to regard the total length of the building as not fixed at 11 m by the surviving evidence.

Several small halls of thirteenth to early fourteenth century date are known from elsewhere in England. That at Lime Tree House in Harwell is thought to have been structurally similar to the Old Abbey Farm hall, consisting of an aisled hall of four bays, measuring approximately 13 m long by 7 m wide internally, together with a later crosswing (Grenville 1997, 130). It has now been interpreted as the homestead of an 8.5 ha peasant yardland (*op cit*), though it seems likely to have been an exceptional rather than a typical peasant house. Smaller halls existed at Manor Cottage, Sutton Courtney (8.75 m long internally) and Til House, Clifton, Nottinghamshire (approximately 6 m long). However, the two bay cruck hall at Manor Cottage was attached to a contemporary three bay crosswing with crown post roof, whilst the Til House hall had an adjoining service bay at its lower end, and a separately framed crosswing at the upper end (Grenville 1997, 130). Both may represent the homes of well-to-do peasants, and should be regarded as housing lower status households than that at Old Abbey Farm. Although Manor Cottage and Til House lie in a different and perhaps more affluent part of England, these parallels give further credence to the idea that the house erected at Old Abbey Farm must have exceeded 11 m in length, or have been provided with separate chamber and service blocks (*see p 157*). This is particularly true given that the hipped roof suggested would have restricted the space available for first floor rooms in the solar or service.

The form of the aisled open hall seems to have been rather archaic when built at Old Abbey Farm in the later thirteenth or early fourteenth century. The nearby aisled hall at Baguley Hall is argued to have been built between the eleventh and early thirteenth centuries (Dixon *et al* 1989, 416). This building is thought to have been at least 15 m long, with the nave 6.5 m in width, and each aisle a further 1.5 m wide. This compares with a nave width of 5.8 m and aisle width of 1.4 m suggested by the span matrix created for the Old Abbey Farm hall. The aisled hall at Baguley Hall was constructed with earthfast aisle posts supported within massive post pits. No post pits were found at Old Abbey Farm; although some features may have been masked below the clay floor and associated external make-up, neither of which could be fully excavated, there were clearly no post pits stratified above the clay floor. It thus seems probable that the aisle posts here rested on padstones, or short transverse plinths extending from the outer walls.

Excavation at Bewsey Old Hall has allowed the tentative identification of another aisled hall in the region, this time sited to the north of the Mersey. There, buildings set on timber sills, possibly with postholes at the corners, may date from as early as the eleventh or twelfth century. However, they were replaced in the second half of the fourteenth century by structures set on sandstone sills. Within the hall, a series of internal postholes was found, parallel with the stone walls, suggesting the possibility that this building may have been aisled. The suggestion is problematic, because of the difficulty of relating the postholes to the stone walls, when they might perhaps pertain to an earlier building of earthfast posts, of which the stone walls might represent an extension outwards (Lewis 2000, 128). Elsewhere, two successive aisled structures have been identified at Norton Priory, but, as with the aisled building at Baguley Hall, these were earlier in date, having been replaced by *c* 1190 (*op cit* 5).

Leaving aside the enigmatic evidence from Bewsey, it seems that the aisled hall at Old Abbey Farm may have been erected in a time of transition in north-west England, lying part way between earlier aisled halls with earthfast posts, and later fully-framed unaisled structures with sill beams. Although in the South and Midlands, aisles had, by the later thirteenth century, been largely superseded by designs intended to remove upright posts from the floor space (Dixon *et al* 1989), the change may have been delayed in north-western England. When the hall at Baguley was replaced in the earlier fourteenth century, its builders did not use a design common in the South and Midlands, but reached their own highly individual solution to the problem of how to achieve a wide hall uncluttered by roof posts (Dixon *et al* 1989). Although the aisled structure at Old Abbey Farm shows few similarities with Baguley Hall, and does not share the use of massive broad, but thin, timbers identified as a regional characteristic, the parallel demonstrates that, in the late thirteenth and early fourteenth centuries, buildings in the Mersey valley might deviate from developments which were common further south and east. However, the lack of evidence for thirteenth century halls in the North West means it is difficult to view the suggested aisled building at Old Abbey Farm within its local context, or to estimate how typical of the region it may have been. Certainly it appears to be the only moated site within the south-west of the historic county of Lancashire for which the detailed constructional characteristics of a possible thirteenth century hall can be suggested (Lewis 2000, 126-132, and table 41).

Land Tenure, Rural Economy, and Settlement Pattern

The historic county of Lancashire has been regarded by many writers as being tenurially distinctive in the three centuries following the Norman Conquest, perhaps by virtue of its geographical isolation, former position within the Kingdom of Northumbria, and treatment after the Conquest, when the lands between the Ribble and the Mersey quickly reverted from Roger de Poitou back to the Crown (Tindall 1985a, 19). The evidence for land tenure has recently been discussed by Dr Jennifer Lewis, as part of her study of *The earthwork sites of West Derby Hundred* (Lewis 2000); the brief review provided here inevitably draws heavily on her work, as does the section below on moated sites, and her assistance in generously providing a text prior to publication is gratefully acknowledged.

Domesday Book records land held by 'thegns' in West Derby and Salford hundreds, 'drengs' in Newton and Warrington, and 'freemen' in Blackburn and Leyland (Tindall 1985a, 18). These titles seem to imply particular forms of land tenure, forms which were to persist to the thirteenth century. The Great Inquest of 1212 demonstrates that almost a quarter of the lands within the hundreds of West Derby, Warrington, and Newton were held in *thanagio* (Lewis 2000, 56); Cadishead, immediately to the east of Culcheth, was held in this way (Farrer and Brownbill 1906, map opp 291), as were the lands of the de Hindleys (Lewis 2000, table 13c), who married into the de Culcheth family in the mid thirteenth century (*see Ch 2*). In Culcheth, as in nearby Atherton and Rixton, lords held their estates by knight service, but even here, study of the rents and terms has suggested that knight service had been imposed on earlier thanage tenures (Farrer 1903, 9). It remains uncertain exactly what, in tenurial terms, was meant by 'thanage', but Lewis suggests that, like the *dreng*, the thane may have been responsible for the supervision of a demesne township, in a manner reminiscent of pre-Conquest Northumbrian administration. Thus, the tenure seems to have been based on the responsibility for the provision of services from the whole vill, rather than on a man's landholding. Certainly, the vill, rather than the manor, was retained as the unit of the Great Survey of 1212 of the county (Lewis 2000, 52).

Throughout the thirteenth century, Pipe Roll references to lands held in lordship within the townships of the Hundred of West Derby refer almost exclusively to a *terra*, *villa*, or simply to 'lands' or 'carrucates'. References to 'manors' become widespread only after 1322 (Lewis 2000, table 13a). This observation holds good whether vills were held by the Crown or Honour of Lancaster, by knight service, or in thanage. Indeed, despite the fact that some lords in the region held their estates by knight service, it has been claimed that nowhere is there clear evidence for the operation of a well-structured system of manorial administration (*op cit*, 59). This may be the case, though in some mid thirteenth century documents, including the '*Gift by William the Butler*' which confirmed the division of Gilbert de Culcheth's estate, the term 'manor' is clearly used (LRO DP 398, Box 2). Whatever the terminology, independently managed, consolidated estates, with intercommoning in neighbouring vills, are visible in the documentary sources, again suggesting to some commentators a much greater similarity with pre-Conquest Northumbrian administration of the countryside than with the manorial exploitation of other parts of England (*op cit*, 59). Likewise, it was quite normal for both the tenants of thanage vills, and the holders of estates by knight service, to make grants out of their estates, especially to members of their families or to monastic orders. Partible inheritance was also clearly

Figure 67: Plan of farmhouse ground floor showing plysical evidence by phase

a feature of lands held by knight service in this area, occurring in the vill of Lydiate as well as in Culcheth (*op cit*, 63), and together, these factors appear to have allowed the proliferation of small, freehold estates in a manner that did not occur in many other parts of the country. It can be argued that the intercommoning often practised after the subdivision of lands was again in accordance with ancient custom.

Tenure by knight service thus appears to have had little effect on the customary organisation of estates. This has significance for consideration of the status of estate centres and moated sites in the region, especially when comparisons are attempted with other parts of England (*see below p 157*).

If the organisation of estates in historic Lancashire was distinctive in the thirteenth century, so also was the pattern of settlement and the rural economy. The pre-industrial settlement pattern of the north-west of England has been characterised as 'dispersed' (Higham 1987, 9). This is a generalisation which does not hold good for all areas: a distinction must be drawn between the south-east and the south-west of the historic county of Lancashire; on the West Lancashire Plain, from the Mersey estuary northwards, the glacial till is covered by Shirdley Hill Sands, 1-5 m deep (Cowell and Innes 1994, 5-6), giving soils more favourable for agriculture and settlement. Here nucleated villages with open arable fields have been identified, with nucleation and dispersal seen in juxtaposed townships (Lewis 1991, 91). Nevertheless, it is clear that considerable areas of the region were ill-suited to large-scale arable agriculture in the medieval period, and that topographical factors often encouraged dispersal of settlement, and hindered nucleation. Away from the coastal plain, as in Cheshire to the south (Higham 1987, 9), niches suitable for arable agriculture were small, discouraging the development of large open fields. When population did start to rise, probably in the thirteenth century, the tendency to clear woodland and moss at the margins of existing agriculture was only likely to exaggerate the dispersal of settlement (*op cit*; Newman 1996, 117).

Much of the area between the Mersey and the Ribble was regarded as 'waste' in 1086, and geological factors have often been held responsible for the creation of an inhospitable landscape of moorland in the north-east, and mossland in the east and north-west (Tindall 1985a, 16). It has been suggested that the natural environment hampered both communications and agriculture, so that much of the region remained a political and economic backwater. However, it would be wrong to suggest that the whole area was unsuitable for arable agriculture. Lewis has estimated that around 10% of south-west Lancashire was cultivated land at the time of the Domesday assessments (Lewis 2000,

69), and the figure for Winwick parish, in which the township of Culcheth lay, appears to have been 11%. Moreover, late twelfth century documentary sources can be used to suggest that the region was well-suited to a mixed regime of cultivation and animal husbandry (*op cit*, 72), and intercommoning of extensive areas of waste may have allowed many estates to be virtually self-sufficient (*op cit*, 75, 76). The mossland and woodland largely ignored by early post-Conquest documentary sources may have been an integral part of a well-balanced economy, as well as providing the potential for future expansion.

The surviving fourteenth century documents relating to landholding in Culcheth township imply a situation which corresponds very closely to this suggested regional pattern of freehold tenure and dispersed settlement, with expansion of agriculture in the thirteenth century. Prior to the division of the estate of Gilbert de Culcheth after 1246, the holding appears to have been coterminous with the township. Culcheth clearly encompassed much of the mossland in the locality (Leah *et al* 1997), as well as areas of woodland, and there seems to have been scope for increasing the area of arable land. One probable mid to late thirteenth century document, surviving in a seventeenth century transcript by Roger Dodsworth (Bod Lib Dodsw v142, f113; MCL L1/51/9/12, f107-9), apparently in settlement of a boundary dispute, states 'that whole waste which is capable of being ploughed and sown between *Sothewode* and *le Westwode*...shall remain to Adam'. This suggests that the Pesfurlong estate was made up of newly ploughed land, as well as perhaps a portion of the arable of the original Culcheth holding. The estate also contained newly enclosed land, with the document stating that 'Adam is to keep all his land and woodland which he has enclosed'. This body of evidence strongly suggests that the new estate of Pesfurlong was substantially a mossland assart, comprising an area of wooded wetland, which was partially cleared, drained, and cultivated in the mid thirteenth century (Newman 1996, 117). It is unclear whether the estate centre itself was founded on existing arable land. The place-name, probably meaning 'the furlong where peas were grown' (Ekwall 1922, 27), might suggest that this was the case, yet the name could easily have been derived from land peripheral to the new estate being applied to the whole area in the absence of another name.

The other new holdings may also be expected to have been made up in part of assarts. Other documents imply (undated) changes in land-use elsewhere in Culcheth by the later thirteenth century, with an apparent progression of part of *Westwod* from common woodland to common pasture (Robert and Ellen's acknowledgement, LRO DP 398 Box 4). This document implies that, within another of the newly created estates, Risley, land was brought into

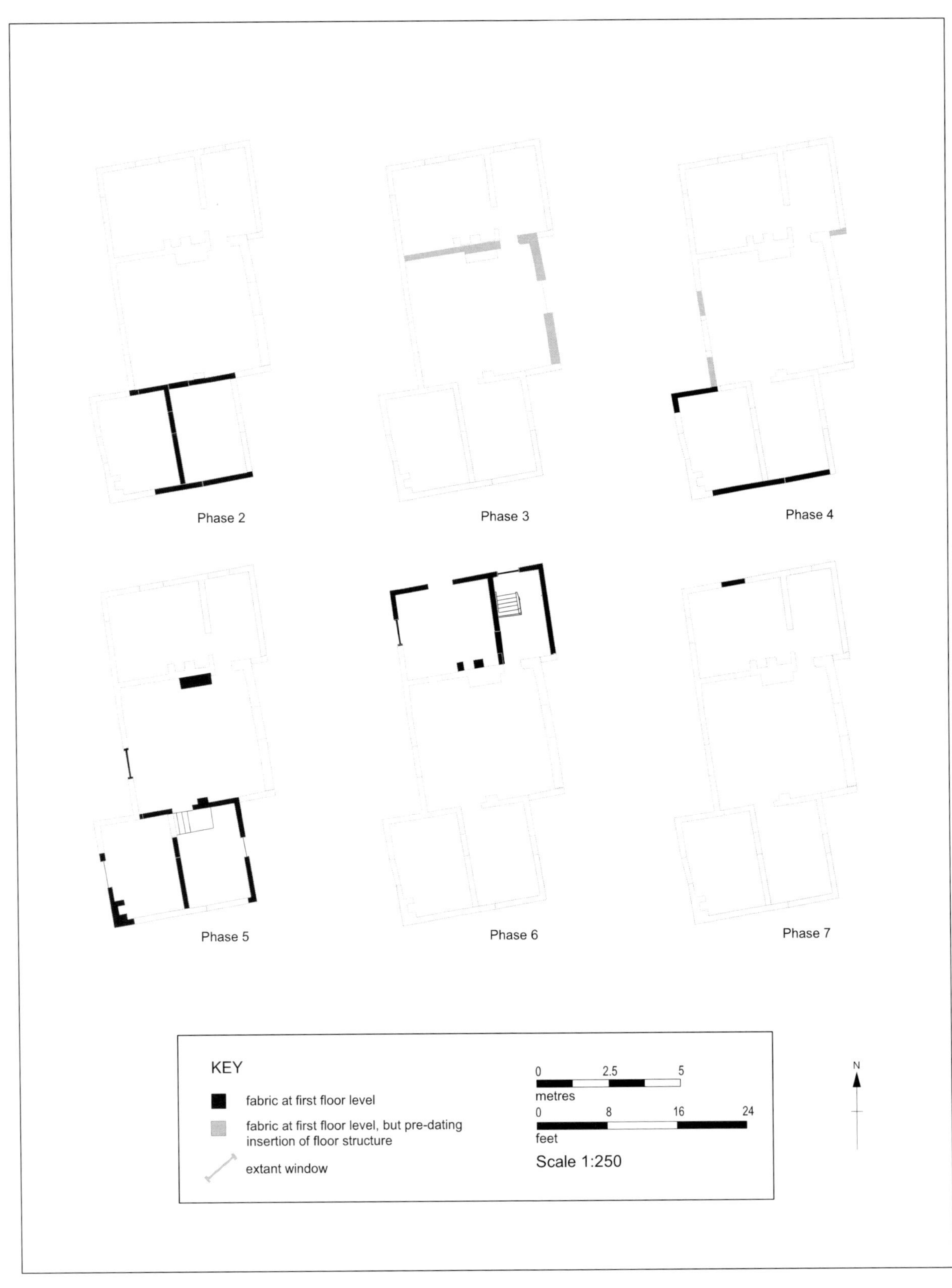

Figure 68: Plan of farmhouse first floor showing physical evidence by phase

more intensive exploitation. Robert and Ellen received 'the waste and deserted place in Culchith [*sic*] township, and also...lands and tenements in the township of Langton...'.

No explicit references to the pattern of settlement within Pesfurlong have been traced; a marriage settlement of 1592 refers to 12 messuages, tenements, and farmholds in Pesfurlong, but none are named (LRO DP 397/25/2). However, several references of grants of small, defined portions of land, presumably to freeholders, seem to imply tenurial arrangements and patterns of landholding more suggestive of dispersed settlement with enclosed fields rather than nucleation and the use of common open fields. These references include the gift of 12 acres of land by Adam to one Giles de Penkit, apparently a discrete parcel of land with its eastern boundary ditched (B Lib BM Add MS 32, 107, f123 item 998); and the lease by Adam son of Hugh del Sargh 'of three acres of land in the township...of Culcheth...as is contained within fixed bounds' (*op cit*, f128, item 1031). These references appear inconsistent with the use of scattered strips within large open fields, and even the place-name 'Pesfurlong' itself does not imply open fields, with the 'furlong' element merely describing an area of land.

A mixed farming regime appears to be suggested by all the thirteenth century documents examined, with references to arable, as well as to woodland and pasture, and indications that some of the woodland and pasture was held in common between estates.

An Estate Centre

The documentary evidence linking Old Abbey Farm with the centre of the manorial estate known as 'Pesfurlong' has been reviewed above (*see Ch 2*). Given this knowledge of the status of the site, it may be helpful to consider Old Abbey Farm in its context as an estate centre, before moving on to discuss the implications of the moat; for, across the country as a whole, it is clear that moats may have surrounded sites of a wide variety of status and function (Taylor 1978, 8). Documentary sources clearly indicate some of the characteristics which a manor or demesne farm might be expected to possess. It may be helpful to review some of these references, although it must be remembered that Pesfurlong was a relatively small estate created on the subdivision of a larger holding, and that manors south of the Mersey may have been rather different to manorial estates in Lancashire, which possibly reflect ancient methods of rural exploitation (*see above p 153*).

For England as a whole, Le Patourel has used documents to reconstruct three generalised models for the layout of moated sub-manors and manors (Le Patourel 1978a, 23). These differ according to whether the house is alone on the moat, or accompanied by other structures, but the elements expected in all models include house, garden, orchard, and agricultural buildings. Manors might additionally have a chapel, fishpond, and park or forest lodge. Documentary sources specifically relating to north-west England suggest the presence of a similar range of features. A record of 1429 lists the following as present at Hulme Hall in Cheshire: 'the lesser chamber, le Pantre, le Buttre, the Larder, le Deyhouse, le Malthouse, le...berne, le Hayberne, le Vyne Yorde, le Night' gale Erber, le Lytell Erber' (Wilson 1987, 147). Fourteenth century records refer to a hall of two chambers and a kitchen, with a barn, stables, and wards beyond the moat, at Broad Oak Farm (Cheshire), whilst the apparently rather richer 'demesne farm' at Ordsall Hall is described as having 'a hall with five chambers, kitchen, chapel, two stables, three granges, two shippons, garner (worth nothing), dovecote (worth 2s a year), orchard (12d), windmill (6s 8d)' (Tindall 1985a, 13). A sixteenth century enquiry into the capital messuage at Baguley Hall, referred to orchards, gardens, barns, a stable, and other buildings (Dixon *et al* 1989, 388). It can be seen that as well as a variety of service and agricultural buildings, gardens and orchards were very common features of manors, and indeed a complex arrangement of earthworks thought to have been associated with a medieval garden has been excavated at Belgrave manor in Cheshire (Turner *et al* 1988).

Although, as stated above (*see p 153*), the Pesfurlong estate was split from an existing manorial estate in the mid thirteenth century, it must have been laid out around a working farm and estate centre, and a variety of service and agricultural buildings must be expected. There may also have been accommodation for a group of manorial servants (as described by Grenville 1997, 116). Adam de Peasfurlong is known to have made several grants of land to individuals who may have lived elsewhere in a landscape which seems to have been characterised by a dispersed pattern of settlement (*see above p 155*), but the early lords of Pesfurlong were not absentees, and the direct management of part at least of the estate must have required the services of men and women outside the immediate family. These individuals may have lived close to the estate centre. The presence of subsidiary dwellings can thus be suggested, although the type of large demesne farm typical of the champion landscapes of, for example, parts of the Midlands should not be expected, as these tend to be associated with open field systems and nucleated villages (Taylor 1983, 125).

Away from the footprint of the hall, and with the exception of the bridge, no certain medieval features

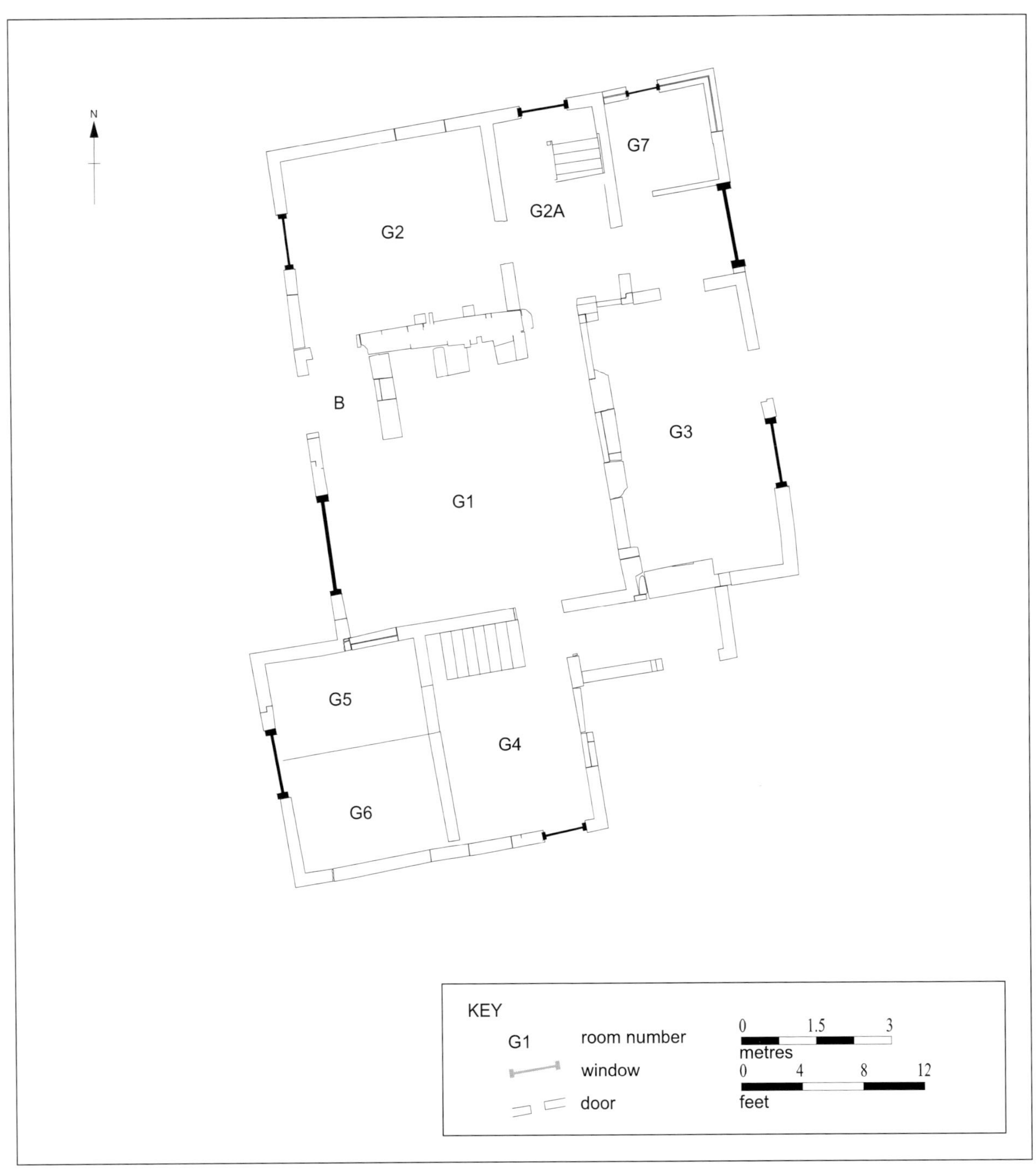

Figure 69: Ground floor room location plan

were revealed by excavation. A small post-built structure, Structure 2 (assigned to Phase 6), might conceivably be medieval, but only if the eighteenth to nineteenth century pottery in one of the posthole fills related to its demolition, and if the seventeenth to twentieth century sherds in the underlying layer were contaminants introduced later by horticulture. There are two explanations for this lack of medieval evidence. Firstly, agricultural buildings, and structures offering subsidiary accommodation, may have been located off the moated platform, in an area only partially sampled by excavation. This seems highly probable, and is discussed further below (*see p 159*)

Secondly, the remains of ancillary medieval structures may not have survived the continuous occupation of the platform into the twentieth century. It can be noted that no trace remained of even the outer walls of the aisled hall itself. This may be due in part to the use of surface-laid sills as the only foundations for many medieval buildings. Records suggest that at Bishop's Manor, Harwell, stone footings were used for a barn erected in 1302/3, but that timber ground sills were used for the hay barn, oxhouse, stable, and sheephouse (Grenville 1997, 120). Closer to Old Abbey Farm, it is clear that a southern *camera* or solar constructed at Baguley Hall, arguably in the thirteenth century, was built on surface-laid sills, only fragments of which had survived protected below a later structure (Dixon *et al* 1989, 412).

It can thus be suggested that there may have been a free-standing kitchen or bake-house, closely associated with the lower end of the hall. Even among the lesser gentry, it is thought highly improbable that the hall was used for cooking (Grenville 1997, 119), and detached or semi-detached kitchens are thought to have been almost universal by the fourteenth century. Certainly, no evidence for any medieval bake oven, which is likely to have been built of stone, was found within the footprint of the farmhouse. Kitchens were vulnerable to fire; no evidence for a disaster of this kind was found at Old Abbey Farm, but nationally, almost all the surviving examples of such kitchens are of stone or brick (*op cit*, 118-9), suggesting the loss of many timber structures. Additionally, if the hall was originally only 11 m in length, it is possible that the service and solar may also have been detached buildings. This would have been typical of the eleventh to twelfth centuries, but a detached chamber may have continued as a response to the difficulty of flooring over the upper end of an aisled hall with hipped roof (Dixon *et al* 1989, 410); locally, it has been suggested that the timber-built range at Rainhill Hall Farm may be a solar which was constructed at right-angles to a former hall (Lewis 2000, 138). A variety of other small structures, such as brewhouse or granary, may also have been located on the moated platform close to the hall, and possibly also servants quarters. However, prior to the fourteenth century, these are unlikely to have been laid out regularly around a rectangular courtyard; this arrangement, sometimes regarded as that of a 'typical manorial complex', appears to have developed on secular sites after *c* 1300 (Clarke 1984, 60; Grenville 1997, 103). It is unlikely that Old Abbey Farm would have been of sufficient status to possess a household chapel.

Moated Sites in North-West England

'Moated sites' have been identified as a distinct type of field monument, and have tended to be discussed collectively (Taylor 1978; Le Patourel and Roberts 1978). Most writers have agreed that the primary reasons for digging a moat were for security (rather than defence) and, perhaps most importantly, to gain and express social status (*eg* Wilson 1987, 148-9). It seems likely that the cutting of moats became fashionable, as members of the gentry, and then landed freemen, sought to emphasise their connection with the aristocracy, who had established castles which were moated, and to stress their separation from the peasantry. A five stage chronology has been proposed, charting the prevalence of the phenomenon from the

inspiration of previous monuments (pre-1150), through the introduction of moated sites (1150-1200), to expansion (1200-1325), decline (1325-1500), and abandonment (post-1500) (Le Patourel and Roberts 1978, 51).

However, across England as a whole, moats can be seen to have surrounded sites of widely differing social status. It is clear that the homesteads of yeoman farmers, the manor houses of the gentry, monastic granges, the estate centres of the lay and ecclesiastical aristocracy, and royal hunting lodges, might all be moated. There are even examples of moats enclosing churches, kilns, and fish-breeding ponds (Taylor 1978, 8). The distribution of moated sites and their status appear to have varied according to geology, settlement pattern, prevalent agricultural regime, and date. It is thus important to pay close attention to location, status, and date, when attempting to draw comparisons between moated sites.

Some writers have found it helpful to adopt a simplified two-fold classification of the status of moated sites, dividing them into 'seignorial' and 'sub-manorial' categories (Le Patourel 1978a; Tindall 1985b). The 'seignorial' sites are thought to represent the capital messuages of lords of the manor, be they barons or senior clerics holding several manors, or members of the gentry whose wealth might be made up largely of a single estate. The 'sub-manorial' sites were at the head of lesser freehold estates, perhaps occupied by the cadet branches of seignorial families, or merchants, their lords not being in possession of true manorial rights. This group appears to have increased in importance from the thirteenth century onwards, as older estates gradually fragmented, and a new class of landowners managed to acquire holdings of their own, often through assarting of waste and woodlands.

In south-west Lancashire, however, this classification may be of limited use, because of the distinctive nature of manorial estates in the region. Here, estates were often small, but they were nevertheless held by well-established families, probably in accordance with ancient customs, rather than rent paying peasants (Lewis 2000, 100; *see p 153*). The Lord seem to have been free to make grants of land from his holdings, or to subdivide them on his death, but the new estates created were often held by junior family members, as with the subdivision of Culcheth (*see Ch 2*). Of the 43 moated sites identified in Warrington Hundred, 28 were in vills held by knight service, nine in vills held by thanage, and the remaining six in vills associated with rectories or held from the crown. The particular nature of the tenure appears not to have affected the ability of freeholders to create moated sites, for in the adjacent hundred of Newton, moats predominated in vills held by thanage (Lewis 2000).

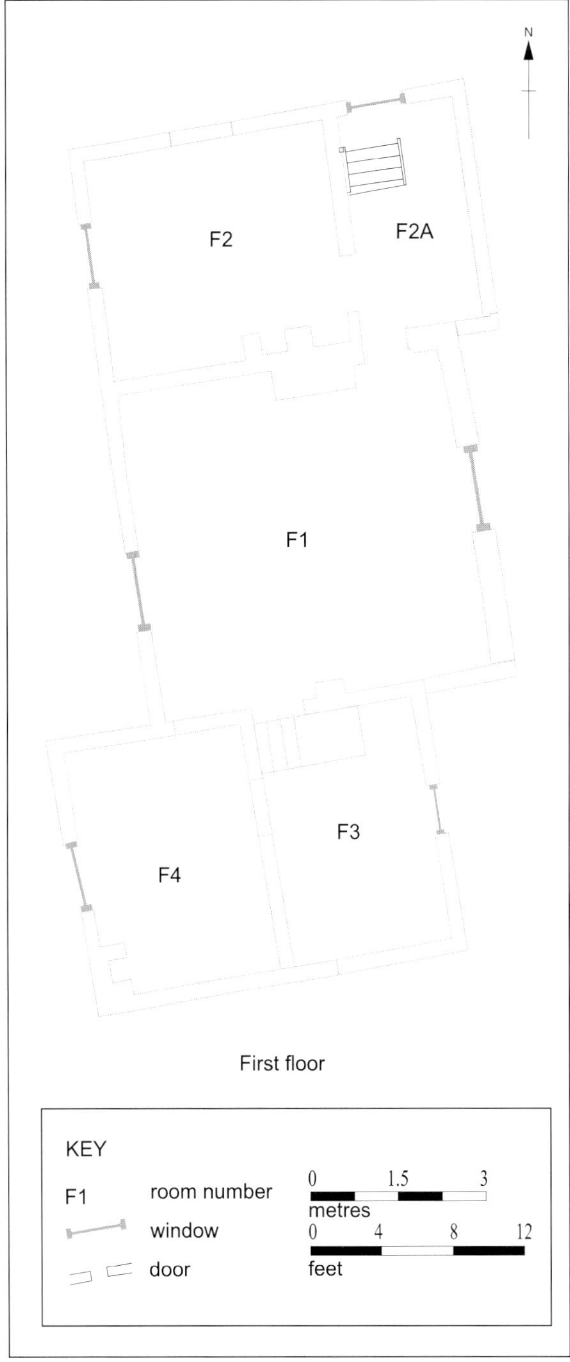

Figure 70: First floor room location plan

A total of 122 moated sites and ditched enclosures can now be identified within the Hundreds of West Derby, Newton, and Warrington, of which 23 have been investigated archaeologically (19%). The distribution is such that, of the 97 vills in the region, 54 have one or more moated site; it can be noted that almost half the vills have no moated site, but conversely, several vills have at least one (Lewis 2000, 94). Moated sites and ditched enclosures are most concentrated in the Hundreds of Warrington (43 sites in 19 of the 26 vills), and Newton (35 sites in 14 of the 19 vills), both lying relatively close to the Mersey. By contrast, West Derby Hundred, extending north from the Mersey estuary

across the West Lancashire Plain, has a lower density of these sites (44 sites in 21 of the 52 vills). The latter area still includes several vills with more than one moat, but the density of such vills is lower, and the area has a significantly higher proportion of vills with no moated site (*op cit*, figs 56, 57).

In view of this distribution, it can be observed that the area with the lowest density of moated sites, close to the western coastal plain, corresponds to that part of the region where the vast majority of named Domesday vills was situated (Tindall 1985a, 17). It seems that this area contained some of the land best suited to medieval arable cultivation, and certainly this is where much of the evidence for open fields and settlement nucleation in south Lancashire is to be found (Lewis 1991). Furthermore, it has been argued the land to the east, in the Hundreds of Newton and Warrington, should be regarded as a zone of secondary colonisation (Tindall 1985a, 17). It is tempting to suggest that most moated sites in this region should be seen primarily as a feature of assarting and the extension of agriculture into marginal areas in the thirteenth century, but this would probably represent an over-simplification.

The western coastal plain is in part capped with permeable sands (Cowell and Innes 1994, 5-6), whereas the area to the east is predominantly covered with boulder clay. Although it is clear that in some cases, moats were deliberately dug through permeable sands and gravels (Lewis 2000, 109), the increased density of moats away from the coastal strip may in part reflect the fact that, here, the geology made it considerably easier to create a moat which held water. Furthermore, although the density of moats was lower than to the east, the distribution of moats in the Hundred of West Derby was still very different to the pattern found in Cheshire. As many as 11 of the 52 West Derby vills had more than one moated site, whereas, in Cheshire, this occurred in only 19 of 540 townships. Where geological conditions favoured moat digging, moats in Cheshire often show a distribution of one per township, and they were often centrally placed, allowing the suggestion that they were predominantly seignorial, and might represent the location of manors (Wilson 1987, 145, 150).

Moreover, if the distribution of moats on the coastal strip of South Lancashire differs from that in Cheshire, it also seems unwise to compare the creation of moats in the Hundreds of Warrington and Newton too closely with other areas of England, in which the close association of moats with assarting has been stressed. Parallels have been drawn with areas of the West Midlands, where moated homesteads appear to be closely associated with woodland assarting by an emerging class of freeman, in areas of agricultural expansion in the twelfth and thirteenth centuries

(Tindall 1985a, 18). A broadly similar process may have been occurring to the north of the Mersey, but there, the new estates and their associated moats were clearly held by lords in thanage or by knight service, rather than by rent-paying peasants (*see p 153*). The character and distribution of moated sites in south-west Lancashire probably owed much to the opportunity for the extension of agriculture into woodland and mossland from the late twelfth century onwards, but it was undoubtedly also influenced by unusual tenurial arrangements, whereby lords seem to have been free to dig moats, and to grant small freehold estates out of their holdings, often to family members.

The township of Culcheth has five, or possibly six, moated sites, and is one of only eight townships in south-west Lancashire with five or more moats (Lewis 2000, fig 56). Three moated sites, and a possible fourth, were at the estate centres occupied after the subdivision of the lands of Gilbert de Culcheth: given that the heirs to the original Culcheth holding had been married to four brothers, it is easy to envisage that competition between the latter may have led to at least three out of four of the new sites becoming moated. Moats have been identified at Old Abbey Farm (Pesfurlong), Culcheth Hall, and Risley Hall, whilst linear features flank Holcroft Hall to the north, east, and south, but could relate to a medieval water mill rather than a moat (*op cit*, 509, 510, 513, 514). The remaining moats were at Old Kingnall Hall, and Tanner's Farm, Twiss Green, both probably the centres of estates in existence since at least the late thirteenth century. The latter appear to have been estates subordinate to Culcheth, held by tenants (*op cit*, 512, 515; Acknowledgement of Richard and Margery, LRO DP 398 Box 4), though it has been suggested that the farm at Kingnall was a tenant holding of Pesfurlong (Freke 1995, 3).

The moat at Old Abbey Farm enclosed a single platform, in common with the majority of moated sites in the south-west of historic Lancashire (Lewis 2000, 121) The platform was subrectangular, measuring approximately 24 m square (*c* 576 square metres), and the moat was 14-15 m wide by 3.2 m deep at the bridging point, where its profile was most fully investigated. It is clear that, by any standards, this represents a very small moated platform surrounded by a relatively large moat. For south-west Lancashire, a significant group of moated sites (30%), have platform areas estimated at 1000-3000 square metres. Of the remaining platforms, 9% were smaller than this, and 27% larger, whilst for 35%, it is impossible to estimate the area (*op cit*, table 39). The majority had ditches 5-10 m wide, or 10-15 m wide, the numbers in each category being roughly equal. In comparison, moated platforms lying in modern Cheshire have been described as in the range of 1000-6000 square metres (Wilson 1987), with most moats 6-15 m wide. For the post-1974 metropolitan county of Greater Manchester, encompassing many of the more easterly south Lancashire sites, it has been suggested that 'over half' the moated platforms fall in the range of 1000-2000 square metres (Tindall 1985a, 11), perhaps suggesting that moat size may diminish towards the east of historic Lancashire. Of the moated sites in Culcheth township, areas can be estimated only for Tanner's Farm, Twiss Green (24 m wide by 30 m long, or 720 square metres), and for Old Kingnall Hall (30 m wide by 40 m long, or 1200 square metres) (Lewis 2000, 210-212).

It is easy to suggest that the size of a moat might correlate with its status, and that the site at Old Abbey Farm may have been relatively socially insignificant. However, other factors may have been at play: it is possible that small moats may be of relatively early date, and that platforms grew in size (Wilson 1987, 146). Although the moat at Old Abbey Farm, perhaps dug in the thirteenth or early fourteenth century, may date to a period which falls within the 'expansion' phase of moat-cutting nationally, it has been suggested that, in the North West, moat-cutting reached a peak rather later. Moated sites have proved extremely difficult to date but, in the south-west of historic Lancashire, only three moats can at present be assigned to a period earlier than the fourteenth century (at Sefton Old Hall, Crosby Hall, and Ince-in-Makerfield; Lewis 2000, 142). Within the modern metropolitan county of Greater Manchester no sites can be said to pre-date the fourteenth century, and it has been suggested that there most moats may have originated in the late thirteenth to late fourteenth centuries (Tindall 1985a, 14-15). The small size of the moat at Old Abbey Farm may thus result from the possibility that this was one of the first such sites to be constructed in this part of England. Certainly the rather larger moat at Tanner's Farm was later in origin, probably being cut around a pre-existing settlement site in the fifteenth century (Freke 1995, 10). For Lancashire as a whole, Lewis has warned against placing too much emphasis on the dimensions of sites, and has found no correlation between size of moated platform, and the tenure by which an estate was held (Lewis 2000, 124).

Moats in Cheshire were sometimes constructed with a bulge in one corner (Tindall 1985a, 11); the significance of this feature is not clear, but the bulge in the south-west corner of the moat at Old Abbey Farm may reflect this tradition. The otherwise square shape of the moat and platform is similar to the majority of sites in the south-west of historic Lancashire, Greater Manchester, and Cheshire; in both counties, moats were typically simple square or rectangular enclosures (Lewis 2000, 121; Tindall 1985a, 11; Wilson 1987, 146). The Old Abbey Farm platform also resembled the majority of moated sites in the North West, in that most of the spoil from the moat must have been dumped off site, rather than being used to raise the platform (Wilson 1987, 152).

It has been suggested above that, being an estate centre, the aisled hall at Old Abbey Farm must have been accompanied by a range of associated buildings, both domestic and agricultural (*see p 157*). This is reinforced by the presence on the site of re-used timbers suggestive of the former presence of a medieval barn (*see Ch 8, above*). Whilst it has been argued that, despite the lack of surviving evidence, a small number of domestic buildings would have stood in close association with the aisled hall, the small size of the platform strongly suggests that agricultural structures lay in an outer court beyond the moat, probably to the west and south of the bridging point, in the same position as buildings shown on post-medieval estate plans (*see Ch 2, above*). This area was sampled by excavation, but not intensively investigated. However, ephemeral remains may in any case have been truncated by the later farmyards which occupied this site until the late twentieth century. If agricultural buildings did lie beyond the moat, this would accord with the suggestion made in 1978 that, nationally, much of the area of a moated platform was typically left empty until a change of fashion in the fourteenth century (Le Patourel 1978b, 43). Excess space within platforms laid out in the thirteenth century might be occupied by an open courtyard (as at Writtle, Essex), or a garden (as at Haddlesey, Yorkshire) (*op cit*, 45).

In north-west England, the supposition that agricultural buildings were often sited beyond the moat finds some further support. A reference to Broad Oak Farm in the *Cheshire Forest Proceedings of 1363* is often quoted, stating that there lay 'outside the moat a barn, stables, wards *etc*' (Wilson 1987, 153). Although the moat may date to *c* 1354, the parallel may be appropriate as this was a site associated with land newly taken into agriculture. Recent excavations in the area of the Mersey valley have produced scant evidence for structures on moated platforms, but no barns or other large agricultural buildings have been found. The early abandonment of the platform at Hough Hall probably accounts for the survival there of structural features. However, although only 7% of the platform there was excavated, the buildings clearly identified appear to represent a small kitchen or bake-house, and another small ancillary structure (Higham 1990, 94). Within Culcheth township, the platform at Tanner's Farm, Twiss Green, probably moated in the fifteenth century, has been completely excavated; this site was again abandoned relatively early, and narrow ridge and furrow seems to have masked and protected medieval features (Freke 1995, 3-4). Although some relatively early structural features had been cut by the moat, the only major structure on

the small platform appears to have been the dwelling house. The evidence for structures at Bewsey Old Hall has been referred to above (*see above p 151*; Lewis 2000). Within Greater Manchester, the only extensively excavated site to have been published is at Buttery House Farm, near Davenport Green (Wilson 1983). There, the excavated evidence for medieval buildings consists of a single structure of post-in-pit construction, perhaps *c* 7 m long, giving little indication of the layout of the site. The historical context of the site is comparable to that of Old Abbey Farm, as it has been linked with the manor house established when an existing estate was subdivided in the later twelfth century (*op cit*, 123-6). However, the platform there seems to have been much larger, measuring *c* 50 m across from east to west.

The paucity of medieval pottery found at Old Abbey Farm, both from the platform and the moat, is typical of many moated sites in the region investigated by excavation. Excavations at Hulme Hall (Wilson 1975), Peel Farm (Wilson 1987), and Willaston Old Hall (Reynolds 1992), all in Cheshire, have each produced predominantly post-medieval and modern pottery. Whilst early in the medieval period, domestic refuse in towns was commonly buried in pits, on rural settlements it seems often to have been stored in temporary middens before being scattered on the land as part of the manuring process. Where medieval layers on moated sites have been truncated by later activity, there is thus little potential for the discovery of pottery. The moats themselves seem to have been cleaned out regularly during the hey-day of moated sites, so that sediment and rubbish typically only started to accumulate once the site had been abandoned, or had fallen in status. A notable exception in north-west England seems to have been the site at Bewsey Old Hall, in the south-west of the historic county of Lancashire, but of relatively high status. There, 1600 sherds of medieval pottery were recovered from the platform and ditch fills during the 1983-5 excavations, with a further 552 sherds being derived from earlier fieldwork (Lewis *et al* forthcoming). However, even there, it has been suggested that much of the material had been deposited at times when extensive alterations were made to the platform and house. This might imply that rather than representing routine rubbish disposal, the concentrations of pottery were the result of reworking of earlier deposits. More modest quantities of medieval pottery were found at Lymm Hall in Cheshire, where 293 potsherds dating from the late fifteenth to sixteenth centuries were recovered from an extensive midden located beyond the moat, adjacent to the driveway (Bearpark and Johnson 1976, 30).

It seems that the moated site at Old Abbey Farm may be typical of many moats in the south-west of the historic county of Lancashire, in that it was held by knight service, but was demonstrably associated with the expansion of agriculture into previously marginal

Phase	Date	Number of rooms	Room functions
Phase 1	*c* 1268	3	Open hall, parlour, service (possible external kitchen)
Phase 2	*c* 1534-1579	5	Open hall, parlour, chamber (?), service (possible external kitchen)
Phase 3	*c* 1615-1635	5+	Open hall, parlour, two chambers (?), service, + possible rear outshut
Phase 4	*c* 1650 - 1720	5+	Open hall, parlour, two chambers (?), service, + possible rear outshut
Phase 5	*c* 1724	7+	Hall, two ground floor rooms in south crosswing, three chambers (?), service, + possible rear outshut
Phase 6	*c* 1750	11+ (9+ excluding agric rooms)	Hall, kitchen in rear outshut, buttery in one of two south crosswing ground floor rooms (?), stock in one of two north wing ground floor rooms (?), three chambers, hayloft, workroom/chamber, + rooms at times subdivided in south crosswing and outshut
Phase 7	*c* 1900+	14	Hall, second reception room, kitchen in rear outshut then south crosswing, one, later two, bathrooms, utility room, four/five bedrooms

Table 5: Development of rooms by phase

areas in the thirteenth century. Its small size may be a product of its relatively early date. The lack of excavation evidence for agricultural or ancillary structures associated with the aisled hall is to be expected on a restricted site occupied into the late twentieth century, but agricultural buildings may in any case have been sited off the moat, with part of the platform perhaps given over to a yard or gardens. Two areas west of the moat were sampled by excavation, but no medieval features were located. The paucity of medieval finds is again typical of many moated sites. However, the evidence for the former existence of an aisled hall of late thirteenth, or possibly early fourteenth, century date is of considerable significance; nowhere else in the south-west of historic Lancashire has such detailed evidence for a possible thirteenth century structure been recorded.

Medieval Development

Phase 1

The survival of the moat, of re-used timbers from what was probably a late thirteenth or early fourteenth century aisled hall, and of documents relating to the subdivision of the original manor of Culcheth, means that we have a relatively good understanding of the establishment of the moated site at Old Abbey Farm. However, very little evidence was found to illuminate the medieval development of the site.

Pesfurlong is known to have passed by marriage to the de Radclyffe family in the early fourteenth century (*see Ch 2*), although we cannot be certain that the aisled hall had been built by this time (*see above p 147*). The de Radclyffes held several estates, and Pesfurlong was at least once settled on a younger son (Hampson 1940, 29-30); it may have declined in status, perhaps functioning as a satellite farm. Unfortunately, the physical development of the house and moated platform in the fourteenth and fifteenth centuries remain largely unknown. The re-used timbers from the aisled hall relate to parts of the fabric of the hall which survived unchanged into the post-medieval period, and are not informative about parts of the structure which may have been altered. The erection of a new timber bridge in or after AD 1455 demonstrates that resources were spent on maintaining the site, but the extent of any modernisations can only be inferred. It is suggested that the aisles of the hall would have been removed to allow the insertion of new windows, and that the end aisles, the inevitable result of the use of a hipped roof, may also have been altered, the roof perhaps being run through to form gable ends. The creation of gable ends would have given more scope for the flooring over of the service and solar, but it is equally possible that no change was made here until one or possibly two crosswings were inserted in the mid sixteenth century. As discussed above, it is considered possible but unlikely that the clay floor (Structure 1; *see Ch 3*), dates to a period after the removal of side aisles. No excavation evidence

Phase	Archaeological evidence	Documentary references	Dating evidence
1 (mid thirteenth to mid sixteenth century)	-re-used medieval timbers in farmhouse and barn suggested presence of an aisled hall (Phase 1a) -moat (Phase 1a) -make-up deposits and clay floor surface beneath farmhouse (Phase 1a) -timber bridge (Phase 1b) -removal of aisles and re-alignment of external walls of open hall inferred from later plan form, and other sites (Phase 1b)	-death of Gilbert de Culcheth, 1246. Culcheth later divided into four smaller manors -Adam de Peasfurlong + wife co-defendants against a suit recorded in the Assize Rolls, 1278 - tenure of Pesfurlong passed to the de Radclyffe family, 1303	-dendrochronological felling dates, for individual farmhouse timbers, of AD 1240+, AD 1249+, AD 1261+, and AD 1268+* -dendrochronological felling dates, for individual bridge timbers, of AD 1448-93, and AD 1455B?*

* Sheffield 1998; Hillam *et al* 1987 for 10-55 sapwood estimate

Table 6: Summary, Phase 1

was recovered for any other medieval structures, with the exception of the bridge, whilst the relatively complete absence of pottery from primary contexts precludes study of the economic contacts of occupants of the site. Late medieval waterlogged deposits within the moat were sampled and analysed. Although plant and invertebrate macrofossils were informative about the vegetation immediately surrounding the moat, they shed little light on the agricultural economy or the refuse of the platform's occupants (*see Ch 10*). However, the range of insect species present within the samples did suggest that the moat held a shallow depth of still or sluggish water.

The well-preserved base of a timber bridge is one of a growing number of such structures recorded in the region. It appears to be very similar to the bridge found at Tanner's Farm, Twiss Green, *c* 3 km to the north, if, as seems very probable, the longditudinal braces on the Tanner's Farm structure are secondary features (Freke 1995, 8-9). As at Old Abbey Farm, two transverse sole plates were found at Tanner's Farm, with a beamslot half way up the inner slope of the moat indicating the position of a third timber. Tanner's Farm appears first to have been moated in or shortly after the fifteenth century, so the two bridges may be of very similar date. Dimensions of timbers and details of any dendrochronological dates obtained were not available in the absence of full publication of the Tanner's Farm site, but it can be suggested that further comparison of the constructional details of the two bridges would be worthwhile.

Elsewhere in the south of historic Lancashire, the remains of a supposedly much earlier bridge were excavated at West Derby Castle in the early twentieth century (Droop and Larkin 1928, 47-55). The gatehouse at Bradley Old Hall, Burtonwood, is thought to have been mid fifteenth century in date, and thus contemporary with the Old Abbey Farm bridge, but it was associated with a drawbridge rather than a fixed bridge (Farrer and

Brownbill 1907, 32, n14). Further afield, the remains of a massive timber bridge were recorded at Willaston Old Hall, near Nantwich, in Cheshire. Dendrochronological analysis suggested that this structure, a drawbridge of 'self stable' type, had been constructed in the period AD 1215-1400 (Reynolds 1992, 17). In north Yorkshire, the remains of four successive timber bridges have recently been recorded during excavation of the manorial moated site at Wood Hall. These were again of rather different type to the Old Abbey Farm bridge. The southern end of the first bridge, probably dating to the mid fourteenth century, was carried on a box frame; the second bridge, of *c* 1458, was supported by two massive horizontal beams. This was replaced in turn, in *c* 1493, by a timber drawbridge with associated stone gatehouse, with the drawbridge section being shortened in *c* 1560/1 (Wood Hall Moated Manor Project 1995).

Post-Medieval and Modern Development

Phase 2

A southern crosswing was built at the upper end of the medieval hall, probably in the period AD 1534-79. It is possible that a northern service wing was built at the same time, also in the form of a crosswing, although the only direct evidence for this was a corner stone possibly deriving from a sandstone plinth. Additionally, the pitch of the hall roof would have been altered, if this had not already been done.

These works to the house can plausibly be linked to the purchase of the estate by Sir John Holcroft, of neighbouring Holcroft Hall, in 1549 (Farrer 1910, 73-4). A new owner might reasonably be expected to make improvements to a property, and the use of close studding in the west gable of the southern wing seems to have been intended to impress. In fact it is suggested that the impression of wealth was an illusion and that, behind the facade, the dimensions of the timbers were much smaller than those within the older hall.

Sir John had an existing family seat at Holcroft, which may have been recently rebuilt; the present house on the site is believed to date to the late fifteenth or early sixteenth century (Lewis 2000, 520). Sir John's will (1559) refers to his new house with a buttery, in his occupation, and also 'my house at Holcroft' (*ibid*). Whether or not the 'new house' is a reference to the purchase of Pesfurlong, it is very probable that the house at Holcroft was much larger than that at Pesfurlong; the will refers to at least ten chambers at Holcroft. Certainly, Pesfurlong was not bought to be the main residence of the Holcroft family, and by 1574, it had been settled on a younger son, Hamlet (Rylands 1887, 13-15). Old Pesfurlong Demesne was probably tenanted from shortly before 1592, and by that year, the manorial seat had been moved to a new site, with the building of New Hall (LRO DP 397/25/2; *see Ch 2*). These are all indications that the house at Old Abbey Farm underwent a rapid decline in status from manor house to dependent farm, over a period of about 50 years. The seeds of this decline may have been sown earlier, when Pesfurlong was one of several de Radclyffe estates, sometimes held by cadet branches of the family.

Several sixteenth century domestic buildings still stand on or adjacent to moats elsewhere in the region, and these include Speke Hall and Lydiate Hall, which share a courtyard plan; both were constructed over or adjacent to earlier houses, but were clearly of much higher status than Old Abbey Farm. However, several smaller timber-framed houses associated with moated sites are also known, and at Moor Hall, Hurleston Hall, and Mossock Hall, as at Old Abbey Farm, box frames were set on low sandstone walls (Lewis 2000, 133). They may date to the late sixteenth or early seventeenth centuries and, standing beyond the presumed position of the associated moats, may have replaced earlier medieval structures on the adjacent moated platforms (*op cit*, 134).

The layout and form of the house at Old Abbey Farm appear to support the suggestion that it was still far superior to the dwellings of most of the local rural population in the sixteenth century, if less grand than the seats of the most important local gentry. Remaining sixteenth century buildings, such as Lightshaw Hall and the houses referred to above, seem to have been owned by men of relatively high status in the locality, whereas the houses of middling farmers in South Lancashire and the Mersey Basin appear not to have survived to the present. Although this may in part represent a lack of fieldwork, it still seems likely that many rural houses may have been largely medieval in tradition if not date, being replaced generally from the later seventeenth century onwards. Furthermore, if comparison is made with a building suggested to be the dwelling of a yeoman or prosperous husbandman in southern England, the relative size of the Pesfurlong house stands out. The Lodge at Coney Weston in Suffolk was built to a progressive design, but its original early sixteenth century build still only offered two ground floor rooms, with a narrow loft above (Johnson 1996, 165), compared with the three ground floor rooms and two first floor rooms with windows at Pesfurlong. At the latter, the medieval open hall with central hearth was retained, possibly with little alteration to the timber framing needed, yet across the country, new houses were still being built with high open halls until the mid to late sixteenth century (Mercer 1975, 5) and, especially in the North, it was common for houses to retain open halls beyond this period. At Baguley Hall, an open central hearth appears to have remained in use until the construction of the south wing in the eighteenth century (Dixon *et al* 1989). The open hall remained appropriate to rural sixteenth century life, and was required to serve a variety of functions, with food now typically cooked as well as eaten there (Johnson 1996, 175).

The addition of the southern crosswing to the Pesfurlong manor house gave the structure a new parlour, with two first floor chambers or store rooms above (Table 5; Figs 64, 65). The possible northern wing, for which there is weak evidence only, may have provided upgraded service facilities. However, the pattern of circulation around the house probably changed little. It is likely that a cross-passage continued to provide entry between the open hall and the service, and with no evidence of alternative access to the southern crosswing, it seems probable that the parlour

Phase	Archaeological evidence	Documentary references	Dating evidence
2 (mid sixteenth - early seventeenth century)	-some timber framing within farmhouse southern crosswing -stone plinth for farmhouse southern crosswing revealed -stone bridge may derive from Phase 2	-Pesfurlong estate purchased by Sir John Holcroft, 1539 -New Hall built by 1592; house at Old Abbey Farm probably already tenanted, and was no longer the manorial seat of Pesfurlong estate	-dendrochronological felling dates, for individual timbers within farmhouse southern crosswing, of AD 1526+, 1534-72, and 1534-?79*

* Sheffield 1998; Hillam *et al* 1987 for 10-55 sapwood estimate

Table 7: Summary, Phase 2

was still reached through the open hall, the hub of the house. Eating, the reception of visitors, and estate business, were almost certainly still carried out in the hall, still something of a public space which might be occupied by those of varied status and, in the sixteenth century, the master and his wife may have continued to sleep downstairs in the parlour (Johnson 1996, 169). It is uncertain whether kitchen facilities would have continued to be housed in an external structure, as is suggested for Phase 1, or if cooking was also now carried out in the open hall.

Elsewhere on the site, there is tentative evidence that improvements were not limited to the farmhouse. Although there is little direct evidence to date construction of a stone bridge, it is suggested above that this may also have been of sixteenth century origin (*see Ch 4*). Additionally, a small number of re-used timbers found within the eighteenth century barn suggested that a cruck-built structure had succeeded a possible medieval barn, and this may have been erected in the sixteenth century. It is known that cruck frames were still being used for new buildings elsewhere in south-west Lancashire (Lewis 2000, 126); a cruck-framed structure of at least three bays has been identified at Speke Hall, and may have been a detached range contemporary with the Great Hall, which has been dated to 1530-31. Timber-framed barns are unusual survivals in the region, but cruck-framed examples are known to have stood at Rainhill Farm, Old Hutt, and Edge Farm (Lewis 2000, 134).

The expansion and increasing internal subdivision of the house at Old Abbey Farm, from Phase 2 onwards (Table 5; Figs 64, 65), can be seen as representative of widespread changes in housing visible across much of England. The changes to the house at this time should not be viewed in isolation, or merely within the context of southern Lancashire. From the sixteenth century to the eighteenth century, the rural houses of the middle ranks of English society, of husbandmen, yeoman farmers, and the lesser gentry, were tending to become larger. This was not because of the growth of households, but resulted from increased segregation, as it became desirable to provide separate rooms for separate people and activities (Johnson 1996, 169). There was also a marked increase in concern for domestic comfort, and the acquisition of movable goods. These changes have often been tacitly explained in terms of progress towards the present, and a 'natural' desire for privacy and comfort as soon as increasing prosperity made this attainable. However, it has recently been argued, convincingly, that the post-medieval development of housing cannot simply be viewed from a modern standpoint, and that changes could only occur because they were symptomatic of much wider social and cultural developments (Johnson 1996, 83, 170). For example, expenditure on domestic comfort was not inevitable and, in previous times, an individual might have been more likely to respond to greater prosperity by giving endowments to the church.

Matthew Johnson has suggested that the development of houses should be seen as just one expression of the transition from a medieval to a modern world, and urged that the open hall be viewed as a manifestation of the way in which, in the medieval period, individuals of different social status might interact within spaces which were physically, though not symbolically, undivided (Johnson 1996, 81). In central England, in particular, clear parallels can be drawn between housing and agriculture. There, open field systems were extensively employed, and physical divisions were absent, yet use of the land was closely governed by local custom, in which the pattern of an individual's strips of land might replicate the layout of tenements in a nucleated village, and ultimately reflect the social relationships of the community. Transactions which might later be purely economic also had a strong social and cultural significance. Although enclosed fields rather than open field systems may have typified the medieval landscape of much of south Lancashire (*see above p 153*), the relationship between houses and the society that created them cannot be ignored.

During the later medieval period, changes began which would contribute to the formation of a very different society. Enclosure gathered pace in many areas, markets with purely economic transactions became more prevalent, and landlord/tenant or farmer/wage labourer relationships replaced the previous bonds (Johnson 1996, 40). An individual's actions were less contained by custom, and could be governed more freely by perceived economic advantage. The social, economic, and domestic spheres of life disengaged, and the homes of the gentry and middling farmers functioned much less as public spaces. Johnson links these transitions with 'closure' in houses, with the master and wife of the household withdrawing into more private rooms, the hall no longer being the main living area, but being replaced by several rooms with specialist functions (Johnson 1996, 79, 169). The process ultimately led to the widespread adoption of 'Georgian' houseplans by the eighteenth century, with rooms independently accessed from central hallways and landings, and with servants relegated to the rear of the house.

The enlarged sixteenth century house, and later eighteenth century farmhouse at Old Abbey Farm, must reflect something of the cultural transitions which were occurring, rather than being merely a product of increased prosperity and a sensible desire to improve comfort and privacy. However, two factors complicate analysis of the development of the post-medieval house from Phase 2 onwards. Firstly, the increase in room numbers and in room specialisation has been identified by studying changes in the houses of specific socio-economic groups over time, yet Old Abbey Farm did not remain the residence of people of a particular class. The decline in the status of the building, from sub-manor and estate centre, to dependent tenanted farm in the eighteenth century, implies a trajectory counteracting the tendency described above for houses to increase in size and comfort. Secondly, the presence of an earlier plan form must have mitigated against the adoption of features shown by contemporary new houses being built locally. However, these two factors are related. Where a house was occupied directly by higher status owners, the funds might be available radically to alter the plan form in line with current architectural practices. This may have happened at Pesfurlong in the sixteenth century (Phase 2). Where a structure was tenanted or otherwise of lower status, the original plan form might remain, with alterations being in the form of repairs to, or replacement of, the fabric, when this became necessary.

Phases 3 and 4

The rebuilding of the walls of the medieval house in brick appears to have begun in the earlier seventeenth century, perhaps around or shortly after the year 1635. Brick had made its first appearance in Lancashire during the sixteenth century, with Salmesbury Hall, rebuilt by Sir Thomas Southworth in the middle of the century, thought to be the earliest brick building in the region (Lewis 2000, 111 n15) There is evidence for brick manufacture in Prescot in 1579 and 1585-6 (Bailey 1953, 82, 99-100), and brick is known to have been employed at Croxteth Hall in *c* 1575 for the construction of two gables (Pevsner 1969, 18). Early use of brick was often associated with the construction of plinths and wall bases, but in the later sixteenth century, it began to be common for brick chimney stacks to be inserted into timber-framed open halls, especially in the south-east of England (Mercer 1975, 130). This seems not to have happened widely in Lancashire before *c* 1600, but in the following century, brick was widely adopted in the county, and entire brick houses were constructed. Carr House Farm, Bretherton, built in 1613, probably represents the house of a member of the minor gentry, but a cluster of brick vernacular buildings of later seventeenth century date has also been identified (*op cit*), for example Leyland Farm, Hindley, built in 1671. In the context of its use primarily for the insertion of a fireplace into a timber open hall, the appearance of brick at Pesfurlong around 1635 can be regarded as early, but not exceptional. Brick tended to be used in chimneys because of the risk of timber structures catching fire. It was initially an expensive material, but once a local kiln had been established, it became cheaper than the alternatives.

The addition of new north and east walls to the house at Old Abbey Farm may have been necessary to remedy defects in the timber frame, and the Phase 4 brick underpinning was almost certainly needed for this reason. Rebuilding up to the existing wall-plates was the most common means of replacing timber framing, and sometimes the wall-posts and first floor structure, where present, were also retained (Lee and Michelmore 1998). This was the case when the southern crosswing was eventually rebuilt a few decades later (Figs 66, 67), and a similar pattern of survival is shown by the remains of the fifteenth century northern wing at Baguley Hall (Dixon *et al* 1989). The use of brick to replace the timber framing of relatively small houses is paralleled locally at Homer Green Farm; probate inventories show that brick was in use in the early seventeenth century in the vicinity of Homer Green Farm (*ibid*), suggesting that the rebuilding could have been contemporary with that at Old Abbey Farm. At Rainhill Hall Farm, the timber frame seems to have been retained, but encased in brick (Lewis 2000, 133).

The rebuilding in brick at Old Abbey Farm occurred in at least four distinct phases spanning slightly over 100 years, suggesting that elements of the timber frame were replaced out of necessity rather than design. The impression that the old walls had begun failing badly is reinforced by the substantial size of the brick foundations underpinning the new brick walls of the central hall. This suggests that the joints of the timber frame were failing, resulting in massive downward thrust via the posts and studs onto the sill beams and sill walls (Lee and Michelmore 1998). Where this had not occurred, the existing sill walls could simply be re-used, as happened when the south and west walls of the southern crosswing were rebuilt.

The partial rebuilding in brick of the central hall in Phase 3 also increased comfort by allowing the insertion of a fireplace with smokehood. Such features had been common in many Pennine open halls built from the late medieval period onwards, with a transverse firewall being flanked by a lateral wall on one side and a five to six foot heck wall on the other. Settles and other heavy pieces of furniture could be drawn up around the fire in winter, screening off a small heated inner space (Mercer 1975, 21).

However, despite the benefits of the improvements, there is no clear evidence that the number of rooms had been increased beyond five by the end of the seventeenth century. The uncertainty relates firstly to the possible existence of a rear outshut, perhaps indicated by the provision of two doors through the new east wall (though any such structure may simply have been a wood store); and, secondly, to whether the northern wing of the house, represented from Phase 4 by two small fragments of brickwork, now had an upper storey (Figs 66, 67). Certainly the building work did little to alter the essentially medieval pattern

Phase	Archaeological evidence	Documentary references	Dating evidence
3 (early to mid seventeenth cntury)	-thick clay-bonded brick walls replaced timber framing to north and east of open hall, with inglenook fireplace and smokehood against new north wall	-Pesfurlong estate bought by Ralph Calveley 1605, but reverted to Holcroft family. Subject to legal dispute, 1605-1661	-dendrochronological felling date for bressumer beam supporting smokehood, AD 1516-35* -mid or late seventeeth century pottery recovered from east wall foundation trench
4 (late seventeenth to early eighteenth century)	-west wall of open hall built in clay-bonded brick, with re-used stone plinth placed on brick foundation -parts of southern crosswing rebuilt in clay-bonded brick -cobbling to west of house; moat allowed to silt	-Thomas Worsley of Hovingham, Yorkshire, is the first tenant referred to by name (1701) possibly resident at Old Abbey Farm; he may have been an absentee	-Phase 4 fabric stratified between Phase 3 and Phase 5 remains, which included dendrochronology-dated timbers -mid or late seventeenth century pottery from cobbling, late seventeenth century pottery from moat fills

* Sheffield 1998; Hillam *et al* 1987 for 10-55 sapwood estimate

Table 8: Summary, Phases 3 and 4

of circulation around the house. Although insertion of the inglenook had in effect created a lobby entry house, the lack of evidence for direct entry into the service wing from the lobby meant that the front door still only provided access into the house via the open hall. The presence of probable stone blocking in the north external wall of the southern crosswing may indicate the provision of a direct entrance into the parlour in Phase 3, and the master bedroom may have moved from the parlour to a first floor crosswing chamber at this time, indicating the beginnings of room specialisation (Johnson 1996, 169). However, a separate kitchen is probably not to be expected in the seventeenth century, and the implication is that cooking may have been conducted in the open hall, in addition to the other activities carried out there.

Whilst the form of the manor house at Pesfurlong may not have been archaic in the sixteenth century, by the seventeenth century elements of the house were certainly becoming outmoded by national standards. It can be suggested that new houses were nowhere being built with high open halls after the late sixteenth century (Mercer 1975, 5). By *c* 1600, the southern farmhouse at Coney Weston had become a four cell unit of two full storeys throughout, with a first floor bedroom now heated, and with circulation along the length of the house possible at first floor level. Access directly to the hall or parlour was possible from the lobby entry. By Lancashire standards, however, the circulation pattern of Pesfurlong, if not the open hall, was still shared by many newly erected seventeenth century houses, and for three cell buildings, a through

passage entry with the parlour reached through the hall/kitchen remained common (*op cit*, 67). Neither was its lack of size unusual for a building of some status in the early seventeenth century; the newly built Skelmersdale Hall provided no more than three ground floor rooms, but was clearly of higher status than the average farmhouse. Lesser dwellings were represented by clam-staff and daub buildings, usually associated with low crucks of light scantling (Harris 1989, 23-5). Yet, if not backward in its regional context, it is clear that the house at Pesfurlong was no longer notable for its size and quality, especially as the seventeenth century progressed. Towards 1800, two storey houses of two to three cells became common on the Lancashire plain to the north. One such was Webster's Farm at Lathom, built of brick in 1682 (Mercer 1975, 31). It seems that the seventeenth century was the period during which the house at Pesfurlong became a middling farmhouse, rather than a gentry residence.

This analysis appears compatible with the evidence of surviving documents. In 1605, Pesfurlong estate was sold to Ralph Calveley, a significant landowner, whose house at Leehill Farm in Cheshire was visited by James I in 1617 (Reynolds and Cocroft 1992). He had also purchased the neighbouring estate of Holcroft by 1619. It seems probable that the rebuilding in brick began under this family's ownership. However, Pesfurlong was one of four estates which was the subject of a legal dispute between the Holcroft and Calveley families, the Calveleys attempting to claim Pesfurlong from 1636 to 1661 (*see Ch 2, above*), and perhaps this blighted development and modernisation. Hearth Tax returns exist for Pesfurlong for the years 1663 and 1666, and members of the Holcroft family head the lists; however, it is to be presumed that their hearths were at New Hall, rather than at Old Pesfurlong Demesne, the name commonly applied to the former manor house prior to the mid nineteenth century. 'Francis Jackson, Gentleman', was second in precedence in the 1666 list; he was recorded as having four hearths, though the figure appears to have been amended from two (LRO MF 1/27, from PRO E 179/250/9/f194; Neil 1998, 23). This individual may have resided at Old Pesfurlong Demesne but, if so, the number of hearths does not match the single seventeenth century fireplace identified by excavation and survey. Alternatively, Old Pesfurlong Demesne may already have dropped even further down the status list by 1666, there being no independent evidence that it was ever occupied by Francis Jackson.

The Pesfurlong estate passed to the Standish family, in *c* 1680, but appears to have been leased for a 50 year period in 1696, by Dame Margaret, widow of Sir Richard Standish, in order to raise money for bringing up her young children. In 1701, 'the manor house of Pesfurlong, commonly called Pesfurlong Hall, and the demesne and demesne lands thereunto belonging' were leased to Thomas Worsley of Hovingham, Yorkshire (LRO DP 397/21/20; Neil 1998, 9). There is some uncertainty as to whether the house referred to was at New Hall or Old Abbey Farm, but the fact that Worsley was identified as being from Yorkshire suggests that he may, in any case, have been an absentee tenant.

The context of ownership disputes, lack of money, and the leasing of the house and its land to individuals outside the owning family helps to explain the piecemeal nature of the brick underpinning of Old Abbey Farm. It appears to explain why no extra rooms were added during the first two phases of building in brick, and why the changes were made within the existing plan form, rather than as part of a more radical modernisation of the house. There is evidence of neglect away from the farmhouse itself. By the late seventeenth century, the moat was no longer being cleaned out, leading to the build up of a thick silting fill against one of the piers of the sandstone bridge. However, the fact that the property was tenanted, and may have suffered from a lack of investment, was probably a major factor in the survival of elements of the earlier medieval hall. Nearby Baguley Hall was also tenanted, and by the eighteenth century, may have been in a similar situation, having no higher a status than any other middling-sized tenanted farmstead (Dixon *et al* 1989).

The quantities of early to mid seventeenth century pottery recovered were far too small for any meaningful analysis of the trading contacts, or consumption and consumerist activities, of the occupants of the farm (*see Ch 10*). The earliest pottery recovered in significant quantities from the site appears to date to the later seventeenth century, and its presence is partly the result of the survival of areas of make-up underlying the later drive and hardstanding in front of the farmhouse. Sherds from vessels in hard-fired black-glazed wares predominate, and some of the forms represented are known to have been restricted in distribution to Cheshire and South Lancashire, a number having been in production at Rainford to the west. Yellow ware plates and dishes were in the Staffordshire tradition, but again could have been produced locally. Few diagnostic early eighteenth century wares were recognised. Certainly the apparent lack of imported finewares seems to confirm that the occupants were of relatively modest social status and financial means by the turn of the eighteenth century, and were not following national fashions.

Phase 5

The central hall was floored over for the first time, but the basic layout of the house was again little altered. The provision of an upper room over the hall, and the subdivision of the ground floor of the southern crosswing, increased the number of identifiable rooms from five to seven, but the existence of an eastern outshut, or of a first floor above the northern service wing, remains uncertain. There is still no archaeological evidence for the existence of a specialist kitchen, and it must again be suggested that cooking may have been carried out in the central hall. In this respect, the house appears to have lagged behind eighteenth century trends, both regional and national. Buttery, pantry, and dairy are presumed to have remained within the northern wing, which, despite evidence for rebuilding in Phase 4, may not have changed in function since the medieval period. Access to the upper storey was via a new staircase installed in the eastern cell of the southern crosswing, but it is not clear how this stair would have been approached. The brickwork of both the internal crosswing partition wall, and of the new southern wall of the central hall, suggested that in both cases these Phase 5 walls had been built initially without doorways. This would imply that the only access to the staircase was via a back door into the crosswing, which seems highly unlikely; it is tempting to imagine that an original doorway into Room G4 must have been obscured by later remodelling. Be that as it may, the new first floor room lay very deep within the structure of the house in terms of access, and it, or the western crosswing cell F4, may have been the master bedroom. It is possible that the western crosswing room G5/6 was used as a private dining room, but its small size, after the partition of the former parlour, may indicate that, instead, food was eaten within the central hall. Thus,

Phase	Archaeological evidence	Documentary references	Dating evidence
5 (early eighteenth century)	-old open hall floored over, re-roofed, and south wall built in lime-mortared brick; earliest internal surfaces -further underpinning of the southern crosswing in lime-mortared brick	-Pesfurlong part of the large Standish family estate	-dendrochronological felling date for roof purlin above former open hall, AD 1724B* -use of 'Yorkshire sash' windows

* Sheffield 1998; Hillam *et al* 1987 for 10-55 sapwood estimate

Table 9: Summary, Phase 5

in summary, although there is some evidence for room specialisation and for privacy, other rooms seem to have remained multi-functional and semi-public.

The evidence for the deposition of thick, waterborne silting fills sealing the remains of the stone bridge remains difficult to interpret. Artefactual and documentary evidence combined suggest that this deposition must have occurred in the earlier eighteenth century. Evidence for disuse of the bridge at this time may correlate with the paucity of diagnostic early eighteenth century pottery, and imply a temporary abandonment of the site. However, the works to the farmhouse in *c* 1724, and again in the mid eighteenth century (*see above, Ch 2*), suggest that any break in occupation was limited, and perhaps of insufficient duration to affect the pottery assemblage. The absence of the known early eighteenth century wares might in any case be explained by the continuing local manufacture and use of the blackwares predominant in the seventeenth century. The artefactual evidence is too imprecise to allow the disuse of the stone bridge to be related to the Phase 5 building works of *c* 1724. However, the construction of the causeway seems more likely to have occurred towards the middle of the century, again on the basis of imprecise artefactual dating evidence, and it seems unlikely that disuse of the bridge and construction of the causeway would be separated by a major phase of building. It is thus suggested that the disuse of the stone bridge may have occurred after the Phase 5 works had been completed.

Phase 6

The unambiguous evidence for a rear outshut, and for the flooring over of the northern wing, means that the number of identifiable rooms increased to 11 or more, fluctuating with the temporary subdivision of the outshut and of southern crosswing room G4. In part this increase may be misleading, because of the possibility that the northern wing had been converted to accommodate stock at ground floor level (with a hayloft above), necessitating the inclusion of previous service rooms into the central and southern parts of the house. However, the increase in room numbers

was also a product of increased room specialisation, with more rooms being used for precise purposes by particular groups of people.

The main entry into the house was still via the central hall, and the first floor was reached by passing through the hall to the staircase in crosswing room G4. In this respect, circulation through the house had not altered. However, for the first time, there is clear evidence for a specialist kitchen, housed in the rear outshut, and provided with a fireplace with associated oven. This can be regarded as a space within the household predominantly occupied by females. The buttery, pantry, and dairy seem formerly to have been housed in the northern wing, but these functions may now have been moved to the southern crosswing. Local people have indicated that the dairy, and beer barrels for harvest workers, were housed in the western crosswing cell, G5/6 (Fig 68), in the 1940s, and this use of rooms may have had its origin in the mid eighteenth century. All these rooms may also have been predominantly female spaces. The central hall, however, seems to have continued to act as a room of mixed function, and the likely accommodation of service functions in the crosswing and possibly of stock in the north wing makes it probable that the hall continued to be used for dining. The masonry at the rear of the fireplace appeared to indicate the former presence of a nineteenth century range, so this room may also have retained a cooking function, though perhaps baking was carried out in the kitchen. Upstairs rooms F1, F3, and F4 (Fig 69) appear to have been bedrooms. The eastern first floor room in the north wing, F2A, lay very deep within the structure of the house, if partitioned from F2 prior to the insertion of a northern staircase in the nineteenth or twentieth century. It may have been a further bedroom, but its function is unknown.

By the mid eighteenth century, the layout of the farmhouse was old fashioned, even by the standards of the North. Double pile houses, of 'Georgian' design, were the most common new farmhouses erected on substantial farms, and these were symmetrically arranged, and divided front and back between family and servants. Fireplaces were often provided in previously unheated rooms (Mercer 1975, 73). The farm at Old Pesfurlong Demesne seems to have been no longer of sufficient status to justify investment by owners in keeping up with fashionable changes in architecture, and tenants presumably lacked the will or resources to do so. Indeed, the likely conversion of the northern part of the house for agricultural use implies dramatically falling status. The kitchen was now to the rear of the house, as in 'Georgian' houses, but this may have been more a function of accident and practical considerations than design. Nevertheless, the house remained large when compared with the cottages of small-holders, labourers, and industrial workers. In the north of England in the eighteenth century, rural cottages of a single storey, and often only one room, were still being built (Mercer 1975, 77). In the south, two-storey, two-cell labourers' cottages appear more common, but even these might have been more cramped than at first appears: documentary references to such cottages at Milton Abbas in Dorset indicate that by 1834 a different family was housed in each room (*ibid*). The use of inorganic roofing materials at Old Abbey Farm also indicates a house of better than average status for a rural situation, since thatch was still very common for the dwellings of the rural poor (Brunskill 1994).

The construction of the Lancashire-type barn, and suggested rebuilding of the north wing of the farmhouse to house stock, may be linked with the slump in the price of corn in the period *c* 1730-60 (Lee and Michelmore 1998). On many farms the emphasis switched from arable farming to stock-keeping, and in the North, older cruck barns were typically replaced by more versatile structures, better able to provide accommodation for breeding stock in the winter, and storage for hay and straw (*ibid*). The building of a new barn implies considerable investment, but use of the farmhouse for stock nevertheless suggests that resources were limited. Perhaps practical expenditure on farm buildings was possible, where spending on updating the farmhouse in accordance with changing fashions and levels of comfort was not. Construction of the barn might appear to be linked with the 1749 agreement between the major landowners in Culcheth

to divide the township's commons and wastes (LRO AE 7/7). However, in reality it appears that little reclamation occurred before the nineteenth century use of the mosses to grow market garden crops for Manchester (Leah *et al* 1997, 39). The first surviving plan of the Pesfurlong estate, dating to 1757, shows the land east of Old Abbey Farm divided into small fields, with Moss Side Farm separating the Old Abbey Farm lands from the Moss (LRO DDRf 11/54(1)). This is thought to suggest a gradual process of piecemeal enclosure and reclamation, which had been going on throughout the medieval and post-medieval periods. This is perhaps supported by the notation...'Intak from following moss' or 'marled croft...'(Leah *et al* 1997, 38). Further reclamation to the east may have had a very limited impact on Old Abbey Farm. The 1757 estate plan has a rather stylised representation of the farmhouse, but also shows further out-buildings to the south and west of the moat. The largest of these appears to have a large centrally placed doorway on the western side, and probably represents the new barn rather than an older structure.

From documentary references, it might appear surprising that there was any investment in the farm at all. Pesfurlong manor was mortgaged for £2000 in 1740. This loan was briefly redeemed in 1768, but the estate soon was remortgaged, the value of the mortgage having increased to £10,000 by 1790. Furthermore, it has been claimed that the young Frank Standish who succeeded in 1756 was more interested in horse racing than the efficient running of his estates (Walker 1990, 35; 1995, 19-23). The tenancy of Old Abbey Farm also appears to have changed three times in the mid eighteenth century, and more frequently in the early nineteenth century. Again, this might imply a lack of investment, or that insufficient resources were available successfully to carry through a programme of investment. Writing in the late eighteenth century, Holt commented that tenants who had to improve the land at their own expense 'are often ruined' (Holt 1795, 22-28; reference provided by J Lewis). Surveys and valuations of the estate name the tenants as Thomas Richardson in 1736, J Warburton in 1750, and T Warburton in 1757 (MCL L1/27/2/1,

Phase	Archaeological evidence	Documentary references	Dating evidence
6 (mid eighteenth-early nineteenth century)	-barn constructed in brick, and northern rooms of farmhouse re-built, ?replacing possible Phase 4 walling -causeway and external brick ancillary structures built; other undated wooden structures demolished (*c* eighteenth-nineteenth century)	-continued Standish ownership, but estate mortgaged from 1740 -1841 Census: house occupied by married couple, two children, two man servants, a man of independent means, and a 'wolin weaver' '-1851 Census: by married couple and nine children	-mock perspective depiction on 1757 estate map shows causeway and brick barn built by this time

Table 10: Summary, Phase 6

Phase	Archaeological evidence	Documentary references	Dating evidence
7 (twentieth century)	-limited re-modelling of the farmhouse and barn	-farm bought by the Wareing family, former tenants, in 1950	-Wareing family documents; recollections of family and other local people

Table 11: Summary, Phase 7

L1/27/2/2, LLHL B/333 Pes). The Richardson family appear to have been working farmers in the lower middling social ranks, similarly the Warburtons.

A significant lack of later eighteenth century tablewares has been identified (*see Ch 10, above*), but this may be due to the consumption patterns of the occupiers, and factors influencing the deposition and location of rubbish, rather than any break in occupation. After the late eighteenth century, white glazed tea and tablewares found in abundance suggest continuous occupation to the late twentieth century. They would have been obtained from a variety of sources, including the Midlands, although redwares were also present, and were probably obtained from relatively local sources (*see Ch 10*).

From 1841, the national Census gives more detailed information about the occupants of the farm for one year in every decade (*see Ch 2*). The presence of a 'wolin weaver' in 1841 represents the only possible evidence for craft specialisation at the farm, and it is not certain that the weaver worked where he lodged. Many of the inhabitants of Culcheth township are known to have been linen weavers in the seventeenth and eighteenth centuries (Farrer and Brownbill 1911, 156). The distribution of the household around the house is uncertain, but it may be that parts of the northern wing had been returned to domestic occupation before the twentieth century, and that one or both of the single men present in 1841 lodged there, perhaps on the first floor, which may have been partitioned in the nineteenth century. In 1851 and 1861, a larger family group was in residence, but no employees from outside the family appear to have been living with the household.

Phase 7

The farm was tenanted by the Wareing family from around 1911 until they purchased it in 1950 (*see Ch 2, above*). The northern wing was back in domestic occupation by the early twentieth century, with a hearth provided on each storey. The total number of rooms was increased to a maximum of 14, plus a small back porch, when the house was subdivided in 1972-3 to provide more private accommodation for the owners' son when he married. There is evidence that, during the twentieth century, direct access was finally provided from the entrance lobby to the northern wing, so that the latter no longer had to be accessed via the central hall.

Conclusion

The Wareing family left the house when Old Abbey Farm was sold to UK Waste Management Limited in 1988. The research programme has shown that, by that time, and despite extensive renewal of the fabric, the house had been more or less continuously occupied for up to 720 years. Yet significantly, it appears only to have been inhabited by, in twentieth century parlance, 'owner occupiers', for the first 40 years and the last 40 years. Soon after passing by marriage to the de Radclyffe family in or before 1303, Pesfurlong seems to have become a satellite estate held by families whose principal residence was elsewhere, albeit one which was from time to time settled on junior family members. Following the construction of New Hall in or before 1590, the former capital messuage seems to have become a secondary farmhouse leased outside the owning family. This decline in status explains the piecemeal renovation and extension of the property, and may in part be responsible for the survival of the evidence for the medieval origins of the building. If the farm had been rebuilt in line with contemporary taste in the seventeenth, eighteenth, or nineteenth centuries, it would probably have been impossible to unravel its complex structural history.

APPENDIX 1

By Jason Wood and Richard Heawood

The Risley Experiment

The 'Risley Experiment' was devised to test the assumptions made by archaeologists when interpreting the results of their work. Focusing on the farmhouse and moated platform, the experiment required that the documentary research, building survey and excavation of Old Abbey Farm were carried out in strict isolation. After a period of almost two years, these three separate strands of evidence were brought together and the results compared. Despite acknowledged deficiencies in the approach, the experiment confirmed that the techniques and interpretative methods upon which the archaeological fieldwork was based were broadly sound. However, the results also highlighted several specific and general concerns about the limitations of building survey and excavation, and the weaknesses of interpretation which may occur if an holistic and integrated approach is not adopted.

Background to the Experiment

As has been explained in *Chapter 1*, LUAU acted as Managing Agent to UK Waste Management Limited, specifying and then overseeing the documentary research, building survey, controlled demolition, materials storage, and subsequent excavation at Old Abbey Farm. Not only did this approach ensure that the archaeological interests were dealt with adequately and that the client met satisfactorily all the obligations of their planning consent, but it enabled a unique research experiment to take place within the confines of the project.

It was agreed that the building survey and excavation would be carried out by two separate teams working in strict isolation, with neither team being aware of the results of the other until after the fieldwork and initial assessment were complete. This exercise would then allow LUAU to compare and contrast the results that each team achieved, and thereby test the validity of the different interpretations derived. Documentary research would be performed by an independent historian. This historical information would also be

withheld from those undertaking the building survey and excavation, in order that comparison could be made between the desk-based and fieldwork results.

The experiment formed the basis of a short television documentary compiled for the BBC's *'Countryfile'* programme, broadcast in July 1996. The project was also a runner-up in the British Archaeological Awards for 1996.

Focus of the experiment

The opportunity systematically to record and demolish an historic building under archaeological supervision, and then to excavate the footprint of that building archaeologically, has been a rare occurrence. More often than not, archaeologists have had to base their interpretations on partial information derived from studying extant historic buildings (or those parts of them affected by refurbishment or repair), or excavating their remaining ground plans and associated deposits. At Old Abbey Farm there was the chance to recover a more-or-less complete record of the site, especially of the farmhouse and the moated platform. The focus of the experiment, therefore, became the farmhouse and its immediate environs.

Briefing the teams

The two team leaders and the historian were all mid-career archaeologists with 10-15 years of experience behind them. The team leaders were briefed on the preliminary conclusions of the 1990 evaluation, which had confirmed the presence of medieval deposits and historic fabric. However, they were given no access to any primary survey or excavation records, or detailed historical documentation about the site. The building survey team was tasked with recording and dismantling the farmhouse and attempting to date it from its building style, materials, and the construction techniques used. The excavation team only had access to the site once the house had been dismantled to ground level, with all remains cleared. They were tasked with excavating the foundations of the house and the moated platform, and describing the accommodation, age, and uses of the building. The historian was tasked with gathering documentary and oral evidence, and achieving an understanding

Plate 21: The BBC Countryfile *crew visiting the site*

of the status and social and economic context of Old Abbey Farm.

For the experiment to work, all communication between the teams, and the historian, was forbidden. The day-to-day findings were held under lock and key, and each team was provided with separate office space for the duration of the experiment - a period of almost two years.

Timetable of events
The building survey and controlled demolition took place between June 1994 and January 1995. The excavation began in March 1995 and was completed by the end of May. The historian worked throughout the whole of this period. In accordance with English Heritage guidelines, the results of the fieldwork and documentary research were subjected to assessment to establish the potential for further analysis and interpretation (English Heritage 1991b). For reasons described below (*see p 176*), assessment of the three sets of records proceeded independently. This assessment phase was completed in February 1996. The findings of each team and the historian were then revealed and discussed at a Research Seminar held at Lancaster in mid-March 1996, and the results debated at a Peer Review Meeting one week later. With the conditions of the experiment now relaxed, a single assessment report, integrating the different

contexts and findings, could be produced. This was submitted in July 1996.

Research Seminar
The three presentations given at the seminar summarised the respective results, phase by phase (starting with the earliest). The historian was asked to present the wider landscape evidence before homing in on the site itself. The leaders of the building survey and excavation teams were asked to illustrate graphically their respective reconstructions of their earliest and latest phases. Following the papers, discussions began to review the evidence as a whole and to compare and contrast the results. The whole event was filmed by the BBC. Indeed, two former occupants of the farmhouse, Hugh Wareing and his sister Alice Sutton, were brought to Lancaster by the BBC to sit in on the seminar and take part in the discussions. Interestingly, they disputed some of the conclusions - but were proved wrong in some cases!

Peer Review Meeting
The Peer Review Meeting was designed to help formulate the assessment of the research potential of Old Abbey Farm. Several specialists in the study of moated sites, medieval settlement, and the dismantling and re-erection of historic buildings, together with other interested parties, were invited to place the work in a wider context.

Comparison of the Assessments

The process of integrating the three separate strands of the project to produce a single phase-by-phase development sequence demonstrated how the results of the two field teams, and that of the historian, correlated. In general terms, despite the differences in the methodological approaches, the conclusions reached by the two teams and the historian were quite similar, indicating a sequence of building development and change from the thirteenth/fourteenth to the twentieth centuries.

The fieldwork investigations succeeded in demonstrating, even before the documentary evidence was added, that the moated site had originally been a medieval residence, probably belonging to a rich freeholder, or member of the gentry. Both the building survey and excavation teams interpreted Phase 1 as being represented by a small, timber-framed structure of probable thirteenth or fourteenth century date, occupying approximately the same site as the later farmhouse, while the documentary research suggested a mid thirteenth century date for construction. However, the two teams differed slightly in their ideas about how the building might have looked and functioned.

Both teams clearly identified the addition of the southern crosswing in Phase 2, and the acquisition of the manor by Sir John Holcroft in 1549 provided a useful historical context for such an addition. Both teams also arrived at an almost identical interpretation of their respective evidence for the Phase 3 partial remodelling of the building in the first half of the seventeenth century. For Phases 4 and 5, the building survey revealed much more about the late seventeenth and early eighteenth century rebuilding than the excavation, though there were some discrepancies. The teams agreed that Phase 6 represented a change of use in the eighteenth/nineteenth centuries, and both concluded that the northern rooms of the farmhouse were rebuilt for agricultural purposes and that the 'services' migrated to the eastern outshut. Likewise there was no disputing the evidence for the limited twentieth century internal reorganisation of the house for domestic occupation in Phase 7.

Specific limitations of the building survey

One significant error generated by the building survey was the identification of the line of large sandstone blocks at the base of the west wall of the farmhouse hall as the remains of a stone plinth for the Phase 1 medieval hall. The blocks lay beneath the clay-bonded brickwork of the west wall, and it was presumed that the brickwork was simply laid on top of an existing dwarf wall, as seems to have occurred when the west and south walls of the southern crosswing were rebuilt. However, excavation of a sondage across the base of the wall demonstrated that the stones had been laid on top of a brick foundation at least three courses high. The stone blocks may have been re-used from the west wall, but equally may have derived from another more recent part of the house. Their presence did not demonstrate the position of the west wall of the medieval hall, nor did they prove that the hall had been built with sill beams resting on stone plinths or dwarf walls.

Of course, a particular limitation was the survey's inability to reveal walls and structures only represented by below-ground remains. Thus, there was no indication that an earlier medieval structure might have existed before the aisled hall identified from study of re-used timbers. Likewise, evidence was not recovered for a complete rebuilding of the southern crosswing west gable in Phase 4, prior to its further rebuilding in Phase 5. In this instance, the existence of a previous build was suspected, but not demonstrated by the evidence. Elsewhere, the former presence of two partition walls was not revealed. These were a brick wall which had subdivided the Phase 6 eastern outshut (Room G3), and a probable wooden partition subdividing Room F3 in the east of the southern crosswing. In both cases, the former presence of these walls was demonstrated by excavation of their foundation trenches. Two external structures which had been demolished were likewise revealed by excavation, but had not been fully identified in the standing building. These were a very substantial external chimney backing onto the fireplace in the south wall of outshut Room G3 (Fig 68), and an external stair north of the farmhouse leading to a first floor door to Room F2. Part of the east wall of the chimney was identified during the building survey and interpreted as the remains of an early build of the crosswing porch. The external stair had left no physical evidence above ground, but was inferred because of the presence of the door above.

Specific limitations of the excavation

In some respects, the limitations of the excavation mirrored those of the building survey. Thus, whilst the survey could not detect the early builds of walls represented only below the foundations, excavation could not be expected to provide anything more than a calculated guess about the features which once survived above the ground level. For example, the insertion of a floor into the open hall in Phase 5 was not detected from the excavated evidence, nor the related changes to the external brick walls of the southern crosswing.

Of more specific concern, however, was a tendency for the stratigraphic relationships between brick walls and stone foundations represented only at or near foundation level to be ambiguous. This sometimes resulted in more constructional episodes being proposed than were demonstrated by the standing structure. Thus, whilst the excavation suggested that the brick partition of the southern crosswing post-dated the Phase 5 construction of the wall to the north, the survey of the standing structure had already demonstrated that the two were contemporary. Likewise, it was not evident that the brickwork of the west wall of the hall and north-west return of the crosswing were contemporary. This ambiguity of relationships between walls was partly the result of there being very few courses of brick or stonework remaining in which to establish a relationship, and partly a function of individual wall foundations being free-standing, although the walls above were clearly built as part of the same rise. The presence of jambs and blocking relating to former doorways also confused interpretation of the foundations. In many instances, the ambiguity was such that it would have been difficult to phase the farmhouse structure correctly on the basis of excavation evidence alone, and in particular, difficult to relate the brick walls of the southern crosswing to those of the hall. Phasing would in part have been reliant on comparison of the bonding material, which was less consistently applied at foundation level than within the walls above.

Plate 22: The excavation team working on the farmhouse foundations

Limitations of the evidence

Some aspects of the development of the farmhouse remain obscure. The date and form of the early service rooms at the northern end of the building was not clearly demonstrated, but the same problem was encountered at nearby Baguley Hall, where an integrated survey and excavation programme produced only the most slender evidence for the probable northern service block pre-dating a fifteenth century crosswing (Dixon *et al* 1989, 412).

Deficiencies of the Experimental Approach

It was accepted that there were going to be deficiencies for the project as a whole in taking such an experimental approach. If a single team had undertaken the entire project, and integrated the various kinds of evidence from the outset, the methodology of recording and recovery of information would doubtless have been different. For instance, under normal circumstances the excavation might have concentrated on solving problems identified during the building survey or seeking specific information to fill gaps in knowledge. However, by not disclosing to the excavation team the evidence retrieved from the examination of the standing fabric, questions which might otherwise have been used to inform the excavation strategy could not be formulated. This is not to say that information might have been missed resulting in the questions remaining unanswered, but that access to the building records might have critically influenced the way the excavation was executed, and certainly avoided replicating recording. One possible way round this potential problem might have been to set up a control experiment on part of the site, but that would have meant the impracticality of isolating part of the building from the rest, as well as isolating yet another team. A more serious flaw perhaps was that by removing all the evidence for the superstructure from the site before the excavation began, the buried archaeological record was compromised in that the normal evidence for decay and/or demolition was not apparent.

The separation of the documentary research from both field teams could also be criticised, as such information often guides building survey and excavation methodologies. This decision was based on the fact that a considerable amount of documentary material already existed in the project archive as the result of the 1990 evaluation and particularly the subsequent Public Inquiry (much more than would normally be expected on a project of this type). To bias the record by introducing too much historical information into the equation prior to fieldwork might have undermined the potential of the experiment. Moreover, it would have been impossible to divide the responsibility for the collection of additional material between the two teams without the obvious problem of each of them encountering information of relevance to the other.

A final problem was knowing when to stop the experiment. Initially, it was thought that the results should be brought together after each team, and the documentary historian, had compiled their respective archives and summary reports, but that would not have allowed them sufficient time to assess the material adequately or introduce specialist studies to back up their interpretations. It was even suggested that for the experiment to be totally valid, it should have continued right through the analysis and interpretation phases leading to the respective parts of the project being published separately! For reasons of cost, as much as anything, this option could not be pursued. The compromise was a coming together of the three component parts of the project after initial assessment. Whatever the deficiencies of the approach, it is considered that the results of the experiment far outweigh the possible loss of information caused by segregation of the three forms of investigation.

Conclusion

The experiment was primarily established to test the validity of different recording, analytical, and interpretative methods used during the examination of a standing building both prior to and during its demolition, compared to those applied during its subsequent excavation. More specifically, the experiment was designed to try to identify the types of problems that occur when buildings are interpreted simply from their ground plans, or the dimensions of earlier phases of building are estimated from re-used material. In general, the results confirmed that the techniques and interpretative methods upon which the archaeological fieldwork was based were broadly sound, although the likelihood that errors or gaps in the evidence would result from use of a single technique alone was highlighted. The fact that the experiment was conducted on a very ordinary building, of a common type, rather than a grand and monumental structure, potentially makes the results of the experiment more applicable and useful to future work elsewhere.

Potential limitations of building survey and excavation techniques

Although the experiment demonstrated the relative importance of applying archaeological recording and analytical methods to surviving historic fabric both above and below ground, there were limitations to the field techniques when applied in isolation.

From our experience at Old Abbey Farm, it could be asserted that building survey may over-simplify the constructional sequence of a stone or brick building, whereas excavation may over-complicate it. Below-ground evidence may be missing from building survey interpretations; former walls may not be known, and indeed earlier structures on the same site may not be revealed. Excavation, by contrast, may generate a mass of evidence which may be difficult to assemble into coherent phases.

However, for timber-framed structures the situation may be reversed. A plinth revealed by excavation may remain unchanged for centuries, but recording of the structural timbers above may indicate that the building has undergone a complex history of remodelling and maintenance. Clearly such situations can play havoc with stratigraphical interpretations. To cite another example, a dwarf wall, for instance, may be dated by reference to material found in its construction trench, or at least to its place within the sequence of structural events. The posthole for its door jamb may be contemporary. Though both features can start life at the same time their subsequent histories may be very different. The wall can receive more than one change to its superstructure; the doorpost, however, might survive all these changes. Another potential stratigraphical pitfall occurs when walls are underpinned. It is entirely possible to invert normal stratigraphic interpretation by, for example, the insertion of a dwarf wall beneath a timber frame.

An archaeologist who wishes to analyse the evidence from excavation must have a clear understanding not only of how to interpret that evidence according to archaeological criteria, but also of how a building of a particular type holds together as a structure and works in terms of space and circulation patterns. Equally important is an understanding of how buildings can develop and function over time within a framework of tenurial, social, cultural, and economic change. Similarly, the building surveyor needs to understand that the structure, as it survives, can be the culmination of one (or very many more) interventions to the original fabric, and that in the course of such interventions both structural and 'cosmetic' features could be demolished, replaced, or enhanced leaving only the merest trace in the fabric itself or on features in its vicinity.

Holistic and integrated approach

Not surprisingly, the experiment confirmed that it would have been difficult to piece together a coherent history of the farmhouse from the excavated evidence alone. The evidence obtained from the standing structure greatly added to an understanding of the structural sequence, whilst the integration of the field interpretations with the historical evidence allowed a much more sophisticated picture of the development of the house to be constructed. Clearly, the best approach to understand the development of a building fully must be to draw on every available source of evidence, using the complementary techniques of documentary research, building survey, and excavation together.

It would be extremely simplistic to imagine that comparison of documentary research, building survey, and excavation undertaken at one site could provide an objective determination of the strengths and weaknesses of the three forms of investigation. However, given that such a 'triple-blind' exercise is unlikely to be repeated on a regular basis, it is felt that the 'Risley Experiment' has provided a useful and educative illustration of the assumptions made by archaeologists when interpreting the results of their work, and of the weaknesses of interpretation which may result if a single technique is used in isolation. Much has been learnt, not just about Old Abbey Farm; hopefully the information will be of value to others working on comparable sites, increasing awareness of the potential pitfalls in under- or over-interpretation of partial evidence.

BIBLIOGRAPHY

Unpublished Primary Sources Cited
Bodleian Library (Bod Lib), Oxford
Dodsw v39, v142 mSS of Roger Dodsworth (1585-1654), predominantly transcripts of deeds then in private hands, often now lost

British Library (B Lib), Manuscripts Department, London
BM Add MS 32,107 Christopher Towneley (1604-74) MSS, 'Book GG'
>f123 item 998 Deed of gift by Adam son of Hugh de Hindeleye to Giles de Penkit [Penketh] of his land in the township of Kulchet, nd [post-1290]
>f139 item 1108 Deed of gift by Giles Rentkit [Penketh] to John son of Robert de Alerton de Selby of all his land in the township of Culchet, nd [post-1290]
>f128 item 1031 Lease by Adam son of Hugh del Sargh' to Richard del Helch[?] de Culcheth and Ellen, his wife, William and John, their sons, and the longer liver of them, of three acres of land in the township and territory of Culcheth, 10th November, 1330
>f131 item 1049 Lease by Adam son of Hugh del Shagh to Thomas son of Hugh del Hirst, for Thomas's life, of all his land between the land which used to belong to Hugh de Dutton on one side, and the way which goes from Westwode on the other side, in the township of Culcheth, 25th May, 1360

Lancashire Record Office (LRO), Preston
Greenwood, C, 1818 *Map of Lancashire*

Enclosure awards
AE 7/7 Enclosure Plan (Map of Twiss Green) and Award, 1749-51

Standish of Duxbury
DDRf11/2 Survey book, property in Lancashire, with notes on rent, repairs, 1807-30

DDRf11/16 Standish Estates Inspection 1900. List of tenants *etc* showing areas, rents, and expenditure in improvements (special) 1896-1900

DDRf11/54 Four plans, Pestfurlong estate, 1750-1850
>(1) Map of the Lordship of Pestfurlong belonging to Sir Frank Standish of Duxbury Baronet, by R Lang, 1757
>(2) Plan of the Pestforlong Estate, reduced and copied by James Derham, ... Chorley, nd
>(3) Pestforlong, small plan, nd

>(4) Pestforlong estate, copied from Mr Thornton's tithe commutation survey of the township of Culcheth by H Mort, surveyor, Tyldesley, nd [*c*1850]

DDRf11/61 Fire insurance particlulars re buildings on Standish estates, 1902-5

DDRf11/63 Sales particulars, Pestfurlong Estate, 6 October 1864

DDRf11/75 Sale particulars, 24 September 1920

DDRf11/77 The Duxbury and Pestfurlong Estates in the County of Lancaster, report by Chas Bailey, 14 July 1853 (stated to be copy of report of May 1848)

Documents purchased
DP 23 Depositions of Leonard Egerton of Shawe, esq, Holcrofte Linford of Little Walden, gent, and John Peers of Glasbrooke, yeoman, in case of Leonard Egerton v John Holcroft of Holcroft, esq concerning money borrowed for the purchase of the manors of Holcroft and Pesferlonge [*sic*]. Copy certified by Hugh Standish and William Berrington, 3 November 1666

DP 397/13/27 Counsel's opinion (?Richard Standish of Barnard's Inn) 'Sir Thomas Standish's case touching his mother's power of leasing' (Pestfurlong and Holcroft), July 1737

DP 397/25/1-4 Holcroft documents, came into collection through interest of Standish family in the manor of Pesfurlong in Culcheth by marriage.

DP 397/25/2 Marriage settlement, for £153 6/6d. John Holcroft of Holcroft and Peter Hetwood of Heywood, estates in Holcroft and Pesfurlong, in lieu of dower, in view of marriage of John Holcroft and Anne, daughter of Peter Heywood. Rental of estates and conditions of maintenance of John Holcroft and his wife, 14 December 1592

DP 397/25/4 Notes on 'defendants title' in lawsuit re manors of, and lands in, Holcroft, Pesfurlong, Culcheth, and Risley, involving Calveley and Holcroft interests. *c*1657

DP 398 Deeds and papers, *c*1270, of the manor of Culcheth, 1250-1845, purchased 1965 (Acc No 1976)

Diocese of Liverpool
DRL 1/21 Tithe apportionment and Map of Twiss Green, 1838

DX 999-1022 Peasfurlong and Holcroft Mosses, and Culcheth tithes, correspondence 1831-38, including:

DX 999 Letter, 9 May 1831, Mr Woodward, Marsh Brow, to Thomas Birchall, esq, Preston arranging meeting at Pestfurlong

DX 1000 8 June 1835, R Woodward, New Brook House, to Thos Birchall, Preston

DX 1001 Letter, 11 March 1836, J L Borron, London, to Wm Birchall, Preston, re Holcroft and Pesforlong Mosses

DX 1002 Letter, 20 May 1836

DX 1003 Letter, 8 June 1836

DX 1004 Letter, 9 February 1837, Joseph Wagstaffe, Warrington, to R Woodward, unable to attend meeting at Pesfurlong

DX 1005 J Birchall to Mr Woodward, copy of letter 17 June 1837, re lack of a meeting

DX 1007 Letter, 22 June 1837, from Thomas Birchall. Reference made to partition deed of 1686, and 'joint manors of Holcroft and Pestforlong'

DX 1008 Reminder re urgent reply required, Wagstaffe to Birchall, 11 August 1837

DX 1009 13 September 1837, Gorst (?) and Birchall to Fitchett and Wagstaffe, 'our client Mr Hall Standish for the sake of avoiding further dispute or litigation upon this subject authorizes us to say that he consents to the adoption of the line of boundary suggested upon our meeting at Culcheth. ..'

DX 1010 Acceptance from Fitchett and Wagstaffe to Gorst and Birrchall, 25 September 1837

DX 1011 F and W to G and B, 20 November 1837, delay in preparing deed due to 'difficulty has arisen respecting the legal title of the Pole family'

DX 1012 Letter, 14 December 1837, Ranken Ford and Longbourne (solicitors for Pole family) to F and W, from Grays Inn, 14 December 1837, advising that the 'difficulty' is only that the Trustees under the will of the late Mr S Pole are trustees for *sale* only

DX 1013-22 Letters 1838, re Culcheth tithes, mainly re postponed meetings and date of completion of Mr Thornton's [tithe commissioner's] valuation

DX 1030 Letter re Fank Standish's extinguishment of the mortgage on Pesfurlong 1768

DX 1200 Rental of Estates of Standish of Duxbury, 1844 Pestforlong included, 'Abbey and Poverties, James Green, arrears 1 October 1843 £2 2/-, years' rent £70

Microfiche
MF 1/27 Hearth Tax 1663, from PRO E 179/250/8/pt 5, and 1666, from E 179/250/9

MF 24/24 from PRO HO 107/524/6 1841 Census

MF 25/66 from PRO HO 107/2204, f194-5 1851 Census

Leigh, and Local History Library (LLHL), Leigh
B/333 PES A survey of lands in Pestfurlong in the parish of Leigh, 1756

B Cul 352 Nor Norbury, W, 1883 Transcripts of Culcheth Town Book, 16 May 1716 to 30 March 1815, also list of constables 1665-1776

Liverpool Record Office (LiRO)
920 MD 74-5 Journal and Disbursements Book of Nicholas Blundell of Crosby

Manchester Central Library (MCL), Archives Department
Papers of Dr William Farrer
L1/27/2/1 A particular of Sr Tho's Standish's Estate. Rental, 1736 of Sir Thomas Standish's estate in the manors of Duxbury, Heapy, Whittle, Anglezark, Heath Charnock, and Pestfurlong, giving names of tenants, number of lives left, ages of lives, and yearly value. f8-9 Pestforlong. Edw Unsworth, the Demesne. Res(erved) R(en)t £100, Yearly value £100

1/27/2/2 A Transcript of all the estates in Culcheth in Lancashire and belonging to Sir Thomas Standish, Baronet, containing their several quantities and valuations as surveyed and valued according to the Act of Parliament for enclosing the Twiss Green, 1750. 18 January 1751 Survey and valuation by Thomas Bird of estates of Sir Thomas Standish, bart in Culcheth as surveyed according to the Act of Parliament for inclosing Twiss Green, 1750 giving the names of tenants, acreage and valuation

L1/27/2/5 Rental of the Duxbury Pestforlong and Eaglescliffe Estates for one year ending 1 October 1842

L1/27/2/8 1845 Rentals of the Lancashire estates of Mr Standish Standish, esq James Green, Abbey and Poverties, £70 yearly, 77a 0r 38p

L1/27/2/11 Report, 1844, on and valuation of Standish estates in Lancs

L1/27/7/1 Case of the claimants of the Standish estates, *c*1820

L1/27/8 Schedule of deeds and documents relating to the property and family of W S Standish [ne Wm Standish Carr], 1686-1841, 27 December 1845, Wiglesworth & Co, Grays Inn

Abstracts and transcripts of documents, made by or for Farrer
    L1/50/1-40 Abstracts and Transcripts of Public Records
    L1/50/10 Land Tax Assessments 1781-1802
    L1/50/28/1-7 Feet of Fines 1 Eliz I to 20 Geo III
    L1/50/28/6 Feet of Fines 38 Eliz - 1655, bdl 59-157
    Farrer f232, bdle 68, m6
    Farrer f314, bdle 96, m1
    L1/50/28/71656-20 Geo III, bdl 158-404
    f496: bdl 204, m11
    f496: bdl 204, m35
    f549: bdl 245, m85
    f553: bdl 249, m32
    f564: bdl 263, m110
    L1/51/9/12 Abstracts and transcripts of deeds of West Derby Hundred: Warrington, Wigan, Winwick, and Leigh

Public Record Office (PRO), London
PRO, 1964 List of the lands of dissolved religious houses: (alphabetically) Kent to Middlesex, *Public Record Office Lists and Indexes*, Suppl Ser **3**, **Pt 2**, Nos 211-221, 38-61

Exchequer
E 179/250/8/pt 51663 Hearth Tax, West Derby Hundred, Pesfurlong and Risley

E 179/250/91666 Hearth Tax, West Derby Hundred, Pesfurlong

Palatinate of Lancaster
PL 6/v24, no 86 Equity proceedings, pleas, 22 March 1665, John Calveley, plaintiff (in Barlow 1989)

PL 6/v41, no 77 Equity proceedings, pleas, re Culcheth, Holcroft, and Pesfurlong, 24 December 1690, Richard Calveley, plaintiff (in Barlow 1989)

PL 7/v42, no 59 Equity proceedings, answers, 22 March 1665, John Calveley, plaintiff (in Barlow 1989)

Warrington Central Library (WCL)
General Register Office, Census of England and Wales. Census Returns for Culcheth, Enumerator Schedules Census 1861-91

M/Film 22, reel 4, copy of PRO RG 9/2801 1861 Census

M/Film 28, reel 6, copy of PRO RG 11/3804 1881 Census

M/Fiche ED 15, fiche 4, copy of PRO RG 12/3085 1891 Census

MF 22, Reel 4 from PRO RG 9/2801, dist 14C, f19 1861 Census

MF 28, Reel 6 from PRO RG 11/3804, dist 14, f62 1881 Census

M/Fiche ED 15, fiche 4 from PRO RG 12/3085, f154 1891 Census

MS 74 Beamont, W, 1864 Abstracts of Charters and Deeds relating to the Family of Culcheth of Culcheth... made ...from the originals in the possession of Thomas Ellames Withington, of Culcheth, given to Warrington Museum... 1879

MS 2549a Tithe Apportionment 1838, copy of LRO DRL 1/21

Wigan Archive Service (WAS)
D/DX EL 122/16 Pestfurlong Estate, sale plan and particulars ... Clayton, Solicitors, Newcastle upon Tyne, 6 October 1864, WAS [and LRO DDRf 11/63] RD Lei/E1/1 Culcheth (Twiss Green) Enclosure Award. Typescript transcript (90pp) and copy plan (1910)

Published Sources

Aberg, F A, 1978 *Medieval moated sites*, CBA Res Rep, **17**, London

Adkins, L, and Adkins, R, 1994 *Archaeological illustration*, Cambridge

Archer, A, and Wilson, D M, 1974 Moated sites in Cheshire, *Cheshire Archaeol Bull*, **2**, 5-9

Ashurst, J, and Ashurst, N, 1988 *Practical building conservation: plasters, mortars, and renders*, Engl Her Tech Handbook, **3**, London

Ashmore, O, 1982 *The Industrial Archaeology of North-West England*, Manchester

Astill, G, and Grant, A (eds), 1988 *The countryside of medieval England*, Oxford

Ayto, E G, 1979 *Clay tobacco pipes*, Shire Album, **37**, Aylesbury

Bailey, F, 1953 *Churchwardens' Accounts*, Record Soc Lancashire Cheshire **104**, Preston

Barker, D, 1986a North Staffordshire Post-Medieval Ceramics - a type series Part One: Cistercian Ware, *Staffs Archaeol Stud, City Stoke-on-Trent Mus Archaeol Soc Rep*, n ser, **3**, 52-7

Barker, D, 1986b North Staffordshire Post-Medieval Ceramics - a type series Part Two: Blackware, *Staffs Archaeol Stud, City Stoke-on-Trent Mus Archaeol Soc Rep*, n ser, **3**, 58-75

Barlow, A, 1989 *Index to the Equity Proceedings up to 1700 of the Chancery of the Palatinate of Lancaster, preserved in the Public Record Office*, London

Beamont, W, 1875 *Winwick: its history and antiquities*, Warrington

Beamont, W, and Rylands, J P, 1879-83 *The Culcheth Deeds in Rose (ed) 1879-83*, **1**, Leigh

Bearpark, P J, and Johnson, B, 1976 Lymm Hall, Lymm, *Cheshire Archaeol Bull*, **4**, 28-30

British Geological Survey, 1980 *Sheet 97 (Runcorn), solid and drift edition (1:50,000)*, Southampton

Brown, A E, and Taylor, C C, 1991 Moats and landscape in northern Bedfordshire, *Medieval Settl Res Grp Ann Rep*, **6**, 5

Brunskill, R W, 1981 *Traditional buildings of Britain*, London

Brunskill, R W, 1982 *Traditional farm buildings of Britain*, London

Brunskill, R W, 1994 *Timber Building in Britain*, 2nd edn, London

Caple, C, 1985 The pins and wires from site S, in *Post-Medieval sites and their pottery: Moulsham Street, Chelmsford* (C M Cunningham and P J Drury), CBA Res Rep, **54**/Chelmsford Archaeol Trust rep, **5**, Chelmsford, 47-50

Carruthers, W J, 1990 Plant remains recovered from daub from a 16th century manor house Althrey Hall, near Wrexham, Clwyd, UK, *Circaea, J Assoc Environmental Archaeol*, **8(1)**, 55-59

Charleston, R, 1975 The glass, in *Excavations in Medieval Southampton 1953-1969. Volume 2 The Finds* (eds C Platt and R Coleman-Smith), Leicester, 204-27

Charleston, R, 1993 The seventeenth century glass, in Ellis 1993, 170-2

Clarke, H, 1984 *The archaeology of medieval England*, London

Cowell, R W, and Innes, J B, 1994 *The wetlands of Merseyside*, North West Wetlands Survey, **1**, Lancaster Imprints, **2**, Lancaster

Crompton, S, 1982 *English Glass*, London

Curzon, J B, 1974 Marton Grange, Marton, *Cheshire Archaeol Bull*, **2**, 26-29

Davey, P J, 1991, Merseyside: The Post-Roman pottery, in The Archaeology of Merseyside (eds P Tomlinson and M Warhurst), *J Merseyside Archaeol Soc*, **7**, 121-42

Davey, P J, and McNeill, R, 1980-81 Excavations at South Castle Street, Liverpool 1976 and 1977, *J Merseyside Archaeol Soc*, **4**, 1-158

Davis, S, 1997 Piecing together the past: footware and other artefacts from the wreck of a sixteenth century Spanish Basque galleon, in *Artefacts from wrecks. Dated artefacts from the Late Middle Ages to the Industrial Revolution* (ed M Redknap), Oxbow Monog, **84**, Oxford, 110-20

Dixon, P, Hayfield, C, and Startin, W, 1989 Baguley Hall, Manchester: the structural development of a Cheshire Manor House, *Archaeol J*, **146**, 384-422

Dobney, K, Hall, A R, Kenward, H K, and Milles, A, 1992 A working classification of sample types for environmental archaeology, *Circaea, J Assoc Environmental Archaeol*, **9**, 24-6

Droop, J P, and Larkin, F C, 1928 Excavations at West Derby Castle, Liverpool, *Annals Archaeol Anthropol*, **15**, 47-55

Egan, G, and Forsyth, A, 1997 Wound wire and silver gilt: changing fashions in dress accessories *c* 1400 – *c* 1600, in *The age of transition. The archaeology of English Culture c 1400 – 1600* (eds D Gaimster and P Stamper), Soc Medieval Archaeol Monog, **15**/Oxbow Monog, **98**, Oxford, 215-38

Egan, G, and Pritchard, F, 1991 Dress accessories *c* 1150 – *c* 1450, *Medieval finds from excavations in London*: **3**, London

Ekwall, E, 1922 The Place-Names of Lancashire, *Chetham Soc*, 2 Ser, **81**/ Publ Univ of Manchester, Engl Ser, **11**, Manchester

Ellis, P (ed), 1993 *Beeston Castle, Cheshire; a report on the excavations 1968-85 by Laurence Keen and Peter Hough*, HBMC Archeol Rep, **23**, London

English Heritage, 1991a *Exploring our past: strategies for the archaeology of England*, London

English Heritage, 1991b *Management of archaeological projects*, 2nd edn, London

English Heritage, nd *Dendrochronology: guidelines on producing and interpreting dendrochronological dates*, London

Farrer, W (ed), 1903 *Lancashire inquests, extents, and Feudal Aids, AD 1205-1307*, Record Soc Lancashire Cheshire, **48**, Preston

Farrer, W (ed), 1905 *Final Concords of the County of Lancaster from the original chirographs, or Feet of Fines ... in the Public Record Office ...,, Part III ... 1377-1509*, Record Soc Lancashire Cheshire, **50**, Preston

Farrer, W (ed), 1910 *Final Concords of the County of Lancaster from the original chirographs, or Feet of Fines ... in the Public Record Office ..., Part IV ... 1510-1558*, Record Soc Lancashire Cheshire, **60**, Preston

Farrer, W, and Brownbill, J (eds), 1906 *Victoria history of the county of Lancaster*, **1**, London

Farrer, W, and Brownhill, J (eds), 1907 *Victoria history of the county of Lancaster*, **3**, London

Farrer, W, and Brownbill, J (eds), 1911 *Victoria history of the county of Lancaster*, **4**, London

Faulkner, P, 1991 Timperly Old Hall: excavations for the third season, 1991, *Archaeol North-West*, **2**, 13-15

Fletcher, J M, and Currie, C R, 1980 The Bishop of Winchester's medieval manor house at Harwell, Berkshire, and its relevance in the evolution of timber-framed aisled halls, *Archaeol J*, **136**, 173-92

Fletcher, J M, and Tapper, M C, 1984 Medieval artefacts and structures dated by dendrochronology, *Medieval Archaeol*, **28**, 112-32

Freke, D J, 1982 *2nd interim report on excavations at Tannner's Farm, Twiss Green*, Rescue Archaeol Unit, Univ Liverpool, unpubl rep

Freke, D J, 1995 *Tanner's Farm moated site excavations, 1982*, Rescue Archaeol Unit, Univ Liverpool, unpubl rep

Freke, D J, and Holgate, R, 1990 Excavations at Winwick, Cheshire in 1980: 1 Excavation of two second millennium BC mounds, *J Chester Archaeol Soc*, **70**, 9-30

Freke, D J, and Thacker, A T, 1990 Excavations at Winwick, Cheshire in 1980: 2 The inhumation cemetery at Southworth Hall Farm, Winwick, *J Chester Archaeol Soc*, **70**, 31-38

Geophysical Surveys of Bradford, 1994 *Report on geophysical survey, Old Abbey Farm, Risley*, GSB rep, **94/127**, unpubl rep

Gooder, E, 1984 The finds from Temple Balsall, *Post-Medieval Archaeol*, **18**, 149-249

Graham, A H, and Davies, S M, 1993, *Excavations in Trowbridge, Wiltshire, 1977 and 1986-1988*, Wessex Archaeol Rep, **2**, Salisbury

Green, J P, 1975 Hallwood Farm, Runcorn, *Cheshire Archaeol Bull*, **3**, 54-55

Grenville, J, 1997 *Medieval housing*, London

Grew, M, and de Neergaard, M, 1988 *Medieval finds from excavation in London: 2. Shoes and pattens*, London

Hall, A R, and Kenward, H K, 1990 Environmental evidence from the Colonia: General Accident and Rougier Street, *The archaeology of York*, **14**(6), CBA Monog, London, 289-434

Hall, A R, and Kenward, H K, 1998 Disentangling dung: pathways to stable manure, *Environmental Archaeol J Human Palaeoecol*, **1**, 123-26

Hall, D, Wells, C E, and Huckerby, E, 1995 *The wetlands of Greater Manchester*, North West Wetlands Survey, **2**, Lancaster Imprints, **3**, Lancaster

Halliwell, J O, 1924 *A dictionary of archaic and provincial words, obsolete phrases, proverbs, and ancient customs, from the XIV century*, 7th edn, London

Hampson, C P, 1940 *The book of the Radclyffes; being an account of the main descents of this illustrious family*, Edinburgh

Harris, R, 1978 *Discovering timber-framed buildings*, Shire Publ, **242**, Princes Risborough

Higgins, D A, 1988-89 Speke Hall: excavations in the west range, 1981-2, *J Merseyside Archaeol*, **8**, 47-84

Higham, N J, 1987 Patterns of settlement in medieval Cheshire: an insight into dispersed settlement, *Medieval Settl Res Grp Ann Rep*, **2**, 9-10

Higham, N J, 1989 Forest, woodland, and settlement in medieval Cheshire: a note, *Medieval Settl Res Grp Ann Rep*, **4**, 24-25

Higham, N J, 1990 Hough Hall: the trial excavation of a moated platform in Mere Township, Cheshire, *J Chester Archaeol Soc*, **70**, 87-97

Hillam, J, Morgan, R A, and Tyers, I, 1987 Sapwood estimates and the dating of short ring sequences, in *Applications of tree-ring studies: current research in dendrochronology and related areas*, (ed R G W Ward), BAR Int Ser, **S333**, Oxford, 165-85

Holt, J, 1795, *General view of the agriculture of the county of Lancashire*, London

Howard-Davis, C, 1985 *The small finds from Furness Abbey*, unpubl rep

Hurst Vose, R, 1994 Excavations at the 17th century glasshouse at Haughton Green, Denton, near Manchester, *Post-Medieval Archaeol*, **28**, 1-72

Johnson, M, 1996 *An archaeology of capitalism*, London

Kaye, W J, and Kaye, Rev E W W, 1905 *The registers of Newchurch in the Township of Culcheth in the county of Lancaster: christenings, weddings and burials, 1599-1812*, Lancashire Parish Register Soc, **22**, Cambridge

Keery, R, 1992 *Historic Culcheth: the story of a village*, Risley

Kenward, H K, 1992 Rapid recording of archaeological insect remains - a reconsideration, *Circaea, J Assoc Environmental Archaeol*, **9**, 81-88

Kenward, H K, 1997 Synanthropic decomposer insects and the size, remoteness and longevity of archaeological occupation sites: applying concepts from biogeography to past 'islands' of human occupation, in Studies in Quaternary Entomology: an inordinate fondness for insects (eds A Ashworth, P C Buckland, and J T Sadler), *Quaternary Proc*, **5**, 135-52

Kenward, H K, and Allison, E P, 1994 Rural origins of the urban insect fauna, in *Urban-rural connexions: perspectives from environmental archaeology* (eds A R Hall and H K Kenward), Symposia Assoc for Environmental Archaeol, **12**/Oxbow Monog, **47**, Oxford, 55-77

Kenward, H K, Engleman, C, Robertson, A, and Large, F, 1986 Rapid scanning of urban archaeological deposits for insect remains, *Circaea, J Assoc Environmental Archaeol*, **3**, 163-72

Kenward, H K, and Hall, A R, 1995 Biological evidence from Anglo-Scandinavian deposits at 16-22 Coppergate, *The archaeology of York*, **14** (7), CBA Monog, York, 435-797

Kenward, H K, and Hall, A R, 1997 Enhancing bioarchaeological interpretation using indicator groups: stable manure as a paradigm, *J Archaeol Sci*, **24**, 663-73

Kenward, H K, Hall, A R, and Jones, A K G, 1980 A tested set of techniques for the extraction of plant and animal macrofossils from waterlogged archaeological deposits, *Sci Archaeol*, **22**, 3-15

Kenward, H, Hughes, P, and Hall, A, 1998 *Plant and invertebrate macrofossils from fills of the moat at Old Abbey Farm, Risley, Cheshire*, EAU rep, **98/23**, unpubl rep

Kenyon, D, 1991 *The origins of Lancashire*, Manchester

Lancaster University Archaeological Unit (LUAU), 1990 *Old Abbey Farm, Risley: an archaeological assessment*, unpubl rep

Langton, W (ed), 1876a *The visitation of Lancashire and a part of Cheshire made in ... AD 1533 by ... Thomas Benalt ...*, Part 1, Chetham Soc, o ser, **98**, Manchester

Langton, W (ed), 1876b *Abstacts of Inquisitions post Mortem made by Christopher Towneley and Roger Dodsworth, extracted from manuscripts at Towneley*, Part II, Chetham Soc, o ser, **99**, Manchester

Le Patourel, H E J, 1973 *The moated sites of Yorkshire*, Soc Medieval Archaeol Monog Ser, **5**, London

Le Patourel, H E J, 1978a Documentary evidence, in Aberg 1978, 21-8

Le Patourel, H E J, 1978b The excavation of moated sites, in Aberg 1978, 36-45

Le Patourel, H E J, and Roberts, B K, 1978 The significance of moated sites, in Aberg 1978, 46-55

Leah, M D, Wells, C E, Appleby, C, and Huckerby, E, 1997 *The wetlands of Cheshire*, North West Wetlands Survey, **4**, Lancaster Imprints, **5**, Lancaster

Lee, C G, and Michelmore, D, 1998 *Old Abbey Farm, Risley: the survey of the timbers from the dismantled buildings*, unpubl rep

Lewis, J, 1991 Medieval landscapes and estates, in The Archaeology of Merseyside (eds P Tomlinson and M Warhurst), *J Merseyside Archaeol Soc*, **7**, 87-103

Lewis, J, 2000 *Medieval earthworks of the Hundred of West Derby*, BAR Brit Ser, **310**, Oxford

Lewis, J, Heawood, R, and Howard-Davis, C, forthcoming *Excavations at Bewsey Old Hall*, Lancaster Imprints

Lynch, G, 1994 *Brickwork: history, technology and practice*, **1**, London

Margeson, S, 1993 Norwich households; medieval and post-medieval finds from Norwich Survey Excavations 1971-1978, *East Anglian Archaeol*, **58**, Norwich

Martin, E, 1989 Medieval moats in Suffolk, *Medieval Settl Res Grp Ann Rep*, **4**, 14

Mercer, E, 1975 *English vernacular houses*, RCHME Monog, London

Metcalfe, V, 1993 Wood Hall Moated Manor Project, *Medieval Settl Res Grp Ann Rep*, **8**, 35-38

Michelmore, D J H, 1983 Interpretation of the buildings of the timber phase, in *Sandal Castle excavations, 1964-1973* (eds P Mayes and LAS Butler), Wakefield, 73-75

Moffett, L C, 1987 The macro-botanical evidence from Late Saxon and early medieval Stafford, *AML Rep, n ser*, **169/87**

Morgan, D E M, 1980-81 The tin-glazed earthenware, in Davey and McNeill 1980-81, 63-76

Moorhouse, S, 1971 Finds from Basing House, Hampshire *c* 1540-1645, Pt 2, *Post-Medieval Archaeol*, **5**, 35-76

Moorhouse, S, and Roberts, I, 1992 Wrenthorpe Potteries, *Yorkshire Archaeol*, **2**, Wakefield

Murray, J A H (ed), 1909, *A new English dictionary on historical principles*, **7**, Oxford

Mytum, H (ed), 1982 *Bibliography of moated sites*, Moated Site Res Grp, Newcastle

Nayling, N, 1998 *Dendrochronological analysis of timbers from Old Abbey Farm, Risley, Cheshire*, ARCUS, **412**, unpubl rep

Neil, N R J, 1998 *Old Abbey Farm, Risley, near Warrington, Cheshire; Documentary Research*, unpubl rep

Nevell, M D, 1994 Late prehistoric pottery types in the Mersey Basin, in *From flints to flower pots, current research in the Mersey Valley* (ed P Carrington), Chester Archaeol Service Occ Paper **2**, Chester, 33-41

Newchurch Girl Guides, 1953 *Culcheth village and its history*, Culcheth

Newman, R, 1996 Medieval Rural Settlement, in *The Archaeology of Lancashire: Present State and Future Priorities* (ed R Newman), Lancaster, 109-24

Noake, P, 1993 The post-medieval pottery, in Ellis 1993, 191-210

Noel Hume, I, 1970 *A guide to Artifacts of Colonial America*, New York

OS, 1843 Ordnance Survey 1st Series 1": 1 mile, Sheet 80 NE, repr in Margary, H (ed) 1989 *The Old Series Ordnance Survey Maps of England and Wales, Scale 1 inch to 1 mile*, 7 (North Central England), Kent

OS, 1849 1st edn 6", 1849 Lancashire Sheet 102, 107, Southampton

OS, 1893 1st edn 2.5", 1893 Lancashire Sheet 109.3, 109.7, Southampton

OS, 1907 rev edn 2.5", Lancashire Sheet 109.7, Southampton

OS, 1928 rev edn 2.5", Lancashire Sheet 109.3, Southampton

OS, 1966 rev edn 2.5", Sheet SJ 6693 and 6793, Southampton

Oswald, O, 1975 *Clay pipes for the archaeologist*, BAR Brit Ser, **14**, Oxford

Pevsner, N, 1969 *Lancashire*, London

Philpott, R A, 1980-81 Mottled Ware, in Davey and McNeill 1980-81, 50-62

Philpott, R A, 1982-83, The finds, in A timber-framed building at 21-23 Eccleston Street, Prescot (Site 30), Archaeology in Prescot 1978-1986 (eds R W Cowell and G S Chitty), *J Merseyside Archaeol Soc*, **5**, 27-33

Reynolds, S, 1992 Excavations at Willaston Old Hall Moated Site, Near Nantwich, *Cheshire Past*, **1**, 16-17

Reynolds, S, and Cocroft, W, 1992 Leahill Farm, *Medieval Settl Res Grp Ann Rep*, **7**, 22-23

Rigold, S E, 1975 Structural aspects of medieval timber bridges, *Medieval Archaeol*, **19**, 48

Robinson, J M, 1991 *A guide to the country houses of the North-West*, London

Rose, J (ed), 1879-83 *Lancashire and Cheshire historical and genealogical notes, reprinted from the Leigh Chronicle 'Scrap Book'*, 3 vols, Leigh

Rust Environmental, 1995 *Building stone catalogue and geology report*, unpubl rep

Rutter, J, and Davey, P, 1980 Clay pipes from Chester, in *The archaeology of the clay tobacco pipe III. Britain: the north and west* (ed P Davey), BAR Brit Ser, **78**, Oxford, 41-272

Rylands, J P (ed), 1887 *Lancashire Inquisitions returned into Chancery of the Duchy of Lancaster, Stuart Period*, Part II, 12 to 19 James I, Record Soc Lancashire Cheshire, **16**, Preston

Smith, W J, 1996 *Old Abbey Farm, Risley: the brick footings and foundations*, unpubl rep

Taylor, C C, 1978 Moated sites: their definition, form, and classification, in Aberg 1978, 5-15

Taylor, C C, 1983, *Village and farmstead: a history of human settlement in England*, London

Tindall, A, 1985a Moated sites of Greater Manchester, *Moated Sites Res Gp*, **12**, Manchester

Tindall, A, 1985b The moated house, in *Country houses of Greater Manchester* (eds JSF Walker and A Tindall), Manchester, 59-72

Turner, R C, Sale, C B, and Axworthy Rutter, J A, 1988 Belgrave Moat, Cheshire, *J Chester Archaeol Soc*, **69**, 59-77

Walker, W, 1990 Duxbury in decline: the fortunes of a landed estate, 1756-1932, *Trans Hist Soc Lancashire Cheshire*, **140**, 33-45

Walker, W, 1995 *Duxbury in decline 1756-1932: a story of the decline of a Lancashire landed estate and the families associated with it*, Chorley

White, D P, 1977 The Birmingham button industry, *Post-Medieval Archaeol*, **11**, 67-80

Williams, J H, 1979 *St Peter's Street, Northampton, Excavations 1973-76*, Northampton

Wilson, D M, 1975 Hulme Hall, Allostock, *Cheshire Archaeol Bull*, **3**, 35-37

Wilson, D M, 1983 Excavation of a medieval moated site at Buttery Lane, Davenport Green, Greater Manchester: a summary report, *Trans Lancashire Cheshire Antiq Soc*, **84**, 121-46

Wilson, D M, 1987 The medieval moated sites of Cheshire, *Trans Lancashire Cheshire Antiq Soc*, **84**, 143-54

Winterburn, J, 1973 *History of Culcheth*, unpubl doc

Winterburn, J, 1974 *The Manor of Peasfurlong*, unpubl doc

Winterburn, J, 1977 *Complete History of Culcheth*, unpubl doc

Wood Hall Moated Manor Project, 1995 *The Wood Hall Moated Manor Project*, Cridling Stubbs

Wrathmell, S, 1989 Peasant houses, farmsteads and villages in north east England, in *The rural settlements of medieval England* (eds M Aston, D Austin, and C Dyer), Oxford, 247-67

INDEX